W9-BFF-624

The Chicago Sports Reader

Sport and Society

Series Editors
Benjamin G. Rader
Randy Roberts

*A list of books in the series
appears at the end of this book.*

The Chicago
Sports Reader

100 Years of Sports in the Windy City

Edited by

STEVEN A. RIESS

AND GERALD R. GEMS

UNIVERSITY OF ILLINOIS PRESS
Urbana and Chicago

© 2009 by the Board of Trustees
of the University of Illinois
All rights reserved
Manufactured in the United States of America
1 2 3 4 5 C P 5 4 3 2 1
♾ This book is printed on acid-free paper.

Library of Congress Cataloging-in-Publication Data
The Chicago sports reader : 100 years of sports
in the windy city / edited by Steven A. Riess and
Gerald R. Gems.
p.   cm. — (Sports and society)
Includes bibliographical references and index.
ISBN 978-0-252-03281-3 (cloth : alk. paper) —
ISBN 978-0-252-07615-2 (pbk. : alk. paper)
1. Sports—Illinois—Chicago—History.
I. Riess, Steven A. II. Gems, Gerald R.
GV584.5.C4C49   2009
796.09773'11—dc22   2008037209

Contents

Illustrations follow page 252

Introduction
The History of Sports in Chicago

STEVEN A. RIESS

Chicago has a long and glorious history as a site of recreational and competitive sport, and has produced some of the finest sporting events and most loyal fans in the United States. Chicago's sporting heritage dates back to Fort Dearborn, where soldiers, French Canadians, and Native Americans participated in such typical frontier sports as hunting and running races. In 1833, when the tiny town of Chicago was established, its mostly male residents hunted wolves and wild fowl, competed in marksmanship contests, sleighed, skated, and played table games at local taverns. Two years later, horse races were staged for purses of up to $1,500. Thereafter, the sporting life began to resemble more established communities, typified by the opening of a two-table billiard hall in Couche's Hotel in 1836.[1]

Chicago became a city in 1837 and rapidly developed into a physically expansive metropolis with a population that reached 29,963 in 1850. Its inhabitants took the same enjoyment in sporting life as the rest of the country, if not more, playing cricket and quoits, going boating, and having footraces. In the 1840s and 1850s American advocates of physical culture were developing a positive sporting creed that justified middle-class participation in clean, moral sports. These views were augmented by the positive example of English, Scottish, and German immigrant athletes, the emergence of new sports like baseball, urban growth, improved transportation and communication, and the impact of industrialization. The result was a great boom in sport after the Civil War.[2]

The first major spectator sports were turf contests, primarily trotting at tavern owner Willard F. Myrick's track laid out in 1837 adjacent to

Lake Michigan at 26th Street. Trotting was the first modern American sport, organized by middle-class men who considered it a democratic and American sport in contrast to aristocratic and English thoroughbred racing. Trotting was very popular in Chicago and there were numerous tracks in the vicinity. In 1840 the Chicago Sporting Club was established, which ran one- and two-mile races for purses up to $200. William B. Ogden, the city's first mayor, served as club president. In 1844 Myrick built the Chicago Race Track, a one-mile course for harness racing. In 1845 he leased it for ten years to Dr. William Tichnor of Kentucky, who built a fence around the course and stands for spectators. The summer and autumn meets featured purses up to $600. In 1854 Platt Martin and the managers of the Garden City Hotel opened the Garden City Course about three miles south of Myrick's track. George A. Green also built a course between Laflin Street and Reuben (now Ashland) Avenue in Cottage Grove, west of the city. It was followed one year later by the Brighton Park Course, about two miles south of Bridgeport, sponsored by the Brighton House and future mayor John Wentworth. These tracks were largely displaced by the Chicago Driving Park, whose president was Daniel Thompson. Women were admitted only with an escort. Last, the designers of the Union Stockyards included space for a racecourse in their plans. In 1867 the Dexter Park racecourse opened on stockyards property at 42d and Halsted with a 1,500–seat grandstand for men and a separate 200–seat grandstand for women. By then the city's population was approaching 300,000.[3]

The male bachelor subculture in antebellum Chicago enjoyed vile resorts like the Prairie Queen, a brothel, which in the 1850s sponsored dogfights and weekly boxing matches. Men also enjoyed watching half-naked women fight each other. As late as 1865, $30,000 was bet on a dogfight.[4] Billiards was apparently popular enough that in 1848 table manufacturer John Brunswick opened a Chicago office, and his artisans crafted beautiful tables that he sold to the wealthy. He also promoted the sport by hiring professionals to compete and give exhibitions. Municipal leaders tried to improve the young city's image by cleaning up the old sporting culture. The 1837 city charter empowered the municipality to license, regulate, or prohibit vile entertainments to encourage wholesome recreation, promote safety and morality, and raise revenue. The 1851 Municipal Code empowered the Common Council to "license, tax, regulate, suppress, and prohibit billiard tables" and all versions of bowling. At one time, the city barred the keeping of billiard tables or bowling alleys, but the revised 1866 code permitted owners to operate by purchasing a $25 commutation certificate per table or alley.[5]

Sport and the Old Immigrants

The local sporting culture was heavily influenced by the coming of immigrants, especially the Germans—who in 1884 made up a third of the city's population—the Irish (18 percent), and to a lesser extent the Scandinavians (8 percent). These "old immigrants" each brought a sporting tradition and organized sports clubs that promoted ethnic pride, sociability, dignity, and status.

Germans brought with them a tradition of physical culture, mainly through the *Turnverein*, that emphasized gymnastics, calisthenics, and German traditions. It provided a positive role model for American and European sportsmen.[6] The Chicago *Turngemeinde*, the city's first Turner unit, was organized in 1852, with a membership that originally included manufacturers, gunsmiths, and blacksmiths. Three-fourths (73.5 percent) of its members who joined between 1852 and 1871 had white-collar occupations, although other societies, some overtly socialist, were mainly working-class.[7]

The Turners gained considerable prestige from their ardent support of the Union during the Civil War, and many Midwestern Turners served in the Twenty-fourth Illinois Volunteers. The Chicago *Turngemeinde* built an impressive two-story Turnhalle on north Clark Street after the war. It was one of the largest buildings in its German neighborhood, where it was also a community center that included a gymnasium, a reading room, a dining room, and one of the largest dance halls in the entire city. Initiation cost five dollars and annual dues were six dollars.[8]

The societies were well known for their cultural, social, and political activities. Turners introduced the teaching of German into the public schools and vigorously opposed the Edwards Law of 1889, which required instruction in English. In 1885 President Louis Nettlehorst of the Chicago *Turngemeinde* convinced the Board of Education to adopt the Turner system of instruction, making Chicago the first American city to adopt a formal program of physical education for public schools. The Turners were also known for promoting working-class interests, often through socialism. They opposed child labor and supported the eight-hour day; compulsory school attendance; the restriction of monopolies; governmental inspection of food, lodgings, and factories; and federal aid to education. The Turner halls provided an important meeting place for labor unions and other working-class organizations. Turners were among the most radical Chicagoans, and three of the eight anarchists imprisoned after the Haymarket Riot of 1886 were members, including August Spies, editor of the *Arbeiter-Zeitung*.[9]

By 1890 Chicago was regarded as the stronghold of the Turners, with thirty-four societies and 5,000 members in the district, the most of any American city. Relations between conservative and socialist Turners blew up after Haymarket, and they went their separate ways, forming their own societies. The precipitating event was the 800–member *Turngemeinde*'s expulsion of Julius Vahlteich for his radical views. He was reinstated by the North American Turner Association (NATA), which was temporarily dominated by radicals. As a result the *Turngemeinde* and three other Chicago branches dropped out of NATA for a year. The left-wingers increasingly devoted themselves to politics alone, reflected by their prominent role in the founding of the Socialist Party of America in 1901. By the later '00s the Chicago Turners were increasingly bourgeois and non-political.[10] The Turners' decline at the turn of the century was because of a drop in German immigration, the widespread acculturation of the second generation, and unwillingness to adapt to the era's prevailing interest in team sports.[11]

Irish-American participation in sports probably surpassed that of all other ethnic groups. The Irish brought to America their male bachelor subculture that glorified manliness and sports like boxing, placing them firmly in the sporting fraternity. Some track-and-field organizations in the 1870s and afterward were affiliated with the secret and violent Clan-Na-Gael. In addition, late nineteenth-century immigrants brought over traditional Irish sports like hurling and Gaelic football that were being revived in the old sod by the Gaelic Athletic Association. They were staged in Chicago at Gaelic Park (37th and Indiana).[12]

The second- and third-generation Irish became very active in mainstream American sports, including boxing, baseball, and track and field. At the turn of the century, many were introduced to organized sports on neighborhood teams run by social and athletic clubs (SACs). These institutionalized youth gangs—usually sponsored by a local politician to promote his political career or a saloon keeper who hoped to host their parties—were very common among many ethnic groups by the 1920s.[13]

The city's preeminent Irish SAC was the South Side Ragen Colts, which began as the Morgan Athletic Club in 1900. Its leader was Frank Ragen, a future Cook County commissioner. The club achieved renown for its athletic prowess, but by the late 1910s it was better known for slugging, intimidating, and terrorizing interlopers into their neighborhood, especially African Americans. They played a prominent and violent role in the Chicago Race Riot of 1919 by attacking black residents.[14]

Scandinavians also brought a sporting tradition that became a cornerstone of certain fraternal organizations like the *Nordsidans skandinaviska Turnerforening* (1867), and the Swedish Sharpshooters Society

(1870), based on similar groups in the old country.[15] There was little love lost between the Swedes and Norwegians (they were ruled by the same monarch from 1814 until 1905, when Norway got its own king), and in 1885 a Norwegian Turner Society was formed, which marked the start of a separate significant Norwegian athletic culture in Chicago. Norwegian sportsmen in America were particularly noted for their winter sports, sponsored by groups like the Athletic Club Sleipner in 1894, which became best known for sponsoring annual ice-skating races. In 1908, 20,000 attended a ski-jumping competition in Humboldt Park in the center of Chicago's Norwegian community. Four years later, the Norge Ski Club's jump at Fox River Grove, about thirty-five miles northwest of Chicago, was the site of the U.S. national ski-jumping championships.[16]

Sport and Class

Upper-Class Sport

In the nineteenth century, social class was a major determinant of sporting activities. An individual's place in the social structure reflected one's occupation, standard of living, education, religion, residency, and social values—all of which influenced one's leisure options. The upper class had a lot of free time and discretionary income, and so they had a lot of recreational alternatives. They preferred expensive sports in restrictive organizations that enabled them to conspicuously display their status and that provided opportunities to improve it. The elite created and organized high-status sports clubs like the Chicago Yacht Club (1875), the Washington Park Jockey Club (1883), the Kenwood Lawn Tennis Club (1884), and the Chicago Athletic Club (1890). The Chicago Yacht Club was probably the most prestigious sports club in the city. It required an invitation just to attend a race, like the prestigious Chicago-to-Mackinac Island race begun in 1898, the world's oldest and longest freshwater sailboat race. It was won by the sloop *Vanenna* over four rivals. The CYC barred Jewish applicants until 1944. Other important aquatic clubs were the Farragut Boat Club, founded in 1872, which limited its membership to 250, and the Iroquois Boat Club, organized in 1887, which accepted only 300. The less restrictive Chicago Athletic Association built a great facility on Michigan Avenue in 1893; it was said to have a waiting list of 3,000 names at the time.[17]

Chicago became an important site for the new sport of golfing, which combined with a fascination with English country life and ample commuter lines to spur construction of suburban country clubs. Stockbroker Charles Blair Macdonald, who had played golf while a student at Scotland's University of St. Andrews, designed a seven-hole course on Senator John Farwell's Lake Forest estate in 1892 after several young university men in the English delegation to the World's Fair Chicago expressed an interest in playing golf. It was the second golf course in the United States, after Shinnecock Hills in Long Island, which opened the year before. Macdonald then persuaded some friends in the Chicago Club, an elite men's club founded in 1869, to help finance a course in Belmont, a municipality later incorporated into the suburb of Downers Grove. The Chicago Golf Club opened in 1893, the first American golf club with an eighteen-hole course. In 1894 Macdonald designed a new, more challenging $28,000, 6,200-yard course for the club in Wheaton, modeled after St. Andrews. It was considered the finest in the United States and hosted the U.S. Open and Amateur championships in 1897. It is currently rated the seventh most prestigious course in the country. Early club presidents included Potter Palmer, Robert Todd Lincoln, and Robert S. McCormick. Macdonald also helped form the United States Golf Association (USGA) in 1894 and won its first U.S. Amateur Championship a year later.[18]

In 1899 fifteen local clubs formed the Western Golf Association (WGA), which became second in stature to the USGA. It sponsored the prestigious Western Open and the Western Amateur. There were twenty-six clubs in the metropolitan area in 1900, which included five public courses for the middle class. The Onwentsia course in Lake Forest was the site of the 1899 U.S. Amateur Championship and the 1906 U.S. Open Championship. Chicagoans were among the nation's best amateur players, and in the 1909 tournament, won by Bob Gardner, seven of the eight quarter-finalists were Chicago-area products, including Charles E. "Chick" Evans Jr., who won both the U.S. Open and the U.S. Amateur titles in 1916. The WGA has made its greatest contribution by administering the Evans Scholars Foundation, established in 1929 to fund college scholarships for caddies.[19]

In the Roaring 1920s, Chicagoland golf was reshaped by super country clubs, particularly the 692–acre Olympia Fields, fifteen miles south of Chicago, founded in 1915 under club president Amos A. Stagg, the football coach at the University of Chicago. It had its four eighteen-hole courses, a clubhouse with an 800–seat dining room, and 100 cottages. It hosted the U.S. Open in 1928 and 2003. Another was the Medinah Country Club in Medinah, Illinois, northwest of the city, which opened in 1925 and soon had 1,500 members. It was financed by Shriners of the downtown Medinah Temple and had a polo field, riding trails, toboggan runs, fifty-three-acre Lake Kadijah, and three eighteen-hole golf courses, including one for women. It has been the site of three U.S. Opens (1949, 1975, and 1990) and two PGA Championships (1999, 2006).[20]

Clubs had very strict admission policies, and applicants could be blackballed by a lone negative vote. Since prosperous German American Jews were barred from prestigious athletic clubs and country clubs, they established their own clubs, including the North Shore Country Club, whose members included Leonard Florsheim, Modie Spiegel, and Julius Rosenwald, while Albert Lasker, the advertising mogul, built his own personal world-class course. The country clubs became important centers of elite sociability, and a place for wives and daughters to play sports. In 1923 when the U.S. Ladies Golf Championship was held in Chicago, Jewish women were barred because the sponsoring Women's Western Golf Association denied full membership to Jewish country clubs.[21]

Elite women participated in sport far more than most other women, because their high status protected them from concerns that athletics would harm their femininity. They played at college, at men's athletic clubs, and at country clubs, which were particularly attractive to elite women who enjoyed golf and tennis and also the clubs' opportunities for socializing. Margaret Abbott, whose father was a member of a Chicago country club, won the Olympic championship for golf in 1900 while on vacation in Paris. In 1898 Belle Ogden Armour and Paulina Harriette Lyon founded the 275–member Woman's Athletic Club of Chicago (WAC), the first private athletic club for women, which two years later opened a downtown gymnasium costing $100,000. The clubhouse had a marble swimming pool, Turkish baths, a gymnasium, a bowling alley, and a running track, along with a parlor, a library, a tea room, and a dining room.[22]

Middle-Class Sport

Chicago's middle class, which made up 31 percent of the workforce in 1900, generally believed in hard work, domesticity, sobriety, and piety and wanted to employ free time for self-improvement and self-renewal. Middle-class men worked a five-and-a-half-day week and had sufficient income to pursue leisure activities. The new middle class of professionals and bureaucrats turned to their pastimes to demonstrate their creativity, self-worth, and manliness at a time when WASP birthrates were declining and culture seemed to be feminized by influential mothers and schoolteachers. This was a big change from the ante-bellum era when the middle class had originally opposed sports because of their violence and gambling, until middle-class reformers in the 1840s initiated the rational recreation movement that sought to substitute moral amusements like clean sports for the evil pleasures of the male bachelor subculture to uplift people, reduce crime, and improve public health.[23]

The middle class took advantage of the city's geography. There was lots of space on the prairie to build huge suburban public parks and baseball diamonds that catered to the middle class, and Lake Michigan provided a great resource for swimming, boating, and fishing. The first Midwestern boating club was Chicago's Pioneer Boat Club (1853), and the city had its first sailing regatta five years later.

The city's middle class relied on the Young Men's Christian Association, founded in 1858 as an interdenominational middle-class evangelical association that sought to protect rural young men from urban vices. It became a leading proponent of muscular Christianity. In 1879 the YMCA set up a gymnasium and baths and shortly thereafter rented an outdoor athletic ground and a baseball park. In 1893 construction began on the thirteen-story Central YMCA on LaSalle Street, which included a bowling alley, swimming pool, and gymnasium.[24]

The middle-class sporting experience was enhanced by the introduction of new sports, particularly baseball, a simple team sport that would supposedly build morality, character, and health. Middle-class men were ardent joiners of voluntary associations, and by 1866, there were 32 teams in the local baseball fraternity, sponsored by men's clubs, occupational groups, companies, and neighborhood organizations. Businessmen like Marshall Field, who had opposed baseball before the Civil War as deleterious to hard work, began to see it as a means to promote teamwork, discipline, sobriety, and self-sacrifice and sponsored company nines. By 1870 wealthy civic boosters raised $15,000 for a professional baseball team, the White Stockings (renamed the Cubs in 1905), to enhance the city's stature. As the game became commercialized, the middle class became ardent baseball fans, having the time and money to attend mid-afternoon White Stockings games.[25]

Thrill-seeking middle-class men in the late 1870s rode the dangerous ordinary, a bicycle with a huge front wheel and tiny rear wheel, over poor roads. Their shared interest in the sport led to the formation of the Chicago Bicycle Club (1879), second-oldest in the USA. In the early 1890s the velocipede was supplanted by the safety bicycle with its equal-sized wheels. There were more than 500 cycling clubs in the United States, and riders became a powerful voting bloc. In 1882 riders successfully ended the ban on riding in Lincoln Park and later voided the law requiring cyclists to dismount when encountering a horse. In 1897, after 100,000 turned out for a cycling show, mayoral candidate Carter H. Harrison Jr. started his campaign with a 100–mile ride to show his identification with cycling interests.[26]

The city became an important center of cycling manufacturing. In 1895 German immigrant Ignaz Schwinn founded a bicycle manufacturing partnership that became Schwinn and Company in 1908, typically producing more than 25 percent of all bicycles made in the United States.

Manufacturers sponsored races to demonstrate their products, including the Chicago-to-Pullman race on Memorial Day that drew some 400 competitors. In time, cycling was supplanted by the technologically superior automobile. Six cars competed in the first great American car race, a round-trip match from Jackson Park to Evanston on Thanksgiving Day, 1895, won by a Duryea, driven by J. Frank Duryea. It was staged in Chicago because of its relatively high-quality cobblestoned streets, the importance of innovative transportation to the World's Fair of 1893 (which had an entire building devoted to the subject), and the sponsorship by H. A. Kohlstaat, a wealthy Chicago booster who owned the *Times-Herald*. The contest inspired future car races and led to the first Chicago Auto Show in 1901.[27]

Middle-class sport was also facilitated by the building of a great park system in 1869 when Jackson, Humboldt, and Garfield Park were constructed. At the time these parks were built, they were in suburbs, which were later annexed. They were accessible by mass transit, but only to people who could afford the carfare. By the 1880s, the city was second only to Philadelphia in total park acreage, with 1,500 acres of park land, but little land was added afterwards, and in 1900 the city was 32nd among all major cities in acreage per population. The parks originally emphasized passive recreation, but athletes defied the ban right from the start. The park district acceded to public demand and in the 1880s laid out baseball diamonds in the parks. In 1886 the first tennis courts were built in the parks, which grew to 300 by 1915. In 1895 the city opened its first public beach at Lincoln Park and required bathers to wear proper attire.[28]

Middle-class women had substantial leisure time, rarely holding jobs and having household servants. There were still Victorian limitations on women engaging in physical exercise, since women were not considered physically fit to participate in sports and because sports were considered a male sphere that promoted aggression and defeminized female participants. Yet as early as 1845 two women's gymnastic academies opened in Chicago. Physicians and female physical educators in the late nineteenth century recommended exercise and feminine sports to improve health and beauty. Feminine sports were those that were not too strenuous, such as golf, tennis, horseback riding, cycling, croquet, and ice skating. These sports also provided opportunities to meet young men. College girls even played basketball using modified rules appropriate to the accepted ideas of women's capacities. Female cyclists particularly enjoyed the activity because it gave them independence. But riding was difficult while wearing traditional long dresses, and sports clothes, such as bloomers and pants, became popular. This threatened many people, particularly males, and the town of Pullman barred women cyclists who did not wear skirts.[29]

A new popular middle-class sport at the turn of the century was swimming, and Chicago, from the 1890s through the 1920s, was a major center of competitive swimming, which began at elite athletic clubs and YMCAs during the 1890s. The Chicago Athletic Association (CAA) built a pool in 1893 and four years later hosted the second annual Amateur Athletic Union (AAU) indoor and outdoor championships. The first great local swimmer was H. Jamison Handy, of the Central YMCA, the Olympic bronze medalist in the breaststroke in 1904. The University of Chicago built a pool in 1904 and hosted the first intercollegiate contest in the Midwest one year later. In the next decade the sport became democratized by settlement houses like the Chicago Hebrew Institute, which had its own pool and developed a strong women's swimming program. The Illinois Athletic Club (IAC) became a major player in competitive swimming under Coach Bill Bachrach. His greatest star was undefeated freestyler Johnny Weissmuller, of working-class Catholic origins, who won three gold medals in the 1924 Olympics and another in 1928, and set a total of 67 world records. He gained wider recognition as Tarzan in twelve motion pictures. Other IAC gold medalists at the 1924 Olympic Games were backstroker Sybil Bauer and freestyler Ethel Lackie.[30]

Lower-Class Sport

Lower-class sporting opportunities were limited by long working hours and low pay, especially among unskilled men, whose workweek in 1900 averaged nearly sixty hours. Employers believed that if workers had more free time and made more money they would only waste their resources at saloons, billiard parlors, or brothels. Options were further limited because many were new immigrants who came to America without any sporting tradition. A third constant was that sporting facilities like baseball diamonds were located at the large municipal parks, far from their crowded inner-city neighborhoods. Blue-collar men who were active in sports like baseball and track and field were primarily either skilled old immigrants or city workers, both of whom worked shorter hours and lived outside the slums. They played for teams sponsored by local politicians, fraternal groups, or occupational organizations. Historian Jerry Gems found that in the 1870s there were twenty-six gymnastic groups that held a monthly festival, and fraternal and political groups sponsored holiday picnics that included sporting contests.[31]

Athletic opportunities were limited for children of the new immigrants whose parents had no interest in sports and lived in the poorest and most crowded neighborhoods far from the great parks. Local progressive reformers, including Jane Addams and other settlement-house workers, lobbied Mayor Carter H. Harrison to open small parks of one to five acres and then the state empowered the South Park District to build thirty-one small parks and playgrounds of ten to sixteen acres with athletic fields, swimming pools, and fieldhouses that became community centers. Youths would play team sports there under adult direction that would presumably build character and discourage juvenile delinquency. This program provided a model for the nation. By 1917 Chicago had more than ninety new parks and more than a hundred playgrounds.[32]

Working-class sport was facilitated in the late nineteenth century by the rise of welfare capitalism, a philosophy that encouraged companies to promote company loyalty and kill off unions by providing workers with a wide variety of services. In the 1880s George Pullman's company town of Pullman had possibly the most comprehensive industrial recreation program in America. The Pullman Athletic Association was open to all members of the town, and 54 percent were blue-collar. The PAA was best known for its nationally ranked cricket, soccer, and rowing teams, which recruited working-class athletes from England and Wales to compete for the club.[33]

Compared to the large eastern metropolises, Chicago had enough empty spaces to facilitate the development of skilled baseball players. It had one of the strongest semipro baseball programs of any American city, with so many teams and leagues that it produced far more major leaguers than its share of the national population. Small-time entrepreneurs, companies, ethnic or church groups, neighborhood organizations, and political leaders like Anton Cermak sponsored teams. In 1906 sports manufacturing magnate Albert G. Spalding's American Sport Publishing Company published a 1,000-page baseball guide devoted just to Chicago ball. The Logan Squares of the City League were so good that they defeated both the White Sox and the Cubs in 1906 after those clubs had played in the World Series. Players in the Chicago Industrial League got $10–20 for Sunday games and often were also given company sinecures. There was a lot of betting on company games by employees.[34]

At the turn of the century, the most accessible sites of working-class sports were billiard parlors and bowling alleys, which were popular hangouts among the male bachelor subculture. Pool halls had a particularly bad public image as lowlife resorts. In 1900 billiards was the most popular commercial blue-collar sport, and by 1910 nearly half of the city's 7,600 saloons had a pool table. The tables were mainly manufactured by John Brunswick, who had opened a local office in 1848. Pool tables were available not only in saloons; by 1920 there were 2,244 licensed billiard parlors, many of which were mainly saloons. That number dropped to 862 in 1922 after Prohibition closed the taverns. The number further fell to 580 in 1936 because of the Great Depression. The fancy, large rooms

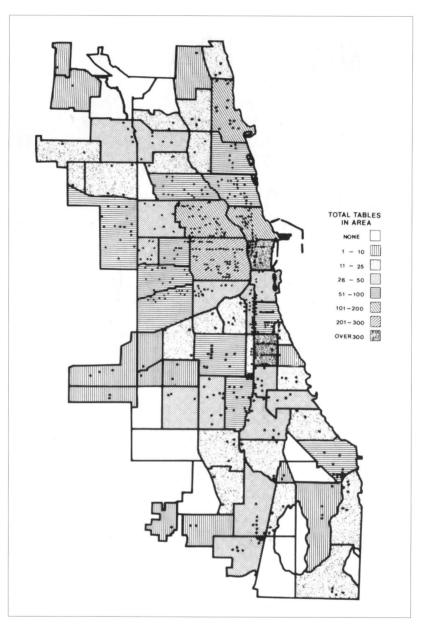

TOTAL TABLES
IN AREA

NONE	
1 — 10	
11 — 25	
26 — 50	
51 — 100	
101 — 200	
201 — 300	
OVER 300	

Distribution of Licensed Billiard Halls in Chicago, 1936. Source: Chicago
Recreation Commission, *The Chicago Recreation Survey, 1937*, vol. 2,
Commercial Recreation (Chicago: Chicago Research Commission, 1938), 58f.

were in the Loop, while smaller rooms were mainly in the Near West Side, the Near Northwest Side, Polish West Town, and the predominantly African American Grand Boulevard. Pool halls were barred from better neighborhoods by zoning laws and licensing restrictions.[35]

Bowling in Chicago was originally a largely German sport. The city's first regulation tenpin alley was installed in the Plaza Hotel (Clark and North) in 1891. Moses Bensinger, the heir to Brunswick, was bowling's biggest supporter. He pushed the Brunswick-Balke-Collender Company in the 1890s to manufacture bowling equipment, hired traveling all-star teams to promote his products, and in 1895 helped organize the American Bowling Congress (ABC). In 1901 Brunswick brought the first ABC national tournament to Chicago, which exclusively used Brunswick products. Bowling became more respectable at the turn of the century with leagues of merchants, clothiers, mechanics, bankers, and jewelers, along with women's tournaments by 1907, but it still had a strong working-class base.[36]

In 1918 there were 139 licensed alleys in Chicago, many associated with saloons. Then one year later the number increased by 40.3 percent in anticipation of the need for an alternative recreation with the impending arrival of Prohibition. Bowling alleys then were very popular with ethnic working-class men and women because they were accessible, sociable, and affordable—a game in the evening cost just twenty-five cents, and there was a lot of gambling in leagues and tournaments. The Loop had more alleys than any other neighborhood, but nearly half were in residential areas on four avenues or streets (Milwaukee, Clark, Halsted, and Broadway). In the 1930s, more than 15,000 local women belonged to the Women's International Bowling Congress. Chicago had more than 500,000 bowlers by the late 1930s, with more than 900 leagues sponsored by companies, ethnic societies, church organizations, and other voluntary associations. After World War II, the sport had a revival, especially among suburban women, who bowled during afternoons at large, well-lit modern facilities, which by the mid-1950s featured automatic pin spotters.[37]

Sport, Race, and the New Immigrants, 1880–1920

The new immigrants from Eastern and Southern Europe came from premodern societies that had little if any sporting tradition. One immigrant group that brought a sporting heritage were Bohemians (from today's Czech Republic), who came from a more developed section of Central Europe. The Czech *sokol* was established in central Europe in 1862 based on the German *Turnverein*, part of a romantic nationalist movement.

The *sokol* was a paramilitary organization promoting a sound body and mind as resistance to foreign control. Chicago was the site of the second American *sokol*, established in 1866, and became the American center of the movement. In 1884 the National Sokol Union was established in Pilsen, mainly by freethinkers.[38]

The *sokol* quickly became one of the most important institutions in Chicago's Bohemian and Slovak communities. The *sokol*s emphasized calisthenic drills and sponsored some gymnastic competitions known as *slets*.[39] *Sokol* leaders found that the American-born preferred competitive American sports and by the 1880s tried to attract them to the ethnic organization by establishing Bohemian baseball teams. As Gems points out, such ethnic teams "allowed ethnics to selectively participate in the American system while retaining their religious and cultural values." In the 1910s they formed Czech soccer teams to compete against other ethnic groups and had enough squads to form their own league in 1917.[40] The *sokol*s provide a model for Greeks, Poles, and Ukrainians, who also established sports clubs to prepare freedom fighters to emancipate their homelands.[41]

Poles in Galicia formed a unit of the Falcons, their version of the *sokol*, in 1867, but because of foreign oppression it was the only such club for seventeen years. In 1887 Felix L. Pietrowicz organized the first American Falcon nest in the parish of St. Stanislaus Kostka, the heart of Chicago's Polonia. It had little success until becoming a department of the Polish National Alliance (PNA) in 1905.[42]

The Polish language press encouraged sports, recommending vigorous athletics to develop good health, sound character, and confidence. By the mid-1920s they were covering sports in English to appeal to the second generation, who were able to identify Babe Ruth better than they were Polish President Józef Pilsudski. The Polish-American youth had only modest success in sports until then, which reflected their poverty and lack of access to sporting facilities. Poles did become very successful in bowling, however. Organizations like the PNA, the Polish Roman Catholic Union, and the Polish Women's Alliance all sponsored leagues, and Polish politicians supported bowling teams. Top keglers who played, and won, tournaments at Casimir Wronski's Lanes on Milwaukee Avenue, the largest in the United States, became local heroes.[43]

Eastern European Jews came from communities where sport was virtually unknown, and the newcomers did not become any more interested on arrival. Like other second-generation newcomers, however, Jewish sons became very interested in sports because they were fun, a means to become acculturated, and a vehicle to display manliness, prowess, and ethnic pride, countering negative stereotypes of Jews as unhealthy, physically unfit, and timid. Top athletes envisioned using their renown to escape the slums to get a good job, become a professional athlete, or get a college scholarship. Many immigrant youths were introduced and trained in sports at settlement houses like Hull House or the Chicago Hebrew Institute (CHI), established in 1903 in the West Side by German Jews, including Julius Rosenwald of Sears, Roebuck, who donated $75,000 to the institute. The CHI's goal was to improve the bodies and minds of Jewish youth so they could readily assimilate, yet maintain a Jewish identity. By 1910 the CHI had a weekly attendance of 11,000 that surpassed Hull House.[44]

Jews made their greatest mark in boxing, beginning with Harry Harris, the world bantamweight champion (1901–1902) and the first Jewish American title holder. Boxing fit in well with their environment because it was a useful skill for inner-city youth who often got into fights with rival ethnics, and it was taught in neighborhood boxing gyms and settlement houses. Tough Jews were considered heroes among the second generation, especially if they defended their fellow Jews. The most famous Jewish fighter was Barney Ross, a product of Maxwell Street, who in 1934 was the first prize fighter to simultaneously hold three championships.[45]

The African American experience in the early 1900s was very different from the immigrants because they grew up in the United States and were familiar with American sports, but they encountered a wall of prejudice regardless of their accomplishments. The black population of Chicago grew from 44,000 in 1900 to 110,000 in 1920. They were segregated into the South Side Black Belt where there were no large parks, and the small parks lacked indoor facilities. Blacks rarely used community centers that bordered small parks for fear of white violence.

Blacks encountered de facto segregation at the YMCA, and as early as 1889, they considered establishing their own branch, but integrationist attitudes at the time blocked that plan. By 1910 white hostility grew to the point that blacks were completely shut out of the local Y. In 1913 renowned philanthropist Julius Rosenwald (the president of Sears) and local meat packers helped fund the $190,000 South Wabash Street Y. The packers supported the Wabash Y to maintain segregation in the YMCA and show their African American employees that the companies were interested in their welfare, so as to discourage unionization.[46]

In the 1910s the newcomers in the Black Belt encountered a lot of opposition when they tried to use public recreational facilities outside their neighborhoods, a common response in cities all across the country. Blacks were afraid to go into white parks, and for good reason. By 1913 youths under adult supervision who ventured into white parks or public beaches were being attacked. Fighting became commonplace at

Washington Park in 1919, which divided the Black Belt from the Irish southwest side. The presence of black baseball players was seen as an infringement into Irish turf and was challenged by Irish SACs.[47]

Racial conflict also occurred at the city's South Side beaches. The only beach open to African Americans was the 26th Street Beach, reflected by the presence of a black director and black lifeguards. On July 27, teenager Eugene Williams inadvertently swam further south to the 29th Street Beach, where he was stoned by white youths. His murder precipitated the Chicago Race Riot that resulted in the deaths of fifteen whites and twenty-three blacks.[48]

There was a lot of community pride around sports heroes like world heavyweight boxing champion Jack Johnson, but also high school stars like Sam Ransom of Hyde Park High School's great 1902 football team, local semiprofessional baseball clubs, and the YMCA basketball team that played white clubs. Blacks lacked access to bowling, since there were no lanes in the ghetto, and were barred from country clubs and golf tournaments; and so they formed their own Alpha Golf Club and country club, which played at public courses. Blacks also formed their own basketball teams that entertained at night clubs before dances, like at the Savoy Ballroom at 4733 South Parkway (now Martin Luther King Jr. Drive). Abe Saperstein transformed them into a touring quintet known as the Harlem Globetrotters.[49]

African Americans responded to discrimination in baseball by forming their own high-quality teams. They got a lot of support from the black press, including Robert Abbott of the *Defender*, who urged that "all race loving and race building men and women should support the negro teams."[50] Chicago's first professional black team was the Unions, established in 1886 by Henry Jones, a future gambling kingpin, and run by future county commissioner Frank Leland. In 1900 the short-lived Columbia Giants began to play, but they went out of business a year later, and its best players joined Leland's aggregate to form the Union Giants. In 1905 the squad went 112-10. The team was bought one year later by black Republican politicians and renamed the Leland Giants Baseball and Amusement Association in 1907. Their star hurler and manager Rube Foster led the team to the city semipro championship. One year later they dominated the prestigious City League, whose other teams were white and included former major leaguers. In 1909 the highly regarded Leland Giants played a three-game series against the Cubs, who swept the Giants in very competitive contests. Internal conflicts led to a restructuring of the team. Foster took the best players, and with white partner John M. Schorling, in 1910 established the American Giants, who played at Schorling Park, the former White Sox field, a short walk from the emerging Black Belt. In 1920 Foster organized the Negro National League, which lasted until 1932. A new NNL replaced it in 1933 and instituted the extremely popular East–West All-Star game at Comiskey Park, which became a highlight in the summer social calendar of Midwestern African Americans, drawing up to 40,000 fans.[51]

Sport and Education

School sports in the nineteenth century were mainly played by middle- and upper-class youth who attended colleges and high schools. Intercollegiate sports in the early nineteenth century were mainly identified with the University of Chicago, then a major sports power. Its teams were coached by Amos Alonzo Stagg, hired in 1892 to put the new university on the map. He was the first football coach tenured as a faculty member. Stagg made the "Monsters of the Midway" into a football power, winning seven Big Ten titles, the last in 1924, compiling a record of 242-112-27. Stagg was a creative coach, an outstanding recruiter who took his teams on national trips, and a successful adviser who placed his players in classes with supportive professors. His innovations included the tackling dummy, the huddle, the reverse and man-in-motion plays, the lateral pass, uniform numbers, and awarding varsity letters. The university was a pioneer in intercollegiate basketball, and in 1896 it defeated Iowa 15-12 in the first five-on-five intercollegiate men's basketball game. The Maroons took six Big Ten titles in basketball, including four straight (1907–10). In 1935 Maroon Jay Berwanger was chosen as the first Heisman trophy winner, and he was the first man ever selected in the NFL draft. Just four years later, in 1939, the school dropped football. The area's other Big Ten Team, Northwestern, in the suburb of Evanston, which started intercollegiate sports in 1882, took five football conference titles by 1936 and won the Rose Bowl in 1949, 20-14 over California. The main Catholic universities, De Paul and Loyola, briefly played football in the 1920s and 1930s, but the sport's cost led them to focus on basketball. Most Catholic fans instead adopted Notre Dame as their favorite team.[52]

Chicago's few high schools in the late nineteenth century became early hotbeds of sport. Students at Hyde Park, North Division, and Lake View high schools formed baseball teams in 1884 and formed a rudimentary football league in 1885. There were even girls' athletic associations at Lake View and West Division high schools in 1887. The sports organizations modeled themselves after local amateur ball clubs and college associations by forming a club, electing officers, organizing a squad, and challenging other schools and amateur teams. In 1889–90, Chicago stu-

dents formalized the Cook County High School League (CCHSL), initiated in 1885, comprising city and suburban public high schools. It was
one of the first such organizations in the United States. It started out with
track-and-field and football championships in 1889 and baseball in 1890.
By 1900 it had added tennis, indoor baseball, and girls' (1895) and boys'
basketball (1900). In 1898 the CCHSL set up a board of control to deal
with such abuses as the use of ringers. Six years later the board removed
all students from their positions of control, yet it failed to eliminate such
problems as eligibility, paid coaches, and traveling. Chicago teams were
proclaimed the mythical national football champions in 1902 and 1903
when Hyde Park high school, which had gone 4-2 during the season (the
losses coming to Big Ten teams), defeated Brooklyn Poly, 105-0, and then
the next year North Division high clobbered Brooklyn Boys high 75-0,
which ended the intersectional series.[53]

The University of Chicago supported high school sports by sponsoring national track-and-field (1902–1933), tennis (1895–1932), and basketball (1917–1930) competitions, which helped it recruit new talent.
The major statewide event was the state basketball tournament, which
the university initiated in 1908. A year later the Illinois High School
Association (IHSA) took over the tournament. Athletic programs in the
1920s commonly had two weight divisions to broaden opportunities
to participate. The biggest single schoolboy event is the Prep Bowl, an
annual match-up between the champions of the Catholic and public
high-school leagues that the mainstream press promoted as an ethnic/
religious competition. Started in 1927, it is the oldest postseason high
school football game in the United States. The 1937 game, which Austin
won 26-0 over Leo, drew 120,000 fans to Soldier Field, the largest crowd
ever to witness a football game in the United States.[54]

The Rise of Commercialized Sport, 1865–1920

Commercialized sport gained popularity after the Civil War and
boomed after the Great Chicago Fire when the city rebuilt and its population skyrocketed. The main sports were baseball, horse racing, and
boxing, with the latter two closely identified with gambling. The national
pastime flourished in Chicago, which entered founding franchises in
both the National League and the American League. Horse racing also
prospered, and by the 1880s, Chicago was the racing capital of the West.
Chicago was also an important center of prize fighting, but it was a sport
that operated on the fringe of the law. Sports entrepreneurs were heavily
involved in local politics, and in the case of horse racing and boxing, often

closely connected to organized crime. Their political clout saved them from undue municipal interference, kept down license fees, provided valuable inside information, and protected them against competition. But these businessmen were not invulnerable, and the city and county halted boxing in December 1904 and horse racing in April 1905.[55]

Prize Fighting and Wrestling

Commercial spectator sports were staged mainly at indoor arenas, racetracks, or baseball parks. Prize fighting had a following as a professional spectator sport even though it was banned everywhere until the early 1890s because of its brutality and the gambling associated with it. John L. Sullivan fought a five-round bareknuckles bout at Dexter Park in 1885. The first fights were held secretly at saloons, and thereafter publicly advertised bouts were staged at Tattersall's (16th and Dearborn), the Battery D Armory (Monroe at the lakefront), and McGurn's handball court (206 W. Division Street), facilitated by men with political clout. Chicago became a major boxing center around the turn of the century when prize fights began to be permitted. Many other famous fighters battled there: Bob Fitzsimmons, the first man to hold three titles; Chicago's own Harry Harris ("the human hair pin") and featherweight champ Terry McGovern. In 1905 the city completely banned prize fighting again because of the gambling, violence, and fixed fights like the McGovern–Joe Gans bout in 1900. Among the top local fighters was world lightweight champion Oscar M. "Battling" Nelson of Hegewisch (1905–6, 1908–10).[56]

Amateur wrestling became popular in the 1890s at athletic clubs and colleges, and after the turn of the century it was very popular at settlement houses, YMCAs, and ethnic sports clubs, including the Greek Olympic A.C. and the Swedish-American Athletic Association. The Chicago Hebrew Institute produced a number of national titlists, including Frederick Meyer freestyle heavyweight bronze medalist at the 1920 Olympics. The first major professional bout occurred in 1887 at the Battery D Armory, when Evan "Strangler" Lewis beat Joe Action to become the first American professional heavyweight wrestling champion. Prize fighting's demise encouraged interest in freestyle professional wrestling. In 1908 Frank Gotch unified the world title in a bout in Chicago by defeating George Hackenschmidt. Their rematch in 1911 drew 35,000 spectators at Comiskey Park. One year earlier, Gotch had defeated Stanislaus Zbysko in two straight falls at the Coliseum (15th and Wabash, built in 1899 by Charles Gunther), winning the first fall in a record seven seconds. The sport lost most of its popularity by the 1930s because matches lasted too long and lacked action. Promoters responded by making it a theatrical exhibition that was so popular that there were nearly 200 shows a year, most notably at the Chicago Stadium on the Near West Side. In the early 1950s, when wrestling was popular on television, many matches were telecast from the Marigold Gardens (840 W. Grace St. in Lakeview) and the International Amphitheater, near the Union Stockyards.[57]

Horse Racing

Horse racing was one of the most important spectator sports of the late nineteenth century. Harness racing was popular after the Civil War at Dexter Park, which was supplanted in 1878 by the West Side Driving Track (across the street from Garfield Park, at the city limits), used for harness and thoroughbred racing. Then, in 1883, 500 leading Chicagoans, about one-third of whom were millionaires, established the prestigious Washington Park Jockey Club. They opened the $150,000 Washington Park Race Track (61st and Cottage Grove) the next year. Washington Park became the Midwest's preeminent track, and its annual American Derby became a classic event. The $50,000 purse paid to winner Boundless in the 1893 American Derby made it the second-richest racing event in nineteenth-century America.[58]

Despite racing's popularity, it had a tenuous existence because of middle-class opposition to gambling. In 1891 Edward Corrigan's West Side Track lease expired, and he built the suburban Hawthorne Race Track to avoid political harassment. A politically connected poolroom syndicate that included Mike McDonald established the outlaw Garfield Park racetrack at the former site, but reform mayor Hempstead Washburne closed it one year later. In 1894 gamblers George Hankins and John Condon opened the new Harlem track in the village of Harlem (now Forest Park), but reformers successfully forced Washington Park to close. Hawthorne and Harlem followed a year later. Harlem reopened in 1897 and the other two tracks were back in business in 1898, and a fourth track opened in southwest suburban Worth. The sport flourished for a few years. Then renewed opposition to the gambling and the new problem of the suburban tracks being bombed by rival betting syndicates led Mayor Carter Harrison II and county officials to halt racing entirely in 1905. The flourishing illegal business of off-track gambling with bookmakers and at poolrooms continued to thrive, particularly under the leadership of Mont Tennes, who dominated the local gambling scene and controlled the national racing wire from 1909 to 1927, when he retired. He sold out to Moses Annenberg, a prominent figure in Chicago's newspaper circulation wars, who controlled the prominent tout sheets and the major racing dailies, the *Morning Telegraph* and the *Daily Racing Form*.[59]

Baseball in Nineteenth-Century Chicago

Professional team sport was introduced in 1870 by the $20,000 Chicago Base Ball Association, founded by Potter Palmer, Joseph Medill, team president David A. Gage, and other leading Chicagoans to boost the city's reputation, copying the example of the Cincinnati Red Stockings of 1869. The team played at Dexter Park, highlighted by a victory over the Cincinnati Red Stockings. In 1871 the White Stockings became a charter member of the National Association of Professional Base Ball Players (NA), the first professional league. They played at the 7,000–seat Lake Front Park on land (today's Grant Park) previously donated to the city by the federal government, stipulating it never be used commercially. The team came in second, finishing on the road after the Great Chicago Fire. Chicago rejoined the NA in 1874 under President William Hulbert, an ardent booster and coal merchant, playing at the Twenty-third Street Park between State and Federal Streets. In 1876 Hulbert organized the National League to put baseball on a businesslike basis. He recruited several NA stars, most notably Albert G. Spalding, who became pitcher/manager for $2,000 and one-fourth of any gate profits. Spalding went 47-13 and led the team to the pennant. But he abruptly quit playing to become team secretary and focus on his year-old A. G. Spalding and Brothers Sporting Goods Company. His company soon dominated the market by manufacturing and heavily advertising a full line of products and cutting costs by mass production. Chicago became a center of this industry, taking advantage of the hides and leathers from the meat-packing industry, another example of which was the Wilson Sporting Goods Company, created in 1913.[60]

Hulbert died in 1882 and Spalding became team president and chief stockholder. In 1883 Spalding built the $10,000 "Palace of the Fans" on the old federal land site where the White Stockings had been playing since 1878. The new field was considered the finest ballpark in the United States, but it had the smallest dimensions in major league history (right field 196 feet, center field 300 feet, and left field 180 feet), which resulted in a record 142 homers in 1884. The team moved again in 1885 after the federal government secured an injunction barring them from using the land, citing the stipulation against using the donated land for a commercial enterprise. The new field was the $30,000, 6,000–seat Congress Street Grounds on the West Side, fifteen to twenty minutes from downtown by streetcar. The audience was mainly the middle class, who had the time and money to attend mid-afternoon White Stocking games. There were no Sunday games until 1893, originally because of league rules and then because owner Albert G. Spalding incorrectly assumed that his middle-class fans opposed public amusements on the Sabbath.[61]

The White Stockings dominated the National League, winning five titles in seven years (1880–82, 1885–86), and by 1887 had accumulated a $100,000 cash surplus. The team's stars were catcher Mike "King" Kelly, a daring base runner and the most popular player of the nineteenth century, and Cap Anson, the first man to make 3,000 hits, and first baseman/manager from 1879 to 1897. He was one of the most prominent racists in organized baseball. In the 1880s he refused on a number of occasions to play against African Americans. Spalding became a major figure in NL councils and led its successful effort in 1890 to undermine the new Players' League established in response to the detested reserve clause. The club played half their games in the following season at South Side Park (Wentworth Avenue and Thirty-fifth Street), and they played every game there in 1892, because of its cheap rent, improved mass transit, and the coming of the World's Fair to nearby Hyde Park. Sunday baseball was introduced one year later at the new spacious $30,000 West Side Park (Polk and Wolcott) with a capacity of 13,000 where the team played exclusively after 1894. From 1876 through 1899, the White Stockings (renamed the Colts in 1890, the Orphans in 1897, and finally the Cubs by 1905) had a league-leading average daily attendance of 3,352.[62]

Chicago's baseball scene was bolstered by the development of sports journalism in its very competitive newspaper market. In the 1880s, Chicago baseball writers like Charles Seymour and Finley Peter Dunne developed a new style of reportage with a lot more personalized style and opinion. This became the dominant style in America. The tradition was sustained a generation later by writers like Ring Lardner, who covered sports for twelve years (1907–1918), especially his column in the *Tribune*, "In the Wake of the News," which gave him the freedom to develop his unique style that was terse and ironic and emphasized dialect. He became a national star with his "Busher's Letters Home," published in the *Saturday Evening Post*. [63]

Baseball in the Early Twentieth Century

In 1900 politically connected Charles Comiskey, a former major league star, moved his St. Paul team in the new American League (formerly the Western League) to Chicago and played at the 7,500–seat South Side Park (39th and Wentworth). Since Chicago's National League club had given up its old nickname White Stockings, Comiskey adopted it, which the press shortened to White Sox in 1902. The team catered to its white ethnic working-class neighborhood and charged just twenty-five cents for bleacher seats. The Sox had the best attendance in the AL for a

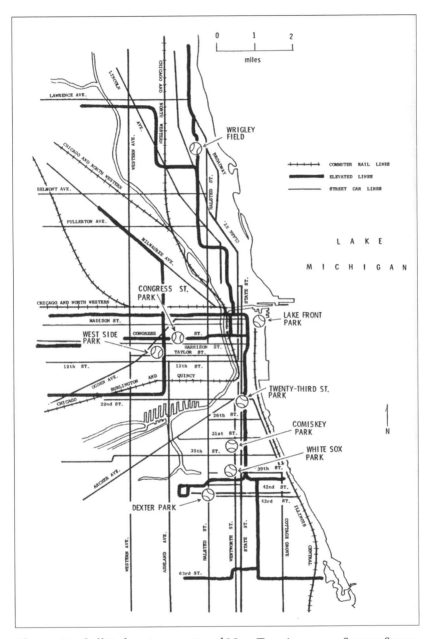

Chicago Baseball Parks, 1870–1916, and Mass Transit, c. 1915. Source: Steven
A. Riess, *Touching Base: Professional Baseball and American Culture in the
Progressive Era*, 2d ed. (Urbana: University of Illinois Press, 1999), 102.

generation and were very successful on the field, winning pennants in 1900 and then in 1901, when the AL proclaimed itself a major league. In 1906 the "Hitless Wonders" batted a league-low .230, yet made it to the World Series with a record of 93-58, where they upset the Cubs, who had gone 116-36, the best record in major league history. This was the first intra-city World Series ever, and the only one in Chicago. In 1910 Comiskey opened his new classically designed White Sox Park (renamed Comiskey Park in 1913) at a total cost of $700,000, the third fireproof park in the majors. Its original capacity was 28,800 and reached 32,000 by 1927.[64]

The Sox won 100 games in 1917 with the AL's best pitching and hitting. Eddie Cicotte led the AL in wins (28) and ERA (1.53). Then they beat the New York Giants in the World Series in six games. They had largely the same roster in 1919, led by Hall of Famers Eddie Collins at second base and Ray Schalk behind the plate, plus left fielder Joe Jackson, who hit .356 lifetime, third-highest in history, and pitcher Eddie Cicotte, who won 29 games. This was the series in which several players conspired to fix the outcome, and the Cincinnati Reds won, five games to three. First baseman Arnold "Chick" Gandil and shortstop Charles "Swede" Risberg orchestrated the conspiracy with the cooperation of pitchers Cicotte and Lefty Williams and center fielder Oscar "Hap" Felsch, because they felt Comiskey had cheated and underpaid them. These five men, utility in-fielder Fred McMullin, and Jackson shared a $100,000 bribe, which was confirmed by grand jury confessions by Cicotte, Williams, and Jackson, who hit .375 for the series. They were all indicted on conspiracy charges along with third baseman Buck Weaver, who knew about the fix but did not participate. In the end, the players were all acquitted on August 2, 1921, largely because the confessions were lost. When Joe Jackson sued for back pay in 1924, the confessions were suddenly found in the safe of Comiskey's attorney. The jury carried the players out of the courtroom on their shoulders as the verdict recertified the integrity of the game that best epitomized the nation. All seemed well again in a country threatened by foreigners, Bolsheviks, and labor radicals. Despite the verdict, Judge Kenesaw Mountain Landis, appointed as the first commissioner of baseball on January 12, 1921, banned the Black Sox from professional baseball.[65]

Meanwhile, on the West Side, Spalding sold the Cubs in 1905 to the team's press agent Charles W. Murphy for $105,000. Manager Frank Chance led the Cubs to at least 99 wins annually from 1906 through 1910, including three straight pennants (1906–1908), and two world championships over the Detroit Tigers, second place in 1909 with 104 wins, and another pennant 1910, when they lost the series to the Philadelphia Athletics. The Cubs were led by Mordecai "Three-Finger" Brown, who won at least twenty games six times, and by the double-play combination of Joe Tinker, Johnny Evers, and Chance made famous by Franklin Adams's poem. The Cubs were the second-best draw in the NL and earned $1,260,000 during Murphy's tenure that ended in 1915.[66]

Major League Baseball's success drew competition from the Federal League, organized in 1913, which proclaimed itself a major league one year later. The Chicago entry, known as the Whales, was owned by restaurateur Charles Weeghman, who built the fireproof $250,000, 14,000–seat Weeghman Park at Clark and Addison, on the newly developing North Side. After the 1915 season, the Federal League merged into Organized Baseball. Weeghman and his syndicate acquired control of the Cubs for $500,000 and his field was renamed Cubs Park. In 1918, chewing gum mogul William Wrigley gained control of the Cubs, who captured the pennant in the war-shortened season with a record of 84-45, but they lost the series against the Red Sox, which was played at the higher-capacity Comiskey Park.[67]

Sport in the Interwar Era

During the 1920s, Chicagoans enjoyed a higher standard of living than ever before. Working hours for industrial workers declined to about fifty hours a week, and even unskilled workers were earning about $1,000 a year. Most Chicagoans had the opportunity to participate in sports or attend spectator sports in "the Golden Age of Sports." Entrepreneurs saw a big opportunity and avidly promoted spectator sports. They secured the legalization of prize fighting and on-track parimutuel gambling on thoroughbred racing. The coming of the Great Depression seriously hampered commercialized sports, but less than most other sectors of the economy, as the public sought escape from the hard times through entertainment. During the depression, when millions had unwanted free time, programs like the WPA repaired and expanded public sports facilities, including pools, ball fields, and skating rinks.

The Democratization of Participatory Sport

In the 1920s working-class Chicagoans played billiards and bowling in their neighborhoods, joined leagues sponsored by fraternal organizations, ethnic groups, and political organizations, and enjoyed sporting opportunities at their workplaces. Labor unions established recreational programs to encourage loyalty and friendship among their members. For example, the Amalgamated Clothing Workers in the 1930s had their own gym and a comprehensive sports program for its 16,000 members. Left-wing groups sponsored gymnastics and soccer to appeal to immigrant workers, but they sponsored American sports as well. Chicago hosted the Communist Labor Sports Union in 1927 and the International Workers' Olympics in 1931 and 1932 (the latter was also known as the "Counter-Olympics"), but the events attracted very small crowds.[68]

Welfare capitalism peaked in the 1920s, providing recreational programs to promote worker loyalty and to fight unions, not just for white men, but also for African Americans and women. In baseball alone, there were some sixty industrial leagues, with roster spots often given workers who had been hired or promoted because of their athletic skills. The Western Electric Hawthorne Works had the biggest program, with 28,000 employees enrolled in its athletic association in 1923. The company sponsored fourteen sports for women, and its annual track meet in 1930 drew more than 10,000 spectators. Promising women athletes of the time, many of whom got their start at park district meets, were recruited by prestigious private organization like the Illinois Women's Athletic Club, founded in 1918, to bring renown to the club.[69] Working-class Chicago women captured national championships in basketball, bowling, swimming, softball, and track. Some working-class women used their athletic skills to get better jobs, but, for most of them, Gems points out, they "found their greatest measure of self-esteem in these leisure activities that provided high visibility, psychic rewards, and peer acknowledgment, if only at the neighborhood level."[70]

During the Great Depression, one-fourth of all American industrial sports programs were eliminated. Nonetheless, in 1937, 233 of the 600 firms studied by the *Chicago Recreation Survey* fielded 1,700 bowling teams, and 264 companies sponsored almost 1,000 softball teams. Softball then was the second most popular participatory sport among men and women. The game originated in 1887 when Chicagoan George Hancock created indoor baseball at the Farragut Boat Club, with an improvised boxing glove and a broomstick for a bat. The game was soon formalized, using a soft seventeen-inch ball, no gloves, and bases twenty-seven feet apart. Within a few years there were over a hundred teams, including high schools and college men and women, but indoor baseball declined rapidly in the 1910s, mainly because of the growing popularity of basketball, and soon disappeared. By 1907 the game, now known as "playground ball," had moved outside and was played by park, school, and church associations using a sixteen-inch ball. Youths in crowded neighborhoods also played stickball and "pinners" or "ledge," a game in which a rubber ball was bounced off a stoop. Sixteen-inch softball became unique to Chicago and was played nightly on nearly every city block in the 1920s and 1930s, promoting cohesiveness and identity in the neighborhood, where leagues were operated by local taverns and small-time gamblers.

Nationally, twelve-inch softball ruled, and at the Century of Progress Exposition in 1933, 70,000 attended the Amateur Softball Association's first national championship. Local men's and women's teams captured the title, and the women repeated in 1934. The city hosted the world's championships in 1936 at Soldier Field.[71]

Spectator Sports

Major League Baseball

Baseball remained the number-one spectator sport. In 1920 Charles Comiskey grossed $910,206, but the Black Sox scandal left him without much of a team. Comiskey spent more than $1 million in the 1920s to recruit talent, but with little success, and the team floundered for decades. Attendance slipped during the Great Depression to just 233,000 in 1932. When Comiskey died in 1931, his son, J. Louis, succeeded him, and after his death eight years later, Louis's widow, Grace Reidy Comiskey took over.[72]

The Cubs fared better, with pennant-winning squads in 1929, 1932, 1935, and 1938. The fans turned out to the park, renamed Wrigley Field in 1927, setting an NL record of 1,163,347 in 1929, when the team went 98-54 with a .303 batting average. The roster team included outfielders Hack Wilson, Riggs Stephenson, and Kiki Cuyler, second baseman Rogers Hornsby, catcher Gabby Hartnett, and pitcher Charlie Grimm. They lost the World Series in five games to the Philadelphia Athletics, one of the best teams of all time. In 1932 they faced the Yankees in the Series and lost in four straight, highlighted by Babe Ruth's alleged called shot off Charlie Root at Wrigley Field. The 1935 squad went 100-54, including twenty-one straight wins in September, but lost the Series in six games to the Detroit Tigers. In 1938, one year after team president Bill Veeck, Jr., planted ivy on the outfield walls, the Cubs won an exciting pennant drive, capped by Hartnett's "homer in the gloamin'." They had to compete against an all-time great Yankees squad in the Fall Classic and were swept. In 1943, when the majors were playing with depleted lineups, owner Philip K. Wrigley organized the All-American Girls' Professional Baseball League with teams in midsized Midwestern cities to sustain interest in the sport. Shortly after the war ended, the Cubs again made the World Series but lost the series to the Tigers in seven. It was their last pennant.[73]

The Turf

The old sport of thoroughbred racing had a big revival in this era. In 1909 former alderman Thomas Carey acquired Hawthorne Race Track and attempted unsuccessfully to revive the sport with mini-meetings in 1909, 1911, 1914, and 1916. Then in 1922 and 1923 he held thriving meets, using oral betting, which the courts ruled in 1924 was legal. The sport began to boom and Charles W. Bidwell's syndicate leased Hawthorne from the Carey family until 1945 when the lease expired. In 1926 Lincoln Fields in Crete and Washington Park in Homewood were opened. Then one year later, the state legalized pari-mutuel betting. H. D. "Curley" Brown established Arlington Park Racetrack in the northwestern suburbs, but there was widespread concern of a possible underworld takeover, and self-made millionaire John D. Hertz of the Yellow Taxicab Company took over the track in 1928 to prevent that. In 1940 control passed to Benjamin Lindheimer, operator of Washington Park. Hertz had a great run as a racer and breeder. In 1928 his Reigh Count won the Kentucky Derby, and his wife Fannie's Count Fleet took the Triple Crown in 1943.[74]

Bettors also enjoyed dog racing in the late 1920s at six tracks. Al Capone controlled the quarter-mile Hawthorne Kennel Club in Cicero and another course in Thornton. His North Side rival Bugs Moran ran the Fairview track, which burned to the ground. But the courts ruled in 1930 that greyhound racing was illegal, and one year later the state legislature turned down proposals to legalize the sport. In 1932 mob lawyer Edward J. O'Hare converted Capone's facility into the half-mile Sportsman's Park, owned by the Bidwell family since 1943. The coming of war curtailed racing because of rationing and manpower needs. Lincoln Fields closed in 1941 and its races moved to Hawthorne; Arlington shut down from 1943 to 1945, shifting its major races to Washington Park.[75]

PUGILISM

Prize fighting, the third major spectator sport, gained a lot of prestige and popularity in the early 1920s after it was legalized in New York and drew large, fashionable crowds to Madison Square Garden. In 1926 Illinois legalized the sport under a State Athletic Commission in response to pressure from ethnic urbanites who enjoyed the sport. Politicians also saw an opportunity for new sources of revenue by licensing big fights like the 1927 Jack Dempsey–Gene Tunney heavyweight championship rematch for newly completed Soldier Field. Back in 1909, the Chicago Plan, drawn up by Daniel Burnham, proposed a multipurpose public facility for athletics and other entertainments on the lake front. The first stage was completed in 1924 by the South Park District and named Municipal Grant Park Stadium. Renamed Soldier Field as a war memorial one year later, the classic-design structure, with its hundred-foot-tall Doric columns, originally seated 45,000, which was more than doubled when finally completed in 1929 at a total cost of $8.5 million, far in excess of comparable municipal stadiums. Today it is mainly remembered for such sporting events as the Army–Navy Game of 1926, attended by 111,000, and the 1937 Prep Bowl, but Soldier Field was also employed for more pedestrian events like the Eighth Annual Track of Field Games of the Chicago Police Department, which attracted 84,000 spectators and raised $200,000 for the Policemen's Benevolent Fund.[76]

The 1927 Dempsey–Tunney fight at Soldier Field drew 104,000 spectators, who paid $2.6 million, a record gate. The scheduled referee was Davey Miller, but he was replaced at the last minute by Dave Barry because it was rumored Al Capone had bet on Dempsey and had taken Miller for a car ride to protect his investment. Dempsey knocked Tunney down in the seventh round but stood over him for five seconds before going to a neutral corner. Barry only then started his count, and Tunney arose at the count of nine. Tunney went on to successfully defend his crown in the "long count" fight.[77]

Chicago was a major boxing town during the Great Depression, with twelve boxing arenas, most notably the 2,200-seat Marigold Gardens (840 Grace St.), which charged as little as 75 cents for admission. There were many boxing gyms for fighters to train, most notably Coulon's (1154 E. 63d Street), founded in 1925 by one-time bantamweight champion Johnny Coulon. Amateurs competed in the Golden Gloves Tournament, started in 1928 by the *Chicago Tribune*, and many trained under the Catholic Youth Organization (CYO), established in 1930 by Bishop Bernard J. Sheil, himself a former star athlete, to fight delinquency, Americanize second-generation ethnic Catholics, and counter the attraction of Protestant organizations. The CYO provided a wide variety of social services but gained most attention from its sports program that serviced over 100,000 participants, claimed the world's largest basketball league (430 teams), and produced many world-class Olympic boxers (three in 1936 alone) and future professional pugilists.[78]

Chicago was also the home of many great fighters in the interwar era, most notably Joe Louis from Detroit, who fought ten of his first twelve professional matches there. In 1937 he captured the heavyweight championship from Jim Braddock at Comiskey Park before 41,675, who paid more than $607,000.[79]

PRO FOOTBALL

Chicago in the interwar years became a major center of professional football, a product of the blending of the blend of sandlots teams, industrial leagues, and sports entrepreneurship. The first pro football player was Yale All-American Pudge Heffelfinger, who in 1892 played for "expenses" for the Chicago Athletic Association in a game in Pittsburgh. Chicago's first fully professional football team traces its history to 1899, when

South Side painting contractor Chris O'Brien established a neighborhood football team, the Morgan Athletic Club. Two years later, he and his brother splintered off with some friends to form the Cardinal Social and Athletic Club, a football club, which in turn became the Normal Athletic Association football team in 1904; it lasted two seasons. Then in 1916 O'Brien established the Racine Cardinals (named for Racine Avenue), and they became a charter member of the American Professional Football Association (APFA) in 1920 (renamed the National Football League two years later). They played at Comiskey Park and renamed themselves the Chicago Cardinals in 1922. Three years later they won the NFL championship. The rival Bears originated downstate as the Decatur Staleys in 1919 to advertise the Staley Starch Company's products and improve employee relations. Former University of Illinois football star and New York Yankee George Halas, a Bohemian lad from Pilsen, ran the Staley athletic program, recruiting players with promises of a full-time job, two hours off from work to practice, and a share of the gate. The Staleys joined the APFA in 1920, coming in second to the Akron Pros with a record of 10-1-2. The company then cut back on its recreation program, but it gave Halas a $10,000 stake to take over the team and move up north to Chicago. Halas made one of his recruits, fellow Illini Edward "Dutch" Sternaman, a partner and sold automobiles to make ends meet. The team played at Wrigley Field, went 10-1-1, and won the championship, but operated at a loss of $71.63 for the season. He paid his players $75–100 per game.[80]

In 1922 the team was renamed the Bears, and three years later, Halas boldly moved to bolster the low status of pro football by signing superstar halfback Red Grange of the University of Illinois. Grange and his personal manager "Cash and Carry" Pyle signed for a guarantee of $2,000 a game, a share of the gate up to 15,000, and 40 percent of ticket sales above that amount. He joined the Bears shortly after the end of his college career, but prior to graduation. Grange was immediately a great gate attraction, drawing 34,000 to his first pro game. The Bears went on a whirlwind eight-game, twelve-day tour, drawing large crowds everywhere, including 73,561 in New York. Grange and Pyle earned $250,000 for the tour, and the Bears made $100,000.[81]

Halas retired as coach in 1930, replaced by Ralph Jones of Lake Forest College, who installed the man-in-motion T formation. The Bears did brilliantly on the field, defeating Portsmouth 9-0 in the NFL championship on December 18, 1932, held indoors on an eighty-yard field in the Chicago Stadium because a five-inch sheet of ice had covered Wrigley Field. The team was led by former Minnesota All-American Bronko Nagurski, who was making $5,000 a year. Halas returned as coach the following season and the Bears repeated as champions with a 23-21 victory over the

New York Giants. They represented the NFL in 1934 in the first College All-Star game at Soldier Field, sponsored by the *Tribune,* which ended in a scoreless tie. The Bears were undefeated that season, going into the championship game on December 9 against the Giants at the icy Polo Grounds. Down 13-3 at the half, the Giants put on basketball shoes to adapt to the poor field condition and scored twenty-seven unanswered points to win the "sneakers game." The Bears lost the 1937 championship game to the Washington Redskins but enjoyed revenge in the December 12, 1940, title game, at which quarterback Sid Luckman led the 73-0 slaughter, the greatest point margin in NFL history. The Bears repeated in 1941 by defeating the Giants 37-9. The 1942 team was undefeated going into the championship but lost to Washington 14-6. But they had their revenge the next year, taking the title against the Redskins 41-21. That season Luckman completed an NFL record of seven touchdowns in a game against the Giants and set a team record of 28 touchdown passes that lasted until 1999, when Eric Kramer notched 29.[82]

Indoor Pro Sport

Indoor professional sports enjoyed a lot of popularity in the 1920s. In 1926 professional hockey came to Chicago when millionaire coffee baron Frederick McLaughlin bought a National Hockey League franchise for $14,000, which he staffed by purchasing the Portland Oregon Rosebuds of the Western Hockey League. Major McLaughlin named the team in honor of his old army unit, the 85th Black Hawk Division. The Blackhawks opened at the 6,000–seat Coliseum on November 17, 1926, defeating Toronto 4-1. Three years later, the Blackhawks moved to promoter Paddy Harmon's new $7 million Chicago Stadium (Madison and Wood Streets), which had opened on March 28, 1929, with the Tommy Loughran–Mickey Walker light heaveyweight championship fight in which Loughran successfully defended his title. The Blackhawks opened their long tenure at the Stadium on December 16, when 14,000 fans saw them defeat Pittsburgh 3-1. The Hawks made the Stanley Cup finals in 1930–31 and captured the Cup in 1933–34 with a dramatic overtime win 1-0 on Mush Marsh's goal. Four years later, despite a 14-25-9 record, the Hawks won another championship, defeating the Toronto Maple Leafs for the biggest upset in NHL history. The Stadium itself struggled during the Great Depression when even the popular six-day bicycle races could not sell out. In 1934 realtor Arthur Wirtz bought the building and rescued it from bankruptcy, mainly through his promotion of Sonia Henie's Hollywood Ice Review.[83]

Professional basketball lagged far behind ice hockey in popularity. Chicago's first team was George Halas's Bruins of the American Basketball League (1926–31), who compiled a record of 101-132. Halas revived the Bruins in 1939 as a member of the Midwestern-based National Basketball League (NBL), composed of teams sponsored by major industrial firms. The Bruins participated in the 1940 Professional World Championship held in Chicago, which the Harlem Globetrotters won. In 1942–43 the Studebakers, a United Auto Workers–sponsored quintet with six black players, represented Chicago in the NBL, followed in 1944–45 by manufacturer Maurice White's American Gears. His roster included veteran pros and local collegians, most notably six-foot-ten All-American George Mikan of DePaul, who led the Gears to an NBL title in 1946–47.[84]

An indoor pseudo-sport that emerged in Depression-era Chicago was roller derby. In 1935 movie publicist Leo Seltzer took over the nearly defunct Coliseum, and, inspired by six-day bike races (first held at the Coliseum in 1915) and the contemporary marathon dance craze, created roller derby as an endurance contest between twenty-five male and female couples. The Transcontinental Roller Derby consisted of 57,000 laps nonstop, eleven and a half hours a day, or nearly 3,000 miles, the approximate distance from New York to Los Angeles. Nine teams finished. Three years later, Seltzer adopted sportswriter Damon Runyon's suggestion to emphasize physical contact between skaters of different teams, which led to the evolution of the "sport" of roller derby. The National Roller Derby League was established in 1949 and became a staple of television programming.[85]

Sports since 1945

After World War II, sport boomed in Chicago, as it did in other cities across the country. There was a pent-up interest from the war years, and people were earning more money than ever before and had a lot of discretionary income to spend on their free time, which reached 6 percent of their income by the 1980s. They attended sporting events in greater numbers than ever before and also watched sporting events on television. In the first decade or two after the war, lower-class Chicagoans devoted relatively more attention to such sports as baseball, boxing, and horse racing while the middle class might be more likely to play golf and attend college football games, but these differences faded away. There was also a big boom in participatory sports, especially after the 1960s, influenced by the fitness fad and feminism.

The rapid suburbanization of the region shortly after World War II did foster significant differences in sporting opportunities, as did racism and life in inner-city Chicago. Suburbanites enjoyed newer and better-financed municipal parks, as well as more and better-funded and more diversified physical education and interscholastic sports programs. The sports powerhouses were no longer city schools, but high schools in Winnetka, St. Charles, and Naperville. New Trier in suburban Winnetka, for instance, won twenty-three state championships between 1996 and 2005.[86]

The changing urban demography was reflected by the weakening performances of Chicago public schools against Catholic school representatives in the Prep Bowl, a game whose significance drastically declined in comparison with the state football championship. There has also been a big change in the sporting culture of African Americans, who became in this era the largest ethnic group in the city. The big sport in that community, long rooted in the rural South, for years was baseball—a sport that until 1947 was segregated at the major league level—but beginning in the 1960s the big sport in black Chicago became basketball, a traditional inner-city sport, whose athletes today are admired for their individual prowess, flair, style, and wealth.

Golf

One of the best known courses in the Chicago area was the Tam O'Shanter Country Club in Niles, where businessman George May began sponsoring professional golf tournaments in 1941, starting with the Tam O'Shanter Open, with a $15,000 purse, the largest in professional golf at the time. He charged only $1 for admission and drew 41,000 spectators. His innovations included grandstands at key locations, refreshments for sale, a dance after the tournament, and slot machines. He established major tournaments for women and in 1945 established the Tam O'Shanter World Championship, with $13,600 to the winner. Club players were the first to use golf carts. In 1953 it was the first nationally televised tournament, and the winner got $25,000, the biggest prize in pro golf. ABC charged May $32,000 to broadcast the competition.[87]

According to golf historian Howard Rabinowitz, Chicago was the national leader in public-access golf. The first public course in the Midwest was Jackson Park in 1899, operated by the Chicago Park District. Today more than half the approximately 275 courses in the area are open to the public. The primary entrepreneur was Joe Jemsek, who bought St. Andrews Country Club in 1939 and built upscale facilities. One of his courses, Dubsdread, opened in 1967 at the suburban Cog Hill club in suburban Lemont, and became the permanent home of the Western Open in 1991 after Butler National in Oak Brook, Illinois, refused to end its male-only membership policy.[88]

Prize Fighting

Postwar Chicago was a major center for prize fighting, hosting more than forty world championships. Title bouts at the Stadium included the Tony Zale–Rocky Graziano middleweight title fight on July 16, 1947, attended by 18,547, who paid an indoor record $422,918 gate. Zale, Gary's "Man of Steel," a member of boxing's Hall of Fame, lost his crown to Graziano on a sixth-round TKO in the fight of the year. On February 14, 1951, Sugar Ray Robinson won the middleweight title from Jake LaMotta on a thirteenth-round TKO, known as the "St. Valentine Massacre," and on May 15, 1953, Rocky Marciano made his first title defense at the Stadium against former heavyweight champion Jersey Joe Walcott, winning with a first-round KO.[89]

Arthur Wirtz and partners Canadian grain merchant James Norris, owner of the Detroit Red Wings, and local African American attorney Truman Gibson established the International Boxing Club (IBC) in 1947, which promoted 80 percent of world championship fights from 1949 through 1955. The IBC also promoted televised fights, which dominated early TV ratings. Televised boxing oversaturated the local market, killing the smaller boxing clubs, and by the 1960s, the local fight game was barely surviving. The Supreme Court dissolved the IBC in 1959 as a monopoly with close ties between leading managers and organized crime.[90]

Horse Racing

After World War II racing resumed with a flourish, and Arlington Park, closed in 1943, reopened in 1946, the same year that Maywood Park opened up as a trotting course. Sportsman's Park added trotting in 1949. Lincoln Fields had been closed during the war, and its races moved to Hawthorne (1943–1947, 1952–1953) and Washington Park (1948–1951). Then a fire closed Lincoln Fields from 1952 to 1954. Benjamin Lindheimer's Balmoral Jockey Club purchased Lincoln Fields in 1955 and renamed it Balmoral. The Balmoral Jockey Club emphasized harness racing and shifted its thoroughbred events to other tracks until 1978. Balmoral helped make Chicago the center of harness racing. Since 1991 the track has been used just for harness racing, and it is currently Chicago's main harness racing track. Since 1987 Balmoral's owners have been George Steinbrenner and Billy Johnson.

In 1960 Marge Lindheimer Everett, Lindheimer's adopted daughter, took over Arlington, Washington Park, and Balmoral. Marge became a principal in one of the worst scandals in Illinois history, admitting she had illegally sold stock at a bargain basement price to Governor Otto Kerner to gain choice racing dates. In 1971 she was compelled to sell her shares in her tracks to Madison Square Garden Corporation, whose parent company, Gulf & Western, sold Arlington to Richard Duchossois's syndicate. A 1985 fire destroyed Arlington Park's grandstand, but it was replaced by the $200 million Arlington International Racecourse, a world-class facility.[91]

Automobile Racing

Chicago has not been known for car racing, but amateur stock-car competition was popular at Raceway Park, a one-fifth-mile asphalt oval in Blue Island, built in 1937 for dog racing. Peter Jenin bought the track in 1948 and promoted stock car racing until 2000 when it was no longer profitable. In the 1950s there were more than sixty races each summer, attended by up to 10,000 fans who paid $1.25 for admission. Drag racing at the time was very popular with teenagers, who held illegal matches on public roads. Legal drag races were staged from 1957 to 1984 at U.S. 30 Dragstrip in Merrillville, Indiana. Soldier Field was a popular site for stock car and midget car racing in the 1940s and 1950s, with crowds of up to 90,000. Racing thereafter lost its attraction until the late 1990s when the national popularity of motor sports encouraged the opening in 2001 of the Chicago Speedway in Joliet for NASCAR events. The $130 million facility has a 1.5–mile oval and seats 75,000.[92]

Ice Hockey

Blackhawks founder Frederick McLaughlin died in 1944, the year the squad lost in the Stanley Cup finals to Montreal. His estate sold the franchise to a syndicate headed by team president Bill Tobin, who mainly turned out to be a front man for James E. Norris, one of the co-owners of the Chicago Stadium since 1936 and the owner of the Detroit Red Wings. The Blackhawks made the playoffs only twice between 1945 and 1958, a period that included several one-sided trades with the Red Wings. On September 11, 1952, the Blackhawks were sold to Arthur Wirtz, James Norris Jr., and James Norris Sr., who died a few months later. Two years later the Wirtz family gained majority control. General manager Tommy Ivan's farm system developed such superstars as Bobby Hull, Glenn Hall, and Stan Mikita. They were the mainstays of Coach Rudy Pilous's second place 1961–62 team that won the Stanley Cup by defeating the Detroit Red Wings in six games. In the 1960s and 1970s, the Hawks, led by Hull, who scored 604 goals in Chicago, were the hottest ticket in town. A ten-time first team All-Star, Hull left the team in a salary dispute in 1972 for the new World Hockey League. The Blackhawks finished the 1966–67 season in first place but lost in the Stanley Cup semifinals. They won eight division championships during the 1970s. Under Coach Mike Keenan they won three Norris Division titles between the 1989–90 and

1992–93 seasons and made the Stanley Cup finals in 1991–92. In 1994–95 the team moved across the street to the $175 million United Center, owned by Bill Wirtz and Jerry Reinsdorf. The Hawks struggled in their new home, and in 1997–98 they failed to make the playoffs for the first time in twenty-nine years.[93]

College Sports

Since the mid-1920s, Chicago college football fans, especially those who were Catholic, looked to Notre Dame in South Bend as their home team, especially with the mediocrity of Chicagoland elevens. The Fighting Irish have captured eleven national championships between 1924 and 1988 and had two great runs in the post-Rockne era, going 149-28-13 from 1934 to 1953 and 278-89-8 from 1964 to 1986. It seems the goal of every outstanding Catholic League football player is to attend the university. When it comes to basketball, there have been few moments of glory for local quintets, and for the most part Chicago loyalty belongs to the University of Illinois in Champaign. Certainly the greatest local achievement was the 1963 NCAA championship won by Loyola, who regularly started four blacks and was the first NCAA team to start an all-black lineup. DePaul also had some outstanding teams, coached by local icon Ray Meyer from 1942 to 1984, with a record of 724-354. His 1944 team led by George Mikan came in second in the National Invitational Tournament. DePaul became a top national team in the late 1970s and amassed an incredible 132-15 record from 1977 to 1982. In 1978–79 DePaul went to the NCAA Final Four, followed up by a #1 ranked team in 1979–80 and 1980–81 that bowed out each year in the team's first tournament game. Meyer coached for 42 years, retiring in 1984 with a record of 724-352, sixth among NCAA coaches.

Professional Basketball

In 1946 major hockey arena owners, looking for an additional attraction, organized the Basketball Association of America, which included the Chicago Stags. Led by All-Star Max Zaslofsky, the Stags had a winning record in all three BAA seasons. In 1949–50, the old NBL and BAA merged to form the National Basketball Association, but the Stags dropped out after one season because of low attendance. In 1961 entrepreneur Abe Saperstein, disappointed that he had never received an NBA franchise, founded the short-lived American Basketball League. The NBA expanded that year, adding Dave Trager's Chicago Packers, who played at the Amphitheater. They were renamed the Zephyrs a year later and played at the Coliseum. In 1963 they moved and became the Washington Bullets.[94]

After several failed attempts to bring back big-time basketball, Dick Klein, a former Gears player, secured an NBA franchise in 1966 for $1.25 million. The Bulls first played at the Amphitheater, coached by former NBA star Johnny "Red" Kerr. All-Stars Jerry Sloan and Guy Rodgers led them to a 33-38 record and an unexpected spot in the playoffs. The Bulls moved to the Coliseum the following year, then to the Stadium in 1968. The franchise was struggling and drew only 891 to the November 7, 1968, game. The team began to improve under Coach Dick Motta's leadership and the great play of forwards Bob Love and Chet Walker. In 1971–72, the team went 57-25, with the league's stingiest defense, but they lost in the playoffs to the Los Angeles Lakers, who had won a record 69 games. In 1972 Bill Wirtz's syndicate bought the team, which in 1974–75 won the Midwest Division but lost the seventh game of the Western Conference championship to the Golden State Warriors.

The Bulls struggled for a decade, and after going 27-55 in 1983–84, earned the third draft pick in the draft, selecting Michael Jordan from North Carolina. Jordan was an immediate sensation, and Coach Kevin Loughery redesigned the offense around him. The squad improved to 38-44 and made the playoffs for the first time since 1981. Jordan averaged 18.3 points, third-highest in the NBA and was Rookie of the Year.

Jerry Reinsdorf became managing partner in 1985, and general manager Jerry Krause rebuilt the team. In 1986–87, under coach Doug Collins, Jordan led the league in scoring with 37.1 points and the team finished at 40-42. Rookies Scottie Pippen and Horace Grant were added the following season, and then prior to the 1988–89 season the much-needed center Bill Cartwright was secured in a trade, putting in place the core of a great team, which sold out every home game. The final piece of the puzzle was the replacement of Collins in 1988 by his untested assistant Phil Jackson, who proved to be an excellent motivator. He employed the triangle offense, which got everyone involved until the fourth quarter, when the ball went to Jordan. The team improved to 55-27 in 1989–90 but lost to the Detroit Pistons in the seventh game of the conference finals.

The Bulls began their remarkable stretch of world championships in 1990–91. Led by Jordan and Pippen, they went 61-21, including 26 straight wins at home. They overcame the Pistons in the Eastern Conference finals in four straight and beat the aging Lakers in the NBA finals, four games to one. They raced through the next season with a mark of 67-15 and finished off the Portland Trail Blazers in the finals four games to one. The team fell to 57-25 in 1992–93 but dispatched the Phoenix Suns in six games for their first run of three straight titles (known as three-peats).

Jordan retired just before the 1993–94 season, yet the team persevered and went 55-27, led by Pippen's outstanding all-around play, advancing to the conference championship. The team moved to the United Center the next season but struggled until Jordan unretired in mid-March. They lost to the Orlando Magic, however, in the second round of the playoffs.

In 1995–96, the team went a remarkable 72-10, the most wins in NBA history. They lost just one game in their first three playoff series and then toppled the Seattle Supersonics in six in the NBA finals. Jordan was MVP in the All-Star game, the regular season, and the playoffs. The Bulls followed the next year with a record of 69-13 and another NBA championship.

In 1997–98, the team went 62-20, as Jordan won his fifth MVP and tenth scoring championship and made the All Defensive team for a record ninth time. The Indiana Pacers took the Bulls to a deciding seventh game in the Conference playoff, the only seventh-game victory the Bulls have ever had in postseason play. The Bulls then faced Utah in the NBA finals, splitting the first two games in Utah, and then at home in game three won by a score of 98-54, allowing the fewest points in the modern playoffs. The Bulls won the next game, but Utah took the fifth. In the decisive sixth game, Utah had a one-point lead with time running out. Jordan tallied on a fierce drive, and then stole the ball, raced up court, and took a jump shot from the right side of the key with five and two-tenths seconds remaining—nothing but net! The Bulls had won their second three-peat, led by Jordan's forty-five points. After the season, Jordan retired, and Jackson followed. Krause thereafter disbanded the squad and began the slow process of rebuilding.[95]

Baseball

Chicago's baseball teams struggled after the war, but announcer Jack Brickhouse of WGN always put a positive spin on Cubs (1943–1981) and White Sox games (1943–1967), first on radio and then on TV. The Cubs did not have a single winning season until 1963 and were considered the "second" team in Chicago. Benevolent owner P. K. Wrigley treated players and fans well and did not try to maximize profits, but the farm system he developed was weak and he did not field competitive teams. The Cubs did not integrate racially, which restricted them from an important pool of talented players. The first African Americans arrived in 1954, second baseman Gene Baker and shortstop Ernie Banks. Banks, "Mr. Cub," won Most Valuable Player awards in 1958 and 1959 and hit 512 homeruns during his career. In 1961 Wrigley tried rotating coaches, instead of using a single manager, but the "college of coaches" was an utter failure. In 1962 the Cubs finished with 103 losses, the most in team history. The Cubs did not begin to improve until after 1966, when fiery Leo Durocher was hired to manage a young team. By 1968 there was renewed fan interest, and attendance surpassed one million for the first time since 1952. Pitcher Ferguson Jenkins won twenty games, and the team finished in third place. The Cubs led the pennant race for most of 1969, with an outstanding lineup. They drew a record crowd of 1,674,993 fans, including a fabled segment known as the "Bleacher Bums," a community of die-hard fans who developed a strong sense of camaraderie. But Durocher overworked his pitching staff, and the eight-and-a-half-game lead in mid-August evaporated as the New York Mets won the pennant by nine games. The Cubs remained contenders throughout Durocher's tenure, which ended in mid-1972, but thereafter they fell on hard times.[96]

P. K. Wrigley died in 1977, and the family sold the team four years later to the Tribune Corporation for $20.5 million to pay inheritance taxes. The new owners were attracted by the potential synergy possible with Cubs afternoon games on WGN-TV, their national super station. In 1982 the owners brought in veteran announcer Harry Caray to replace Brickhouse; Caray had just left the White Sox when they moved to cable TV. Caray became a fan favorite, broadcasting Cubs games until his death in 1997. In 1981 the Tribune Company hired Dallas Green as general manager. Green's excellent trades brought in second baseman Ryne Sandberg and pitchers Rick Sutcliffe and Dennis Eckersley, who led the team to the 1984 division championship. The Cubs took the first two playoff games against the San Diego Padres, only to lose the final three. In 1988, the Tribune Company got the City Council to permit night games, primarily for broadcasting purposes, and the first evening game was played on August 9. The team won the divisional championship in 1989, but again lost the NL championship series, this time to the San Francisco Giants. There were few highlights in the 1990s, other than Sammy Sosa's sixty-six homers in 1998 (now marred by a suspicion he used performance-enhancing drugs) and a spot in the playoffs. Under manager Dusty Baker, the Cubs did take the division in 2003, and beat the Braves in the divisional series, but lost to the Florida Marlins in the league championship series four games to three. Since then, the Cubs under Dusty Baker fell out of contention despite high-priced players. Even so, attendance soared to more than three million in 2004 because of fan loyalty, the enjoyment of Wrigley Field's beauty and ambience, and post-game entertainment in the gentrified surrounding neighborhood. In 2007 and 2008, the club under skipper Lou Piniella won their division.[97]

The Sox were the much more popular team in the postwar era, with seventeen straight seasons in the first division. In 1948 Grace Comiskey made her twenty-four-year-old son Charles A. Comiskey vice president, and he brought in Frank Lane as general manager. Lane in five years traded, bought, and sold 223 players, including 1951 Rookie of the Year

Minnie Minoso, an Afro-Cuban and the first player of African descent to play major league ball in Chicago. The family sold their controlling interest in 1959 to Bill Veeck's syndicate for $2.7 million, and that year the Sox, under manager Al Lopez, won the pennant, finally beating the hated Yankees, after regularly finishing second or third in the 1950s, with a record of 94-60. The club had a weak hitting lineup that featured infielders Nellie Fox and Luis Aparicio, but excellent defense. The pitching staff was the finest in the AL, led by Early Wynn's twenty-two victories. The Sox lost the World Series to the Los Angeles Dodgers in a thrilling six-game series. But the Pale Hose could not keep up the momentum, plagued by bad trades and Veeck's tight purse strings. Over the next fifteen years, attendance declined, the team started losing, and Veeck sold out to his former business associate Arthur Allyn Jr. and his brother John Allyn. The team did bring in the humorous, opinionated, fun-loving broadcaster Harry Caray in 1971 to succeed the "Old Commander" Bob Elson, who had broadcast the Sox since 1934.[98]

The imaginative Veeck returned in 1975, purchasing 80 percent of the Sox stock for $8.55 million, which enabled him to depreciate the players' value from his taxes. He staged a series of promotional events, including the disco demolition of July 12, 1979 (a spectacular ritual destruction of disco dance recordings), which resulted in a riot and a forfeited game. Veeck had little capital and could not compete for free agents or top amateurs. He sold the Sox on January 29, 1981, to real-estate developer Jerry Reinsdorf and media entrepreneur Edward Einhorn for $20 million. They promoted the team as family-oriented entertainment, suspending beer sales and building up security, which alienated the traditionally rowdy fans.

The Sox in 1983 took the Western Division championship, "winning ugly" (a modestly talented roster with inconsistent pitching, fielding, and batting) with a record of 99-63, but they failed to advance in the playoffs. They drew 2.1 million while playing at the oldest park in the majors in Bridgeport, a working-class white ethnic neighborhood that was close to the city's largest black ghetto. The fan base was overwhelmingly western suburbanites, who were uneasy going to a game near a black neighborhood, and the team considered moving. Municipal leaders sought a publicly financed ballpark to keep the franchise and promote urban development. The Sox seemed bound for St. Petersburg, Florida, when politicians in Chicago and Springfield established the Illinois Sports Facilities Authority to build a new $167 million stadium adjacent to the old field. The new Comiskey Park (renamed U.S. Cellular Field in 2003 at a cost of $68 million to be paid over 23 years) opened on April 18, 1991, with positive reviews; the Sox drew 2,934,154, that year, a team record. The good feelings continued in 1993 when the team went 94-68, led by MVP Frank Thomas and Cy Young winner Jack McDowell, but the Sox lost in the playoffs to the Toronto Blue Jays. But new Comiskey lacked the intimacy of other new ballparks like Baltimore's Camden Yards and Jacobs Field in Cleveland. Fans disliked the sharp 35–degree slope of the upper deck, and there were major access problems for suburban commuters. Furthermore, fans felt a lot of resentment against the owners, who had helped foment the 1994 players' strike that ended the season prematurely with the Sox in first place. The Sox thereafter struggled at the gate and on the field. They turned it around in 2000, winning 95 games under manager Jerry Manuel, but they were swept in three straight in the playoffs by the Seattle Mariners. In 2004 Ozzie Guillen was hired as manager and with General Manager Ken Williams's astute trading, the team made enormous strides forward, and in 2005 shocked the baseball world by winning the World Series in four straight over the Houston Astros. Attendance reached 2.3 million, the highest since 1993, a mark surpassed in 2006, with a franchise record attendance of 2,957,414.[99] In 2008, the Sox won a playoff with the Minnesota Twins and won the Central Division, but they lost in the ALDS to the Tampa Bay Rays in four games.

Football

In football, the Cardinals were owned since 1932 by Charles W. Bidwell Sr., a vice president of the Chicago Bears, who had bought the team from Dr. David Jones for $50,000. Jones had bought the Cardinals from Chris O'Brien in 1929. The Cardinals struggled for years, until finally jelling in 1947, winning the NFL championship over the Philadelphia Eagles, who defeated the Chicagoans in a title rematch one year later. Nonetheless, the Cardinals remained far behind the Bears in popularity; both played at Wrigley, but the Cardinals had the lowest broadcast revenues in the league, and by 1958 attendance had dropped to 96,000. In 1959 the Cardinals played four home games at Soldier Field and two in Bloomington, Minnesota, a suburb of Minneapolis, which was seeking an NFL expansion franchise. After having achieved just one winning season in the 1950s, Violet Bidwell, the team's owner since her husband's death in 1947, moved the Cardinals to St. Louis in 1960.[100]

The Bears won the NFL championship in 1946, their fourth in seven years. Ten years later they captured the Western Conference title in 1956, only to lose the championship game 47-7 to the New York Giants. Halas had retired as coach before the 1956 season but returned in 1958 and led the Bears back to the NFL title in 1963 over the New York Giants, 14-10. Halas ended his coaching career in 1968 with a record of 321-142-31, leaving a team with superstars Gayle Sayers, who scored six touchdowns in one game in 1965, and Dick Butkus, the finest middle linebacker of all time. In 1971 the Bears moved to the renovated Soldier Field. Halas remained as owner and president of the team until his death in 1983, when grandson Michael McCaskey became the new team president. Two years later, the great 1985 team, coached by Mike Ditka and led by Jim McMahon and Walter Payton, perhaps the best all-around halfback in NFL history, went 15-1 and decimated the Boston Patriots on January 26, 1986, 46-10 at Super Bowl XX. But the team could not maintain their excellent level of play, and subsequent Bear teams enjoyed modest success. In 2003 the new $632 million 61,500–seat Soldier Field reopened within the pillars of the original structure, financed by $432 million in tax-backed bonds and $200 million in private funds. The original edifice was designated a National Historical Landmark in 1987, but lost that status because of the drastic renovations that created an eyesore on the lake.[101]

Chicago joined the professional soccer world in 1975, when businessman Lee Stern established the Chicago Sting of the North American Soccer League. They played at Soldier Field, Wrigley Field, and Comiskey Park with a fan base mainly composed of European immigrants and suburban soccer families. The Sting won the Soccer Bowl in 1981 against the New York Cosmos and again in 1984 against the Toronto Blizzard, the final year of the NASL. The team also played in the Major Indoor Soccer League in the 1980s. The team went out of business in 1988, but in 1998 Philip Anschutz, former chairman of Qwest, secured an expansion franchise in the three-year-old Major Soccer League. The Chicago Fire played at Soldier Field, winning the championship in their first season, but they were defeated 2-1 by the Kansas City Wizards in the 2000 title match. The team moved to Toyota Park in Bridgeview, a soccer-only facility seating 22,000, in 2006.[102]

The Revival of Recreational Sport

Beginning in the late 1960s, interest in physical fitness, health, beauty, the passage of Title IX of the Educational Amendments of 1972 (which barred sexual discrimination in all educational activities), and a desire among young adults to socialize promoted a lot of participatory sporting activity, especially among (weekend) athletes living in fashionable neighborhoods in the city and suburbs. They are the face of contemporary Chicago, the prosperous white-collar middle class, who have supplanted blue-collar Chicago, city of the big shoulders. Thousands of people trained at the Y, community centers, and health clubs, like the fashionable downtown East Bank Club (founded in 1980). Their facilities included treadmills, stair climbers, stationary bicycles, and rowing machines, as well as offering aerobic dance classes and yoga. Several tennis clubs opened up, including the Midtown Tennis Club (1969), the Lakeshore Athletic Club (1972), and the Edens Athletic Club (1976). The Grant

Park Recreation Association, catering to workers in the Loop, provided competition in five sports, which included 682 softball teams in 1968. Cycling and running clubs also flourished, reflected by the development of the Chicago Marathon (1980), one of the largest participatory events in the world, which has grown to have more than 40,000 competitors.

Conclusion: Chicagoland Sports at the End of the Century

Chicago since its earliest days was an important site for the development and expansion of sport. The sporting world there underwent important changes over time, as participatory and spectator sports became increasingly democratic in the twentieth century. The old working-class sports of billiards and bowling have lost most of their popularity, but now there are some 850,000 golfers in Chicagoland, and business is brisk at public and semipublic golf courses.[103] Spectators crowd major professional golf tournaments, most notably the Western Open (from 1991 to 2006 at the Dubsdred Course at the Cog Hill Golf Country Club in Lemont), which celebrated its 100th anniversary in 2006, but the Professional Golfers Association discontinued that great event.

Public interest in Chicago remains closely tied to professional sports. Two of the old bygone standards of professional sport are struggling today, horse racing and boxing, as they are in the rest of the country. The decline of inner-city slums has hurt prize fighting more than public outcries against the sport's brutality, while thoroughbred racing has been hurt by the sale of top racehorses around the world to distant locations like Dubai and by the proliferation of the state-operated lottery and legalized gambling at riverboat casinos.

Access to spectator sports is influenced by the cost of spectating, which is going through the roof. In 2003–2004, the Bears' average ticket was $66, with a Fan Cost Index (FCI) for a family of four of $370. The Bulls' costs were $51 and $293, respectively, and the Blackhawks', $50 and $286, respectively. In 2006 the Cubs' average ticket price was $34.30, and an FCI for a family of four was $219.21, both second-highest in the major leagues, while the Sox came in ninth with an average ticket price of $26.19 and an FCI of $191.26.[104]

Today the city has sixteen professional teams, including franchises in all four major sports (baseball, football, basketball, and ice hockey), including the newest venture, the Chicago Skye of the Women's National Basketball Association. Chicago professional sports fans are among the most ardent of any city from the vantage point of audience size at games and on TV and radio (including sports talk radio), and purchases of team paraphernalia. Chicagoans are long-suffering fans whose clubs, except for the Bulls (who did falter when Jordan left), have been mediocre products at high prices. Chicago is one of only three cities with two major league baseball teams, neither of which had won a World Series between 1917 and 2005. This is a pretty dismal record despite the lofty fiscal values of local teams. As recently as 2001, the Cubs, located in the nation's third-largest market, were thirteenth out of thirty teams in payroll expenses, and the Sox were seventeenth. By 2006 both teams had bolstered their salaries closer to the top echelon, at which time *Forbes* estimated the Cubs were worth $448 million and the Sox, $315 million. Among the other major teams, the Blackhawks, have won only one Stanley Cup since World War II and no longer sell out, and even the beloved Bears, who always sell out, have won only two NFL championships since 1946.[105]

Politics remains an important factor in commercialized sports, even though politicians are rarely themselves sports entrepreneurs, as the dollars necessary to buy a team have skyrocketed into the stratosphere. In recent years, clout and the threat of teams leaving resulted in the construction of publicly financed stadiums for the White Sox and the Bears. Commercial sports are very much on the political agenda. Issues like adding more night games at Wrigley Field, the expansion of the ballpark, and the rooftop spectator stands on privately owned buildings around Wrigley dominate the baseball pages. Furthermore, another major issue is the enhancement of racetrack betting options to compensate for competition from legal wagering.

In the early twenty-first century, local fans remained fanatic Bear supporters, despite a long plunge into mediocrity until 2006, when the team went to the Super Bowl, and despite the fans' inability to move beyond memories of 1985, Ditka, and "da Bears." Chicago fans have proven extremely loyal time and again. Today still, North Siders identify with the Cubs, and South Siders with the White Sox. This fascination with spectator sport provides residents a common interest through which separate class, ethnic, racial, religious, and gender identities merge into a pluralistic and multicultural identity as Chicagoans. And that's pretty darn good.

Notes

1. Bessie Louise Pierce, *A History of Chicago*, vol. 1, *1673–1848* (Chicago: University of Chicago Press, 1937), 20, 206–8, and Jacqueline Peterson, "The Founding Fathers: The Absorption of French-Indian Chicago, 1816–1837," in Melvin Holli and Peter D. Jones, eds., *Ethnic Chicago: A Multicultural Portrait*, 4th ed. (Grand Rapids, Mich.: Eerdman's, 1995), 17–56.

2. On the development of a positive sporting creed, see John R. Betts, "Mind and Body in Early American Thought," *Journal of American History* 43 (March 1968): 787–805 On the making of an urban sporting culture, see Steven A. Riess,

City Games: The Evolution of American Urban Society and the Rise of Sports (Urbana: University of Illinois Press, 1989) , 3–5, 7, 26–30, 34, 46.

3. *American Turf Register and Sporting* Magazine 11 (October 1840): 237; *Spirit of the* Times 24 (25 February 1854): 18; *Chicago Tribune*, 16 June 1867, 1, 25 August 1863, 4, 26 August 1863, 4; Melvin Adelman, *A Sporting Time: New York City and the Rise of Modern Athletics, 1820–70* (Urbana: University of Illinois Press, 1986), 55–73; Herbert Asbury, *Gem of the Prairie: An Informal History of the Chicago Underworld* (New York: A. A. Knopf, 1940), 31–32, 36; James H. B. Robertson, *The History of Thoroughbred Racing in America* (Englewood Cliffs, N.J.: Prentice Hall, 1964), 80; Louise Carroll Wade, *Chicago's Pride: The Stockyards, Packingtown, and Environs in the Nineteenth Century* (Urbana: University of Illinois Press, 1987), 52, 55, 56; Pierce, *History of Chicago*, vol. 1, 207; John Hervey, *Racing in America*, vol. 2 (New York: Jockey Club, 1944), 236–38; Gerald R. Gems, *Windy City Wars: Labor, Leisure, and Sport in the Making of Chicago* (Lanham, Md.: Scarecrow Press, 1997), 9. On early harness racing in Chicago, see Marie Fisher, "Horse Racing in Old Chicago," Box 83, Federal Writers Project, Abraham Lincoln Presidential Library, Springfield, Ill.

4. Gems, *Windy City Wars*, 14–15.

5. Edmund J. James, *The Charters of the City of Chicago*: vol. 2, *Part 2: The City Charters, 1838–1851* (Chicago: University of Chicago Press, 1899), 148–49.

6. Fred Eugene Leonard and George B. Affleck, *A Guide to the History of Physical Education* (Philadelphia: Lea & Febiger, 1947), ch. 11; Robert K. Barney, "Knights of Cause and Exercise: German Forty-Eighters and *Turnvereine* in the United States during the Antebellum Period," *Canadian Journal of History of Sport* 13 (December 1982): 282n7. The Turners who remained in Germany formed the *Deutsche Turnerschaft* in 1860, which became fervidly nationalistic, conservative, and eventually also highly anti-Semitic. They also became ardent opponents of modern sport with its characteristics of instrumental rationality. The Turners felt that sport promoted self-pride, the development of an asymmetrical and unhealthy physique (soccer was decried as barbaric), and undue concern with record keeping and specialization. Sport was also castigated for hindering moral improvement and the building of nationalism. They preferred noncompetitive mass displays of exercises. See Allen Guttmann, *Games and Empires: Modern Sports and Cultural Imperialism* (New York: Columbia University Press, 1994), 143–45.

7. Theodor Jannsen, *Geschichte der Chicago Turn-Gemeinde* (Chicago: M. Stern, 1897), 9-13; Data on occupations was drawn from the Chicago City Directory and from Hugo Gollmer, *Namensliste der Pionieres des Nord Amerikanischen Turnerbunds der Jahre 1848-62* (St. Louis: H. Rauth, 1885). For Newark Turners, see Susan E. Hirsch, *Roots of the American Working Class: The Industrialization of Crafts in Newark, 1800–1860* (Philadelphia: University of Pennsylvania Press, 1980), 100; for Milwaukee Turners, see Kathleen Neils Conzen, *Immigrant Milwaukee, 1836–1860* (Cambridge, Mass.: Harvard University Press 1976), 179-80. Milwaukee's first Turner society was organized by prominent businessmen: 77.8 percent of fifty-four pioneer Turners who joined between 1853 and 1860 were white-collar. A significant bourgeois membership was undoubtedly a factor in renaming the Socialistischer Turnerbund von Nord-Amerika, the original national Turner society organized in 1851, as the Nordamerikanischer Turnerbund in 1856. Nonetheless, it remained supportive of left-wing politics. On socialist Turners in Chicago, see Pierce, *History of Chicago*, vol. 2, *1848–1871*, 187; Ralf Wagner, "Turner Societies and the Socialist Tradition," in Harmut Keil,

ed., *German Workers' Culture in the United States, 1850 to 1920* (Washington, D.C.: Smithsonian Institution Press, 1988), 225, 230, 232–36; Bruce C. Nelson, *Beyond the Martyrs: A Social History of Chicago's Anarchists, 1870–1900* (New Brunswick, NJ: Rutgers University Press, 1988), 195–96; Henry Metzner, *A Brief History of the American Turnerbund* (Pittsburgh: National Executive Committee of the American Turnerbund, 1924), 29–30; Benjamin G. Rader, "The Quest for Subcommunities and the Rise of American Sport," *American Quarterly* 29 (1977): 360. For a history of the American Turners in English, see Metzner, *Brief History of the American Turnerbund*; and Carl Wittke, *Refugees of Revolution: The German 48ers in America* (Philadelphia: University of Pennsylvania Press, 1952), 147-58.

8. Metzner, *Brief History of the American Turnerbund*, 17–23; Gollmer, *Namensliste der Pioniere*; *Chicago Times*, 20 January 1873; *Illinois Staats-Zeitung*, 26 August 1861, 3 October 1881, in Federal Writers Project, Illinois, Chicago Foreign Language Press Survey, typescript (Chicago, 1942), Special Collections, University of Chicago Library (hereafter cited as CFLPS). A microfilm copy is available at the Chicago Public Library.

9. On the Turners and socialism, see Wagner, "Turner Societies," 221–40; Metzner, *Brief History of the American Turnerbund*, 25–27; Wittke, *Refugees of Revolution*, 156-57; *Chicago Arbeiter-Zeitung*, 2, 8 September 1879, 4 February 1888, CFLPS; Gerald Robert Gems, "Sport and Culture Formation in Chicago, 1890–1940" (Ph.D diss., University of Maryland, 1989), 55; Nelson, *Beyond the Martyrs*, 58, 138, 151. In June 1879 the Bohemian Sharpshooters rented Silver Leaf Grove on the Southwest Side for a picnic. Unfortunately the outing deteriorated into a violent inter-ethnic fray. Just when the band began to play for a dance, Irish hooligans invaded the grove, throwing rocks at the revelers, who shot back with bullets. Twenty-three people were arrested. Nelson, *Beyond the Martyrs*, 137-39.

10. *Chicago Tribune*, 20 February, 22 May 1891, 2 May 1892; Jannsen, *Chicago Turn-Gemeinde*, 75-76: *Chicago Abendpost*, 17 September 1891, CFLPS. In 1887 there were 26,722 members of 235 Turner societies in the United States. Donald E. Pienkos, *One Hundred Years Young: A History of the Polish Falcons of America, 1887–1987* (Boulder, Colo.: East European Monographs, 1987), 20. On the Valteich affair, see Hartmut Keil, "German Working-Class Immigration and the Social Democratic Tradition of Germany," in Keil, ed., *German Workers' Culture*, 5; Wagner, "Turner Societies," 235; Nelson, *Beyond the Martyrs*, 73, 85, 125, 160, 196, 217, 221; *Chicago Tribune*, 2 May 1892.The Chicago *Turngemeinde, Sudseite Turngemeinde*, the Central *Turnverein*, and the Germania *Turnverein* together with two out-of-town clubs formed the short-lived National Turner Alliance, which had 1,450 members in 1892. See Wagner, "Turner Societies," 235, 239n.39. In 1911 Vahlteich became editor of the *Chicago Arbeiter Zeitung*, which was the Socialist Party's outlet in German. See Klaus Ensslen and Heinz Ickstadt, "German Working-Class Culture in Chicago: Continuity and Change in the Decade from 1900 to 1910," in Hartmut Keil, ed., *German Workers in Industrial Chicago, 1850–1910: A Comparative Perspective* (DeKalb,: Northern Illinois University Press, 1983), 249.

11. Klaus Ensslen, "German-American Working-Class Saloons," in Keil, ed. *German Workers' Culture*, 176; Ensslen and Ickstadt, "German Working-Class Culture in Chicago," 244. *Chicago Arbeiter-Zeitung*, 30 June 1908, CFLPS; Gems, "Sport and Culture Formation," 266; Dominick Pacyga, "Chicago's Pilsen Park

and the Struggle for Czechoslovak Independence," in Leo Schelbert and Nick Ceh, *Essays in Russian and East European History: A Festschrift for Edward C. Thaden* (Boulder, Colo.: East European Monographs, 1995), 126. In New York City the German-American Athletic Club, founded in 1884, was disbanded in 1917 in reaction to anti-German passions. See Pamela Lynne Cooper, *The American Marathon* (Syracuse, N.Y.: Syracuse University Press, 1999), 78; Ensslen and Ickstadt, "German Working-Class Culture in Chicago," in Keil, ed., *German Workers' Culture in Chicago,* 244.

12. Paul Darby, "Emigrants at Play: Gaelic Games and the Irish Diaspora in Chicago, 1884–c.1900," *Sport in History* 26 (April 2006): 47–63; Carl Wittke, *The Irish in America* (Baton Rouge: Louisiana State University Press, 1956), 164-65, 269; Sheilah Post, "The Role of Irish National Sports in the History of Irish Immigration in America" (seminar paper, HIST 444, "American Sport History," Northeastern Illinois University, 1980); Charles Fanning, Ellen Skerrett, and John Corrigan, *Nineteenth Century Chicago Irish: A Social and Political Portrait* (Chicago: Center for Policy Study, Loyola University of Chicago, 1980), 33; Charles Fanning, ed., *Mr. Dooley and the Chicago Irish: An Anthology* (New York: Arno, 1976), 95, 99, 103–4; *Chicago Tribune,* 26–28 September 1892.See also Charles H. Hermann, *Recollections of Life and Days in Chicago: Recollections of Life and Doings in Chicago from the Haymarket Riot to the End of World War I, by an Old Timer* (Chicago: Normandie House, 1945), 30–31; *Chicago Daily News,* 20 March 1885, 12 January 1886; *Chicago Times,* 17 November 1889, 6 July 1891; *Brooklyn Eagle,* 13 October 1897; Jack Curley, "Boxing around Chicago in Those Good Old Days," *Ring Magazine* 5 (July 1926): 7; Herman Kogan and Lloyd Wendt, *Bosses in Lusty Chicago: The Story of Bathhouse John and Hinky Dink* (Indianapolis: Bobbs-Merrill, 1943), 123.

13. On social and athletic clubs, see Frederick Thrasher, *The Gang: A Study of 1,313 Gangs in Chicago,* abr. ed. (Chicago: University of Chicago Press, 1963), especially 13, 48, 52, 60, 124, 315–18; Riess, *City Games,* 95–96; Liz Cohen, *Making a New Deal: Industrial Workers in Chicago, 1919–1939* (Cambridge, U.K.: Cambridge University Press, 1991), 145–46. On Jewish basement clubs in the late 1920s, see Isadore Zelig, "A Study of the 'Basement' Social Clubs of Lawndale District," Paper for Sociology 270, 1928, Ernest Watson Burgess Papers (hereafter cited as EBP) Box 139, Folder 3, Special Collections, University of Chicago Library. Zelig studied four clubs, which each had a distinctive membership and its own special focus: socializing, sports, crime, and charity. See also S. Kirson Weinberg, "Jewish Youth in the Lawndale Community: A Sociological Study, Paper for Sociology 269 (1932), EBP, Box 139, Folder 3, pp. 50–79, 397.

14. Gems, *Windy City Wars,* 105–7; Chicago Commission on Race Relations, *The Negro in Chicago: A Study of Race Relations and a Race Riot in 1919* (Chicago: University of Chicago Press, 1922), 237.

15. Ulf Beijbom, *Swedes in Chicago. A Demographic and Social Study of the 1846–1880 Immigration* (Stockholm: Läromedelsförlaget, 1971), 270; Odd S. Lovoll, *A Century of Urban Life: The Norwegians in Chicago before 1930* (Northfield, Minn.: Norwegian American Historical Association, 1988), 100. The Swedish Sharpshooters Society was organized at German Hall by thirty Svea members and was probably soon incorporated into the Chicago National Guard prior to the Great Fire of 1871. Beijbom, *Swedes in Chicago,* 271.

16. Lovoll, *Century of Urban Life,* 132–33, 135, 249, 251–53. On the early history of Nordic skiing (cross-county and ski-jumping) in America and its boom in

the 1920s, see John E. B. Allen, *From Skisport to Skiing: One Hundred Years of an American Sport, 1840–1940* (Amherst: University of Massachusetts Press, 1993).

17. Gems, *Windy City Wars*, 34, 37–38.

18. Ibid., 35; Herbert Warren Wind, "Golfing in and around Chicago," *Chicago History* 4 (Winter 1975–76): 244–50; "The 100 Most Prestigious Private Clubs in America" *Golf Connoisseur* (Spring 2006), cited in "Chicago's Most Prestigious Golf Club," http://chicago.about.com/od/sportsrecreation/a/030106_golf.htm.

19. Wind, "Golfing," 247–48; Gems, *Windy City Games*, 37; Riess, *City Games*, 62; Howard Rabinowitz, "Golf," *Encyclopedia of Chicago.* http://www.encyclopedia.chicagohistory.org/pages/525.html (accessed 12 July 2006).

20. John H. Long, "Olympia Fields, IL," *Encyclopedia of Chicago.* http://www.encyclopedia.chicagohistory.org/pages/930.html (accessed 4 August 2007); "Medinah Country Club," http://www.medinahcc.org/Default.aspx?p=Generic ModuleDefault&modID=83640&modtype=&ssid=47702&vnf=1 (accessed 4 August 2007).

21. *Jewish Daily Forward,* 5 May 1926, 16 July 1923, CFLPS; Michael Ebner, *Creating Chicago's North Shore: A Suburban History* (Chicago: University of Chicago Press, 1988), 233.

22. Steven A. Riess, "Leisure," *Encyclopedia of Chicago.* http://www.encyclopedia.chicagohistory.org/pages/735.html (accessed 15 October 2006); Celia Hilliard, *The Woman's Athletic Club of Chicago: A History—1898–1998* (Chicago: Women's Athletic Club, 1999); Bertha Damaris Knobe, "Chicago Women's Athletic Club," *Harper's Bazaar* 39 (June 1905): 537–46. Tiffany Crate, "Fitness and Athletic Clubs," *Encyclopedia of Chicago,* http://www.encyclopedia.chicagohistory.org/pages/459.html (accessed 10 July 2006).

23. Cindy Sondik Aron, *Ladies and Gentlemen of the Civil Service: Middle-Class Workers in Victorian America* (New York: Oxford University Press, 1987); John S. Gilkeson Jr., *Middle-Class Providence:1820–1940* (Princeton, N.J.: Princeton University Press, 1986); Barton Bernstein, *The Culture of Professionalism: The Middle Class and the Development of Higher Education in America* (New York: Norton, 1976); Stuart Blumin, *The Emergence of the Middle Class: Social Experience in the American City, 1760–1900* (Cambridge, U.K.: Cambridge University Press, 1989); Burton J. Bledstein and Robert D. Johnston, eds. *The Middling Sorts: Explorations in the History of the American Middle Class* (New York: Routledge, 2001).

24. Paula Lupkin, "Young Men's Christian Association," *Encyclopedia of Chicago* http://www.encyclopedia.chicagohistory.org/pages/1393.html (accessed 11 July 2006); Emmett Dedmon, *Great Enterprises: 100 Years of the YMCA of Metropolitan Chicago* (New York: Rand McNally, 1957); Elizabeth Halsey, *The Development of Public Recreation in Metropolitan Chicago* (Chicago: Chicago Recreation Commission, 1942); Gems, *Windy City Wars*, 16–17.

25. Stephen Freedman, "The Baseball Fad in Chicago, 1865–1870: An Exploration of the Role of Sport in the Nineteenth Century City," *Journal of Sport History* 5 (1978): 42–64.

26. George D. Bushnell, "When Chicago Was Wheel Crazy," *Chicago History* 4 (Fall 1975): 167–75; Richard Harmond, "Progress and Flight: An Interpretation of the American Cycle Craze of the 1890s," *Journal of Social History* 5 (Winter 1971): 235–57; Gems, *Windy City Wars*, 38–40.

27. Bushnell, "Wheel Crazy"; Cord Scott, "The Car Race of the Century," *Journal of the Illinois State Historical Society* 96 (2003): 37–48.

28. Gems, *Windy City Wars*, 78–81.

29. Harmond, "Progress and Flight," 235–57; Gems, *Windy City Wars*, 39–40.

30. Gems, *Windy City Wars*, 144, 145.

31. Ibid., 26.

32. Ibid., 76–77, 82; Michael P. McCarthy, "Politics and the Parks: Chicago Businessmen and the Recreation Movement," *Journal of the Illinois State Historical Society* 65 (Summer 1972): 158–72; Riess, *City Games*, 138–40.

33. Wilma Pesavento, "Sport and Recreation in the Pullman Experiment, 1880–1900," *Journal of Sport History* 9 (Summer 1982): 38–62; Stanley Buder, *Pullman: An Experiment in Industrial Order and Community Planning, 1880–1930* (New York: Oxford University Press, 1968); Gems, *Windy City Wars*, 44–47.

34. On semipro baseball, see *Spalding's Official Baseball Guide, 1906* (New York: A. G. Spalding, 1906); Ray Schmitt, "The Semipro Team That Beat the Champs," in Emil Rothe, ed., *Baseball in Chicago: A Celebration of the Eightieth Anniversary of the 1906 World Series* (Cooperstown, NY: Society for American Baseball Research, 1986); Ray Schmidt, "The Golden Age of Chicago Baseball." *Chicago History* 28, 2 (2000): 38–59; Steven A. Riess, *Touching Base: Professional Baseball and American Culture in the Progressive Era*, 2nd ed., rev. (Urbana: University of Illinois Press, 1999), 177–78, 182–83.

35. Riess, *City Games*, 73–77; Gems, *Windy City Wars*, 42–43; Perry Duis, *The Saloon: Public Drinking in Chicago and Boston, 1880–1920* (Urbana: University of Illinois Press, 1983), 247–48.

36. Riess, *City Games*, 76–77; Gems, *Windy City Wars*, 43–44, 142–43, 149.

37. Gems, *Windy City Wars*, 142–43, 191; Riess, *City Games*, 78–81. On bowling as a working-class sport, see Paul W. Kearney, "Ten Million Keglers Can't Be Wrong," in Herbert Graffis, ed., *Esquire's First Sports Reader* (New York: A. S. Barnes, 1945), 226–38.

38. Guttmann, *Games and Empires*, 149–50; Vlasta Vlaz, ed., *Panorama: A Historical Review of Czechs and Slovaks in the U.S.A.* (Cicero, Ill.: Czechoslovak National Council of America, 1970), 22-26, 133-36; Joseph Hanc, "Who Are the Sokols?" in *Souvenir Journal Commemorating the Fiftieth Anniversary of the Organization of T. J. Sokol Fuegner* (Long Island City, N.Y.: n.p., 1936), 9, 11; J. J. Zmrhal, "The Sokols Abroad and Here," *Sokol Americky* (August 1937): 53-55; Jarka Jelink and Jaroslav Zmrhal, *Sokol: Education and Physical Culture Association* (Chicago: American Sokol Union, 1944), 43–44, 47, 51; *Svornost*, 12 August, 6 September, 25 November 1878, CFLPS. The National Sokol Union later moved to New York. A second national organization based in Chicago was Zupa Fuegner-Tyrs in 1897. The two associations merged in 1917 to form the American Sokol Union in Chicago. An auxiliary ladies' gymnastic society was started in 1883. *Svornost*, 8 November 1883, CFLPS. On the success of the women's program, see ibid., 12 March 1890.

39. Jakub Horak, "The Assimilation of Czechs in Chicago" (Ph.D diss., University of Chicago, 1920), 92; Vlaz, ed., *Panorama*, 133, 136, 145-46; On plans for the 1893 World's Fair gymnastics demonstration, see *Svornost*, 2 February 1892, CFLPS. On the Sokol use of Pilsen Park, see Pacyga, "Chicago's Pilsen Park," 121. On July 4 celebrations, see *Denni Hlasatel*, 28 June 1913, CFLPS. Sokol participation at the 1913 Chicago Olympics is detailed in *Denni Hlasatel*, 30 May, 30 June 1913, CFLPS. The first slet in America was held in New York in 1879 (Vlaz, ed., *Panorama*, 133).

40. *Svornost*, 8 April 1890; *Denni Hlasatel*, 2 April 1910, 16 September 1911, CFLPS. Anton Cermak contributed to the sporting life of the community when

he was an alderman and member of the Chicago Athletic Commission. He constructed a ballpark in the Czech community in 1922 for his semiprofessional team, which included many Bohemian Americans. It was a business venture as well as a means of increasing his political support. See Alex Gottfried, "Anton J. Cermak, Chicago Politician: A Study in Political Leadership" (Ph.D diss., University of Chicago, 1952), 284–86, *Denni Hlasatel*, 30 April 1922, CFLPS. See also Gems, *Windy City Wars*, 110–12, 226 (quote).

41. Andrew T. Kopan, "Greek Survival," in Jones and Holli, *Ethnic Chicago*, 112–13, 132–33; Jane Addams, *Twenty Years at Hull House* (New York: Chautauqua Press, 1911), 442–44. For a fascinating study of the Ukrainian Athletic Association, *Sich*, founded in 1902, with a branch in Chicago in 1917, see Myron Bohdon Kuropas, "Ukrainian Chicago: The Making of a Nationality Group in America," in Jones and Holli, *Ethnic Chicago*, 165-73. Kuropas traces the Sich's evolution into a paramilitary, anti-Communist organization that organized gymnastics, military drills, and field maneuvers. By 1930 the Sich even had its own "air corps."

42. *Dziennik Sziazkowy*, 15 September 1915, 21 March 1928, CFLPS; Arthur L. Waldo, "The Origin and Goals of the Falcons," in *Polish Falcons of America, 60 Years of District IV (1904–1964)* (Pittsburgh: Polish Falcons of America, 1965), 5-7, 71; Pienkos, *One Hundred Years Young*, 3–4, 23–24, 32–33 35. Their motto was "Unity As Life, Disunity Death." See *Zgoda*, 23 August, 29 November 1893, CFLPS; *Dziennik Chicagoski*, 4 February, 14, August 1892, CFLPS. In 1914 there were 30,000 Falcons in Galicia, 14,000 in Poznan, and 25,000 in the United States (Pienkos, *Polish Falcons*, 23–24, 35).

43. *Dziennik Chicagoski*, 10 August 1896, 8 October 1904, 27 June 1915; *Dziennik Zwiazkowy*, 8 April 1908, 22 April 1922, CFLPS; *Dziennik Chicagoski*, 8 October 1904, 19 October 1906, CFLPS. Polish sport historian Casimir Wronski claims that the Royal Colts, a baseball team that included Poles and various old immigrant players, defeated Foster's Leland Giants in 1908. Casimir J. B. Wronski, "Early Days of Sport among Polish Americans of Chicagoland," in *Poles of Chicago, 1837–1937: A History of One Century of Polish Contribution to the City of Chicago, Illinois* (Chicago: Polish Pageant, 1937), 146-48; Gems, "Sport and Culture Formation in Chicago," 223–24. On the geographic distribution of bowling alleys in the 1920s and 1930s, see Chicago Recreation Commission, *The Chicago Recreation Survey, 1937*, vol. 2, *Commercial Recreation* (Chicago: Works Progress Administration, 1938), 54, 58ff.; Gems, *Windy City Wars*, 111–12, 177.

44. The CHI was originally located on Blue Island, but it moved five years later to Taylor and Lytle Streets. Irving Cutler, "Jews of Chicago," in Holli and Jones, *Ethnic Chicago*, 56, 69; Irving Cutler, *Jews of Chicago: From Shtetl to Suburb* (Urbana: University of Illinois Press, 1996); Hyman L. Meites, ed., *History of the Jews of Chicago* (Chicago: Jewish Historical Society of Illinois, 1924), 470-71. The German Jews saw the Chicago Hebrew Institute (later renamed the Jewish People's Institute) as an appropriate alternative to the YMCA or settlement houses. *Chicago Messenger*, 1 November 1909, CFLPS. In 1927 the JPI moved to Lawndale, following the Russian Jewish migration to that neighborhood, and built a $1.3 million building. Ibid., 25. See also S. Kirson Weinberg, "Jewish Youth in the Lawndale Community: A Sociological Study," EBR, Box 136, Folder 3-4, pp. 231–36. Weinberg also examines in brief the sports programs of the Better Boys Republic and the American Boys Commonwealth, which broke off from the Better Boys Republic in 1922 (pp. 236–42). See also *Chicago Jewish Courier*, 23, 28 August 1912, 26

April 1914; Chicago Hebrew Institute, *Observer*, November 1912, December 1913, January 1918, January 1919, CFLPS; Gerald R. Gems, "Sport and the Forging of a Jewish-American Culture: The Jewish People's Institute," *American Jewish History* 83 (March 1995): 15–26; Barney Ross and Martin Abrahamson, *No Man Stands Alone: The True Story of Barney Ross* (Philadelphia: Lippincott, 1957); Douglas Century, *Barney Ross* (New York: Schocken, 2006). Ironically, one aspect of Jewish involvement in the national pastime strengthened anti-Semitism. The 1919 World Series was fixed by eight Chicago White Sox in concert with various gamblers. One of the go-betweens was Abe Attell, a Russian Jew from San Francisco who had been featherweight champion from 1904 to 1912. Attell was associated with Arnold Rothstein, the fabled New York gambler, who helped finance the fix, although he had not initiated it. Anti-Semites like Henry Ford blamed underworld Jews for the fix, which reflected the supposed Jewish undermining of American morality and institutions. F. Scott Fitzgerald memorialized Rothstein as Meyer Wolfsheim in *The Great Gatsby* (New York: Scribner, 1925).

45. Mark Haller, "Organized Crime in Urban Society: Chicago in the Twentieth Century," *Journal of Social History* 5 (1971–72): 221-27; Daniel Bell, *The End of Ideology* (Glencoe, Ill.: Free Press, 1960), 127-50; Riess, *Touching Base*, 188-89; Landesco, *Organized Crime*, 231-32. Samuel J. "Nails" Morton was a World War I veteran, a street fighter, and a gangster who was a hero to second-generation West Side Jews in Chicago, despite his sordid occupation, because he helped protect them against rival ethnic groups. He died in 1923, falling off a horse while riding with underworld kingpin Dion O'Bannion. His associates, in typical gangland style, retaliated and killed the horse. See *Chicago Tribune*, 1 May 1923, 1; Elizabeth Bernstein, "Jewish Chicago Story: A Nostalgic Look Back at Some Kosher-Style Capones," *JUF News* (June 1993): 63. On Jewish American Gangsters, see Albert Fried, *The Rise and Fall of the Jewish Gangster in America* (New York: Holt, Rinehart and Winston, 1980); Jenna Weissman Joselit, *Our Gang: Jewish Crime and the New York Jewish Community, 1900–1940* (Bloomington: Indiana University Press, 1983); and Robert A. Rockaway, *But He Was Good to His Mother: The Lives and Crimes of Jewish Gangsters*, rev. ed. (New York: Gefen, 2000). The Miller Brothers included Davey, a West Side ward politician, gambler, and boxing referee; Harry, a policeman; and Max and Hirschie, who were gangsters. They owned several restaurants and night clubs, beginning with the E & M at 3216 Roosevelt Road, opened in 1909, the 2539 Club at Milwaukee and Kedzie, and another downtown at Clark and Randolph, across the street from the famous Sherman House. In January 1924 Davey Miller was critically shot at the LaSalle Theater by Dion O'Banion, presumably a result of gang warfare involving brother Hirschie, but Davey survived (*Chicago Tribune*, 21 January 1924, 1; Bernstein, "Jewish Chicago Story," 64); Walter Roth, "Scrapbook Provides Glimpses of an Unusual Chicago Jewish Life," *Chicago Jewish History* 14 (Winter 1991): 1, 7–9; "Runyon on Davey Miller," *Chicago Jewish History* 14 (Winter 1991), 9; Davey Miller Scrapbook, copy at Spertus College Library, Chicago, Ill. On Chicago Jewish boxers, see Harry Harris, "Scrapbooks, 1897-1908," 3 vols., Special Collections, American Jewish Archives, Cincinnati, Ohio (microfilm copy, New York Public Library); Thomas H. Jenkins, "Changes in Ethnic and Racial Representation among Professional Boxers: A Study in Ethnic Succession" (M.A. Thesis, University of Chicago, 1955), 85-89.   For the history of Chicago boxing, see the twenty-four volume *Scrapbooks on Boxing*, Chicago Historical Society. Chicago prize fighting in the late nineteenth century is discussed in Curley, "Box-

ing around Chicago," 7. Boxing was blighted after the turn of the century by the apparently fixed match between Joe Gans and Terry McGovern of 13 December 1900. See *National Police Gazette*, 5, 12 January 1901. The last legal fight in Chicago occurred on 7 October 1904, ibid., 28 October 1905. On the legalization of boxing in 1925, see Don S. Kirschner, *City and Country: Rural Response to Urbanization in the 1920s* (Westport, Conn.: Greenwood Press, 1970), 98-108. For a discussion of Jewish fighters Jackie Fields (who named himself after the department store), Barney Ross, and Kingfish Levinsky, who were prominent in the 1920s and 1930s, see Ira Berkow, *Maxwell Street: Survival in a Bazaar* (Garden City, N.Y.: Doubleday, 1977), 98, 141-48, 183-88. See also Ross and Abramson, *No Man Stands Alone*.

46. James Grossman, *Land of Hope: Black Southerners and the Great Migration* (Chicago: University of Chicago Press, 1989), 81, 128, 142, 150, 200–202, 228; Riess, *City Games*, 114–15.

47. Allan H. Spear, *Black Chicago: The Making of a Ghetto, 1890–1920* (Chicago: University of Chicago Press, 1970), 205–6; Chicago Race Commission, *Negro in Chicago: A Study of Race Relations and a Race Riot* (Chicago: University of Chicago Press, 1922), 271–97; *Chicago Defender*, 15 June 1917, 2; correspondence from Jerry Gems, 9 April 1995.

48. Spear, *Black Chicago*, 214. Grossman points out that the *Defender* used to brag about African American access to well-equipped playgrounds and open access to Lake Michigan beaches (Grossman, *Land of Hope*, 86). For a full discussion of the riot, see Arthur I. Waskow, *From Race Riot to Sit-In: 1919 and the 1960s* (Garden City, N.Y.: Doubleday, 1966); and William Tuttle, *Race Riot: Chicago in the Red Summer of 1919* (New York: Oxford University Press, 1970).

49. On Jack Johnson, see William H. Wiggins Jr., "Jack Johnson As Bad Nigger: The Folklore of His Life," *Black Scholar* 2 (1971): 35–41; Al-Tony Gilmore, *Bad Nigger! The National Impact of Jack Johnson* (Port Washington, N.Y.: Kennikat, 1975); and Randy Roberts, *Papa Jack: Jack Johnson and the Era of White Hopes* (New York: Free Press, 1983), which makes extensive use of classified FBI files to give a complete and well-rounded picture of Johnson. On the geographic distribution of bowling alleys, see Chicago Recreation Commission, *Chicago Recreation Survey*, 2: 66ff. For the origins of the Globetrotters, see Ben Green, *Spinning the Globe: The Rise, Fall, and Return to Greatness of the Harlem Globetrotters* (New York: Harper Collins, 2005). On the first black golf tournament, see *Chicago Defender*, 16 October 1915.

50. Quoted in Robert Peterson, *Only the Ball Was White* (Englewood Cliffs, N.J.: Prentice Hall, 1970), 66.

51. Sol White, *Sol White's History of Colored Baseball with Other Documents on the Early Black Game 1886–1936*, comp. Jerry Malloy (1907; repr., Lincoln, NE: University of Nebraska Press, 1995), 26, 28; Jerry Malloy, "Introduction: Sol White and the Origins of African American Baseball," in ibid., xxxvii, xli–xlii.; Peterson, *Only the Ball Was White*, 59, 62–66, 82, 107–8; Neil Lanctot, *Fair Dealing and Clean Playing: The Hilldale Club and the Development of Black Professional Baseball, 1910–1932* (Jefferson, N.C.: McFarland, 1994), 14–15, 31–34, 165–66; Phil Dixon, with Patrick J. Hannigan, *The Negro Baseball Leagues: 1867–1855, A Photographic History* (Mattituck, N.Y.: Amereon House, 1992), 96–97; Michael E. Lomax, *Black Baseball Entrepreneurs, 1860–1901: Operating by Any Means Necessary* (Syracuse, N.Y.: Syracuse University Press, 2003); Linda Ziemer, "Chicago's Negro Leagues," *Chicago History* 23 (1994–95): 36–51. On player/owner

Rube Foster, see Robert Charles Cottrell, *The Best Pitcher in Baseball: The Life of Rube Foster, Negro League Giant* (New York: New York University Press, 2001). While most historians have dated the origins of the Chicago Unions to 1886, there is some evidence it dated back to the late 1870s. See *Indianapolis Freeman*, 13 March 1909, cited in Lanctot, *Fair Dealing and Clean Playing*, 243–44, n.6.

52. On Stagg, see Robin D. Lester, *Stagg's University: The Rise, Decline, and Fall of Big Time Football at Chicago* (Urbana: University of Illinois Press, 1995), 1–150, 165–67.

53. Gems, *Windy City Wars*, 66–68, 98–99; Robert Pruter, "Sports, High School," *Encyclopedia of Chicago*, http://www.encyclopedia.chicagohistory.org/pages/1185.html (accessed 12 July 2006); Thomas W. Gutowski, "Student Initiative and the Origins of the High School Extracurriculum: Chicago, 1880–1915." *History of Education Quarterly* 28 (Spring 1988): 49–72.

54. Gems, *Windy City Wars*, 148, 178; Gerald R. Gems, "The Prep Bowl: Football and Religious Acculturation in Chicago," *Journal of Sport History* 23 (Fall, 1996): 49–72.

55. On the politics of urban sport, see Riess, *City Games*, 171–202.

56. Benjamin G. Rader, *American Sport: From the Age of Folk Games to the Age of Televised Sports*, 5th ed. (Upper Saddle River, N.J.: Prentice Hall, 2004) , 97–104; Riess, *Touching Base*, 185; Charles H. Hermann, *Recollections of Life and Days in Chicago* (Chicago: Normandie House, 1945), 30–31; *Chicago Daily News*, 20 March 1885, 12 January 1886; *Chicago Times*, 17 November 1889, 6 July 1891; *Brooklyn Eagle*, 13 October 1897; Curley, "Boxing Around Chicago," 7; Kogan and Wendt, *Bosses in Lusty Chicago*, 123; Robert Pruter, "Boxing," *Encyclopedia of Chicago* http://www.encyclopedia.chicagohistory.org/pages/159.html (accessed 8 July 2006).

57. Robert Pruter, "Wrestling," *The Encyclopedia of Chicago* http://www.encyclopedia.chicagohistory.org/pages/2213.html (accessed 11 July2006).

58. Steven A. Riess, "Horse Racing in Chicago, 1883–1894: The Interplay of Class, Politics, and Organized Crime," in Ralph C. Wilcox, David, Robert Pitter, & Richard L. Irwin, eds., *Sporting Dystopias: The Making and Meanings of Urban Sport Cultures* (Albany: SUNY Press, 2003), 116–41.

59. Ibid., 131–32; John Landesco, *Organized Crime in Chicago*, part 3 of the *Illinois Crime Survey, 1929* (1929; repr. Chicago: University of Chicago Press, 1968), 46–48, 50–61; Riess, *City Games*, 186, 194; William Poundstone, *Fortune's Formula: The Untold Story of the Scientific Betting System That Beat the Casinos and Wall Street* (New York: Hill and Wang, 2005), 1–12; Allan May, "The History of the Race Wire Service," http://www.crimemagazine.com/racewire1.htm (accessed 3 April 2006).

60. On the White Stockings, see Federal Writers Project, Illinois, *Baseball in Old Chicago* (Chicago: A. C. McClurg, 1939), 7, 9, 13; Riess, *Touching Baseball*, 59–63; Peter Levine, *A. G. Spalding and the Promise of American Sport* (New York: Oxford University Press, 1984); Robert K. Barney and Frank Dallier, "'I'd Rather Be a Lamp Post in Chicago Than a Millionaire in Any Other City': William A. Hulbert, Civic Pride, and the Birth of the National League," *Nine* 2 (Fall 1993): 42.

61. *Chicago Tribune*, 5 February 1885, 6, 31 May 1885, 17, 7 June 1885, 14; Riess, *Touching Base*, 100–103, 135–37.

62. Riess, *Touching Base*, 61–62, 103–4, 162–63; Levine, *Spalding*, 29–48. On the role of Anson in segregating baseball, see Jerry Malloy, "Out at Home: Baseball Draws the Color Line," *National Pastime* 2 (1983): 22–28.

63. Riess, *Touching Base*, 16; James Diedrick, "Ring Lardner and Chicago Sports Reporting, *Encyclopedia of Chicago*, http://www.encyclopedia.chicagohistory .org/pages/2409.html (accessed 28 June 2006).

64. Riess, *Touching Base*, 63–64, 66, 117–19; Bernard A. Weisberger, *When Chicago Ruled Baseball: The Cubs–White Sox World Series of 1906* (New York: William Morrow, 2006).

65. Eliot Asinof, *Eight Men Out : The Black Sox and the 1919 World Series* (NY: Holt, Reinhart, and Winston, 1963), is the standard narrative, but lacks sources. John Sayles's outstanding film, *Eight Men Out* (1988) is very true to Asinof's story. For a more scholarly view, see Harold Seymour, *Baseball*, vol. 2, *The Golden Age* (New York: Oxford University Press, 1971), 294–339. For biographies of two of the men who claimed their innocence, see Irving M. Stein, *The Ginger Kid: The Buck Weaver Story* (Dubuque, Iowa: Elysian Fields Press, 1992), and Joe Gropman, *Say It Ain't So, Joe! The True Story of Joe Jackson*, 2d rev. ed. (Secaucus, N.J.: Carol, 1999). For a new analysis that examines the image of the event and the participants over the years, see Daniel A. Nathan, *Saying It's So: A Cultural History of the Black Sox Scandal* (Urbana: University of Illinois Press, 2003).

66. Riess, *Touching Base*, 64–69; John Findling, "Chicago Cubs," in Steven A. Riess, ed., *The Encyclopedia of Major League Baseball Teams*, vol. 1, *The National League* (Westport, Conn.: Greenwood Press, 2006), 65–68.

67. Riess, *Touching Base*, 120–22.

68. Gems, *Windy City Wars*, 188–90; William J. Baker, "Muscular Marxism and the Chicago Counter-Olympics of 1932," *International Journal of the History of Sport* 9 (1992): 397–410.

69. Gems, *Windy City Wars*, 144–45, 148, 149.

70. Ibid., 154. On welfare capitalism in Chicago in the 1920s, see Lizabeth Cohen, *Making a New Deal: Industrial Workers in Chicago, 1919–1939* (Cambridge, U.K.: Cambridge University Press, 1990), 159–211.

71. Terrence Cole, "'A Purely American Game': Indoor Baseball and the Origins of Softball," *International Journal of the History of Sport* 7 (1990): 287–96; Gems, *Windy City Wars*, 190–91; Riess, *City Games*, 87–88; Kathryn Jay, *More Than Just a Game: Sports in American Life since 1945* (New York: Columbia University Press, 2004), 14, claims that a women's game at Wrigley Field drew over 30,000 fans.

72. Richard Lindberg, "Chicago White Sox," in Steven A. Riess, ed., *The Encyclopedia of Major League Baseball Teams*, vol. 2, *The American League* (Westport, Conn.: Greenwood Press, 2006), 535–63.

73. Derek Gentile, *The Complete Chicago Cubs* (New York: Black Dog & Leventhal, 2002); Jerome Holtzman and George Vass, *Chicago Cubs Encyclopedia* (Philadelphia: Temple University Press, 1997); Findling, "Chicago Cubs," 72–77; John Skipper, *The Cubs Win the Pennant: Charlie Grimm, the Billy Goat Curse, and the 1945 World Series Run* (Jefferson, N.C.: McFarland, 2004); Charles N. Billington, *Wrigley Field's Last World Series: The Wartime Chicago Cubs and the Pennant of 1945* (Chicago: Lake Claremont Press, 2005); Doug Feldmann, *Miracle Collapse: The 1969 Chicago Cubs* (Lincoln: University of Nebraska Press, 2006).

74. Steven A. Riess, "Horse Racing," *Encyclopedia of Chicago* http://www .encyclopedia.chicagohistory.org/pages/601.html (accessed 28 June 2006); Riess, *City Games*, 188.

75. *Chicago Tribune*, 20 April 1931, 6; Riess, "Horse Racing"; Riess, *City Games*, 191–92.

76. Riess, *City Games*, 144; *Chicago Tribune*, November 28, 1926, 1, August 26, 1929, 25.

77. Roger Kahn, *A Flame of Pure Fire: Jack Dempsey and the Roaring '20s* (New York: Harcourt Brace, 1999), 412–23; Bruce J. Evensen, *When Dempsey Fought Tunney: Heroes, Hokum, and Storytelling in the Jazz Age* (Knoxville: University of Tennessee Press, 1996), 106–10; Elliott Gorn, "The Manassa Mauler and the Fighting Marine: An Interpretation of the Dempsey-Tunney Fights," *Journal of American Studies* 19 (1985): 27–47; Randy Roberts, *Jack Dempsey: The Manassa Mauler* (Baton Rouge: Louisiana State University Press, 1979), 212–335. On Davey Miller, see Steven A. Riess, "Tough Jews: The Jewish American Boxing Experience, 1890–1950," in Steven A. Riess, ed., *Sports and the American Jew* (Syracuse, N.Y.: Syracuse University Press, 1999), 87–89, 93–94.

78. Pruter, "Boxing"; Gems, *Windy City Wars*, 182–85, 215; Gerald Gems, "Sport, Religion, and Americanization: Bishop Sheil and the Catholic Youth Organization," *International Journal of the History of Sport* 10 (August 1993): 233–41. Jewish boys had a similar group in the B'nai B'rith Youth Organization (BBYO).

79. Lewis Erenberg, *Greatest Fight of Our Generation: Louis v. Schmeling* (New York: Oxford University Press, 2006).

80. Joe Ziemba, *When Football Was Football: The Chicago Cardinals and the Birth of the NFL* (Chicago: Triumph, 1999); Richard Whittingham, *The Chicago Bears: A 75-Year Celebration* (Dallas: Taylor, 1994), 19, 21–23; George Halas with Gwen Moran and Arthur Veysey, *Halas by Halas: The Autobiography of George Halas* (New York: McGraw-Hill, 1971); George Vass, *George Halas and the Chicago Bears* (Chicago: Regnery, 1971).

81. John C. Carroll, *Red Grange and the Rise of Modern Football* (Urbana: University of Illinois Press, 1999); Vass, *George Halas and the Chicago Bears*; Whittingham, *Chicago Bears*, 17–33; Robert A. Gallagher, "The Galloping Ghost: An Interview with Red Grange," *American Heritage* 26:1 (1974): 20–25, 93–99.

82. Whittingham, *Chicago Bears*, 119–30, 141–43.

83. Paul Greenland, "Blackhawks," *Encyclopedia of Chicago*, http://www.encyclopedia.chicagohistory.org/pages/144.html (accessed 25 June 2006). John Chi-Kit Wong, *Lords of the Rinks: The Emergence of the National Hockey League, 1875–1936* (Toronto: University of Toronto Press, 2005), 101–02, 134–35, 139–40; Michael Kirby, *Figure Skating to Fancy Skating: Memoirs of the Life of Sonia Henie* (Raleigh, N.C.: Pentland Press, 2000).

84. Robert Pruter, "Basketball," *Encyclopedia of Chicago*, http://www.encyclopedia.chicagohistory.org/pages/117.html (accessed 25 June 1906); Ted Vincent, *The Rise and Fall of American Sport: Mudville's Revenge* (Lincoln: University of Nebraska Press, 1994), 291.

85. David H. Lewis, *Roller Skating for Gold* (Lanham, Md.: Scarecrow Press, 1997), 28–29, 61–71.

86. Doug Huff, "Best by State: The Top High School Athletic Programs in America," *SI.com magazine*, 11 May 2005, http://sportsillustrated.cnn.com/2005/magazine/05/11/top.high.map0516/index.html (accessed 5 August 2007).

87. Al Barkow. *The History of the PGA Tour* (Garden City, N.Y.: Doubleday, 1989), 86–92; Tom Govedarica, *Chicago Golf: The First 100 Years* (Chicago: Eagle Communications Group, 1991).

88. Rabinowitz, "Golf."

89. *Chicago Tribune*, 17 July 1947, 1, 15 February 1951, B1, 16 May 1952, 1.

90. Barney Nagler, *James Norris and the Decline of Boxing* (Indianapolis: Bobbs-

Merrill, 1964). For sociological studies of Chicago prize fighting, see S. Kirson Weinberg and Henry Arond, "The Occupational Culture of the Boxer," *American Journal of Sociology* 57 (March 1952): 460–69; Nathan Hare, "A Study of the Black Fighter," *Black Scholar* 3 (November 1971): 2–8; Loic Wecquant, "The Social Logic of Boxing in Black Chicago: Toward a Sociology of Pugilism," *Sociology of Sport Journal* 9 (September 1992): 221–54.

91. Riess, "Horse Racing"; Hank Messick, *The Politics of Prosecution: Jim Thompson, Marge Everett, Richard Nixon, and the Trial of Otto Kerner* (Ottawa, Ill.: Caroline House, 1978), 152–58, 163–65, 195; "History of Arlington Park," http://www.arlington park.com/node/1811 (accessed 15 June 2008).

92. Robert Pruter, "Motor Sports," *Encyclopedia of Chicago*, http://www.encyclopedia.chicagohistory.org/pages/2188.html (accessed 4 September 2006); *Chicago Tribune*, 4 September 2006, sec. 2: 5; "Chicagoland Speedway History," http://www.chicagolandspeedway.com/cgi-bin/r.cgi/cls_history.html? (accessed 1 August 2008).

93. Daniel Greene, "United Center," *Encyclopedia of Chicago*, http://www.encyclopedia.chicagohistory.org/pages/1285.html (accessed 12 July 2006).

94. Alex Sachare, *The Chicago Bulls Encyclopedia* (Lincolnwood, Ill.: Contemporary Books, 1999).

95. Ibid.; David Halberstram, *Playing for Keeps: Michael Jordan and the World He Made* (New York: Random House, 1999).

96. Peter Golenback, *Wrigleyville: A Magical History Tour of the Chicago Cubs* (New York: St. Martin's Press, 1996); Jerome Holtzman and George Vass, *Baseball, Chicago Style: A Tale of Two Teams, One City* (Los Angeles: Bonus Books, 2005); Holtzman and Vass,*Chicago Cubs Encyclopedia*; Findling, "Chicago Cubs," 75–80; David Claeraut, *Durocher's Cubs: The Greatest Team That Didn't Win* (Dallas: Taylor, 2000), 83–104; Feldmann, *Miracle Collapse.*

97. Holtzman and Vass, *Chicago Cubs Encyclopedia*; and Findling, "Chicago Cubs," 80–86.

98. Lindberg, "Chicago White Sox"; Richard Lindberg, *The White Sox Encyclopedia* (Philadelphia: Temple University Press, 1997).

99. Ibid.

100. "Chicago Cardinals," http://www.sportsecyclopedia.com/nfl/azchi/cardschi.html (accessed 1 September 2006).

101. Armen Keteyian, *Ditka: Monster of the Midway* (New York: Pocket Books, 1992); Jeff Davis, *Papa Bear: The Life and Legacy of George Halas* (New York: McGraw-Hill, 2005); John Mullin, *The Rise and Self-destruction of the Greatest Football Team in History: The Chicago Bears and Superbowl XX* (Chicago: Triumph Books, 2005); Gale Sayers with Fred Mitchell, *Sayers: My Life and Times* (Chicago: Triumph Books, 2007); Steve Chapman, "A Stadium Deal That Is Hard to Bear," *Chicago Tribune*, 14 September 2003. http://infoweb.newsbank.com.rwlib.neiu.edu:2048/iwsearch/we/InfoWeb?p_product=NewsBank&p_theme=aggregated5&p_action=doc&p_docid=0FD910C29D92E3B9&p_docnum=1&p_queryname=2

102. Dave Litterer, "Chicago's Soccer History, http://www.sover.net/~spectrum/chicago.html (accessed 1 September 2006); Clemente Lisi, "The Man behind the Curtain: Patience Is Most Certainly a Virtue for MLS's Mysterious Patriarch, Philip Anschutz—Major League Soccer," *Soccer Digest* (October–November 2002), http://.findarticles.com/p/articles/mi_m0FCN/is_4_25/ai_92201934 (accessed 18 June 2008); Graham Bowley, "Goal! He Spends It on Beckham," *Inter-*

national Herald Tribune, 22 April 2007, http://www.iht.com/articles/2007/04/22/ yourmoney/22anschutz-webonly-ASIA.php (accessed 18 June 2008).

103. Rabinowitz, "Golf."

104. The FCI includes two adult average price tickets, two child average price tickets, four small soft drinks, two small beers, four hot dogs, two programs, parking, and two adult-size caps. Paul Bannister, "Family Costs for a Day at the Game," http://www.bankrate.com/brm/news/advice/20041119b1.asp (accessed 4 August 2007); "Major League Baseball 2006," http://www.teammarketing.com/ fci.cfm (accessed 4 August 2007).

105. Kurt Badenhausen and Jack Gage, "Bronx Cheer," *Forbes* 177 (8 May 2006): 64.

Chicagoans participated in turf sports even before the city was established, primarily harness racing. Thoroughbred racing struggled until the formation of the elite Washington Park Jockey Club in 1883, which built the outstanding Washington Park Race Track one year later. The Jockey Club made Chicago the Midwestern center of thoroughbred racing, featured by the prestigious American Derby, one of the most lucrative races in North America. The sport's success encouraged entrepreneurs to establish profit-oriented tracks that tried to attract a broader audience. The big profits came primarily from the gambling, which was permitted at the tracks but barred by law off the tracks. The gambling encouraged the expansion of syndicate crime, led by Mike McDonald, which was protected by powerful political connections. These gambling operations were a key source of revenue for organized crime. Racing in Chicago was very successful until 1905, when the authorities halted all racing, and racing was not resumed for a generation. The closing of the local tracks was expected to hurt business for poolrooms (illegal off-track betting parlors) and handbooks (off-track bookmakers who took bets in saloons, cigar stores, and other male hangouts) because those races received the most local publicity and press coverage. The off-track betting operations continued to flourish, however, with the cooperation of local politicians and police by taking bets on out-of-state tracks whose results were quickly reported by the racing wire. Bettors had less information about those races, but they loved to gamble, and the poolrooms and handbooks made it convenient for them.

1 Horse Racing in Chicago, 1883–1894

The Interplay of Class, Politics, and Organized Crime

STEVEN A. RIESS

This chapter will examine how horse racing provided a nexus between urban machine politics and organized crime in Chicago, the second largest city in the nation, and the site where organized crime reputedly first emerged in the United States. The rise of organized crime in the late nineteenth century reflected the growing political clout of urban political machines and the growing demands of citizens in increasingly anonymous urban enclaves to secure illegal services. Organized crime refers to crime syndicates that are protected by political connections. This is a symbiotic relationship in which the criminal gangs are protected from the criminal justice system by political cronies who forewarn them of occasional police raids and guarantee lenient treatment by friendly judges in the unlikely event of an arrest. The politicians gain from this sources of campaign financing, party workers, and bribes. The primary activities of organized crime in the late nineteenth century were in gambling and prostitution, victimless crimes in which the participants were willing clients. These were moral violations that large segments of the population felt should not be criminalized, and there was rarely a great deal of pressure upon the police to enforce such violations.[1]

In Chicago, the man who is credited with organizing the first crime syndicate was Michael Cassius McDonald, born in Niagara Falls in 1839. He became a swindler at age 16, selling fruit, candy, newspapers, and fake prize packages to railroad passengers for John R. Walsh, a politically connected Chicago publisher. In 1857 Mike became a gambler on the Mississippi, returning in 1860 to Chicago, where he became prominent along Gamblers' Row as a partner in several gambling houses and became known as the leading dice and cards man in the city. McDonald then went into the liquor business, where he became connected with powerful German brewers. In 1873, he opened "The Store," a deluxe downtown gambling emporium at 176 Clark Street, across the street from the county building. The first floor housed a cigar store and saloon that became the center of the local male bachelor subculture. The second floor housed McDonald's elegantly furnished gambling operation, which got a lot of business from traveling businessmen as well as local sports. McDonald and his fellow gamblers formed a syndicate, or trust, that compelled newcomers to the trade to pay them a percentage of their profits to stay in business. Among the other leading gamblers, originally outside the syndicate, were the Hankins brothers and Harry Varnell. The Hankins had an elegant gambling hall on Clark Street that purportedly made $20,000 a month in the 1880s. Another important ex-rival, Varnell, had a downtown gambling operation with over 90 employees that was open 24 hours. Varnell had a brief political career, serving in 1880 as warden of the Cook County insane asylum, which he transformed into a clubhouse for politicians and where several county commissioners lived. His political clout enabled him to run his gambling business with little interference from the authorities.[2]

From the mid-1880s, the McDonald-Hankins-Varnell bookmaking syndicate dominated Chicago and Indiana racetracks. They maintained a slush fund to support their political interests. One pool operator reportedly made $190,000 in 1889 alone. A few bookmakers, friends of McDonald's, were permitted to operate outside of the alliance, most notably Big Jim O'Leary and Silver Bill Riley. O'Leary was the son of a woman whose cow many thought had started the Chicago Fire. At the turn of the century, he was the preeminent handbook operator on Chicago's South Side. Riley's poolroom reportedly was the first gambling enterprise in the 1880s to focus exclusively on horse racing.[3]

According to the *Chicago Herald*, Mike McDonald was a political boss "who never held office, but he ruled the city with an iron hand. He named the men who were to be candidates for election, he elected them, and after they were in office they were merely his puppets."[4]

McDonald first became prominent in politics in 1873, when he helped found the People's Party, a coalition of Democrats and others interested in protecting personal freedoms that were under attack by moralists in post-fire Chicago. The coalition succeeded in electing Mayor Henry Colvin, who promoted a wide-open city. For the next several years, McDonald had several friends on the county board. Nonetheless, in 1876, a reform Republican mayor was elected in reaction to the wide-open city. Mayor

Monroe Heath made matters hot for the gamblers, with frequent raids, despite the presence of their friend, Mike Hickey, who was general superintendent of police. Underworld figures relied on McDonald and his trust to provide protection, advance information about raids, secure favorable witnesses, and avoid heavy sentences in the police courts. McDonald was recognized as the man to see for bailouts from jail, to arrange payoffs to policemen, or to influence a judge to release arrested gamblers or assess them token fines.[5]

The gamblers' interests became more settled with the mayoralty of Carter H. Harrison I, a blue blood who supported the concept of personal freedom. During Harrison's tenure as mayor (1879–1887), the gamblers were largely left alone. He believed that Chicagoans should be allowed to enjoy their vices, as long as they did not harm anyone else. Harrison refused to enforce anti-poolroom laws, because that would cause worse evils, and the gamblers would move to hotels, clubhouses, and saloons. The *Tribune* felt that he was wrong, albeit honest and outspoken: "He told no lies and made no excuses. He behaved like a man, defending a bad cause with courage and ability."[6]

Historians debate the extent to which McDonald influenced Harrison, who was an old friend. In 1882, when McDonald was indicted on gambling charges, the mayor appeared on his behalf as a character witness, testifying that he had often called on him. McDonald would appear with candidates at athletic halls and public meetings, and he helped raise campaign funds by requiring each gambler to put up $500. McDonald claimed at one time that his support was worth 5,000 votes.[7]

According to Mayor Harrison's biographer, McDonald was a constant supporter who "figured in nearly every convention which nominated him, and was one of the leading spirits in one of them." In the 1893 campaign, when Harrison ran for a fifth term, he denounced McDonald for his political activity, likely for political purposes, since the mayor did not want the public to think he was controlled by the underworld. Nevertheless, McDonald or someone else collected funds from gamblers for Harrison's campaign. The *Inter-Ocean* claimed that $300,000 to $500,000 had been amassed. Harrison told campaign manager Adolf Kraus why he had taken their money. "Why a gambler votes with his money. If I refuse their money, they withhold their votes. I accept their money, get their votes, and after election return their money. I want their votes, not their money."[8]

After around 1885, McDonald reputedly sought more legitimate endeavors to gain social acceptance for himself and his children. In addition, he eventually became involved in downtown real estate, construction, and traction interests, most notably Charles T. Yerkes's Lake Street el, and, for two years, the *Chicago Globe* newspaper. According to

Chicago police historian Richard Lindberg, his syndicate reputedly fell apart around 1889, when there were important police scandals, organized gambling in Chicago became less centralized, and gamblers began to cut their own deals. However, as the history of Chicago's racetracks indicates, the reported demise of the McDonald syndicate was premature.[9]

Organized Crime and Horse Race Gambling

By the end of the Civil War, gambling on horses in Chicago surpassed the traditional riverboat games such as stud poker, faro, and craps. At first, horse race gambling in Chicago primarily took place on racetracks, where auction pool operators dominated the business. In this form of betting, the man taking bets set up a pool and "auctioned off" each horse to the highest bidder. The bettor whose horse won the race took the pool, less a commission of about 5 percent to the bet taker. The city had a couple of second-rate tracks, but the big boom in the turf came in 1884 with the opening of Washington Park Racetrack, perhaps the finest in the Midwest, which was operated by the prestigious Washington Park Jockey Club. The track originally was located south of the city limits in the town of Lake, which was annexed in 1889 by a growing Chicago. The jockey club's members were the leading citizens of the city, including three-fourths of its millionaires, and the opening of the track became the major event of the summer social season. The American Derby, the signature race of the Chicago meet, became one of the preeminent sporting events in the United States.[10]

During this era, the auction pool betting system, which was largely limited to well-heeled bettors, gave way to bookmaking, in which individuals set odds on all of the horses in a race. In 1887, for example, Washington Park had 36 bookmakers' stalls, 4 pari-mutuel machines, and 2 auction pools. The sport was under a lot of pressure from anti-gambling forces that felt that betting was ruining families and encouraging embezzlement. An anti-pool law was passed, but it permitted gambling at the tracks. But even worse than betting on the tracks was the illegal gambling away from the facilities, which reflected that the gamblers' main concern was betting, not enjoying the sport.[11]

The leading Western tracks were organized into the American Turf Congress, whose goals included prohibiting the telegraph transmission of results to hinder off-track poolrooms that were taking a lot of business away from the tracks. Downtown Chicago was the primary locus for off-track Midwestern betting parlors in the mid-1880s. After Carter Harrison left office in 1887, having served four terms, his successor, Republican Mayor John Roche, came into office with the goal of elevating public morality and stopping gambling. He ordered the police to close six of the more notorious downtown poolrooms, and they remained shut during his term.[12]

Prior to the 1889 mayoral election, the gamblers offered both political parties a deal, trading permission to gamble in return for votes and campaign contributions. They worked hard for Democrat DeWitt Cregier and contributed about $6,000 to him. According to the *Tribune*, the gamblers were instrumental in getting him elected:

> This is an open secret to everybody at all versed in the unwritten history of the campaign. Cregier was a defeated man until within a week of the election. His Campaign Committee was destitute . . . and there was no prospect of getting enough to pay the expenses of printing the tickets and peddling the same. Cregier was apparently irreconcilably opposed to the reopening of the gambling houses which had on their walls the accumulated cobwebs of two years while Mr. Roche was mayor. Friends came to his rescue and induced him to promise that the gamblers should be permitted to resume business at their old stands.
>
> Michael C. McDonald, the eminent philanthropist and rare diplomat, had left Chicago in disgust, and was at this time in Philadelphia looking after some railroad interests. He was summoned to Chicago. . . . Mr. McDonald exercised the talents which have made him famous and wealthy.[13]

Under the Cregier regime, gaming houses that were closed for two years now reopened, and they remained so, except for a day or two to help out the administration's bad public image. The *Tribune* asserted, "While there is not and cannot be any written proof of a bargain, there is sufficient circumstantial evidence to show that one was made between the gamblers and some one who held Cregier in the hollow of his hand. During his term, while he kept some of his promises to the gamblers, he did encounter pressure to close up the lesser faro games. Overall, the Cregier years were not as good for gamblers as Harrison's four terms."[14]

Downtown poolrooms flourished in the 1890s and hurt local tracks, even if most only posted out-of-town events. The selling of pools on foreign events was a specialty of gambler Joseph Ullman, who often ran afoul of the Hankins-McDonald syndicate. They demanded 60 percent of his profits for protection, while Ullman refused to go over 40 percent. In 1890, the *Tribune* urged the Cregier administration to shut them up. Typically some pool operators would be fined; they would appeal, and often the violation would be forgotten. Journalists wondered if the mayor and police were afraid to act.[15]

The grand jury, in the summer of 1890, was concerned that the mayor, police chief, and staff were not suppressing gambling. A gambling war was emerging, in which political influence played a significant role. The press reported that Edward Corrigan, owner of the proprietary West Side Racetrack adjacent to Garfield Park at the city's western border, was persecuting downtown poolroom men to make them operate at his track where they would have to pay him fees. The mayor and the city police sided against Corrigan on the pool selling issue. Corrigan meanwhile used his Pinkertons to protect the West Side Track against outside interference. On July 28, for instance, Pinkertons tried to kick some intruding constables and city police off the track. A truce was supposed to be arranged in the gambling war, but Corrigan got warrants against the downtown bookies. In response, the poolroom men orchestrated a raid on Joseph Ullman's racetrack poolroom. The truce ended after the last race, when fighting broke out.[16]

The *Tribune* was very down on the city for "its open siding with the downtown poolrooms in the war." It also took to task the state's anti-pool law that did not apply to racetrack pools because it permitted pool selling on the grounds of an incorporated racing association one day prior to the opening of a meet and while races were in progress. The *Tribune* hoped to see both sides of the fight eat each other up:

> One must be protected because the gamblers are interested in it, and the gamblers control the Mayor, who controls the police, who put their heavy hands on one set of scoundrels while protecting, encouraging, and supporting the other—for a consideration.
> The down-town pool-rooms are backed by that syndicate of gamblers who made, and run, the present City administration. The Law Department gave an accommodating opinion that the state law might be unconstitutional, and was risky to enforce. Yet it was apparently constitutional to break up the foreign books at the track. This is the most shameless confession yet of the ownership of the City Administration by the gaming trust. The people have seen the police force restrained from raiding protected halls. They have seen it making raids on those which were not protected. But they never before have seen it ordered out publicly to fight the battles of these gamblers, and to assist them, in conjunction with an auxiliary force of constables and private detectives, in suppressing their adversaries while defending the trust.
> It is the lowest depth of degradation which has been reached yet by any City Administration. But if the gamblers demand still stronger evidence of servility they will doubtless be forthcoming. And it is to this the "moral scratchers" have brought the city—its patrolmen obeying openly the orders of Hankins and McDonald, the real Chiefs of Police.[17]

On July 30, Corrigan secured an injunction against Mayor Cregier and the police chief to prevent interference with his track. There had been no interruptions in 1889, but since opening up nine days before, Chicago officials had threatened Corrigan and his associates with arrests. Corrigan indicated that poolrooms were operating in the city contrary to law but were "kept open pursuant to an agreement and understanding made between the owners and operators . . . and DeWitt C. Cregier, Mayor of Chicago, Frederick H. Marsh, Superintendent of Police of Chicago, and sundry other persons connected with said defendees, wherein and whereby said pool-sellers in the city of Chicago contribute a certain percentage of their profits . . . for so-called police protection" on a weekly basis. The mayor was irate and denounced the charges. Corrigan asked the poolroom men to observe the same policy for his track as Washington Park, but they refused. "We have done enough for Cregier in shutting down during the Washington Park races, so that he might keep faith with some of his political backers. We do not propose to close down for you, even if the Mayor should ask us." When Corrigan threatened to enforce anti-poolroom laws, Hankins and McDonald responded with threatened raids: "We can turn [Police Captain] Hayes loose on you." The *Tribune* noted: "They evidently spoke with authority. They are putting their threat into practice. They control the police force. That is clear. Cannot Mayor Cregier see that they do?"[18]

The *Tribune* found it embarrassing for the city's chief executive to encounter such charges, using "hackneyed and stereotyped line of defense once cleverly employed by Mr. Harrison, but stupidly persisted in too long." The mayor's claims of having effected the closing of poolrooms were disingenuous. Indeed, "It is hard to get to City Hall without running into a poolroom."[19]

According to a *Tribune* editorial, "The original contract made with the gamblers was that their places should not be unmolested. Nothing was said of pool-selling. Therefore, when the trust demanded protection for the pool-rooms . . ., the mayor should have refused permission." But instead he yielded miserably, trying to hide his surrender by securing a judgment from the law department that the law could not be enforced. Then when rival poolrooms outside the trust began operations, the gamblers insisted that the police close them, which was done. The editorial continued: "So the lawful pool sellers are suppressed and the unlawful pool sellers are protected by the police. Whatever the outcome of Corrigan's accusations may be, these facts are enough to condemn the administration that has surrendered unconditionally and is the mere puppet and tool of a handful of gamblers."[20]

Cregier's motivation for closing the poolrooms during the Washington Park meet is unclear. According to one story, some of his main backers were interested in the Washington Park races and threatened to blow Cregier "out of the water" unless the rooms were closed up. Pat Sheedy's poolroom was raided for the first time, possibly because it became known that he had paid attorney Richardson to help prosecute Corrigan and Ullman. The *Tribune* continued to take Cregier to task for allowing six downtown rooms to operate that Mayor Roche had closed, and it criticized City Prosecutor May (a former attorney for the gamblers) as practically being an attorney for the Gambling Trust.[21]

The *Tribune* unfavorably compared Cregier to his immediate predecessors. Harrison had been wrong in his actions, but at least he had stood up like a man for his point of view. Then came Roche, who had carried out his plan to curtail gambling. Cregier, on the other hand, had decried gambling as a great evil that should be stopped, but he had not, either because his orders were not obeyed or they were not respected. Consequently, the *Tribune* claimed, the public saw him as insincere or incompetent.[22]

In late October Judge Murry F. Tuley ruled that pool selling was illegal, and that the state and city laws permitting it at the tracks were also void, because gambling everywhere was the same. This contradicted prior courts that had held that pool selling was not gaming within the meaning of the general statute on gambling.[23]

The *Tribune* applauded Tuley's righteous action that promised to wipe out the privileged class of gamblers, putting off-track pool sellers and bookmakers on the same level without a legal leg to stand on: "It would remove dangerous and insidious temptations from the path of young men. It will tend to make businessmen more secure in the honesty of their employees. It will remove the shameful spectacle of gamblers protected by police authority. It will place gambling of every kind where it can be reached by the law. It also opens up a golden opportunity for his Honor, Mayor Cregier, as it gives him the power to suppress gambling of every description and save him from the trouble of regulating it."[24]

Corrigan's West Side lease expired in the fall of 1890 and would not be renewed. Corrigan then was under a lot of political pressure to move from politicians tied to the gambling syndicate. For instance, on February 12, 1891, state Senator Sol Van Pragg, a Chicago poolroom operator, introduced legislature aimed at harassing Corrigan. The bill proposed limiting racing meets to 30 days and taxing the tracks 5 percent of their gross receipts. Corrigan dismantled his buildings and prepared to move his operations to another site southwest of the city.[25]

Mayor Cregier was up for reelection that spring against the reform Republican candidate Hempstead Washburne. Cregier sought financial support from the gamblers, who knew that Washburne was sure to oppose them. The Gamblers' Trust and its allies purportedly amassed a $25,000 fund to support Cregier's retention. The trust was monopolizing Chicago faro banks, and other forms of gambling, including policy, under the Democratic regime. However, despite the aid from organized crime, Cregier was defeated by the reform-minded Washburne.[26]

In April 1891, Mayor Washburne came into office and turned the screws on gambling. Police were instructed to warn gambling rooms to close up or expect to get raided and have their property confiscated. They virtually all complied, not all willingly. Some bookmakers left Chicago for southern tracks, while others announced the start of handbook betting with 150 workers immediately available, since they had lost their old jobs.[27]

On May 20, Corrigan's Chicago Racing Association opened for business just outside of the city limits at the border of the village of Hawthorne and the town of Cicero. His partners in the new Hawthorne Racetrack included former West Park Commissioner John Brenock, a man with some political clout. Hawthorne opened in the spring, charging 75 cents to $1 admission, but it closed early in the summer, when Washington Park held its meet.[28]

After Corrigan had left the West Side, two North Siders leased the site where the old racecourse still stood, with a 10–year option. A new $300,000 West Side track known as Garfield Park was planned at Madison and 40th Street [present-day Pulaski Road]. It was named for the beautiful suburban park adjacent to the track. This was a "bookmakers' track," run by the Hankins syndicate, with Democratic politician Washington Hesing, publisher of the *Staats-Zeitung*, serving as track president. The stockholders included Mike McDonald (who had invested $20,000), B. J. Johnson ($15,000), George V. Hankins ($35,000), Al Hankins ($10,000), Jeff Hankins ($10,000), William J. Wightman, Harry Varnell, Harry Romaine, Sidney McHie, and John Condon, a fixer for the McDonald syndicate, who had run his own gambling hall in the late 1880s. They budgeted $150,000 for a 20,000–seat grandstand, with a fine clubhouse, sheds for 800 horses, and running tracks that measured ¾ of a mile and 1 mile. But when the track opened, the grandstand built in 1878 was still employed. Nonetheless, one thing Garfield Park had going for it was its location. It was situated much closer to the center of the city's population and was more accessible than either Washington Park or Hawthorne. It was just sixteen minutes from Union Depot by special Wisconsin Central trains and thirty-five minutes by cheaper streetcars. The other thing going for the track was the political clout of McDonald, the Hankins, and Varnell.[29]

Moral reformers opposed the establishment of Garfield Park. They found support from the West Chicago Park Commissioners, who sought an injunction on June 20 to block construction. The commissioners claimed that the Park Act gave them the power to forbid horse racing, gambling, or any offensive activities within 400 feet of the park and the West Side boulevards, as well as a 50–foot easement for a building line around the park. They further argued that the track would harm the usefulness and benefits of the park and neighborhood, bringing in "vast crowds of objectionable persons and necessitate an increase in the park police force." Neighborhood property owners living within 400 feet of the site also filed for an injunction, complaining that virtually all of the track owners were pool sellers or bookies, including many notorious keepers of common gambling houses. They pointed out that the new track was not intended to improve the breed, to develop speed, or for sport, but purely to promote gambling. Local landlords pointed out that Corrigan's racetrack had been a nuisance, with foul odors and noise, drawing to their neighborhood "thieves, confidence men, loafers, tramps, beggars, and adventurers. . . . Women and children could not venture from their house for fear of violence or insult at the hands of this mob. Dog fights and prize fights were other attractions offered. Property has depreciated to such an extent since the new track was talked of that there is no sale for lots and people who can are moving out of the neighborhood." Property owners expected nothing better and a lot worse from the new promoters. It would attract "all classes of low people, thieves, prize-fighters, abandoned women, tramps, and other disreputable characters." The efforts of the park commissioners, moral reformers, and neighbors failed to block the sporting venture, and Garfield Park was leased to the bookmaking syndicate for $60,000 over three years.[30]

Garfield Park track operated in direct competition with Corrigan's new Hawthorne course. Neither track drew the best horses that raced at Washington Park, and purses were about the same at both tracks. Garfield quickly developed a reputation for dubious integrity, as bookmakers regularly bet against horses they owned. They competed for the more plebeian audiences, with Garfield usually coming out ahead, averaging over 7,000 each day, and drawing as many as 22,000 one afternoon. Admission cost 75 cents to $1, but each scheduled a number of free dates. Garfield's ticket sales were modest, often no more than $200, partly because so many people got in on passes. However, it made up for small admission fees with large profits from the betting.[31]

Hawthorne operated until early September. Its meet was described by the *Spirit of the Times*, a leading sporting weekly of the day, as a "heroic struggle against peculiarly adverse circumstances." Corrigan and his partners were said to be losing a lot of money each day, despite Hawthorne's integrity and good training facilities, hurt by the expensive and infrequent public transit. What saved them was that Corrigan's horses made $25,000 during the meet, and their bookmaking on foreign (out-of-town) races brought in $55,000.[32] The *Spirit* also blamed politics for many problems:

> Then again, the Tweed and Tammany rings of New York in their palmiest days were babies in comparison to the clique of Chicago, who have strained every source known to the order to down Mr. Corrigan. Every dive, barroom, and thug ugly of the Garden City were in league against him, in fact so bitter has been this element that most of the public resorts boycotted his racing cards, so that patrons were obliged to wait the morning papers to see the entries at Hawthorne. Almost every respectable racing stable of the West stuck to him until the flag was furled, and few men in Chicago to-day have more friends among horsemen than Edward Corrigan.[33]

Garfield's proprietors reputedly made a fortune during the three-month meet, even though the track had provided only $43,280 in stakes and purses. The foreign book alone took in $600,000, with total profits at $1 million. The owners announced plans for a winter meet, which encountered strong public opposition, led by the local press. Their plans were strongly opposed by Mayor Washburne, who in the fall put a lot of pressure on the city council to prevent Garfield from reopening in the spring. On December 3, 1891, he secured the passage of a city council ordinance forbidding the reopening. McDonald and the racetrack crowd expected their allies on the council to subsequently emasculate the law and keep them in business. In the meantime the police, under orders from the park commissioner, stepped in at the scheduled three-month season on December 12 to halt operations, claiming the one-mile track infringed on the protected boulevards around Garfield Park. (Actually, the racing occurred at the three-quarter-mile track that was legally far enough away.) The *Inter-Ocean*, a paper that normally supported racing, as well as some other papers, stopped printing results from Garfield Park, stating that "the racing at Garfield Park is not honest and it is cruel." The city council continued to put pressure on the bookmakers. One ordinance, which did not pass, sought to run streets through the track. Another was approved to ban bookmaking and pool selling at tracks inside the city limits, but its constitutionality was uncertain, since it contradicted the state law that permitted betting on all regular tracks.[34]

In the spring of 1892, the press, particularly the *Chicago Times*, vigorously criticized Chicago racing, particularly McDonald and the Garfield Park crowd. The *Chicago Times* proclaimed: "Mike McDonald is an unscrupulous, disreputable, vicious gambler, a disgrace and menace to the city. He should be driven from the city and the racetracks closed up forever." The strong critique by the *Times* surprised many observers, because it was owned by former Mayor Harrison, McDonald's old friend.[35]

Mayor Washburne indicated that he intended to close Garfield, which had optimistically enlarged its grandstand to seat 17,000. Management tried to get a three-month license but, like the other tracks in the area, it was only granted a 30–day permit. The owners encountered considerable pressure from the mayor, and they failed to secure an injunction to prevent Washburne from interfering with the pools, foreign books, and local books. Garfield Park opened its spring meet on May 21 with free admission for the 4,200 in attendance. There were also twenty uniformed policemen and detectives, who did not interfere with the gambling. But they offered a stronger presence two days later when there were only 1,200 spectators. The track subsequently closed until just before Decoration Day, when the owners presumed that the authorities were too busy with parades and crowds elsewhere to interfere. The holiday event attracted 5,000 racing fans and 42 bookmakers. The foreign books were raided the next day, but they were soon back running. The biggest day of the spring meet was the $17,000 Garfield Park Derby for three-year-olds on June 18.[36]

Washburne thereafter stepped up his fight against Garfield Park. Alderman John Cooke, an administrative spokesman in the city council, presented an ordinance on July 18 to close up the racetrack, because "This is a residential district and the residents complain that the betting pools cause disreputable men and women to loiter in the neighborhood." The track's interests were protected by machine politicians such as Bathhouse John Coughlin, the colorful First Ward alderman and Democratic committeeman that the bookmakers helped elect in early 1892 to protect their interests. Coughlin himself was a racing fan who owned a small stable of thoroughbreds and had a box at Garfield Park. He developed into one of the most notorious political bosses in Chicago history, who took full advantage of the grafting opportunities of his wide-open Levee district. Bathhouse John staunchly stood up for Garfield Park: "You can't do that. . . . You can't shut up a man's property. . . . It's unfair. . . . It's. . . . un-American, that's what! Why gentlemen, think of the money racing brings to Chicago, the millions of dollars. You can't get an order like this through the council, and I tell you, Me? Maar, I'm going to vote against it, and I know every man here will do the same." The proposal to close the track and make permanent the anti–Garfield Park law was sent to the judiciary committee. One week later, the committee reported that the plan was unfair, and it suggested closing all of the other tracks although the only track in the city limits was Washington Park.[37]

Varnell tried unsuccessfully to get the city collector to issue him a ninety-day license, and his colleagues then sought an injunction to require the city to give them the license. Their efforts were rejected by Judge James Horton, who denounced all horse racetrack gambling, particularly at Garfield Park.[38]

The council passed a bill in late July before its summer recess to circumvent the mayor's licensing powers in the racing business. Councilman Johnny Powers of the Nineteenth Ward, chairman of the finance committee, and the "Prince of Boodlers," recommended a plan to permit a racing association to hold meets between May 1 and November 1 for a $200-a-day license fee. "We must have races in Chicago," said Alderman Powers. "It is a sport center, and the great majority of people favor racing." The Powers bill was approved by 38 aldermen and sent to the mayor for his approval. Washburne, as expected, immediately vetoed the bill, criticizing the measure for leaving the authorities with insufficient control to close a racetrack, should it become a menace to public order. McDonald, that afternoon, tried to get a license for the track, but because of the veto, he was out of luck.[39]

The council recessed for the summer, which halted any additional action, on the racing license issue. The track owners were certain that Washburne would not take action until the council reconvened in September, so they reopened Garfield Park in early August.[40]

When Garfield Park reopened, local citizens organized to protest. Bishop Fallows claimed that most of the embezzling in Chicago was a consequence of betting losses, and another commentator judged the gambling at Garfield worse than the infamous Louisiana Lottery. The meet attracted about 40 bookmakers, compared to only about 11 at Hawthorne, and there was a lot of betting. Of course, "The four hundred are not out in force at Garfield."[41]

On Friday, September 2, the racing situation came to a head. Acting on a petition from local businessmen and clergymen, Police Chief R. W. McClaughry ordered a raid on Garfield Park for operating without a license and for permitting gambling. The track was surrounded after the first race by Inspector Lyman Lewis, leading 100 officers and 13 paddy wagons. Nine Pinkerton guards were ordered away from the front gates and placed into some of the wagons. Thirty-three people were arrested, including track manager M. Lewis Clark, his secretary, the race starter, nine Pinkertons, and the 13 jockeys who raced in the opening event. Coughlin and Varnell bailed them out, charging that Corrigan and ex-Mayor Carter Harrison, who they believed was part owner of Hawthorne, were behind the raid. Mayor Washburne later testified in court that Corrigan's partner and secretary, James E. Burke, had told Chief McClaughry early in the summer that Hawthorne would pay big money to the Republican Party if Garfield was closed up, and that the chief had passed the offer to the mayor, which Washburne rejected out of hand. The chief admitted that he had known Burke for fifteen years, but he denied that Burke had offered $50,000 to close up the competition. He did admit taking advice from Burke, whose brother, a bishop, had frequently visited McClaughry at home. Burke retorted, "Why I'm a good Democrat. What would I be doin', givin' dough to the Republicans?"[42]

The press applauded the raid. The *Tribune* described the track as a vile resort of the lowest type, a nest of thieves, burglars, confidence men, and lewd folk: "It has been a veritable charnell-house for morals, a den in which were killed off all the good and noble sentiments that were originally entertained by its frequenters, and for them substitute vile ambitions, a test for wicked enjoyments, and an admiration for the ethics of the thief and libertine."[43]

On Saturday, despite the raid the day before, and the presence of 150 police officers, 8,000 attended the races. The start was delayed for three hours with Inspector Lewis in front of the starter's stand. As soon as George Hankins finally rang the starter's bell, the police moved in, arresting Hankins, Varnell, and as many employees as they could catch. McDonald blamed the raid on Corrigan, who he claimed was tight with Chief McClaughry and the Republicans, and he urged all racing fans to vote Democratic in the next election.[44]

The track was closed on Sunday for the Sabbath. On Monday, September 5, Pinkerton guards closed and bolted the front gates once the crowds were in to keep out the police. Two races were staged without interference, but then around 3:30 P.M., five wagon loads with several hundred police officers arrived, having received reports that gambling was going on inside the track. They stormed and smashed the gates with axes, raced into the track, and surrounded the betting ring with paddy wagons. They arresting 25 gamblers, 25 jockeys, Col. Clark, George Hankins, Varnell, and Michael Coughlin (Bathhouse's older brother). In all, 800 people were detained, and 125 were locked up. This was one of the largest raids in the city's history. McDonald made bond for the track officials.[45]

On the following day, attendance was down to 1,500. Shortly after 3 P.M., the police moved into the park and fired their pistols into the air. Among the men in the crowd was noted horseman and former Texas sheriff Jim Brown, well known as a tough guy, who sat up on a barn roof where his horses were stabled, twirling his .44 (which had 12 notches for men he had killed) and shouting that no one was going to stop the races. Brown fled, but when he was cut off by Officer John Powell, he shot and killed the policeman. Brown tried to escape but ran into Officer William Jones, whom he also tried to shoot, but his gun jammed. Jones shot and killed Brown.[46]

This bloody event precipitated the end of Garfield Park, confirming Chief McClaughry's determination to close the track. "If police officers cannot enter the park in the discharge of their duty without being killed, it is time the park was closed." Reformers ranging from the daily press, clergymen, and women's clubs all called for the end of Garfield Park.[47]

Garfield's last breath came on September 12, when the city council considered Washburne's license veto. Prior to that vote, a test vote was taken on a bizarre resolution proposed by Alderman Henry Eller and backed by Coughlin, which praised the courage of ex-sheriff Brown and demanded an investigation of the police and the reported bribe offers from Ed Corrigan and Jimmy Burke. The resolution failed, and the veto was upheld by a vote of 60 to 3. Newspaper headlines screamed, "The Reign Is Ended."[48]

The closing of Garfield did not mean the demise of Chicago racing, or of the bookmakers and organized crime. Several of the Garfield Park investors, including John Condon, Harry Varnell, and Paddy Ryan, simply moved their business in November to Roby, Indiana, one mile across the state border. Roby was accessible by water transport and a half-hour train ride from Chicago. The new track's president was Chicago Alderman Ernest Hummell. The Garfield crowd invested money in the local Democratic campaign chest to ensure noninterference and to gain influence in the state legislature.[49]

Horse race gambling was an issue in the next mayoral campaign. The Democratic candidates were former Mayor Cregier, Washington Hesing, denounced by the *Times* as "the candidate of the Garfield Park gang and the management of their racetrack," and *Chicago Times* publisher Carter H. Harrison, who was running for a fifth term. He did not oppose pool selling on the tracks and admitted making wagers and buying pools. Harrison did not believe that gambling could be eliminated, and he sought to regulate it when it was too obnoxious (betting on foreign races, late closing hours, juveniles at the track, free liquor given as enticements, etc.). He was targeted by the press for having failed to squash the gambling interests in his prior terms.

Harrison felt that the elite Washington Park merited special consideration, because it ran short, one-month meets, was less accessible, and was owned and operated by prominent moral men: "I should judge that the class of patrons of Washington Park can much better afford to lose their money than those who go to Garfield. At the former track I have seen the majority of the crowd to be respectable people, while at the latter they are very disreputable. At Washington Park it is a great sight to see a well-dressed society lady betting on her favorite horse and clapping her pretty hands when he comes in first. At Garfield, this cannot be seen, for the demi-monde prevails."[50]

Harrison won the nomination and then the general election over Republican Samuel Allerton, a wealthy meatpacker. He got to preside over the Columbian Exposition, but his term was cut short in 1894 by an assassin.

In the short run, racing did very well in Chicago after the closing of Garfield Park. Racing enjoyed a banner year in 1893, benefiting from the excitement and tourism surrounding the World's Fair. Hawthorne was open for 260 dates, while at Washington Park stakes and purses amounted to $378,000, twice more than in 1892. The American Derby was attended by 47,000 spectators and was won by Boundless, who earned a record $50,000 for his victory. Nonetheless, the track encountered a lot of negative press, particularly from the crusading *Chicago Daily News*, which considered Derby Day to have been a disgrace, with many respectable women seated "in the presence of scores of harlots, most of whom are drunk and all of whom are loudly dressed and otherwise act their infamous callings." The *Daily News* commenced a vigorous crusade against Washington Park, complaining about minors betting, the presence of loose women, the integrity of certain races, and declining property values near the track.[51]

In 1894 there were three major tracks in the metropolitan area after George Hankins, John Condon, and the former associates of Mike McDonald established the proprietary Harlem Race Track southwest of the city (in present-day Forest Park). The pressure on Washington Park heated up in 1894, led by local Protestant clergymen and the newly formed Civic Federation. South Side businessmen petitioned Democratic mayor Hopkins not to renew its license.[52] In May the South Side Anti-Race Track Association organized a mass meeting at which one speaker took to task the elite Washington Park track:

> The chief difference between [the] Washington Park racetrack and the Garfield track is in the character of its members. The Washington Park track includes the same bad elements, the gambling, the evil association, the disreputable elements are all there, but there is a sprinkling of respectability who use these races as a cover to their vices. Yearly at its meetings are dumped on a respectable and quiet residence community a mass of humanity, gamblers and disreputables, and the offscourgings of the earth. . . . It is a well-known fact that this racetrack has greatly degenerated in morality and is becoming decidedly "tough."

> This club becomes the common meeting-ground between supposed respectability and total depravity. Women of loose character swarm the grounds and hold sway where the young men of the city are here led into gambling and evil associations, and the air of semirespectability given it by its list of prominent members and their attendance, example, and sanction is a large factor in leading them on.[53]

Washington Park's spring meet started out well with the $20,000 American Derby, which drew more than 35,000 spectators. But the rest of the meet was a struggle, with light attendance and modest betting, affected by the ongoing depression, the lack of exciting horses, and the Pullman strikes that briefly halted the Illinois Central Railroad.[54]

The reform movement was further bolstered that spring by the publication of William T. Stead's *If Christ Came to Chicago*, a muckraking account of local vice that sold 100,000 copies in its first two weeks. Then, on June 30, 1894, a grand jury indicted several leaders of Washington Park, including President George Wheeler, for keeping a gaming house.[55]

In late September the Civic Federation commenced a crusade against Chicago gambling, with daily raids on local poolrooms and even a raid at the Hawthorne track. The Civic Federation was supported by the local press, the Chicago Trade and Labor Assembly, the American Federation of Labor, and Mayor John P. Hopkins.[56]

Shortly thereafter the WPJC Board of Directors decided to halt operations. They were influenced by the growing public pressure and harassment, the declining condition of the turf, Wheeler's arrest, and the inability of the state legislature to pass enabling laws similar to the Ives Act in New York to protect racing interests. Furthermore, many club members, few of whom were active horsemen, wanted to separate the social and racing aspects of the club.[57] Finally, its leaders did not have the intestinal fortitude to stand up and fight the reformers, perhaps because throughbred racing was not all that encompassing to them. These upperclass Chicagoans had other ways to certify their status and demonstrate their manliness and were not prepared to go to the barricades to protect the sport, especially if it meant working with the bookmakers and entrepreneurs who ran the local proprietary tracks.

The tracks had a checkered career over the next few years because of pressure from moral reformers, particularly the Civic Federation. Washington Park did not reopen until 1899, concerned about the growing presence of a less desirable element at the track, possible grand jury indictments, and the needs for funds to secure supportive legislation in Springfield. Harlem held a brief meet in 1895 and then closed until 1897. Hawthorne closed after a short run in 1895 and did not reopen until 1898, the year when the new Worth course was established. Thereafter, thoroughbred racing had several excellent years until 1905, when the mayor aand the county closed all the tracks, and they remained virtually shut until the 1920s.[58]

Bookmaking, on the other hand, thrived, from the downtown poolrooms to the hundreds of handbooks found in most working-class neighborhoods. Handbook backers, who took bets of a dollar and up, did not seem worried about the racetrack woes, getting their information on out-of-town races from Western Union. Chicago became a national center for off-track betting, second only to New York.[59]

Conclusion

Horse racing in Chicago and in other parts of the United States provided a key nexus for organized crime and machine politics. This often meant ownership of racetracks, participation in racing stables, and management of legal wagering, and always control of illegal, off-track gambling. Machine politicians needed financing and votes from the underworld, while the gangsters needed protection for illegal gambling networks and speedy information on the results of races. These findings are similar to that previously discovered for New York and New Jersey, where urban machine politics and crime were integral elements of late-nineteenth-century and early-twentieth-century horse racing. In metropolitan New York, the most prestigious tracks were not owned by professional politicians or the underworld, but the legality of horse racing was tied to the political clout of well-to-do horsemen allied with Tammany Boss Richard Croker, himself a famed owner of outstanding thoroughbreds. More importantly, there was an extensive off-track betting business controlled by the Gambling Trust, prominent figures in Tammany Hall, which included Big Tim Sullivan, number two man in the machine, and Frank Farrell, the leading gambling impresario in New York. In New Jersey, racing in the late nineteenth century was intimately tied to the Democratic political machines in Hudson and Gloucester counties, home of the notorious Guttenberg and Gloucester racetracks. These outlaw tracks were owned and operated by prominent Jersey pols. Similarly, in St. Louis, Cincinnati, and New Orleans, urban political machines and syndicate crime played a prominent role in the turf. Yet the alliance was not omnipotent, as outlaw tracks in New Jersey and Illinois were closed despite the owners' political influence, and racecourses in most major racing areas were slammed shut for varying periods of time.[60]

Notes

Reprinted by permission from "Horse Racing in Chicago, 1883–1894: The Interplay of Class, Politics, and Organized Crime," by Steven Riess, in *Sporting Dystopias: The Making and Meanings of Urban Sport Cultures* edited by Ralph C. Wilcox et al, the State University of New York Press, c. 2001, State University of New York. All rights reserved.

1. On the history of organized crime, see, e.g., David Johnson, *Policing the Urban Underworld: The Impact of Crime on the Development of the Police, 1800–87* (Philadelphia: Temple University Press, 1977), and David Johnson, "A Sinful Business: The Origins of Gambling Syndicates in the United States, 1840–1887," in D. H. Bayley, ed., *Police and Society* (Beverly Hills, Calif.: Sage Publications, 1977), 17–47.

2. Richard Lindberg, *To Serve and Collect: Chicago Politics and Police Corruption from the Lager Beer Riots to the Summerdale Scandal* (New York: Praeger, 1991), 90–95; Herbert Asbury, *Gem of the Prairie: An Informal History of the Chicago Underworld* (New York: A. A. Knopf, 1942), 142–44; Herbert Asbury, *Suckers' Progress: An Informal History of Gambling in America* (New York: Dodd, Mead, 1938), 296–302; Lloyd Wendt and Herman Kogan, *Lords of the Levee: The Story of Bathhouse John and Hinky Dink* (Garden City, N.Y.: Doubleday, 1940), 28; Bessie L. Pierce, *A History of Chicago*, vol. 3, *1871–1893* (Chicago: University of Chicago Press, 1953), 305. On the Hankins brothers, see, e.g., *Chicago Tribune*, 16 June 1890, 6, 17 June 1890, 4, 23 July 1890, 8.

3. Steven Longstreet, *Chicago, 1860–1919* (New York: McKay, 1973), 209; Asbury, *Sucker's Progress*, 299; Pierce, *History of Chicago*, 476–477.

4. Quoted in Longstreet, *Chicago, 1860–1919*, 201.

5. Ibid., 42–44.

6. *Chicago Tribune*, 9 Aug. 1890, 1, 10 Aug. 1890, 1, 12.

7. Claudius O. Johnson, *Carter Henry Harrison I* (Chicago: University of Chicago Press, 1928), 139; Lindberg, *To Serve and Collect*, 94–95; Asbury, *Gem of the Prairie*, 146–147.

8. Johnson, "Sinful Business," 187–188 (quote); Kogan and Wendt, *Lords of the Levee*, 67.

9. Lindberg, *To Serve and Collect*, 96–98; Asbury, *Gem of the Prairie*, 158

10. *Spirit of the Times*, 106 (22 Dec. 1883): 625, (5 Jan. 1884): 689, (12 Jan. 1884): 720, 107 (28 June 1884): 680, 684, (5 July 1884): 710, 711, (12 July 1884): 736, 108 (3 Jan. 1885): 713; Herma N. Clark, *The Elegant Eighties: When Chicago Was Young* (Chicago: A. C. McClurg, 1941), 205. On the history of American horse racing, see W. H. P. Robertson, *The History of Thoroughbred Racing in America* (Englewood Cliffs, NJ: Prentice-Hall, 1974); C. B. Parmer, *For Gold and Glory: The History of Thoroughbred Racing in America* (New York: Carrick and Evans, 1939).

11. *Chicago Times*, 28 June 1887, 2. See also *Chicago Tribune*, 16 April 1887, 1.

12. *Chicago Tribune*, 9 Aug. 1890, 1, 10 Aug. 1890, 1, 12.

13. *Chicago Tribune*, 3 Apr. 1891, 1–7.

14. *Chicago Tribune*, 13 Aug. 1890, 4, 3 Apr. 1891, 1.

15. *Chicago Times*, 3 Nov. 1889, 12, 11 Nov. 1889, 3; *Chicago Tribune*, 4 May 1890 12; *Spirit of the Times* 118 (31 May 1890): 830, 118 (7 June 1890): 865, 119 (26 July 1890): 1; *Clipper* 37 (9 Aug. 1890): 347, 37 (8 Nov. 1890): 554.

16. *Chicago Tribune*, 25 July 1890, 2, 29 July 1890, 1.

17. *Chicago Tribune*, 30 July 1890, 4.

18. *Chicago Tribune*, 31 July 1890, 1, 4 (quote).

19. Ibid.

20. Ibid.

21. *Chicago Tribune*, 31 July 1890, 1, 1 Aug. 1890, 1, 4. The six rooms were owned by Al Hankins, Sid McHie, Corrigan, J. H. Levy, Shepard and Argo, and Pat Sheedy. On Mayor Roche's early efforts against Chicago gamblers, see *Chicago Tribune*, 16 June 1887, 1.

22. *Chicago Tribune*, 9 Aug. 1890, 1, 10 Aug. 1890, 1, 12.

23. *Chicago Tribune*, 14 Aug. 1890, 8, 15 Aug. 1890, 7, 31 Oct. 1890, 1, 1 Nov. 1890, 4.

24. *Chicago Tribune*, 1 Nov. 1890, 4.

25. *Chicago Tribune*, 24 Jan. 1891, 6, 13 Feb. 1891, 7.

26. *Chicago Tribune*, 3 Apr. 1891, 1.

27. *Chicago Tribune*, 29 Apr. 1891, 1; *Spirit of the Times* 120 (16 May 1891): 743.

28. *Chicago Tribune*, 19 June 1891, 1; *Chicago Times*, 20 July 1891, 3, 23 July 1891, 6, 24 July 1891, 2, 26 July 1891, 4, 3 Aug. 1891, 2, 7 Aug. 1891, 8, 23 Aug. 1891, 1.

29. *Chicago Tribune*, 5 June 1891, 6, 27 June 1891, 8.

30. *Chicago Tribune*, 21 June 1891, 5, 17 June 1891, 3 (quotes); *Chicago Times*, 4 July 1891, 4, 8 July 1891, 9, 11 July 1891, 5.

31. *Chicago Times*, 20 July 1891, 3, 23 July 1891, 6, 24 July 1891, 2, 26 July 1891, 4, 3 Aug. 1891, 2, 7 Aug. 1891, 8, 23 Aug. 1891, 1; *Spirit of the Times* 121 (9 Sept. 1891): 330; 123 (2 July 1892): 995.

32. *Spirit of the Times* 121 (9 Sept. 1891): 329, 330 (quote).

33. Ibid., 330.

34. *New York Times*, 10 Dec. 1891, 5; *Spirit of the Times*, 121 (5 Dec. 1891): 717, (12 Dec. 1891): 787, (19 Dec. 1891): 818 (*Inter-Ocean* quote), (26 Dec. 1891): 857, (16 Jan 1892): 996. On street closing, see *Spirit of the Times* 121 (6 Feb. 1892): 86.

35. Kogan and Wendt, *Lords of the Levee*, 15, 21, 27–28, 50 (*Chicago Times* quote).

36. *Chicago Tribune*, 21 May 1892, 6, 22 May 1892, 6, 24 May 1892, 6, 31 May 1892, 6, 1 June 1892, 7, 12 Sept. 1892, 3, 27 Aug. 1903, 4.

37. Kogan and Wendt, *Lords of the Levee*, 15, 21, 27–33, 50 (quotes), 52. Coughlin's older brother had worked as a teenager at the tracks, where he was befriended by many touts and jockeys and had become a good handicapper. He was responsible for getting Bathhouse John interested in the turf.

38. Kogan and Wendt, *Lords of the Levee*, 50.

39. Kogan and Wendt, *Lords of the Levee*, 51; *Chicago Tribune*, 27 July 1892, 4, 30 July 1892, 8.

40. Kogan and Wendt, *Lords of the Levee*, 51–52; "Mayor's Veto of Ordinance Licensing the Tracks," July 28, 1892, filed September 12, 1892, #3901. Proceedings Files of the City Council of Chicago, Illinois Regional Archives Department, Northeastern Illinois University.

41. *Chicago Tribune*, 1 Aug. 1892, 7, 3 Aug. 1892, 7, 10 Aug. 1892, 6; *Clipper* (6 Aug. 1892): 349; (13 Aug. 1892): 365; *Spirit of the Times* 122 (3 Sept. 1892): 223.

42. *Chicago Tribune*, 3 Sept. 1892, 1, 9; Kogan and Wendt, *Lords of the Levee*, 54 (quote); *New York Times*, 7 Sept. 1892, 1.

43. *Chicago Tribune,* 4 Sept. 1892, 28–29; *New York Times,* 3 Sept. 1892, 3.

44. Kogan and Wendt, *Lords of the Levee,* 54.

45. *Chicago Tribune,* 6 Sept. 1892; *New York Times,* 6 Sept. 1892, 3.

46. Kogan and Wendt, *Lords of the Levee,* 55–56.

47. *New York Times,* 7 Sept. 1892, 1; Kogan and Wendt, *Lords of the Levee,* 56.

48. *Chicago Tribune,* 12 October 1892, 7.

49. *Chicago Tribune,* 1 Aug. 1892, 2, 7 Aug. 1892, 4 Aug., 22 Sept. 1892, 6; *Brooklyn Eagle,* 1 Aug. 1892, 2; *Spirit of the Times* 124 (12 Nov. 1892): 607.

50. *Chicago Daily News,* 17 Feb. 1893, 8; *Chicago Tribune,* 5 Apr. 1893, 1; Johnson, *Carter H. Harrison,* 188, 257–258.

51. *Spirit of the Times* 126 (29 July 1893): 36; *Chicago Daily News,* 26 June 1893, 1, 4, 27 June 1893, 1, 28 June 1893, 1, 6, 29 June 1893, 1, 30 June 1893, 1, 1 July 1893, 1, 6 July 1893, 3, 18 July 1893, 3.

52. *Chicago Daily News,* 30 Apr. 1894, 4.

53. *Chicago Daily News,* 8 May 1894, 1, 10 May 1894, 1.

54. *Chicago Tribune,* 24 June 1894, 28, 23 July 1894, 7; *Chicago Daily News,* 23 July 1894, 2; *Spirit of the Times* 128 (21 July 1894): 6.

55. William T. Stead, *If Christ Came to Chicago* (Chicago: Laird & Lee, 1894); Chicago Civic Federation, *First Annual Report* [1894] Chicago: Author, 1894), 86; *Spirit of the Times* 128 (29 Sept. 1894): 358;*Chicago Tribune,* 1 July 1894, 12.

56. *Chicago Tribune,* 23 Sept. 1894, 4, 24 Sept. 1894, 2, 29 Sept. 1894, 7; 14 Oct. 1894, 1; *Chicago Daily News,* 24 Sept. 1894, 2, 28 Sept. 1894, 1; *Spirit of the Times* 128 (29 Sept. 1894): 358; Chicago Civic Federation, *First Annual Report,* 85.

57. *Spirit of the Times* 128 (29 Sept. 1894): 358, 128 (20 Oct. 1894): 466, 480; *Chicago Daily News,* 2 Oct. 1894, 2, 15 Oct. 1894, 1, 2 Nov. 1894, 8; *Chicago Tribune,* 14 Oct. 1894, 14; *New York Tribune,* 15 Oct. 1894, 4; *New York Times,* 15 Oct. 1894, 1.

58. *Chicago Tribune,* 28 Aug., 1895, 7; 12 July 1897, 4; 14 Apr. 1898, 7; 15 Apr. 1898, 4.

59. *Spirit of the Times* 132 (19 Dec. 1896): 670.

60. Steven A. Riess, *City Games: The Evolution of American Urban Society and the Rise of Sports* (Urbana: University of Illinois Press, 1989), 185–87; Steven A. Riess, "Sports and Machine Politics in New York City, 1890–1920," in Raymond Mohl, ed., *The Making of Urban America* (Wilmington, Del.: Scholarly Resources, 1988), 105–10; Steven A. Riess, "The Turf in the Garden State: The Politics of New Jersey Horse Racing, 1870–1894." Southern Historical Association, Louisville, Ky., Nov. 12, 1994.

Bicycling was an enormously popular fad in the late nineteenth century. The first bicycles were difficult to ride and dangerous, starting with the "boneshaker" or velocipede in the mid-1860s, supplanted in the mid-1870s by the "ordinary," with its high (fifty-four-inch) front wheel and tiny rear wheel. But in the early 1890s, the English safety bicycle was mass-produced. It was lightweight and had equal-sized front and rear pneumatic tires and efficient coaster brakes. It was not cheap, costing around one hundred dollars, which would be equivalent to $2350 in 2008 dollars, but it became enormously popular. By 1896 there were four million cyclists in the United States. Chicago, home of one of the first bicycle clubs, became an important center for riders, races, and also bicycle manufacturers.

The bicycle became a symbol of progress that provided riders with an alternative mode of transportation that could enable them to escape the city. Cycling became very popular with middle-class women, who rode for exercise and independence. Conservatives saw the bicycle as a threat because women riders wore less-restrictive sports clothing (such as bloomers or pants), it made them too autonomous, it promoted coed socializing, and it was said to encourage housewives to shun domestic duties.

Bicycling also thrilled riders with speed. As the technological revolution transformed modern society, cycling offered one means to test human capabilities and overcome natural restrictions. Bicycle racers and recreational speedsters, known as "scorchers," challenged records and, in the latter case, pedestrians and horse riders in the parks. Chicago built a velodrome to accommodate racing in Humboldt Park on the West Side, and cyclists formed a national organization, the League of American Wheelmen, as early as 1880, which lobbied successfully for paved roads long before the advent of the automobile.

2 | When Chicago Was Wheel Crazy

GEORGE D. BUSHNELL

The fad of cycling began with only a few hardy males in the 1870s but, within twenty years, Chicagoans of all ages and both sexes were indulging in a heady love affair with the bicycle. By the 1890s, the "wheel" had become a means of both recreation and transportation for almost everyone with enough balance to stay on and enough strength to push the pedals. The entire city, it seemed, was caught up in the cycling craze.

In fact, for Chicago as well as the entire nation, the golden age of cycling had begun. In 1895, the normally reserved *New York Times* marked the discovery and development of the bicycle as "of more importance to mankind than all the victories and defeats of Napoleon." In April of that same year, a writer for *Harper's Weekly* estimated that four hundred thousand bicycles had been manufactured since the first of January and predicted that production would continue to soar in 1896.

The precarious high-wheeler, or "ordinary" of the 1870s, had a six-foot-high front wheel which inspired little confidence in the observer as it rolled along Chicago's streets or out into its countryside. The smallest stone or rut could pitch an unwary rider forward over the wheel to the ground in a nasty fall, steering was difficult, and a quick turn was almost impossible. The ordinary and the sport of cycling were the exclusive preserve of the adult male.

Developments in England were to change all this and make cycling a sport for everyone. In 1884, an inventor named John Kemp Starley designed the first "safety" bicycle, a machine with two much smaller wheels of equal size joined by a tubular frame. The rider sat on a saddle in the center of the frame and applied foot power to the pedals, which were connected to the rear wheel by a chain. A few years later, John B. Dunlop invented the pneumatic tire, which provided a far less bumpy, air-cushioned ride. American cycle makers also imported England's lighter hollow steel tubing and, in 1894, the invention of the coaster brake completed the evolution of a bicycle very similar to today's models.

Chicago in the Gay Nineties was an ideal climate for cycling. By 1893, there were a million and a half residents in the city proper, and two thousand miles of roads, many paved. Cyclists in or near industrial areas had additional incentives to mount their wheels. The air and the buildings of their neighborhoods were grimy from the ceaseless pall of smoke which hung like a low cloud, belched forth from factories, houses, and railroad yards, and from the stubby steam engines which ran the "Alley El" route from Congress Street to the Columbian Exposition's 63rd Street station. But escape was as close as Lake Front Park (now Grant Park), and to the north and west were tree-lined streets and an absence of industrial pollution, all easily reached by bicycle.

Best of all, the bicycle was relatively inexpensive. It cost far less than a horse, and it required little upkeep. In the Nineties, Chicago's cyclists could buy a Columbia made by the Pope Manuacturing Company or an A. G. Spalding bicycle for $100. An inseparable twosome could buy an American tandem, advertised at $150 in the *Chicago Inter-Ocean*, and bargain hunters could pick up a "good used" Monarch for $50 or a "shopworn" model for $35.

Many customers preferred to buy a Schwinn, a Chicago brand still familiar to cyclists. Arnold, Schwinn & Company was founded in 1895 by German immigrant Ignaz Schwinn and Chicago meat packer Adolf Arnold. At 29, five years earlier, young Schwinn had left a promising job at the Heinrich Kleyer cycle factory in Frankfort-on-the-Main to find opportunity in America. Attracted to Chicago by the city's promise as a major bicycle manufacturing center, Schwinn worked first for Hill & Moffat, maker of the Fowler cycle, and then began Arnold, Schwinn & Company's long career in rented space at the northwest corner of Lake and Peoria streets. The enterprise prospered, and the company bought the March-Davis Bicycle Company in 1899 at a receiver's sale, moving to its site on Chicago's western edge. In 1908, a new factory was built on adjacent land at 1718 North Kildare Avenue.

Accessories were more limited in the Nineties than now. The well-equipped cyclist bought a brass kerosene lamp for $2.25, a tire repair kit for a nickel, and a spare tire for $6.50. For 25¢, Rothchild & Company offered a doublestroke cycle bell. By 1895, nocturnal cyclists were buying the new carbide lamps fueled by acetylene gas to light the roads and ruts ahead. West Madison Street became Bicycle Row in the 1890s: there cyclists could buy a new or used wheel, have repairs made quickly, inflate tires, and perhaps even meet a young cyclist of the opposite sex.

The women really were there on Bicycle Row, because cycling helped them take a giant step towards emancipation. Chicago's women, ready to throw off the Victorian restraints of the era, quickly related to the fetching Gibson Girl, a beautiful, self-possessed young woman who could and did join her male friend for a spin. Modishly dressed in a fetching sailor hat, a shirtwaist with a mannish collar, leg-o'-mutton sleeves, and bloomers or divided skirts, the ladies enthusiastically took to the roads.

Judy O'Grady and the colonel's lady were equals on the bicycle, as *Wheel Talk* testified in 1895. Even Princess Maud of Wales, the magazine reported, "when she mounts a wheel, is no better off than other girls." In May 1897, the *Chicago Post* reported that young society women were indeed awheel: "The fashionable girl no longer lolls about in tea gowns and darkened rooms, but stands beside you in short skirts, sailor hat, low shoes and leggings, ready for a spin on the wheel."

Whether bloomers were proper garb, however, was a controversial matter, even among the women. By the late 1880s, the drop-frame cycle model was available to them, and the modified design did solve the problem of an entangled skirt, even though a typically brisk Chicago wind might suddenly blow a skirt back to outline the female cyclist's limbs. Two lady cyclists, who prudently used only their initials, debated the bloomers issue in the Lake View Cycle Club's monthly magazine *The Cherry and Black* for April 1896. Said the pro-bloomers writer, apparently something of a prophet, "We girls are not always going to stick around the home like they did in olden times."

Outing summed up the bicycle's role in female emancipation in verse:

> The maiden with her wheel of old
> Sat by the first to spin
> While lightly through her careful hand
> The flax slid out and in.
> Today her distaff, rock and reel
> Far out of sight are hurled
> And now the maiden with her wheel
> Goes spinning round the world.

But the old guard died slowly. In June 1895, Gyda Stephenson, a teacher at Humboldt School, put on knickers, cycled, and then wore the same garb into her classroom. In the ensuing skirmish with the school board, Stephenson made it clear that what she chose to wear while cycling or teaching was entirely her affair. Surprised by her resolute stand, the board dropped the matter.

Bloomers were a boon to the homely girl according to a poet writing on the subject for the *Sunday Inter-Ocean*. He averred that although her face stopped not only clocks but streetcars as well, she found a solution:

> And so she got some bloomers
> And now with eager zest
> She rides a cycle daily
> And looks like all the rest

Not only the apparel manufacturers benefitted from the craze. Cosmetic manufacturers were also quick to seize an opportunity. To sell a variety of beauty aids—creams, pomades, and soaps—the merchants advertised their concoctions about the effect of wind and weather on delicate skin. One unguent, not content to advertise that it was "a sure and pleasant protection against the flying particles of sand, cinders, grit and other abrasives," also informed readers that it was an effective shield against the "destructive rays of the sun."

The male cyclist had a simpler time dressing than his opposite number. The proper male attire for a spin consisted of knickers, a sack coat or sweater, a shirt and tie, high-top shoes, and a cap with visor. As spring approached, the city's newspapers advertised sales of cycling garments, among them Frederick M. Atwood, the proprietor of a clothing store at Clark and Madison streets who featured "extra strong knee pants with reinforced seats."

Touring to new places became popular by the mid-1890s, and a timely article by James B. Townsend in *Harper's Weekly* in 1896 listed the materials needed by a cyclist making an excursion. Considered essential was a copy of the road book published by the League of American Wheelmen, because of "the absence of sign posts and the impossibility of depending, as a rule, upon information as to the condition of roads, distances, etc. from the average person one meets . . ."

In addition, the author suggested that the touring cyclist should take a waterproof coat, a change of underwear, and toilet articles. And to be fully equipped, he should pack court plaster, needles, thread, safety pins, a bottle of Pond's Extract (the Universal Pain Extractor), and salve. Last, but certainly not least, he should carry a small flask of whiskey or a bottle of Jamaica ginger, to be added to water from roadside wells or pumps. The whiskey was to be used sparingly: Townsend admonished the touring cyclist never to indulge in liquor "except perhaps at the end of the day at dinner." Champagne, apparently even more dangerous, was to be "shunned as poison."

The cyclist out for a shorter spin could simply wheel to the Saddle and Cycle Club, Fisher's Beer Garden on the north end of Lincoln Park, or to the Auditorium Hotel for dinner. And whatever the mileage, cycling received the physician's stamp of approval. As one doctor wrote, although "the bicycle has come among us with such volcanic suddenness as a new social force . . . it is inducing millions of people to take regular exercise who could never be induced to take it by any means hitherto devised."

After buying a wheel, most Chicago cyclists joined one of the city's cycle clubs. By 1895, there were five hundred clubs of varying size, each with its own colors and a distinctive uniform for endurance rides and competitive events. Club members could enjoy reading rooms, group outings, and a variety of social events from conventions and banquets to dances.

The Chicago Cycling Club, founded in 1879, was the nation's largest and oldest organization. At first, the club shared the quarters of the Racquet Club at 185 Michigan Avenue, but in 1888 it moved to a three-story flat at 57th Street facing Jackson Park, "convenient to both steam and cable cars." The club's 1895 prospectus lured prospective members with the statement that "Our runs are on the beautiful boulevards and avenues of the South Park System."

Other Chicago clubs active in the decade were the Aeolus, at 174 Evergreen Avenue; the Columbia Wheelmen, at 311 West Division Street; the Lake Park Cycling Club, which met at the Post Office; and the Atlas Cycling Club, at 244 Lincoln Avenue. North Side cyclists joined the Lincoln Cycling Club and West Siders belonged to the Illinois Cycling Club.

Typical of Chicago's large cycling organizations was the Hermes Club, which charged a $5 initiation fee and monthly dues of 50¢. The club's colors were blue and silver gray; its uniforms consisted of a light brown corduroy coat buttoned to the neck, breeches of the same material, a white flannel shirt with blue lacing, dark blue stockings and belt, low blue shoes with yellow leather trim, and a dark blue hat with a visor and two ornamental bands around the crown. The club's badge depicted Hermes, the winged messenger of the gods, engraved on a gold disc the size of a quarter.

Although the clubs were primarily dedicated to cycling and social activities, at least one proposed to use its political influence in the cause. The Viking Cycling Club's prospectus announced tersely that "This club and its associates control 1,800 political votes and will support those candidates favorable to wheelmen and wheeling."

A variety of publications served the city's cyclists. In 1896, a nickel bought a copy of the small but jam-packed *Chicago Cycler's Guide,* which listed fifty of the principal clubs, their addresses and colors, and the names and addresses of repair shops throughout Chicago and in such popular suburbs as Evanston, Joliet, and Geneva. The *Guide*'s list of low-priced hotels included Miller's Hotel in Downers Grove, which charged 25¢ for a meal and $1 for lodging. The remarkable little book also included mileage from the city courthouse to forty cities and suburbs, named the best routes to take and the streets to avoid, and reminded its readers of the two most important rules of the road for cyclists—riding single file and not exceeding eight miles an hour. Several pages covered first-aid procedures for sprains, fainting, shock, and broken legs and arms.

Wheel Talk, another publication, included articles and diagrams showing the do-it-yourself cyclist how to repair bent handle bars. And it paid $10 to readers who sent in helpful articles, a generous sum for those days. The Lake View Cycling Club's handsome monthly *The Cherry and Black* was filled with cycle-shop advertisements and included letters, news of coming road races, brief reports of cycle shows, paragraphs about members' accomplishments, minutes of club meetings, and profiles of its officers. A yearly subscription cost only 50¢.

Chicago's cycling boom also created a new kind of riding academy. Beginners signed up for a series of seven lessons. They began on a cycle with training wheels, progressed to a "duplex"—two cycles joined side by side—with a front steering wheel and, finally, rode a safety. A half-hour lesson cost 50¢, but the academies charged a lower rate for the full series.

Bicycle racing attracted huge audiences. In Chicago, the principal event was the Pullman Road Race, held on Memorial Day from the Leland Hotel at Michigan Avenue and Van Buren Street to the Pullman community on the South Side. From two to three hundred racers, mostly members of clubs, took part.

Racing produced its own athletic heroes, as well known then as any modern-day football or baseball star. A leading Chicago racer was Joseph F. Gunter of the Lincoln Cycling Club, who won 95 gold bars and secured for his club the 1,000–mile record. At first, the Chicago cycle racers were amateurs, sparked only by the thrill of competition and the glory of winning for self and cycling club. By the late 1890s, however, the top-ranking racers were full-fledged professionals, subsidized by bicycle manufacturers. Among the best were Arthur A. Zimmerman, Harry C. Tyler, and Willie Windle, who ranked with the fastest riders in the world.

The races were so popular that in 1893, during the Columbian Exposition, a track was built at South Side Ball Park, 35th Street and Wentworth

Avenue, for a week of cycle competition. By the spring of 1897, the *Inter-Ocean* included a regular cycling section in its sports pages, and other Chicago newspapers were giving the sport regular and full coverage. Nor did the immense popularity of racing escape aspiring politicians. In 1897, a young candidate named Carter H. Harrison II, making his first try for mayor of Chicago, launched his campaign by riding his "century"—one hundred miles—from his West Side home to Waukegan, Wheeling, and Libertyville, and back—in just nine and one half hours.

Chicago maintained a squad of cycle police, ostensibly to protect cyclists from heedless carriage and wagon drivers but more probably to catch fast cyclers, or "scorchers," in the act. Offenses brought prompt penalties. In May 1897, for example, E. W. Ballard of the Chicago Cycling Club was arrested and whisked away in a police wagon to the closest station house. Ballard, who protested that he was only riding at a rate of two miles in eighteen minutes, was released after an hour, but the knowledgeable *Inter-Ocean*, which had predicted that the city's special patrol would "soon be a feature of every police system in the country," observed that Ballard's claim of so modest a speed "raised a laugh among his brother wheelmen." In January 1896, a hundred thousand Chicago cycle buffs flocked to the city's third annual cycle show, an event which testified to the profitable aspects of the wheel. Potential customers inspected the products of the show's 225 exhibitors and collected brochures, catalogs, and souvenirs, including pins, buttons, spoons, watch chains, and tiny knives. Show visitors marveled at a bicycle built for an American millionaire, complete with a name plate set in diamonds, lugs covered with gold inlay and precious stones, a frame decorated with boat racing, horse racing, and hunting scenes, and encrusted with rubies, diamonds, and pearls.

There were even bloomer girls, employed by the Fowler Bicycle Company to tout its cycles and accessories. On the final night, January 11, the city's cycle clubs turned out en masse, with the skirl of bagpipes, the blare of trombones, and enthusiastic club yells.

Chicago cyclists had at least one clash with the power structure of the time. In 1897, the traction moguls wanted a city franchise to lay streetcar tracks down the center of Jackson Street. The cyclists hurriedly organized against the proposal, which had already been introduced by two aldermen, urging instead that Jackson Street become a boulevard, that streetcars, wagons, and trucks be banned, and that traffic be restricted to cycles and pleasure vehicles. They flooded the city with yellow ribbons, inscribed "Jackson Street Must Be Boulevarded," and the city fathers bowed, adopting what was called the "Yellow Ribbon Ordinance" and, at least temporarily, making Jackson Street into a boulevard for cyclists.

Chicago's cyclists had a powerful ally in the League of American Wheelmen. Founded in 1880, at Newport, Rhode Island, the League had fifteen thousand members and chapters in every principal city in the nation by 1890. Besides fostering the sport of bicycling, the League was an effective crusader for better roads, respect for the cyclist, and special hotel rates for touring riders. Early in the 1890s, the League's Chicago and Illinois chapters helped shelve an Illinois bill which would have compelled cyclists to dismount when they came within a hundred yards of a horse—and, adding insult to injury, to stand off the road until the horse had passed. The League also fought back when, in 1897, the Lincoln Park commissioners declared that the bicycle had become a threat "to the peace of mind and safety of body necessary to the pursuit of happiness."

Even as the cycling craze reached its peak, experiments with the gasoline-powered horseless carriage were foreshadowing the era of the automobile. By the first decade of the twentieth century, the automobile had displaced the bicycle as the citizen's means of transportation. The newfangled vehicle, however, freely acknowledged its debt to the wheel, which had pioneered not only the pneumatic tire, differential gear, and chain drive, but had fought for better roads and created new vistas for the home-bound citizen.

This article, George D. Bushnell, "When Chicago Was Wheel Crazy," appeared in the fall 1975 issue of *Chicago History* magazine.

In 1891 J. Frank (1870–1967) and Charles (1861–1938) Duryea began tinkering with gasoline-powered cars, and two years later Frank made the first outdoor test run in Chicopee, Massachusetts. In 1895 Charles established the Duryea Motor Wagon Company, the first American manufacturer of gasoline automobiles. He built thirteen a year later, one of which was bought by New Yorker Henry Wells, who in May 1896 collided with a bicyclist and was arrested. This was the first reported traffic accident in American history.

The first formal car race, in 1895, ran from Paris to Rouen, and the first in the United States took place on November 28, 1895, a 53–mile round trip from Chicago to Evanston, won by Frank Duryea in 10 hours and 23 minutes. On the same date the Studebaker Company held an auto show displaying twelve motor vehicles at its wagon and buggy showroom on South Wabash Avenue. Horseless carriages had first been displayed in Chicago at the 1893 World's Fair, a Morrison electric car and a German gasoline-powered car. In the next few years, Chicago became an early site for car manufacturing, with twelve companies in production by 1900. Automobiles then were toys for the rich, cost several thousand dollars, and were not very reliable. In 1901 the city hosted the first Chicago Automobile Show, which evolved into the largest and most frequently held car show in North America.

3 | The Car Race of the Century

CORD SCOTT

The twenty-eighth of November 1895 was the worst possible day for an automobile race. On this Thanksgiving Day the city of Chicago had been hit with an early season blizzard and the roads were covered in snow and slush, and the "motocycle" (as the automobile was popularly called at the time) was considered by the city's newspapers to be nothing more than an aberration. It was predicted to be a passing fad, unlike the other new form of transportation, the bicycle. However, the automobile race that was to take place that day would cause residents to change their attitudes. The race would establish the automobile as the transportation technology of the future, and Chicago's connections to the automobile. In addition, this "Race of the Century" and the drivers who participated in it would help to establish the ties between the car and masculinity, social class, and the city. The race and, in a larger sense, the automobile, would fundamentally change life in Chicago.[1]

One might first ask why Chicago was chosen for the Race of the Century rather than the larger cities of New York, Philadelphia, or San Francisco. There were many logical reasons for choosing Chicago. First and foremost, throughout its history, Chicago had served as a hub for transportation. Since 1849 Chicago had been a central crossover point for the rail and river shipping lines throughout the country.[2] This gave the drivers in the 1895 race the opportunity to ship their cars to Chicago via rail or ship, assemble and test them, and then officially enter the car into the race without much fuss or extra bother. Furthermore, Chicago's ample and well-kept city street network allowed the racing cars to be run on relatively smooth cobblestones.[3] This would allow drivers (in theory) to race at higher speeds with minimal risk of damage to the suspension system of the cars, or to the wheels, which were made of solid rubber in most cases. Some of the drivers, however, used pneumatic tires, which later proved to be of substantial advantage on the day of the race.[4]

The second reason for Chicago being chosen for the Race of the Century was its ties to the World's Columbian Exposition of 1893. The Colombian Exposition highlighted several new forms of transportation that would gradually eliminate the horse as the chief form of propulsion in America and around the world. The idea of eliminating the horse was an active one to most residents since every horse deposited about thirty pounds of manure each day on the city's streets. In addition to the waste issue, the city faced another problem when the animals died. The horses used to pull heavy wagons for the disposal of garbage and to deliver supplies and were used to haul buggies for private use. It was not uncommon for overworked horses to drop dead in the streets. The carcasses then had to be hauled off by other horses before they caused hygiene and odor problems. Housing the animals also created a problem. The presence of tens of thousands of horses in 1890s Chicago posed a logistical nightmare in a city that was already facing a housing shortage for its burgeoning human populations.[5]

New forms of transportation . . . included cable cars, the "El" (elevated trains), and electric trolleys. All of these public transportation systems would help the city as a whole and their promises brought people to the Exposition, especially to the Transportation Hall at Jackson Park. Inside the building (and its annexes) the exhibits were divided into railroads, marine transportation, and vehicles for work and pleasure. It was in this last division that people took notice of the "horseless carriage." But what really drew people to the hall were the displays of the bicycle, the transportation craze of the 1880s.[6] Many people at the fair saw the bicycle as the personal transportation vehicle of the future. It did not pollute as the horse did, it allowed for exercise and personal fitness, which was important during a time when personal hygiene and strength were obsessing many in the nation and, most important, it caused enthusiasts to pressure legislators to support the construction of paved roads. Bicyclists claimed that most city streets were in terrible condition, especially those roads made of dirt, which would turn into mud whenever it rained. They argued that the roads needed to be paved to allow for smoother, better transportation. This in turn would benefit the whole economy.[7] The bicycle was a featured system of transportation in the exhibits at the Columbian Exposition, and the police in both New York and Chicago discussed it as a possible vehicle for use by law enforcement.[8]

The third reason for Chicago hosting the Race of the Century regards the sponsorship of the event. The race was the brainchild of H. A. Kohlstaat, a Chicago booster who had made his fortune in the restaurant industry during the 1870s. He eventually made enough money to buy a controlling interest in the *Chicago Times-Herald*. In 1893 he was responsible for drumming up support for the transportation exhibits at the Columbian Exposition when they were initially not well attended. He learned that, in 1894, Count LaBose and several French newspapers (such as *Le Petit Journal*) had sponsored an automobile race of from Paris to Rouen. Kohlstaat seized upon this idea and announced in July 1895 that the *Times-Herald* would sponsor a race that would allow horseless carriage drivers to race from Chicago to Milwaukee. The race would be held on 2 November 1895 and prize money totaling five thousand dollars would be offered.[9] It was Kohlstaat's vision and enthusiasm that brought the race to the citizens of Chicago and the Midwest.

The fourth reason for choosing Chicago for the Race of the Century was the promise that large crowds would witness the race and, most important to Kohlstaat, buy the *Times-Herald* to read about the exploits of the jaunty men and their machines. Close to one hundred teams expressed interest in the 2 November race; however, when the deadline for entries approached, many did not register. In fact, the original date of the race had to be pushed back three weeks, to 28 November, because of the lack of drivers.[10] Many of those who originally expressed an interest in participating were not able to meet the deadline because their newly-designed cars had to be handmade and were not ready to race by early November. The entrant cars also had to pass a preliminary test of road-worthiness inside a building owned by Kohlstaat. Those cars that did not pass the inspection were not allowed to run.[11] This further cut down the number of cars actually running in the race. On 2 November only two cars were fully ready to race. The *Times-Herald* noted, on that day, organizers ran a "special exhibition race," but pushed the larger one to 28 November. The city's other newspapers, such as the *Chicago Tribune*, made a mockery of the 2 November "race" and Kohlstaat's attempt to cover his unmet promises. The *Tribune* stated that, "only five hundred spectators turned out at Jackson Park to witness the beginning of the race." The reporter derisively noted that Kohlstaat was 499,500 *shy* of the 500,000 spectators predicted by the *Times-Herald*. And most of the "spectators were actually commuters on their way to work, who soon disappeared."[12] The paper then went on to describe how the vehicles of the future could not make it up a small incline, which allowed the course to cross over the Chicago, Burlington, and Quincy Railroad tracks. The autos had to be pushed over the hump by several people. It was further commented that, as the reporters followed the cars on a tandem bicycle, they had to apply their brakes so as not to overtake the cars, which averaged just six miles per hour.[13] In the end, the Gottlieb Benz-built car driven by Oscar Mueller of Decatur, Illinois, won the exhibition race on 2 November. The other contestant in the first race, J. Frank Duryea, did not finish, because his car developed a steering problem.[14] While the two drivers were given accolades by the *Times-Herald* and were derided by the *Tribune* and the *Chicago Inter-Ocean*,[15] no one could dispute the fact that they represented a certain entrepreneurial spirit that permeated the late nineteenth century. The drivers and their designers and judges all came from decidedly specialized backgrounds and could certainly be called "artisans." Their specialization of workmanship and the fact that they necessarily needed money to purchase such playthings as racing autos would lead one to assume that the early racing car drivers would have come from the ranks of the wealthy.

In fact, the vast majority of people in the United States and in Europe saw the first automobiles as little more than interesting toys for the rich. The automobile needed all sorts of extra items that the other forms of transportation of the day did not.[16] In contrast to the horse and the automobile, the bicycle had become a new economical form of transportation for "the masses." The bicycle did not need to be fed or stabled or watered like a horse. It just needed lubrication for the chain, repairs if the balloon-style tires developed leaks, and a flat surface on which to run. The bicycle was also a convenient way to get around the streets of a city and provided an acceptable form of socialization for both men and women during the otherwise restrictive Victorian era. The bicycle also had its own form of socializing and sports. By 1895, bicycling clubs throughout the United States were sponsoring races, as well as dances, football leagues, and other events.[17] The automobile, on the other hand, required rubber tires, gasoline, water (for the cooling system), and most importantly, the knowledge of what to do to keep the car operational. In addition, an automobile cost a good deal more than a bicycle: nearly five hundred dollars in 1895 as opposed to just one hundred dollars.[18] The actual cost of the automobile was probably higher, as very few cars actually existed, and available parts were either hand crafted or small in quantity. By the time the production of automobiles came about, only the rich could afford one. The prohibitive expense of the early automobiles was due to the hand-assembled, craftsman-like production. It is interesting to note, therefore, that the participants in Chicago's 1895 Race of the Century had working-class backgrounds. The race actually allowed the designers and drivers to cross social classes.

The driver who won the exhibition race of 2 November, Oscar Mueller, was a prime example of a hybrid man who worked with his hands, yet had enough money to invest in a car. He drove a Benz-built car that had been made in, and imported from, Germany. However, Mueller had made such extensive modifications to the car that he considered it his own design. The judges for the race noted this, and the car was listed as a Mueller-Benz on the official race entry.[19] Mueller had to have been mechanically inclined. The other drivers showed similar social patterns.

J. Frank Duryea, along with his brother Charles, developed racing automobiles and had a similar background to Mueller. Both brothers started off in a coach and sedan business in the late 1880s and eventually went into the development and construction of working automobiles. By the early 1890s, the brothers took divergent paths, however. Charles settled in Peoria, Illinois, while Frank started on his construction of an engine, clutch, and gears assembly that found their way into the car that he would eventually race in Chicago. When Frank arrived in Chicago for the race he began testing the car; he eventually altered the engine from a two-stroke to a four-stroke engine. This allowed the car to produce more speed, as well as run much more smoothly.[20] During both races, the Duryea car experienced part failures. This meant that, because the automobile had been hand-made, new parts had to be fabricated during the race. These repairs to the car would hinder Duryea during the 2 November race; he hit a horse team, damaged the steering, and was forced out of the race, making Mueller the sole contestant and winner of the exhibition.[21]

Duryea's repair of a broken steering arm while crossing the Rush Street Bridge during the official race on 28 November was an example of how adaptable and mechanically-minded these racers had to be. He stopped, ran to a blacksmith shop, reformed and repaired the arm, and reassembled the car in order to continue the race. He also had to forge a new igniter for the car. Toward the last quarter of the race, the igniter on the engine started to fail, causing the car to lose power. Duryea drove at slow speed until he found a tinsmith's shop, where he stopped. The smith was not in the shop, so Duryea drove to the smith's house, roused him, took him back to the tinsmith's shop, forged a new igniter, and was back on the course in fifty-five minutes.[22] While this variation from the course should have technically disqualified Duryea, it definitely showed his determination and ability to adapt.

Another man who was directly involved with the race and who showed an entrepreneurial spirit was Charles King. King served as a judge aboard the Mueller car during the 28 November race.[23] He was originally a pneumatic toolmaker and had received a medal for his exhibition at the Columbian Exposition in 1893. He was also involved in designing and building engines for boats as well as for cars. King initially planned to enter a car in the Race of the Century, but his design was not ready in time. He was later responsible for developing several different items for automobiles, including improved engines. He was eventually able to complete the construction of his own racing car and was driving it in Detroit the next year.[24] King was recognized as an influential figure in the field of automobile construction and was asked to be an umpire for the 28 November race aboard the Mueller-Benz car. Following a rather bizarre incident, in which Mueller passed out while driving, King pushed Mueller aside, and proceeded to pilot the car, and finished the race.[25] King also had a background as an artisan; he helped Henry Ford with engine designs before forming the King Motorcar Corporation. As with the other designers/drivers/engineers, King's vehicles featured marked improvements over previous designs, and included left hand steering, center control gearshifts, and improved lamps for driving at night. All of these inventions added to the function of the car, but also required that the inventor get his hands dirty.

Several of the cars, while not finishing the race, were design innovations. Many of the cars built for the race utilized propulsion systems that have become desirable in the early twenty-first century because of their positive environmental qualities. One of the cars was steam powered, and was built by A. C. Ames of Chicago's south side. The car used two bicycle frames and a sleigh body for its chassis, with the engine toward the rear of the car. It was an interesting design and was technically an entrant in the race. However, it was really only displayed because its steam engine limited its travel to a few hundred feet.[26] Two of the cars used an electric power plant. One was the Sturges Electric Car, built and driven by Harold Sturges on Thanksgiving Day. The power from the batteries was sufficient to propel the car at low speeds, but, because of the heavy snow and ill-plowed streets, the car only ran from Jackson Park to Lincoln Park, where the batteries finally failed.[27] Henry Morris and Pedro Salom built the other electrically powered car. The Electrobat, as it was called, was built in Philadelphia. It also had propulsion problems because of the weather conditions. It finally ran out of power near the Rush Street Bridge. The car made an impression on the judges of the race, however, and was awarded the *Times-Herald* Gold Medal Award for general efficiency. This angered several other racers, as the Electrobat neither finished the race, nor went as far as the Sturges.[28] The umpire aboard the Electrobat was Hiram Maxim. Maxim was the creator of the Maxim gun, one of the first functional machine guns of the nineteenth century.[29] Another judge for the race was Henry Timkin, who later went on to great fame in the field of transportation for his invention of enclosed ball bearings.

In the gasoline-powered division, many of the builder/drivers had Chicago connections, and utilized the Chicago bicycle designs to help increase the performance of their cars. The automobile driven by Max

Hertel, which had the smallest displacement engine of all the cars, did not perform well enough to even start the race on 28 November. E. J. Pennington's car was, much like many of the others in the race, based on two bicycle frames welded together, but his auto was most important for its innovative tires, which were of the balloon type. This was in stark contrast to the solid rubber tires used by most of the contestants. In fact, several of the racers, King included, noted that Pennington's balloon tires gave both a smoother ride and a better handling performance in the snow.[30]

G. W. Lewis, an inventor from Chicago, had a car that featured a front deflector/dash board, which prevented some street debris from hitting the driver. It was unfortunate that his car was unable to compete on race day because of mechanical difficulties. The last notable designer/driver was Elwood Haynes of the Haynes-Appleton Car Company. Haynes started the Thanksgiving Day race driving a car of his own design. However, it was damaged and he had to withdraw before the finish. Before the race, Haynes's car had been pulled over by a Chicago policeman who chased him down on a bicycle. The incident occurred before the 28 November race and was most likely a publicity stunt. Haynes later became a prominent member of the Chicago Automobile Association.[31]

Some of the drivers in the race, of course, were not the designers or the builders of their automobiles but were wealthy sportsmen who purchased their cars for the fun and leisure associated with the racing. However, even they had to have some mechanical abilities because, when their cars broke down, they would often have to make on-the-spot repairs. Like the bicycle before it, the automobile became associated with a sporting and leisure culture. But, also like the bicycle, the automobile's reputation suffered from a rough beginning. The original bicycles were unwieldy because of their huge front tires. With the invention of the British safety bike (which had the same size tire front and back, as well as a chain propulsion system) in the 1880s, the bicycling craze exploded. Bicycling soon grew into an acceptable social pursuit for both men and women. For some men, however, the overall appeal of the bicycle was in its potential for racing. In Chicago, some five hundred bicycle clubs had formed by the mid 1890s, with primary race days on Sunday. Racing bicycles became a status symbol for the middle and upper classes.[32] It was a logical transition for bicycle enthusiasts to transfer their interests to automobiles.

Bicycle and automobile racing also gave some men the thrill of being pitted in a battle against the forces of nature and against other men. Early racing cars were entirely open to the elements. The drivers, therefore, had to take special precautions (such as wearing specialized clothing). Surviving such hardships allowed drivers to show the world that nothing could get in their way of finishing the race and reaching their goals. Each of the drivers in the Thanksgiving Day race, even those who did not finish (and only two actually did so), had proved themselves by taking on the elements for at least eight hours with little food, no rest, no heat, and in cold snowy, blustery winds. It was probably a good thing that the course had been shortened from the originally proposed Chicago–Milwaukee run; the 28 November race course only went from Chicago to Evanston and back to Chicago (a total of fifty-three miles). The *Times-Herald*, as well as many of the drivers, noted that even "King Winter" could not stop them on that day.[33] This battle against the elements also worked against the racers, however. Only about sixty spectators showed up in Jackson Park for the start of the race. The *Times-Herald* was no doubt disappointed at the turnout. The poor turnout was due not only to the adverse weather conditions; many who might have enjoyed the race were in Lincoln Park partaking in another spectator sport and passion of the day: football. The University of Michigan and the University of Chicago were in a heated rivalry at the time, and their game drew approximately ten thousand spectators, who eventually rioted when the University of Michigan won over the hometown team.[34]

Many of the race's few spectators were probably attracted by the prospect of danger or even death. Most of the cars in the race did not have brakes. This was not a concern for most, however, since the cars were traveling at such low speeds (the average speed was around six miles per hour; most people can walk at a speed of four miles per hour). But it was still difficult for the cars to stop on slippery surfaces when something unexpected occurred. A large number of cars that were disabled both before and during the race had to withdraw. Duryea, for example, certainly had his share of broken parts. But the driver who should be singled out for having the most inopportune luck during the race was Jerry O'Connor; he was driving a Benz car, sponsored by Macy's Department Store of New York. O'Connor had a total of three accidents on the day of the race. The first involved a collision with a horse-drawn streetcar near the Art Institute; the second accident involved a horse-drawn cutter, which was carrying Frederick Hass, a driver of one of the withdrawn cars, and A. E. Richter, a reporter for the *Times-Herald*. The third collision involved a hack (a horse-drawn taxi) near Douglas Park. The damage to O'Connor's car in the third collision (four bent wheel spokes, damage to the wheels themselves, and damage to the steering gear) caused O'Connor to finally abandon his quest.[35]

In addition to the dangers posed by the weather and by other vehicles on the roads, the drivers also had to deal with trouble-making spectators. A couple of mischievous boys threw snowballs at the drivers, particularly at Mueller. Mueller's story during the race, it turns out, is probably the most dramatic. After spending several hours in the driver's seat, Mueller became despondent when one of his passenger/umpires, Charles Reid, was transferred to a relief wagon after he fell unconscious because of the cold weather. Soon afterward, Mueller himself passed out while driving! King, in an attempt to keep the car from becoming disqualified, squirmed into the driver's position by sliding Mueller over, and held on to Mueller with his right arm while he steered the car with his left arm. King finished the race for Mueller, but Mueller remained in the car, still exposed to the elements. The rules of the race stipulated that the car must finish with its driver still in the car.[36]

The Race of the Century certainly posed problems for drivers that twenty-first century racers do not have to face. Today's drivers have crews that handle the mechanical requirements of the car while, back in the early days, drivers did much of the mechanical work themselves. Another difference between the early races and modern ones is that, in the early days, entrants started at staggered times in order to prevent accidents. A race was not necessarily meant to be an all-out event, but an endurance run. Still, the thrill of the race was definitely a "rush" for those involved. Had the weather conditions been different for the Thanksgiving Day race, the events probably would have transpired much differently. Mueller, for instance, had installed a "high speed clutch" that, at one point, caused his car to careen down the Chicago streets at an unprecedented speed of sixteen miles an hour; more favorable conditions might have allowed even more speed.[37] By today's standards those speeds seem insignificant, but in an age of solid rubber tires, leaf springs, and cobblestone streets, the constant bumps and strains would have tested the abilities of any driver, then or now.

Following the race, the drivers, builders, umpires, and other participants met and founded the American Motor League, which was the world's first automobile association. The league was established to develop new ideas for travel on streets and highways, share ideas and designs for automobiles, give legal protection to drivers, and promote safe roadways. This organization, in turn, prompted the organization of similar clubs in Paris and London.[38] It was apparent to the drivers and builders in the Race of the Century that it had been a successful endeavor for horseless carriages. But other people, particularly the Chicago papers and transportation officials, did not agree. Most of the newspapers did not carry any news of the Thanksgiving Day race. Of those that did, the reports varied from those that were impressed by the prowess of the drivers ("driving through the mud and slush for a feat horses would not have been able to match in endurance"), to scathing criticism.[39] The

Chicago Tribune was the most vicious, opining that the race itself was an abomination. The staff writer took particular note of the fact that five of the cars were lost during the race, "wandering aimlessly about the streets . . . or lying wrecked in some gutter along the way." He also noted that the spectators at the end of the race consisted of two reporters.[40] The *Times-Herald* reported that, while the crowds were thin ("not fifty people"), they were enthusiastic, and that more and better races would soon emerge.[41] The race even contained the elements of a spy novel; the *Times-Herald* noted that builders feared "invention pirates" who would steal their designs before they could perfect and patent them. As the American Motor League noted, many of the designers eventually did share their ideas. For example, King discussed his engine innovations with Henry Ford, who had wished to enter the race but could not convince anyone to loan him the money to ship his car to Chicago.[42] While Ford, Duryea, and King became names associated with the early automobile industry in the United States, only a few of the carmakers from the race are remembered. However, those who raced that day were pioneers of automobile racing and of American culture.

The race had wide-ranging effects for auto racing, both in the United States and in Europe. Following the Chicago Race of the Century and the French contests of the previous year, automobile racing became much more common and more popular. By 1896, Frank Duryea entered and won the London-to-Brighton, England, race, as well as the Cosmopolitan race held in the United States.[43] The number of United States car races continually expanded and, in 1902, a Championship Auto Racing Team (CART) series of races was instituted at various locations. The establishment of CART coincided with the Vanderbilt Races, which were held at various locations around the United States (including Crown Point, Indiana) and further brought cars, and car races, to the Chicago area. The legitimacy of auto racing in the United States was firmly established in Indianapolis in 1911 when the Indianapolis 500 race was held for the first time in its current format.[44]

The Race of the Century also brought another mainstay to the Chicago calendar, the Chicago Auto Show. The first organized show was held in 1901, with Samuel Miles as its manager.[45] The show was associated with *Motor Age,* a new magazine dedicated to the car and its benefits. People such as Charles Duryea, who by the early 1900s had become enmeshed with the Duryea-Stevens Auto Company, continued to laud the benefits of auto ownership. Doctors, priests, and even housewives, he argued, could all benefit from the new auto.[46] As with the bicycle, young people of both sexes soon saw the car as a place where they could liberate themselves from the watchful eyes of parental control. Despite the predictions by the newspapers, the Race of the Century in Chicago turned out to be important, not only to Chicago, but to the nation as a whole. It is impossible to imagine the development of the United States without the automobile. And Chicago became the place, not only where the race was held, but the place where part of the American Dream had its start.

Notes

"The Race of the Century-1895 Chicago" by Cord Scott in *Journal of the Illinois State Historical Society* 2003 96(1): 37–48. © 2003. Illinois State Historical Society. Reprinted with permission.

1. "The Recent Storm," *Chicago Tribune*, 1 November 1895, 1.

2. Don Miller, *City of the Century: The Epic of Chicago and the Making of America* (Chicago: Touchstone Books, 1986), 180.

3. John Alford, *A Report to the Street Paving Committee of the Commercial Club on the Street Paving Problem of Chicago* (Chicago: R.R. Donnelly, 1904), 6.

4. Charles King, *Personal Sidelights of America's First Automobile Race* (New York: Super-Power Printing, 1945), 20.

5. City Clerk of Chicago, *Report on Horses in the City* (Chicago: City of Chicago Press, 1909), 3.

6. Department of Publicity and Promotions, ed., *World's Columbian Exposition Catalogue*, Vol. 7, part 7 (Chicago: W. B. Conkey, 1893), 791.

7. Stephen Goddard, *Getting There: The Epic Struggle between Road and Rail in the American Century* (Chicago: University of Chicago Press, 1994), 48.

8. "Put Police on Bicycles," *Chicago Tribune*, 30 November 1895, 10.

9. "Race to Be Held," *Chicago Times-Herald*, 12 July 1895, 2; George May, "The Thanksgiving Day Race of 1895," *Chicago History* (October/November 1982), 177.

10. "Run Is Postponed," *Chicago Times-Herald*, 2 November 1895, 1.

11. "Proves Its Worth," *Chicago Times-Herald*, 3 November 1895, 1–2.

12. " Race Is a Bust," *Chicago Tribune*, 3 November 1895, 3.

13. May, "Thanksgiving Day Race of 1895," 178.

14. Frank Duryea, *Data Relative to the Development of America's Gasoline Automobile* (Springfield, Mass., 1941), 20.

15. The *Chicago Inter-Ocean* did not directly report on the race, but did publish a cartoon ridiculing the car, comparing it to antiquated political practices. Cartoon, *Chicago Inter-Ocean*, 3 November 1895, 1.

16. Donald B. Meyer, *Sex and Power: The Rise of Women in America, Russia, and Sweden* (Middleton, Conn.: Wesleyan University Press, 1987), 280–81.

17. Various ads and columns in *Chicago Tribune* and *New York Times*, November 1895.

18. Ad for Cleveland Bicycle, *New York Times*, 17 November 1895, 15. The car price was quoted for a sedan car, minus the engine, in 1896. Ad in *Columbian Exposition Catalogue*, 791–820.

19. May, "Thanksgiving Day Race of 1895," 177.

20. Duryea, *America's Gasoline Automobile*, iii, 18.

21. "Race Is a Bust," *Chicago Tribune*, 3 November 1895, 7; "Proves Its Worth; *Chicago Times-Herald*, 3 November 1895, 3.

22. Duryea, *America's Gasoline Automobile*, 22.

23. King, *Personal Sidelights*, 20. King took over when Mueller passed out during the race, and was the driver of the Mueller-Benz when it crossed the finish line.

24. *Detroit Free Press*, 1896, as cited in King, *Personal Sidelights*, 46.

25. King, *Personal Sidelights*, 20.

26. Ibid., 22.

27. "Duryea Is First," *Chicago Times-Herald*, 29 November 1895, 3; King, *Personal Sidelights*, 23, 34.

28. "Making Final Tests," *Chicago Times-Herald*, 30 November 1895, 1; King, *Personal Sidelights*, 32.

29. King, *Personal Sidelights*, 32.

30. Ibid., 20.

31. Ibid., 40.

32. Miller, *City of the Century*, 297.

33. "Duryea Is First," *Chicago Times-Herald*, 29 November 1895, 1.

34. "Chicago-Michigan Game a Battle," *Chicago Tribune*, 29 November 1895, 1–3.

35. King, *Personal Sidelights*, 30.

36. "Duryea is First," *Chicago Times-Herald*, 29 November, 1895, 5.

37. May, "Thanksgiving Day Race of 1895," 179.

38. King, *Personal Sidelights*, as quoted from *the Charter of the AML*, p. 41.

39. "A Motocycle Triumph," *Chicago Press Journal*, 29 November 1895, 4.

40. "Duryea Wins the Race," *Chicago Tribune*, 29 November 1895, 8.

41. "Duryea Is First," *Chicago Times-Herald*, 29 November 1895, 1.

42. May, "Thanksgiving Day Race of 1895," 179.

43. Duryea, *America's Gasoline Automobile*, 43–44.

44. Giuseppe Guzzardi and Enzi Rizzo, *Century of Automobile Racing* (New York: Barnes and Noble, 1999), 22, 236.

45. "Testimonials," *Leslie's Weekly*, 11 February 1909, 126.

46. Duryea published a book of testimonials for the automobile in general, and the Duryea in particular. Charles Duryea, *The Real Pioneer* (New York: Simon and Schuster, 1945), 6–13.

Amos Alonzo Stagg was an All-American football player at Yale, where he studied religion with the intent of becoming a clergyman. He was uncomfortable as a public speaker, however, and instead found his mission as a coach who would build muscular Christians. He was hired in 1892 to coach the University of Chicago football, baseball, and track programs (and later added the new game of basketball) at a salary that exceeded what nearly everyone on the faculty was making. Such an appointment rationalized the inclusion of coaches as faculty members, allowing administrators to assume greater control over the previously student-run athletic teams. He was also the first coach ever granted tenure. Such developments created the modern framework for athletic coaches in American institutions of higher education.

Stagg coached at the University of Chicago until he was required to retire because he reached the age of seventy in 1932. His 1905 team was considered the national champion and his teams won seven Big Ten titles. He went on to coach the College of the Pacific through 1946 and assisted his son at Susquehanna for six more years after that. He assisted at Stockton Junior College until the age of 98. He is credited with 314 victories and many important tactical innovations, including the man in motion and the lateral pass. Stagg was elected to the College Football Hall of Fame as a player and coach in its first class in 1951. In this chapter from his outstanding book, **Stagg's University,** *Robin Lester, former headmaster at such noted independent high schools as Trinity (of New York) and the Latin School of Chicago, examines how Stagg recruited his players, kept them eligible, and promoted football as a popular spectator sport in late nineteenth and early twentieth century Chicago.*

4 The Rise of the Spectator, the Coach, and the Player, 1895–1905

ROBIN DALE LESTER

Rockefeller gifts were celebrated like football victories, and football victories like the Second Coming.
—*Milton Mayer*

Our profession is one of the noblest and perhaps the most far reaching in building up the manhood of our country.
—*Amos Alonzo Stagg*

I have no more fun in practice games. It isn't amusement or recreation any more. It is nothing less than hard work.
—*Chicago player, 1897*

Harper's university fostered the growth of football so successfully at the turn of the century that Chicago gained the leadership of western intercollegiate football and won the national championship in 1905. Maroon football had two extraordinary assets. First, located in the largest city of the Midwest (and by 1900 the nation's second most populous), the university could count on many players and spectators. . . . those spectators ensured the end of the players' innocence, the cessation of play as an end in itself, and the beginning of play as an instrument of larger economic and cultural values. Second, Amos Alonzo Stagg was the perfect athletic entrepreneur to complement William Rainey Harper's academic entrepreneurial movements.[1]

The Rise of the Spectator

The most significant development during the period was the rise of the spectator—the widespread acceptance and use of the Chicago football enterprise by the students, faculty, and alumni of the university community and by the larger civic community. The use and enjoyment of football by American "witnesses," not participants, for whatever civic, social, economic, or vicarious cultural reasons were barely remarked upon, even though they constituted an enormous change from the British educational model. After all, Chicago did not invent these practices, rather it had eagerly transferred eastern collegiate forms and folkways to the Midway in as intact a fashion as possible. In the event, the university became very successful in selling its athletic product and even at applying monopolistic principles as a kind of "athletic Darwinism." Although some academics grew chary of the strong community interest and nascent control by 1900, most judged that the activity was useful to the university's larger mission.[2]

Certainly President Harper was keenly aware of the relationship between philanthropy and football victory. He dramatically appeared in the Maroons' dressing room at halftime of the 1895 Wisconsin game, with his players down 0 to 12. He challenged the players: "Boys, Mr. Rockefeller has just announced a gift of $3 million to the University. . . . He believes the University is to be great. The way you played in the first half leads me to wonder whether we really have the spirit of greatness and ambition. I wish you would make up your minds to win this Game and show that we do have it." Chicago won 22–12.[3]

The period is replete with a kind of yellow sports journalism. Frank Luther Mott notes that "emphasis on sports was characteristic of the yellow press," and that editors "developed for that department a slangy and facetious style." William Randolph Hearst developed sports journalism when he challenged Joseph Pulitzer for New York circulation leadership in 1895. American intercollegiate sports coverage evolved into a permanent feature on the "sporting page" after the turn of the century, displacing the earlier method of including collegiate activity within the social elite's leisure news. The "windy city" newspapers maintained their civic booster reputation with unsupportable claims for Stagg's teams. The journalists themselves were a prime market for the game, even as they became the chief salesmen; they soon believed and printed virtually everything that Stagg told them.[4]

Boosterism came full circle in 1902 when the first "Gridiron Fest" was sponsored by the Chicago Press Club. Coaches, athletic managers, football officials, and players joined the propagandists in the formal unification of the press and the new intercollegiate football industry. The banquet was termed "an entire success" from the "social point of view" by the *Chicago Daily News*, which interpreted the event as changing the "atmosphere entirely between the men actively engaged in football, the greatest of all college sports, and those who have this same game to report for the mass of enthusiasts."[5]

The university's strategy in taking the game to the Chicago civic community was divulged by Horace Butterworth, manager of Maroon athletics, when he discussed schedule-making and the market. He reasoned that early season victories promoted attendance and enthusiasm for the later contests, an approach that accounts for the scheduling from 1896 to 1905 of teams that managed only twenty-seven points in thirty-six early season games while Chicago scored 1,116 points. Butterworth described the Chicago marketplace as possessing two elements—the "society element" and the public. Athletic Director Stagg added a third constituency, "the college people" (he estimated fifty thousand), by which he meant citizens who had attended other institutions and whose loyalty might be partially transferred to the Chicago Maroons. All of these groups, including the press and the noncollege "subway alumni," were addressed carefully as markets.[6]

The city of Chicago was a limited football marketplace in the early 1890s because few Chicagoans knew the game either as players or spectators. Public interest in football picked up when the sport was introduced into the secondary schools during the 1890s, but the greatest single influence on public perception was the football enterprise that Harper and Stagg marketed. Between 1896 and 1905 almost 90 percent of all Chicago games were played at home, and persistent publicity argued that the honor of the collegiate and civic community was at stake on the Maroon gridiron.

Chicago students readily accepted the idea that the team was "theirs" and that the games provided valid institutional comparisons. The autumn placement of the sport was especially advantageous. Games became a weekly meeting place for the new and old members of the university and promoted a community reconfiguration each autumn. The campus suffered and rejoiced communally over the team's performances: "Rockefeller gifts were celebrated like football victories, and football victories like the Second Coming."[7]

Student support for the Maroons was formally expressed by carefully composed and rehearsed songs and cheers. The prime example, a song entitled "John D. Rockefeller" (sung to "Daisy"), was both audacious and defensive regarding Rockefeller's relationship with the university. The first stanza is brassy.

> There Is a Varsity out in the West Chicago, Chicago
> Founded by capital, backed by the best
> Go it Chica-a-go.
> Headed by wisdom that knows no bounds
> She's making a wonderful show
> And others are longing to share the lot
> Of Chica-go, Chi-ca-go-go.

The second verse is defensive regarding the school's origins.

> They say that he made it by forming a trust
> Chica-go, Chica-go,
> That may be true but its use is most just
> Of this man we are all proud
> Be it high or low
> For to him we owe our all
> At Chica-go, Chica-go-go.

The panegyrical chorus sublimates any unease that might remain.

> John D. Rockefeller
> A wonderful man is he,
> Gives all his spare change
> To the U. of C.
> He keeps the ball a-rolling
> In our great varsity
> He pays Dr. Harper
> To help us grow sharper
> To the glory of U. of C.

An additional stanza was added within a short time and reiterated the chauvinism of the first.

> We advise you, kind friends, keep an eye on this place,
> It has entered the race and it will set the pace,
> Go it, Chicago!
> The recourse is long, the world it includes,
> And all who would start at the blow,
> Must train here with us for many a year,
> At Chicago! Chicago-go![8]

These positive and defensive words were no doubt prompted by the widespread image of the new institution as flying the "Standard Oil Colors" and of the team termed the "Rockefellerites."[9]

Rockefeller was also honored with a short yell used during the 1890s:

> Who's the feller
> Who's the feller
> Zip-boom-bah
> Rock-e-feller
> He's the feller
> Rah! Rah! Rah![10]

John J. MacAloon has used the modern Olympic Games to discuss Émile Durkheim's proposition that modern secular societies require secular rituals that provide them meaning and solidarity. The football festival of

the campus weekend developed by college communities, with its atten-
dant rituals and abnormal behavior, also meets Durkheim's prescription.
Certainly the outlines of Chicago student behavior toward the team were
clear and fixed by 1905. Pregame rallies, school songs, football banquets
and receptions, celebratory bonfires and parades—all the spectatorial ac-
coutrements to the Chicago football industry—were begun, developed,
and refined during the period to such a degree that they changed little
over the next decades.

Careful rituals were developed for pregame mass meetings by 1903.
The meeting for that year's Michigan game became the prototype; it was
planned by six committees, held in Mandel Hall, led by a prototypical
cheermaster, Arthur E. Bestor (later to become one of America's leading
cultural historians and critics), and followed a special four page program
of the nineteen separate steps of the evening's observance. The meeting began with step one, "The Procession," of fifteen campus organizations whose three hundred members all sat on the stage and concluded
with "a series of fights between the freshmen and sophomores," which
would have been the twentieth step had it been placed in the program.
The alumni met earlier in the evening at a nostalgic dinner that was to
become a staple for returning team members and their supporters. The
mass meeting was described as the "biggest and most enthusiastic in the
history of the University of Chicago," a claim that would be repeated
with uniform monotony in future football seasons.[11]

The women of the university took the lead in producing cheers. Dean
Marion Talbot, "in behalf of the girls," announced a prize contest for the
"best gridiron lyric." As "chairman of the committee on musical cheer,"
Talbot expected that the assembled students would practice new compo-
sitions weekly to improve team support on Saturdays. The committee
was none too sure of the quality of the entries. A scale of prizes was set
up for the "best composition": $10 if the composition was "satisfactory"
and only $5 if "it is satisfactory or not." The women were working out
their peculiar role as major athletic advocates on the American campus.
Only two years before, the psychologist G. Stanley Hall had dared provide
the pioneer analysis of football and female supporters: "Glory, which is
the reward of victory and makes the brave deserve the fair, is . . . never
so great as when it is the result of conflict; and while the human female
does not as in the case of any animal species look on complacently and
reward the victor with her favor, military prowess has a strange fascination for the weaker sex, perhaps ultimately and biologically because it
demonstrates the power to protect and defend. Power . . . has played a
great role in sexual attraction."[12]

Women were shut out of what was becoming one of the surest means
to social acceptance on the American campus—intercollegiate athletic

participation. The role of women in intercollegiate football and the larger society was graphically evident in 1902 as female students helped lead a rally for the beaten Chicago team in 1902 after the second consecutive loss to Fielding Yost's dominant Michigan squad. The university community met "to show their appreciation for the great fight put up." Over the caption "Coed Rouses Spirit of Defeated Maroons" the *Tribune* ran a photo of Agnes Wayman encircled with posies. Many students and faculty spoke of the discouraged team's courage and pluck, but it remained for Agnes Wayman to strike the right note of comfort and encouragement. She said, "The harder the defeat, the more tender ought to be the treatment the team received at the hands of the university students." She retailed the "faith the coeds had in the team" and concluded with the prediction of great success and joy for the Maroons. Then the *Chicago Chronicle* expressed surprise that "even the coeds had something to say."[13]

The football team's relations with the faculty and alumni also became more regular and formalized during the period. Faculty leaders made frequent appearances at football mass meetings, and some could be counted upon for stirring rhetoric. The 1902 meeting after the Michigan defeat was also noteworthy for faculty response: "Almost every department furnished a representative" to aid the team in assuaging their despair, and none was more convincing than the sociologist Albion Small. The professor mused that everybody connected with the team's valiant effort should be praised, "from substitute to Captain Sheldon and from highest soprano to cheer leader. Rubber, scrubber and cook deserve it, too." Small concluded that "football has got to be played with a combination of brain and muscle" and left no doubt with his audience in which element he felt Chicago superior to her opponents. Law Dean Joseph H. Beale, recently arrived from Harvard, offered "a stirring speech" at the same meeting, and Philip S. Allen, the initiator and managing editor of *Modern Philology*, neatly encapsulated the university's twofold purpose to the delight of his listeners. The two purposes, according to the former Maroon star, were "to spread the light of knowledge over the western world and to 'lick' Michigan."[14]

University Registrar and Secretary of the Board of Trustees Thomas Goodspeed, called "Chicago's oldest rooter," keynoted the largest mass meeting of the 1903 season with rampant enthusiasm and analogy. Michigan could be beaten, he insisted, if Chicago would fight with "the same spirit that animated the old Norse sea kings." Dean George E. Vincent addressed the same audience alliteratively as "heroes, heroines, and heelers."[15]

Both President Harper and Dean Vincent hosted celebratory dinners and receptions. For some years Harper held a postseason dinner for the football team at which the captain for the next season was elected; in

1903 he added a midseason "Victory dinner" at Hutchinson Commons and five hundred male students attended. That same year Vincent's annual Thanksgiving Eve reception for the team members had evolved into a rather formal event by invitation only. The invitations, sent sparingly to the university community and "friends," allowed the recipient "to meet the University of Chicago football team" from 7 to 10 on the eve of the battle. The occasion had the unmistakable air of using the team as a corporate asset.[16]

Professors who showed anything less than wide-eyed, uncritical enthusiasm for the Maroons courted swift unpopularity. The day after an 1896 victory over Michigan, a crowd of two hundred students roamed the halls, cheering and interrupting lectures. Only once did they meet a professorial check, and that by geologist Rollin D. Salisbury, who "shoved the offenders out the door." The students chanted derisively in response, "What's the matter with Salisbury? He's all-right! Nit!" President Harper emerged from his office and ended the confrontation by enthusiastically contributing $10 to start a fireworks fund for the evening rally.[17]

A more serious campus upheaval resulted from a Thanksgiving victory over Brown University in 1899. A number of the faculty, including the political economist J. Laurence Laughlin, required their classes to meet the next day, despite the custom of granting the students a holiday after a Thanksgiving win. Several hundred students spilled into Cobb Hall, where most of the classes were meeting, and shouted for the offending lecturers to dismiss their students. The reserved, anti-imperialist Laughlin's classroom became the focus of this demand, and the man described by a colleague as "the essence and flower of good form" came to the classroom door. "'Mr. Laughlin, give us a speech. Expansion. Expansion.' chorused the students." A shoving match resulted, followed by the use of the professor's fists and a chair he lifted to defend his classroom. These methods having failed, Laughlin demanded the names of the offenders, who boldly handed over their identity cards and continued chanting. President Harper arrived at a poky run, spoke persuasively to the leaders, and the crowd began to drift from the building, accompanied by Laughlin's mutterings of "rowdyism" and "ungentlemanly exhibitions." Most of the campus appeared willing to accept Secretary Goodspeed's judgment that the episode was "simply an outbreak of natural boyish enthusiasm."[18]

The development of consistent support by alumni occurred later than the development of student and faculty support and was contemporaneous with the support of the larger civic community. Chicago was in a unique position during the 1890s; although it opened and functioned as a fully staffed university with a comparatively large student body, it took about a decade of graduations to produce a sufficiently large and interested group of supportive alumni. By the 1902 season 1,866 degrees (70 percent of which were undergraduate) had been awarded. There was also a sizable number of students who had attended the institution during the first decade without taking a degree. The Chicago alumni were joined around 1900 by other universities' alumni to provide enthusiastic backing for Stagg's teams and a collateral desire to demand victory regardless of means.[19]

During the first decade, alumni interest in the athletic fortunes of university teams was informal, and little organization beyond the seating of alumni in the Chicago section of the stands was accomplished. The local alumni club, the largest and most active chapter, planned a dinner in honor of the football team as early as 1899. Soon after, a more formal dinner before the Thanksgiving game became a regular feature. The first successful concerted effort by the alumni to influence athletic policy occurred at that annual dinner in 1902, where some critical remarks were directed to Stagg's alleged ineptitude at recruiting top high school athletes. This alumni influence, combined with the increasing sense of team ownership felt by the civic and journalistic communities, was so strong that Stagg and his staff were stirred to more active recruiting and periodic reports to the alumni. In return, the alumni-civic coalition provided long-running protection for his winning program and rendered Coach Stagg a campus untouchable. Harper and Stagg were more than willing to go along with the demands for victory, even when the result was the bending and warping of the original stated values of their intercollegiate athletic program.[20]

The selling of the Maroon football team went well at Harper's university. The rise of the spectator on the Midway and in the city was so marked that the Maroons did not leave Chicago once for their twelve matches in 1902. They began with two games in September, wedged six contests into October, and finished with four in November. From 1903 through 1905 Stagg scheduled twenty-eight games in Chicago, five away. Football revenue had so outgrown football expenses that the surplus was devoted to maintaining the other activities in the Department of Physical Culture and Athletics. Increasingly, the dependence on football was becoming a major argument for maintaining the large commercial football enterprise at Chicago and elsewhere.[21]

The Rise of the Coach

Amos Alonzo Stagg rose to a position of considerable power in Harper's university. The growing influence of a coach at such a university is perhaps initially difficult to fathom, considering that in 1892 Stagg was an untried administrator and shaky academic surrounded by eminent administrators and scholars. Stagg's rise was due to his special relationship to Harper, his dominant personality, the precedentless department that he headed, the innovative "profession" of coaching of which he was a pioneer, and the enlargement of his national reputation based upon his unparalleled entrepreneurial and football genius.

President Harper and Coach Stagg grew increasingly close and mutually dependent. It was a good marriage because they knew what to expect from each other, and both endeavored not to let the other down. Harper was constantly vigilant about the best way to present the Maroon football show to the paying customers. In 1897, he suggested to Stagg the addition of "a bulletin board" (scoreboard) on the field so that "all can see and understand" the progress of the game and then wondered, "Should there not be a band at the Michigan game Thanksgiving day?" The next day he wrote to Stagg again, this time to ask, "If you could get the team together at any time secretly, without its being public, I should like to make a little talk to them. . . . It must of course be absolutely quiet." He also requested Stagg's presence at the morning Thanksgiving service—"and have all the boys with you." Stagg almost always carried out his president's requests promptly and diligently.[22]

The relationship also had its trials. Harper showed unhappiness over his coach's management in 1895 when a university summer baseball team (one of Stagg's delights was to play in these more informal games), comprised partially of nonuniversity students, played teams the president deemed inappropriate: "We have had a series of games with negroes etc. which has brought disgrace upon us." Stagg seems to have sorted out the baseball issue by the summer of 1896, although many questions are left unanswered. Few African Americans played for him, but few were enrolled at Chicago. Perhaps the most celebrated was Henry Dismond, one of Stagg's sprinters who held a world record.[23]

The Harper-Stagg colleagueship was severely strained at times because the coach was frequently at the heart of a campus imbroglio and often the focus of antagonism. People sometimes viewed his insistence upon what he considered points of "principle" as overly forceful or even tactless behavior. Stagg was a man of imperious character, and he saw issues more simply than his faculty colleagues; he committed himself completely to a position, sometimes squelching those who were less committed or sure of a solution. His sense of personal and departmental prerogative grew with his enhanced reputation, and he became more bold when he dealt with his superiors and increasingly sensitive to what he considered any infringement of his preserve. A number of times his resistance to any interference with the affairs of the athletic department came to the fore, and on occasion his letters reveal a regrettable brashness. For example, Stagg wrote an assertive letter to President Harper in 1896 regarding what he considered the impertinence of University Comptroller Henry Rust in requesting justification for some of Stagg's expenditures. "I understand that I am not to be hampered in any way in my work through this arrangement of finances; that Major Rust is not to request *reasons why* this or that expenditure; that I am not compelled to *explain* to him for what ever purpose certain money is to be used. . . . and am not to be called to account by *him* for the same."[24] Harper backed Stagg, and it was not until many years later when the University Council and board of trustees investigated Stagg's special autonomy that his department was brought into line with others.

Another episode occurred when the university's extension department sought the use of the gymnasium bleachers for an outdoor event. Stagg's chief assistant had granted the request, and plans went forward for the occasion; Stagg then denounced the agreement and stipulated a rental fee for the stands. Harper gingerly wrote to his coach that perhaps Stagg was "a little rigid with the University in this matter," confessed that he did "not see why one department should rent timber from the other," and suggested they discuss the issue "as a matter of principle." Stagg's reply was a marvel of technicality, obfuscation, and patent self-denial. He found an analogy in the nonlending of "house furniture" of the university he admitted "to a degree" the worth of the promise made to the other department but did not feel "absolutely committed"; and he pictured the extension department as disingenuously attempting to "get around" the issue of damage by paying the rental fee he demanded.[25]

Stagg's relationship to the governing Board of Physical Culture and Athletics evolved during the period. Early on, the coach took care and time to establish his dominance. For example, during Stagg's 1895 summer vacation his assistant Horace Butterworth kept him informed of the board's doings. He reported a good deal of dissatisfaction over Stagg's management among such prominent members as Assyriologist Robert Harper (President Harper's brother) and divinity professor Shailer Mathews. Butterworth described them as "men anxious to make a display of authority," noted that an important meeting of the board was imminent, and predicted that they would "try to take management of affairs out of your hands" and then "crow over it." Butterworth's report stirred Stagg, who began a heated, handwritten letter to President Harper with "I hope that you will see to it that the Board does not act upon important matters of policy in my absence." He continued "Frankly, I do not consider some members of the Board capable of wise action, and I don't care to have the work of the Physical Culture Dept. made more burdensome." Stagg finished his argument by referring to the control of policy as "my particular charge . . . for which I have thought and labored and prayed a great deal." Harper acquiesced, and Stagg acquired a virtually impregnable position as a result of this and other test cases.[26]

Stagg's impatience with those who might challenge his point of view was not confined to his relations with university officials. His dealings with the representatives of other universities led to complaints that he had behaved imperiously toward them. The Intercollegiate Conference of Faculty Representatives, the Midwest's pioneer athletic governance organization, had been formed in 1895–1896 and provided the context for such protests. President C. K. Adams of the University of Wisconsin leveled extensive charges against Stagg in 1898 to the effect that Stagg's duplicity had ruined athletic relations between Wisconsin and Chicago. A year later Adams wrote a longhand "Personal and Private" plea to President Harper regarding the "assumption of superiority" he felt Stagg had demonstrated toward him, University of Illinois President Andrew S. Draper, and Michigan Professor Albert H. Pattengill at a conference meeting. That Chicago alone was represented by an instructor in athletics rather than Harper or one of the traditional academics at Chicago was an issue that would receive airing and resolution within a decade.[27]

Coach Stagg's successful athletic career and his early physical education training at Springfield had prepared him to serve as the pioneer of a new profession, the college coach. In this development, he was in advance of the gentlemen-scholars who became the businessmen-superintendents of America's public schools in their new profession. The same societal forces behind the "cult of efficiency" that was to convert the schoolmasters into superintendents was a part of the culture that produced the nation's football coaches. Their vulnerability to "the great strength of the business community and the business philosophy in an age of efficiency" was considerable, and these influences molded their work. Few were allowed to remain simply as coach-educators. The professionalization of the college coach is illustrated by Stagg's career. He moved from the player-coach of the first generation of coaches (from around the 1880s through 1900) into the "scientific" coach-manager (from around 1900 through 1920) and the celebrity-entrepreneur-coach (the 1920s) stages of successive generations. Many other coaches followed his model at each generation. Football coaches, for example, assumed control over all other intercollegiate activities as "athletic directors" because of football's dominant economic position on campuses about twenty to thirty years after Stagg had assumed the title. Stagg even led the chosen few toward the final coaching stage—the celebrity-entrepreneurs of twentieth-century

American universities. These powerful coaches often occupied a cultural and financial niche well above their college president or state governor and at this stage of development Knute Rockne took the leadership from the aging Stagg. Stagg and his fellow first- and second-generation coaches, especially in the old, elite Anglophile eastern universities, would seem tailor-made to fit T. J. Jackson Lear's description of antimodernism. The coaches were antimodernist, and they claimed to capture "real life" for sixty minutes on the gridiron much as Lears's "pre-modern craftsman, soldier" and "saint" did in their endeavors.[28]

By 1905, Athletic Director Stagg was the best known figure in intercollegiate athletics west of the Appalachians, and Walter Camp had already named him the "dean" of western football. The fame he had gained as a Yale undergraduate was not of a transient nature because he made new conquests of the popular fancy throughout his career as coach and athletic director.[29]

Stagg was lauded by a leading Chicago newspaper, the *Chronicle*, in 1902 as "better known than anyone connected with the University of Chicago, Dr. W. R. Harper and John D. Rockefeller alone excepted." The panegyric continued, "Stagg is hardly ever out of the public eye" and concluded that he was "the genius of the university advertising department." The public enjoyed reading about the spartan Maroon coach. In one earlier case, a journalist described how Stagg coached from the sidelines while holding plump Alonzo Junior in his arms. When needed, he hastily handed the baby to his all-American Clarence Herschberger and "plunged into the lineup." The enthusiastic observer concluded that the "grave coach, carrying the youngster in his arms and initiating the green ones into the mysteries of football is a sight not soon to be forgotten." A mystique surrounded his activities on the gridiron and extended well beyond its perimeter, where Stagg's abstemious behavior was appreciated. It is probable that he personified, for many Americans, a purer, less materialistic, Christian America that had been lost.[30]

Stagg's preeminence lay in the acquaintances and contacts he maintained in the East, as well in his position as a leading coach and athletic director. His coauthorship of the first avowedly "scientific" football book, *A Scientific and Practical Treatise on American Football for Schools and Colleges*, in 1893 had also brought him considerable attention. He knew most of the eastern athletic authorities, and the East continued its hegemony of the West in athletics during the early years of the century. In 1904, Stagg became the first noneastern representative on the Football Rules Committee, which legislated the rules of the sport for the entire nation. The Intercollegiate Conference had elected Stagg as representative in the hope that his prestige and friendship with the six-member Rules Committee might induce his inclusion. Walter Camp soon wrote the Rules Committee's acceptance of the familiar Stagg.[31]

University of Chicago football teams became nationally known because of their precedent-setting inter-regional trips and games. Stagg's 1894 West Coast marathon was followed four years later by a significant eastern foray. The 1898 game with Pennsylvania at Philadelphia's venerable Franklin Field was not only an important Chicago institutional milestone, but also the match "that put western football on the map." Penn was considered the best team in the country that year based on a twenty-four-game winning streak and the presence of three all-Americans. Chicago, featuring the play of back Clarence Herschberger, led at the half and surprised Penn with a new style of play that featured deception and quickness (despite Penn's victory). Walter Camp wrote, "Stagg brought out of the West a decidedly advanced style of play," and the veteran observer Caspar Whitney ranked Chicago equal to the best of the East that year. At the end of the season, Herschberger became the first noneastern player (i.e., the first not educated at Harvard, Yale, Princeton, Pennsylvania, or Cornell) selected by Walter Camp for his all-American team. Chicago football teams met eastern opponents seven times in the four seasons from 1898 to 1901 and served as the first western host of an eastern team. Local journalists expected only path-breaking material from Stagg: In 1904 the Maroons' match with the University of Texas was hailed incorrectly as the first football game between teams of the Southwest and the North.[32]

Perhaps an instinct for profits as well as desire for renown accounted for the fact that Stagg's football teams consistently played more difficult schedules than those of their opponents. Well-known, successful opponents ensured greater revenues, and Chicago regularly played two or three times the number of major opponents as the other conference members. For example, Chicago's 1904 schedule included seven major university teams out of eleven opponents; Michigan played two major opponents in nine games, Wisconsin two of seven, Illinois four of ten, and Minnesota two of ten.[33]

The fact that Stagg's demands were granted regularly despite his occasional rudeness to superiors and peers indicates the esteem in which he was held. The 1903 construction of state-of-the-art Bartlett Gymnasium, with its medieval lines and stained glass, was due to the coach's dogged insistence on the best from Harper. When a well-known sports authority accused Stagg in 1903 of using players who were not amateurs, the charge brought a swift defense from one of the university's most renowned professors. Albion Small angrily termed Stagg's detractor "a cad sport lacking in manhood" in a speech before five hundred at President Harper's 1903 football dinner. As Small warmed to his subject, he stated, "I want to tell you that in this cad sport's whole body there is not as much of the making of a man as Stagg leaves on his shaving paper each morning." Small's remarks demonstrate the depth of Stagg's support among Harper's administrators and some faculty. Stagg took deep pride in his position as football coach: "Our profession is one of the noblest and perhaps the most far reaching in building up the manhood of our country."[34]

The Rise of the Player

The most concise statement of the change in the place of football in the lives of players at Harper's university came from a Maroon veteran in 1897: "I have no more fun in practice games. It isn't amusement or recreation any more. It is nothing less than hard work." This development no doubt relieved many American minds; set against their distrust of organized sport, any physical training that could be seen as work (or later, as war) was welcome. Hence, the status of players changed, as well as those of spectators and coaches, and the period from 1895 to 1905 saw student-players become player-students. By 1905 football was viewed as the most jealous mistress of college sports; a *Harper's Weekly* commentator compared football with the older sports baseball and rowing and then concluded, "In those sports high excellence is not incompatible with a residue of strength applicable to other pursuits. Current first-class football seems to take, while it lasts, everything a lad has in him. The game is his work. His recreation he finds in the hospital."[35]

The role of the football player was becoming an identifiable one; it can be described as the twofold development of the player as a "campus commodity" and as a "campus physical elite." The attitude of the young student-player who complained of the businesslike manner with which he was expected to approach the sport of football in 1897 became an anachronism by 1905, for by then players were required to continue football training year-round.[36]

The basis for Stagg's new cult of player efficiency can be seen in his explanation of the award of the coveted C monograms to Chicago athletes—the Order of the C was "the first athletic-letter club ever formed," he wrote. Stagg controlled the awards, which were based upon "merit, amount of work done, and usefulness to the team and the university." The form letter of notification of membership in the Order of the C was built upon the concept of "athletic service to the university." Hence, "usefulness" and "athletic service" spelled out the rationale for the rise of the player as a campus commodity.[37]

Just as the city of Chicago afforded the university the preeminent football marketplace of the West from 1895 to 1905, an excellent supply of college-level players was also available locally. Chicago was in the median enrollment position among Intercollegiate Conference schools, and after 1902 Stagg had excellent players for years. For example, the Maroons of 1896 averaged 173 pounds; those of the 1905 aggregation, 186 pounds; and the size and quality of the players increased almost yearly. The player commodities were supplied by the high schools and by the Chicago Football League, which sponsored a "prairie" (sandlot) game for youths. Both of these agencies, especially the former, grew rapidly from 1895 to 1905 and were similar to the sources the eastern colleges used.[38]

The Recruitment of the Campus Commodities

Stagg and Harper developed a number of recruiting methods that enabled them to improve the quality of Chicago's football teams markedly. Shortly after the turn of the century they sought to create a special relationship with interscholastic players and officials. Harper himself presented an ingenious plan (no doubt produced by Stagg) to the Board of Physical Culture and Athletics addressed to the "reorganization of the Physical Culture work." The seven resolutions were passed in May 1902 in a form both dignified and vague enough to pass faculty review; their effect was the widespread recruitment of schoolboy athletes. Six of the seven resolutions served as Stagg's manifesto to recruit in a more open manner, and they formed an outline of his future recruitment activities.[39]

Harper proposed using the nine previously "affiliated" university prep schools in Illinois and Indiana as places of future employment for Maroon athletes and as athletic "feeder" schools. Another recommendation cleared the way for using the public schools in much the same way. Recommendation number five was the most cryptic and significant of the seven: "That a system be devised for obtaining information in regard to athletics in secondary schools." The text would appear to provide for a kind of data-gathering regarding secondary school athletic programs. In truth, this recommendation led to a comprehensive card file on high school athletes to whom recruitment letters were sent and followed up. Dr. Joseph Raycroft, a member of the board, provided the rationale for the resolution: "The university, to protect itself, must engage actively in a canvass for new students. Others did it, and we must do it, too."[40]

Finally, the sixth recommendation passed in May 1902 legitimated an event that Stagg had already planned and scheduled. The vague proposal was "that interscholastic meets be held of the Academies and high schools in relationship to the University." Within eight days the "First Annual Interscholastic Track Meet" was history, and about two hundred athletes from forty schools—youngsters who had won state meets in Illinois, Michigan, Wisconsin, and Iowa—competed at Marshall Field. Stagg's varsity track team was put on display for the school as the Maroons engaged the University of California on the same field. The visiting "young prospectives" were housed in university fraternity houses and entertained in "great style" by the athletic management and by enthusiastic student groups.[41]

The coaching staff's decision to engage in a recruitment drive and capture beefy, speedy campus commodities constituted a change from their public position on the matter. Stagg had often railed against "scouting by other universities and their alumni; in 1900 he argued that recruiting was contrary to the "spirit of amateurism." Two unsuccessful football campaigns later, Stagg and the board "discovered that something had to be done if Chicago expected to compete with other western universities." He and Raycroft admitted that their "conversion" came chiefly in the hands of Chicago graduates, who challenged them publicly at the 1901 alumni football dinner to initiate thorough recruiting. An older Stagg was to assert that the alumni of the American universities were "the most active agents in developing athletic immorality," even though he had assiduously courted just such a development.[42]

The Chicago coaches, the football captain, and interested faculty members met periodically to assess their recruitment progress. They reviewed past communication with the prospects, charted new letter-contacts, and prepared for the fall season. The prospects for the 1902 season had been poor, but the number of football aspirants grew from thirty to nearly sixty by early October. The recruitment success of 1902 was enlarged in 1903 with the prophetic "Maroons Sound Doom of Yost's Great Eleven" due to the snaring of "one of the greatest collections of giants ever collected in the West." Earlier in the spring, "unusual activity" by "several old alumni" was credited, along with the track meet, for the "very fertile" athletic prospects of the freshmen of 1903.[43] Chicago newspapers greeted each Midway acquisition as a civic resource and with bold headlines: "Stagg Gets Sprinter," "Hogenson Captured for the Maroon Team," "Stagg Secures Good Guard," "Stagg Gains Another Star Prep Athlete," and "Stagg Secures Star."[44]

President Harper worked with the coaching staff to initiate the recruiting system. He led the formal organization of the university alumni early in 1904, when he addressed them along with C monogram-winners, faculty, and the team at his annual football dinner in the Reynolds Club on campus. "Bring in freshmen athletes" was the motto Harper "unreservedly adopted" in his speech. "We have 6000 alumni in and about Chicago," he challenged the one hundred alumni guests. "Why do not these alumni see that the university gets its fair share of the athletic material?" Harper then urged that a committee be appointed to organize the alumni into "a recruiting organization." The alumni complied within days.[45]

The interscholastic track meet grew rapidly in its importance for the Chicago football enterprise. In its second year Stagg's meet more than doubled in size, and representatives from Indiana, Ohio, Missouri, and Minnesota joined the states that had previously sent athletes. "Stagg's Interscholastic" was the premier meet in the West by 1905, as Nebraska and Kentucky joined the throng; seventy-five schools were represented.[46]

A battle between Chicago and Michigan erupted in 1903 over recruiting prominent Chicago high school players. It was difficult to make a head count, for some of Stagg's new wards had not completed high school, and it was not always easy to pry them into the university. Coach Fielding Yost of Michigan also recruited his share of Chicago public high school juniors in 1903. Yost had early demonstrated the value of proselytizing player talent for his teams—he had managed to shanghai some of his West Coast stars (including the legendary Willie Heston from a neighboring California college) when he made the change from Stanford University to a new academic home at Michigan. President David Starr Jordan of Stanford addressed the North Central Association of Colleges and Secondary Schools in 1903 and recalled Yost as a practitioner of the "kind of corruption" in intercollegiate athletics that colleges should eschew.[47]

This undignified recruiting scramble by two major universities drew some criticism, but not from the eminent academics within those institutions. The criticism came from the public press and from high school administrators and officials. One respected columnist, Henry M. Bates, had described late in 1902 the "new and dangerous development of semi-official recruiting bureaus" as a part of the University of Chicago. Bates argued that even if such recruitment were confined to the supposed "legitimate methods," the activity was "most unworthy of the dignity and purposes of a great institution of learning." Another critic perhaps captured the proper spirit when he suggested that the school boys "should . . . be numbered and driven into an inclosed field," after which the coaches of the Intercollegiate Conference would have a drawing for the lot.[48]

The most telling indictment of the player recruitment chaos came from Chicago Superintendent of Schools Edwin G. Cooley. Cooley was an alumnus of the university (Ph.B., 1896) and an acquaintance of President Harper. The superintendent described the Chicago–Michigan approaches to Chicago school boys in 1903 as "practically stealing boys out of high

school for athletic purposes before their high-school courses are completed." Cooley claimed, "There are in the University of Chicago three
pupils who are on the team who did not complete their high-school
course. At the University of Michigan there are two, while the other
universities are also bad offenders."[49]

Cooley and a committee of secondary school teachers and principals
drew up a set of resolutions that were presented to the Intercollegiate
Conference for approval. The resolutions consisted of three rather general
statements regarding "a higher standard of morality in athletics" and two
specific ones that required a change in university behavior toward high
school athletics and athletes. The Intercollegiate Conference responded
by noting that the high school officials should address the individual
universities, because the conference had no jurisdiction over admissions
policies.[50]

Cooley's committee next addressed the universities individually. At
least two of the conference schools indicated a desire to cooperate, but
the response from Chicago was ambiguous. President Harper did not
acknowledge receipt of the committee's January letter until April; he admitted that he had not even presented it to the Board of Physical Culture
and Athletics, and yet his conclusion seemed promising: "the conditions
which now hold in interscholastic and intercollegiate athletics are so
bad that they need the earnest co-operation of all forces—secondary and
collegiate—to keep them within proper bounds. You can always count on
the University of Chicago joining forces with other faculties and institutions in any effort to better athletic conditions."[51] Events were to prove,
however, that such assurances represented the diplomatic duplicity of the
athletic entrepreneur rather than the considered judgment of a leader of
a major university. There is no record that Harper presented the Cooley
Committee's communication to any Chicago faculty group.

President Charles R. Van Hise of the University of Wisconsin presented a plan similar to the Cooley Committee's to Harper, and the
response was again disappointing. Van Hise wrote twice before the Chicago leader answered his proposal that all athletes should spend a year in
residence before competing in intercollegiate athletics. Harper dismissed
the proposal with "one serious objection": "The inevitable result will be
to send all men who are interested in athletics to eastern colleges. The
eastern institutions are now vying with each other to secure material
from the west. This will be playing into their hands. If we could have the
east join with us in this rule, this difficulty would be avoided, but there
is little hope that they will do this, and if they do not it is practically
an abandonment of the athletic field."[52] The Board of Physical Culture
and Athletics, in a rare display of difference with Harper, discussed the

Harper–Van Hise correspondence at their next meeting and voted to support Van Hise's reform idea.[53]

Vagabond players peddled their football abilities to the highest-bidding school at the turn of the century, and in the absence of standardized eligibility regulations, the bidders were many. For example, two candidates for the 1902 Chicago team practiced one week, disappeared, and emerged at the Michigan practice field. One of the tourists returned to Chicago's team, followed by the other; Wisconsin was then rumored to have captured their fancy. Finally, one went to Ann Arbor to play, and the other remained at Chicago.[54]

The most difficult recruitment for Chicago's football enterprise occurred in 1905 with the acquisition of Walter Steffen, future all-American, from a Chicago high school. His attendance at the Midway did not end the battle for his services, however, for if the universities of the Midwest attempted to lure young athletes before high school graduation, they did not scruple to recruit athletes enrolled at another institution. According to his father, Steffen had "matriculated, paid his tuition, bought his books and attended classes for a week" at Chicago when he left for Madison, Wisconsin. He was accompanied by Wisconsin coach Philip King and the Wisconsin captain, who had journeyed to Chicago ostensibly to see a Chicago game with Iowa. Steffen's announced reason for the visit was an earlier promise made on one of his two previous trips "to see what they had." To that end, he attended football practice to ascertain the football future that Wisconsin, and perhaps he, could expect. Steffen returned to Chicago after a three-day absence. He claimed that the journey was made "entirely against my will" and that he "was ashamed to make the trip and hoped to get up there and get back before any one would know about it." Captain Vanderboom of Wisconsin retorted that the Madison sojourn "was done on Mr. Steffen's own initiative." When the valuable young man returned to the Maroon practice field, President Harper quietly forgot his threats to require an explanation for Steffen's absence from President Van Hise of Wisconsin; Coach Stagg stated that the athletic department would take "no official notice" of Steffen's confused behavior.[55]

The Retention of the Campus Physical Elite

Retaining players proved as difficult as recruiting them, and the elevation of players to a special status in order to retain their services produced physical elite on the Midway. The new athletic meritocracy within American higher education should not be viewed as a sole aberration against the backdrop of a pure academic meritocracy. Indeed, that academic meritocracy was itself instituted during the late nineteenth century within the social meritocracy (based upon one's birth, piety, and behavior) of the earlier American college.[56]

In 1896 Thomas W. Goodspeed encapsulated the attitudes that led to the rise of football players at Chicago as physical elite: "What we like about our team is that they are men. They are clean upright men and we are not ashamed of them in the classroom, in the parlor, among men or upon the gridiron." He proclaimed them "heroes, every one of them" and promised that "anything the university had they could have." Goodspeed's promise proved remarkably prescient.[57]

The specter of ineligibility was constant for the Chicago players. At least five of the best players on the 1900 team were found academically deficient in July. One leading player was frustrated enough to charge that "he was flunked by a professor who is opposed to athletics." The charge would be difficult to prove because the Chicago faculty generally showed a benign interest in the football team. Indeed, the player who complained was given a special makeup examination by history professor O. J. Thatcher, who was in constant attendance at team practices. The errant player was soon back on the field.[58]

Special examinations administered by a football enthusiast were only part of the indication of faculty kindness. Another valuable player for Chicago journeyed with the team to West Point, New York, for the 1903 Army game although when he departed he was ineligible. The player's eligibility was reinstated by telegram to Stagg from Dean George Vincent after the team's arrival in New York: "Parry reports satisfactory eligible to play best wishes to team."[59]

The departure of an ineligible player with the team may appear questionable, but the ruling was no more precipitate than those made the morning of a game. Eleventh-hour eligibility decisions were usually made by a small subcommittee of the Board of Physical Culture and Athletics. The composition of the committee during one particularly busy period consisted of three physical culture department members (Stagg, Raycroft, and Butterworth) with the ubiquitous Professor Thatcher as chair. The *Chicago Inter-Ocean* surveyed the arrangements at the Midway and concluded, "It seems safe to say that no really valuable man will be lost to the team on account of any little educational deficiency." Another newspaper noted wryly later that season that none of the players was ineligible for the Thanksgiving game with Yost's Michigan team.[60]

The regular academic program consisted of three majors of course work each quarter for undergraduates. Chicago undergraduates could take a baccalaureate degree upon completion of four academic years only if nine quarter majors were earned each year. The academic records of the 1903 football team during the fall quarter show that only three of twenty-three members were registered for the normal three majors of work, and only two of the three members received credit for their majors (the third was in a law program that extended into the next quarter). The athletic and academic authorities exercised "careful supervision" over the athletes to limit their course work to two majors. Eighty-three final grades were given the twenty-three members (most were given separate final grades for "class work" and for examinations). The team maintained a 2.01 grade point average (on a four-point grade scale) as a group, or a C average for the quarter if all final grades are weighted equally. There were few A grades (three, two by one team member, F. G. Burrows, a substitute lineman) and few failing grades (i.e., four no-credit grades, two by Walter Eckersall).[61]

That the players were indeed carefully supervised can be seen also in the memoirs of a young history instructor. When Elizabeth Wallace offered her initial course in Latin American history she found "Most of my students were athletes." Because Spanish was not a prerequisite, and all relevant readings were in Spanish, she recalled, "It was logically concluded by the keen undergraduate mind that the course would be a lecture course and therefore what was known as a snap. It was."[62]

Coach Stagg himself kept a watch on his players and was not above using an informal conversation with an instructor as an appeal for a player's eligibility. When his captain flunked a course after the instructor had told him, he claimed, that the player would pass, Stagg wrote a protest to Harper. The coach stated he thought the case justified his breaking "a rule of my own not to intercede in behalf of any delinquent athlete." He questioned whether the player's failure after his coach had been told the man would pass was "according to rule and whether it is fair treatment." Because there is a paucity of explanatory materials on the many delinquent players it is unclear how often Stagg felt it necessary to abridge his rule "not to intercede."[63]

The physical elite were given other special considerations as well. Early in the century a set of chimes was installed in newly constructed Mitchell Tower, and Stagg had the idea of a special playing of the carillon for the Maroon athletes, especially for those who tended to miss curfew, and gave a sizable gift toward that end. His gift was to provide "a nightly curfew to the men in training." As he explained, "The thought came to me and filled me with the deepest satisfaction, 'Why not have a good-night chime for our own athletes—to let its sweet cadence have a last word with them before they fall asleep, to speak to them of love and loyalty and sacrifice for their University and of hope and inspiration and endeavor for the morrow.'"[64]

The special nightly ringing of the carillon for the benefit of the athletes was consistent with the new elitist status of the group. The concern
for the football players' welfare led to a special diet for them at a "training
table." The original training plan was to ask all football candidates to
live on or near the campus to enable them to eat together. The concept
was extended to their living quarters in 1896, when two flats of a private
apartment house were engaged as a training center where the "candidates,
coaches, and trainers" would "spend all of their time when not in the rec-
itation-room or on the athletic field." That hope vanished by 1897, when
local landlords claimed that the footballers had "played such havoc" that
they would not be accepted as tenants again. The university countered
this refusal by putting a portion of Snell Hall at the disposal of Stagg's
men, and by 1902 the newest and most luxurious residence hall was reserved for the intercollegiate athletic teams. Hitchcock Hall, termed the
"millionaires' den," became the site for the training table and quarters
for about thirty players. Every resident athlete had to sign a "Training
Quarters Agreement," which incorporated the spirit of Stagg and the peculiar calling of the young Maroon athletes. Each athlete pledged "not to
bring in nor use" alcohol or tobacco and not to gamble; the "good name
of the athletic men of the University" was to be preserved in order to
make Hitchcock "a clean, sweet and beautiful athletic home."[65]

The separation of the football team from the rest of the student body
was accomplished with no discussion of its effect upon student life and
values. The idea of separate and unequal training facilities for the players
was viewed simply as an efficient use of the physical elite. But students
petitioned the faculty overseers of the Men's Commons to move the
athletes and their training table to the midst of the commons so that
mutual-acquaintance and "school spirit" could develop properly. Their
argument asked for the return to a time when student-athletes were not
restricted as to the sphere of their activities and when student spectators
were acquainted with the players for whom they cheered. The plea was
to no avail.[66]

If the physical man was furnished at the training table and at the training quarters, the mental and emotional man was also served. Academic
advice came from the faculty members most interested in the success of
the team and from Coach Stagg, who watched his men's study habits carefully. President Harper inaugurated a special tutorial program for football
players by requesting instructors to coach them in troublesome areas.
The emotional balance of the football team was sometimes strained during the season as the pressures for winning mounted. When the Maroons
suffered "Nervous Fits" in 1905, Stagg suspended practice sessions and
took the team for a carriage ride through Jackson Park. Later in the season

when "lack of sleep and general nervousness" bothered the team before an important contest they were whisked to exclusive Onwentsia Golf Club in Lake Forest for a weekend of relaxation at university expense.[67]

The administration and many faculty members were lavish in their praise of the function the new physical elite performed on campus. The football captain was elected at President Harper's annual dinner and became the most revered undergraduate figure. Maroon captains were usually rewarded with the position of convocation student marshal as "an evidence of the esteem" in which they were held by their university, according to President Harper.[68]

Many members of the university community caught the openhanded spirit promised by Secretary Goodspeed; the *Chicago Tribune* observed after one season that the "gridiron warriors have not yet descended to the level of ordinary students," for they still had "distinctions shown them to which the common 'grinder' cannot lay claim." The players were given post-game theater parties, dinners, and trips to other campuses to view football games, accompanied by proud professors and paid for by the game receipts. Such use of game revenues had clear, if casual, precedent. Philip S. Allen, a language instructor and former captain, recounted the immediate use of gate receipts in 1895 to feed the team at a French restaurant on Clark Street after every game. The Thanksgiving dinner after the traditional Michigan game had an important place on the players' calendar, especially when select female students were included as guests of the young gladiators and themselves became an auxiliary elite.[69]

President Harper and many others on the Midway viewed the players as having greater responsibilities to the institution and the other students because of their position as campus elite. Harper scolded academically conditioned and flunking athletes as lacking in "genuine college spirit" at his football banquet in 1903; he charged that such students did not have "the interest of the university at heart." And athletes were held to a higher standard of behavior, much as the nineteenth-century class deacons at Yale. When ice cream was stolen from a class reception and carried to Hitchcock Hall, three athletes who did not participate in the theft but who helped eat the ice cream were immediately suspended as examples to the student body.[70]

Player Profile: Walter Eckersall

The rise of intercollegiate football players as campus commodities and as campus physical elite can be illustrated in the career of Walter

Eckersall, the most acclaimed intercollegiate athlete in University of Chicago history and a consensus all-time all-American quarterback.[71]

The future star was born and grew up in the Woodlawn area of Chicago, adjacent to the university. "We little fellows couldn't buy footballs," Eckersall later recalled, "but we caught the spirit of the game from watching Stagg's players racing around in practice and in real games. We had bully times those days. I guess we all dreamed of being football heroes."[72] The youngster's rare physical gifts became apparent at Hyde Park High School. Eckersall set a ten-second-flat Illinois hundred-yard dash record in 1903 that stood until the future Olympian Ralph Metcalfe broke it in 1928. The football teams on which he played there were nationally ranked and contributed many noteworthy players to American collegiate football. One year Hyde Park played Brooklyn Tech, the best eastern school team, for the "high school national championship" and won 105-0 (fifteen-year-old Knute Rockne sneaked into the ball park to see his boyhood idol Eckersall play that day). Eckersall was the quarterback and leader of those teams and already a favorite with intercollegiate coaches when he was midway through his secondary school work.[73]

Coach Stagg precipitately announced in the autumn of 1902 that he had secured "Eckersall's promise to enter the Midway school" the following year. That claim upon Eckersall was recalled in June of 1903, when it was reported that "Michigan has had secret embassies calling on Eckersall" and that "rare inducements have been offered." An outraged member of Chicago's athletic management was quoted as charging that the "Wolverines have violated every ethic of intercollegiate sport" and have "been stooping to the lowest practices to steal Eckersall from us."

Stagg was probably the strongest inducement for Eckersall to remain in Chicago for his intercollegiate career. An important, if not crucial, factor in Eckersall's decision was Stagg's defense of the young player's "amateur" status during the summer of 1903, when the Amateur Athletic Union suspended Eckersall for playing on a professional baseball team. Stagg was the chief public defender (Yost of Michigan also joined the defense) of Eckersall's amateur status, and he was later reinstated. In the event, the uncertain young man did not make his college decision until just before the opening of the two universities in 1903, and he was aided mightily by Stagg, who later admitted grabbing Eckersall off the platform before he could entrain to Ann Arbor.[74]

Eckersall was the best-known athlete to leave a Chicago high school up to 1903; his athletic records and the AAU contretemps had brought him more notoriety before he had played a game for Chicago than most collegiate performers ever gain. The slight, quiet boy seemed to be made in the hero's mold on and off the gridiron. He even saved the life of a yachtsman in the summer of 1904 after the sailor's boat capsized in Lake Michigan.[75]

Young Eckersall served well as player commodity. He was a selfless performer, marked by complete dedication to the purpose of the American intercollegiate game—victory. Well, almost always. Once he decided to refuse. In a play to be used when the Maroons were within five yards of the goal line, the linemen were to hurl the 136–pound Eckersall goalward through the air. On the first practice attempt, he landed a scant three yards away on his back. The winded and bruised quarterback commented, "The Old Man has gotten up this fine play, but I will be damned if I am ever going to call it." Eckersall's commitment to victory was never more noticeable than in the 1904 game with Michigan, when he fainted of exhaustion in the carriage returning home. His academic dean George E. Vincent said in a speech to students and faculty, "I have noticed that he has always shown extraordinary indifference to the grandstand, and a splendid loyalty to his team." The Eckersall dedication to the game infused his teammates magnificently, according to Stagg: "In his playing, Eckie was very intense and hard working, and he had no patience with a loafer. On the field, and running the team, he was a dominant personality and carried the team along with him. He snapped out his signals quickly and incisively with the command of a general, and did not stand for any dilatory tactics on the part of any of the players."[76]

Walter Eckersall brought more publicity to the University of Chicago than any other student in the institution's history, with the possible exception of the kidnap-murderers Nathan Leopold and Richard Loeb. From his freshman year, when a disappointed Wisconsin newspaper headlined a Chicago victory with "Eckersall, 15; Wisconsin, 6," the young man had a heavy burden of fame to carry.[77]

Intercollegiate football provided the authentic folk hero for the university which it had lacked. The students had gamely tried to make the cadaverous Rockefeller a hero with their songs and praise, but the attempts were characterized by a defensiveness and unease hardly appropriate to a hero's status. Eckersall was a figure who could not be gainsaid, even by the enemy. Michigan composed an Eckersall chant that was wishfully fatal but implicitly laudatory:

> Eckersall, Eckersall!
> running with the ball,
> You will get an awful fall,
> Eckersall, Eckersall!
> Eckie, Eckie, break your neckie,
> Eckersall![78]

Unfortunately, Walter Eckersall was living on borrowed time; he compiled an atrocious academic record but was permitted to pursue that path until his football eligibility ended. In 1905 *Collier's* termed him as "simply an 'athletic ward'" of the university, whose qualifications were well short of the "most poorly prepared freshman." From his first quarter at Chicago as a subfreshman (he had not completed college preparatory work), Eckersall led his teammates off—as well as on—the field in failing grades and total absences from classroom work. He registered for courses with the same instructors the next quarter (winter 1904), but his political science instructor, Charles Merriam, reported that "he never appeared in class" during the quarter. His work in English showed a C average, although he again led the class in absences. Eckersall continued to participate in athletics after his disastrous first quarter at the university. In fact, he and six other first-year students who were flunking participated in intercollegiate track meets for freshmen. Their participation and the press coverage prompted an embarrassed University Council to reconsider the basis of eligibility for freshmen, but the inquiry petered out when Harper assumed responsibility with Stagg for the involvement of the errant students.[79]

The reconstruction of Eckersall's eligibility began during the spring quarter of 1904 to ensure his football play that autumn. He was enrolled in two history courses for Senior College (upper-division) students. His enrollment in "The Renaissance Age" would appear peculiar because the course was described as appropriate for those wishing to do graduate work in history, and such students were advised to take the course in their third year at Chicago. Eckersall's registration would appear peculiar, that is, if the teacher were other than the Chicago athlete's friend, Oliver J. Thatcher. Eckersall was given a C for his work by Thatcher, who did not flunk a single student in the class of sixty-seven, which included a good number of athletes, some of whom had previously experienced academic difficulty. The other course Eckersall enrolled in was "History of the United States: The Later Constitutional Period," taught by Francis Shepardson, a future member of the Board of Physical Culture and Athletics and secretary to President Harper. Work in the course was acceptable for graduate credit, and the largest division of students represented were in the Senior College. Eckersall received a C for his work in the course, which enrolled sixty-six and flunked but one.[80]

Although quarterback Eckersall's football career continued along extraterrestrial lines during the remainder of his four seasons at Chicago, the hapless young man fell to earth and further behind his classmates in his academic career. He maintained his eligibility in intercollegiate athletics but found that after three and two-thirds years of higher education he was still classified in the Junior Colleges (lower division). His lack of the full secondary school preparation for his college work was partly responsible; at least eight of his courses were applied toward making up his admissions deficiencies. At the end of the autumn quarter of 1906, the all-American had earned only fourteen course majors of credit toward the thirty-six required for graduation. He no doubt viewed his academic future with considerable anxiety; the completion of his degree program would have required many years of further study even though his program, the Ph.B. in the College of Commerce, was the least taxing field of study.[81]

By 1905 Eckersall had captured the complete fancy of football officials, sportswriters, and the public. His appearance in the lobby of the Chicago hotel where the Intercollegiate Conference was meeting reportedly provoked a spontaneous ovation. Sportswriters honored him with paeans for special games or performances. Most of the efforts were forgettable sports page doggerel, but one was more revealing than intended. "The Man with the Toe," written before the 1905 game with the Michigan Wolverines, was prefaced with an apology to Edwin Markham and began:

> Bowed by responsibility he's poised
> Upon his toe and gazes at the ball,
> Resolution stamped upon his face,
> And on his back the burden of maroon.
> Who made him dead to censure or applause,
> A man who grieves not and who always hopes,
> Clever and cool, a brother to the fox?
> Who loosened him among the wolverines?
> Whose was the mind that taught him how to kick?
> Whose word that coached his docile brain?[82]

Eckersall was consistently portrayed as the Chicago team leader and star player: "Everything revolved around the skilled kicker," asserted the *Chicago Journal.* The *St. Louis Post-Dispatch* headlined an article regarding Eckersall, "Chicago Sets More Store by Eckersall's Toe Than Rockefeller's Money." The article claimed that "greater even than Mr. Rockefeller's tainted tin about Chicago University is the terrible toe of Walter Eckersall." *Collier's Weekly* thought Eckersall's play was "without a flaw" and that "as captain of a team and field general he has no equal." The *New York Globe* wrote of Eckersall's place in intercollegiate football at the close of his career: "The passing of Eckersall is not only a loss to western football but the eclipse of the brightest star in the football firmament. When it comes to handling the palm to any one player for individual brilliancy Eckersall has no rivals, according to critics of all sections of this country."[83]

The student body gathered in a giant rally to demonstrate their affection and appreciation for Captain Eckersall the day before his last game in 1906. The *Daily Maroon* reported that at the "most enthusiastic mass meeting that has been held this year the cheers for the little captain lasted at times for minutes." The report continued:

> Actual tears stood in Eckie's eyes as he told how much gratitude he owed to Coach Stagg, as he praised the team, as he thanked the student body for its loyal support of him and as he expressed his wish for Chicago's success in the future. He had planned to say more, but his emotion made him leave the platform abruptly. He said in speaking of Director Stagg: "It is a privilege to be on such a team as Chicago has. I cannot tell you how great a privilege it has been to spend four years under Coach Stagg. I owe what success I have had to him. He not only trains his men in athletics but he trains their character."

An accompanying *Maroon* editorial spoke of Eckersall's football playing abilities and asserted that "his loyalty, his modesty, his qualities of leadership . . . have endeared him to his friends." Students at the university were encouraged to "pay tribute" to their hero "by purchasing the beautiful six-color, 25 x 29, autographic poster of Eckersall." The buyer was instructed to "hang it up in your room, and always have a material remembrance of him."[84]

Dean Vincent praised the strength of Eckersall's character in a speech to that student rally, and the university faculty reinforced his assessment at the player's last game. The faculty presented Captain Eckersall a "timepiece" as a "token of appreciation" of his "services in the University." Thomas Goodspeed presented him with a gold watch in front of the grandstand during half-time of the Nebraska game. The moment was frozen by a photograph: Eckersall, sheathed in a Maroon blanket, accepts with becoming modesty as he shakes the hand of Secretary Goodspeed, whose round face frames eyes crinkled with pleasure; one prepubescent boy lays his hand gently upon the laces of Eckersall's football shoe as if to imbibe the wondrous powers within, and another boy gingerly begins his grope for a share in the anointment. Eckersall expressed his formal thanks to Acting President Harry Pratt Judson (Harper died early in 1906). "It is a gift," he wrote, "I shall cherish as long as I live, not alone for its value as a gift, but also for the memories it carries with it." The admiration that prompted the gift, and the gratitude the young man felt toward the donors, were to evaporate within two months.[85]

The last term in which Walter Herbert Eckersall was enrolled was the 1906 autumn quarter, during which he completed his football eligibility. He did not register for the 1907 winter quarter and never again resumed

his studies at the university.[86] Eckersall faded rapidly from the pages of
the newspapers that he had dominated such a short time before. The last
athletic exploit recorded of Eckersall on the Midway was as spectacular
as his earlier ones. Bowling in the interfraternity tournament, he broke
the university record handily as he rolled a 245 game score. Within days
his difficulty was hinted, but not explained, when the *Maroon* announced
that his bowling scores for his fraternity, Alpha Delta Phi, had been abrogated due to his being ruled ineligible because of his "non-residence."[87]

The demise of Walter Eckersall at the University of Chicago was su-
perficially sudden, but the crisis was seemingly long in the making. The
troubles he experienced must have gone beyond the academic for some
time, but the extant records are spare and coded. We do know that a bitter
rupture between Eckersall and university officials occurred; a notation
dated January 25, 1907, on his official transcript reads, "*Mr. Eckersall is
not to be permitted to register in the Univ. again—for cause. By Order of
Acting President Judson.*"[88]

The fullest explanation available of this whole affair is contained
in a four-page letter written to President Judson on March 14, 1907, by
an older friend of Eckersall, George Buckley. Buckley wrote as a representative of some Chicago alumni, who had heard that Judson was
"contemplating drastic action" to demonstrate his "disapproval of the
many deplorable and unfortunate actions of Mr. Eckersall." Buckley explained that Eckersall had informed the alumni group of a letter he had
written to the president. Eckersall, Buckley reminded Judson, had "the
object of removing himself from your jurisdiction as well as to call your
attention to the fact that the University, through its officers, has been
derelict in its duty. Derelict in so far as their having knowledge of his
loose morals, and yet willing to use him for advertising purposes until
he had completed his college career."[89]

Buckley did not continue this theme of thinly veiled attack on
Judson's university. Instead, he admitted the truth of the grave charges
against his friend Eckersall, which included bad debts, traitorous personal friendships, and the athlete's letter, which Buckley termed "a nasty
thing," to Judson. Buckley undertook to guarantee the reformation of
the football star with the help of the other interested alumni and a legal
undertaking by Eckersall "assigning every cent of his salary and income
for one year to a person who will see to it that all debts contracted by
Eckersall in the past will be paid." The goal was that Eckersall execute
a "right about face" and "clean house morally."[90]

Buckley alluded no farther to the circumstances under which Eckersall was recruited by the university community and encouraged to put
the life of the body before the life of the mind; Judson, after all, had been

a major official in the university when Eckersall was at the institution. Instead, Buckley kept his purpose firmly in mind and eased the tone of his letter considerably from his opening; Eckersall became at once victim and victimizer: "He is not altogether to blame; he has never had the right way pointed out to him until the University took action. He had come to regard his friends and admirers merely as persons from whom something was to be had for nothing. In other words, he has been a grafter as well as a monumental liar." Buckley concluded with a plea that no public expulsion or similar action take place until the group of alumni and friends of Eckersall had an opportunity "to make Eckersall a man." There is a bitter irony here, for both Stagg and Eckersall had claimed for four years that such manufacture occurred daily at the football field. Buckley's plea is strong, touching, and patronizingly hypocritical, with, "We believe you do not want to do anything which would in any way handicap this boy in the years to come." Buckley's plea for mercy brought a swift response from Judson—by return mail he asked Buckley to come in for a conference. President Judson subsequently made no public statement regarding Eckersall, and there is no further official university record of their most famous student-athlete.

Walter Eckersall soon became a successful football correspondent for the *Chicago Tribune*, a task in which he could still trade upon his athletic career. He also became a widely employed football game official, frequently of the same game he was covering for the *Tribune* (and earning considerably more at the game as an official than as a writer). He was one of many sportswriters who practiced this conflict of interest, but he seems to have been particularly popular in the role, especially with Knute Rockne, who often successfully managed the selection of officials for his own games and even paid sportswriters as publicists for the games they were assigned by their newspapers. In *Shake Down the Thunder: The Creation of Notre Dame Football,* Murray Sperber notes that Eckersall even practiced "triple-dipping" (as paid game publicist, game official, and game reporter) for Rockne, and that coaches gave many writers (including Eckersall) free tickets, which they resold for a handsome profit.[91]

Although Dean Vincent warned Stagg off further relations with the disgraced Eckersall in 1908 ("It would seem unfortunate to have any association with him or recognition of him by the University"), the coach found it difficult advice to follow. He subsequently took Eckersall with him to help former Maroon halfback and teammate Hugo Bezdek install the forward pass at the University of Arkansas. However, the relationship must have cooled subsequently, because in 1924 Stagg asserted that the sportswriter "has given me the go bye for years." And a long-due loan for $20 and Eckersall's national promotion of cigarette smoking did not help

the relationship during the 1920s. There is no record of Stagg's response
to the tobacco campaign, but other coaches were outraged: Coach Bill
Roper of Princeton attacked what he termed this "exploitation of football
for commercial purposes," and Knute Rockne, offered $2,000 for the same
advertising campaign, refused: "This attempt . . . to build up increased
business at the expense of the youth of the land cannot be condemned
sufficiently." The ghost of Eckersall's past as the prototypical player commodity and gridiron hero seems to have pursued him, however, according
to an undated memorandum dictated by his old coach Stagg: "In ____, I
visited 'Wallie' Eckersall at the St. Luke's Hospital, where he was in very
great danger of dying as the result of a very severe case of heart dilation
brought on as a result of dissipation. I said to him, 'Eckie, you are going
to turn over a new leaf now, aren't you?' and he said 'Yes, Mr. Stagg, I am.'
It is several years now since this incident occurred, and Eckie has been
true to his word. He hasn't touched liquor since his hospital experience
and he has become a dependable and good citizen."[92]

Somehow the need for a proper ending to the Eckersall story took
precedence over the truth of his obloquy on the Midway. In 1921, a scant
fifteen years later, George Matthew Adams, a leading writer of twentieth-
century success manuals and a nationally syndicated columnist, confidently wrote: "Many years ago, when Eckersall, the brilliant quarterback
for the University of Chicago, finished his college course, he paid this
tribute to Mr. Stagg: 'Stagg teaches character, as well as football.'"[93] The
apocrypha was enough to warrant that a Walter Eckersall Memorial Stadium be built by the city of Chicago in 1947.

Walter Eckersall received his apotheosis soon after his early death
in 1930. It was fitting, perhaps, that this poetic remembrance of him be
written in the turgid style of the sports page:

THE QUARTERBACK

It's a long way back o'er the beaten track,
To the football of yesteryear,
Over hill and dale winds the long, long trail
That's misty at times, and drear,
There are lots and lots too, of gladsome spots
Though the gladness just now is stayed
When we think of the cheers not unmixed with tears
When young Walt Eckersall played.
Not the bulky type but your heart would gripe.
When he flashed through a broken field,
And he knew the trick of a placed drop-kick
When a score was a drop-kick's yield.
Reckoned near and far as the quarterback star

O'er the Styx he's gone unafraid,
And the old time grads will say they were lads,
When young Eckersall played.
But he's old Walt now and that battered brow
Is stilled 'neath its laurel and bay.
What can be that roar from the nearing shore?
Why it's men not the Milky Way.
Friends are in the crowd, 'God they're crying' out loud?"
They await him, bedecked, arrayed?
Be sure they recall in Valhalla's hall
When young Walt Eckersall played.[94]

The patronage of President William Rainey Harper, the spectator and player supply that the city of Chicago offered, and the single-minded "saintly" coach had combined to ensure that the University of Chicago football enterprise was hugely successful by 1905. President Harper had adopted university founder John D. Rockefeller's Darwinian modus operandi closely enough to recruit professors and players alike and to use them successfully in promoting the new academic creation. It was, moreover, Harper's and Stagg's keen sense of the basics of the institution and their artful collaboration in the athletics of Darwinism that promoted football within and without the university. The institution and the sport were now synonymous, stable, and famous. And the fixity of the football undertaking was soon demonstrated, for Stagg and Chicago football were tested severely in 1905–6, along with the national game.[95]

The rise of the spectator, coach, and player over the generation ending in 1905 demonstrates that the order of primacy in American football had been reversed—the student-player lost control of his surpassingly enjoyable pastime—the adults snatched the joy from him, and his campus enjoyment became his campus employment. The voracious appetite of the consumption economy began to take over adolescent sport—the man/child had begun to lose the natural joy of sport to the yawning maw of the acquisitive society.

Notes

From *Stagg's University: The Rise, Decline, and Fall of Big-Time Football at Chicago.* Copyright 1995 by the Board of Trustees of the University of Illinois. Used with permission of the University of Illinois Press.

1. This chapter demonstrates the factors of modern sport at the collegiate level that Allen Guttmann defined and argued in *From Ritual to Record.* Guttmann posited secularism, equality, specialization, rationalization, bureaucratization, quantification, and the keeping of records as the elements that characterize modern sport. And he applied his proposition to American sport in *A Whole New Ball Game: An*

Interpretation of American Sports (Chapel Hill: University of North Carolina Press, 1988). His discussion of the intercollegiate form is especially helpful.

2. On the evolution of a community of participants into a community divided into watchers and the watched, see Daniel J. Boorstin, *The Creators* (New York: Random House, 1992), 206–13, and Allen Guttmann's survey and interpretation of the centuries and the literature, *Sports Spectators* (New York: Columbia University Press, 1986).

3. Amos Alonzo Stagg, *Touchdown!* (New York: Longmans, Green, 1927), 203; also Stagg to "Dr. Goodspeed," no date, which described (Thomas) Goodspeed's half-time talk to the boys as well as Harper's, box 24, folder 24, Papers of Amos Alonzo Stagg, Department of Special Collections, University of Chicago Library (hereafter cited as Stagg Papers).

4. Frank Luther Mott, *American Journalism: A History of Newspapers in the United States through 250 years, 1690–1940* (New York: Macmillan, 1941), 443, 579; Lewis, "American Intercollegiate Football Spectacle," 117–18 and 124–28, for the expansion of periodicals due to greatly expanded advertising and favorable postal laws; and Michael Oriard, *Reading Football: How the Popular Press Created an American* Spectacle (Chapel Hill: University of North Carolina Press, 1993), 62–85, 274–76.

5. *Chicago Daily News*, Nov. 29, 1902. The program, menus, and guest list are affixed to Scrapbook, vol. 28, Stagg Papers. Cf. *Chicago Chronicle* and *Chicago Journal*, Nov. 29, 1902.

6. *Chicago American*, Oct. 16, 1902, Dec. 1, 1902; Stagg, *Touchdown!* 173–74. Edwin Cady delineated the game constituencies in *The Big Game: College Sports in American Life*, (Knoxville: University of Tennessee Press, 1978), 11–12.

7. Milton Mayer, "Portrait of a Dangerous Man," *Harper's Magazine* 193 (July 1946): 60.

8. "Thanksgiving Day Songs and Cheers," Scrapbook, vol. 3, 118, Stagg Papers; Scrapbook, vol. 34, Stagg Papers: loose pamphlet. The additional stanza appeared in *University of Chicago Songs* (Chicago: University of Chicago Press, "Published by the Glee Club," 1897), 4–5.

9. *Minneapolis Tribune*, Oct. 13, Nov. 4, 1900. The Rockefeller song appeared as a leading composition in the university songbook until 1920, when it was demoted to appear as the eleventh song. It was finally dropped in 1921.

10. "Thanksgiving Day Songs and Cheers," Scrapbook, vol. 3, Stagg Papers. Cf. the student description of Rockefeller in the yearbook, *Cap and Gown*, 1895, dedicated to him.

11. John J. MacAloon, *The Great Symbol: Pierre de Coubertin and the Origins of the Modern Olympic Games* (Chicago: University of Chicago Press, 1981); "Football Mass Meeting," Scrapbook, vol. 33, between pages 64 and 65, Stagg Papers; *Chicago Tribune*, *Chicago Inter-Ocean*, and *Chicago Record-Herald*, all Nov. 25, 1903.

12. *Chicago Inter-Ocean*, Oct. 8, 1902; *Chicago Record-Herald*, Nov. 21, 1902; G. Stanley Hall, "Student Customs," *Proceedings of the American Antiquarian Society* 14 (1900): 119, quoted in Frederick Rudolph, *The American College and University: A History* (New York: Vintage Books, 1962), 393.

13. *Chicago Chronicle*, Nov. 17, 1902; *Chicago Tribune*, Nov. 18, 1902. The persuasive Wayman served as captain of the women's basketball team at Chicago and as assistant instructor in the women's gymnasium at the University Settlement House, where she conducted a gymnasium class for "the children of the stockyards district," *Chicago Chronicle*, Nov. 18, 1902; *Chicago Tribune*, Nov. 24, 1903. The students were segregated by sex at the rallies, with the men in the choic-

est seats. On the changing and contradictory attitudes toward women as football supporters, see Lynn D. Gordon, *Gender and Higher Education in the Progressive Era, 1890–1920* (New Haven, Conn.: Yale University Press, 1990), 118. Chicago women outperformed their male classmates in the one realm in which they were permitted to compete equally—the classroom. Women made up 56.3 percent of the Phi Beta Kappa chapter, even with a smaller total enrollment. Gordon, *Gender and Higher Education,* 112.

14. *Chicago Chronicle, Chicago Record-Herald,* and *Chicago Record-Herald,* all Nov. 18, 1902.

15. *Chicago Tribune* and *Chicago Inter-Ocean,* Nov. 25, 1903; *University Record* 8 (Nov. 1903): 201.

16. *Chicago Times-Herald,* Dec. 4, 1896; *Chicago Record-Herald,* Nov. 3, 1903; Invitation, Scrapbook, vol. 33, Stagg Papers.

17. *Chicago Tribune,* Nov. 28, 1896.

18. *Chicago Times-Herald,* Dec. 2, 1899; Elizabeth Wallace, *Unending Journey* (Minneapolis: University of Minnesota Press, 1952), 93, describes Laughlin; *Chicago Daily News,* Dec. 2, 1899.

19. *Alumni Directory, the University of Chicago, 1861–1910* (Chicago: University of Chicago Press, 1910), ix.

20. *University Record,* Nov. 10, 1899, 191; *Chicago Tribune,* Nov. 20, 1902; *Chicago American,* Nov. 23, 1902; *Chicago Record-Herald,* Nov. 21, 25, 1902.

21. *Minneapolis Tribune,* Oct. 12, 1900; *Chicago Record-Herald,* Nov. 27, 1903; *Chicago Tribune,* Nov. 13, 1904; *Twelfth Census of the United States* (Washington: Census Office, 1901), 1: 455. Total football receipts had exceeded expenses by about $41,000 from 1892 to 1902, see the *President's Report, 1892–1902* (Chicago: University of Chicago Press, 1903), 365–66; *Chicago American,* Nov. 26, Dec. 1, 1902; *Chicago Inter-Ocean,* Dec. 25, 1902; *Chicago Record-Herald,* Jan. 17, 1904; Financial Statements, box 11, folder 3, and Department Financial Reports, boxes 21 and 22, in Stagg Papers.

22. Harper to Stagg, Nov. 22, Nov. 23, 1897, box 9, folder 2, Stagg Papers.

23. Harper to Stagg, July 27, June 6, June 24, Aug. 1, 1895, and Stagg to Harper, July 11, 1896, box 9, folder 1, Stagg Papers; Harper to Stagg, June 1, June 15, 1897, box 9, folder 2, Stagg Papers. Spencer Dickson, as early as 1896–97, Dismond, and Cecil Lewis ran the 440-yard dash for Stagg, see Arthur R. Ashe, Jr., *A Hard Road to Glory* (New York: Warner Books, 1988), 63–66.

24. Stagg to Harper, March 24, 1896, Athletics folder 1, UPP, 1889–1925, Stagg's emphasis. Contrast Stagg's views and actions here with the following statement: "Because Stagg considered his department similar to the other departments of the University, he believed that all funds received and disbursed by his department should be put in the keeping of the regular business officer of the University." Kooman Boycheff, "Intercollegiate Athletics and Physical Education at the University of Chicago, 1892–1952," (Ph.D. diss., University of Michigan, 1954), 22–23. Boycheff cites only a speech Stagg gave in 1923; he cites nothing from Stagg's long administrative career.

25. Harper to Stagg, July 31, 1905; Stagg to Harper, Aug. 8, 1905, A. A. Stagg folder, William Rainey Harper Papers, Special Collections, University of Chicago Library (hereafter cited as WRHP).

26. Butterworth to Stagg, July 22, 23, 1895, box 11, Stagg Papers; Stagg to Harper, July 25, 1895, Athletics 1 folder, University Presidents' Papers, Special Collections, University of Chicago Library (hereafter cited as UPP), 1889–1925.

27. Adams to Harper, July 16, 1898, and accompanying memoranda, Francis W.

Shepardson to J. C. Elson, June 15, 1898, Stagg to Harper, Aug. 8, 1898, all in Athletics 5 folder, UPP, 1889–1925.

28. Raymond E. Callahan, *Education and the Cult of Efficiency* (Chicago: University of Chicago Press, 1962); see Rudolph, *The American College and University*, 389–92, for the context of the rise of the coach; and Ronald A. Smith, *Sports and Freedom: The Rise of Big-Time College Athletics* (New York: Oxford University Press, 1988), ch. 11. Samuel Haber, *The Quest for Authority and Honor in the American Professions, 1750–1900* (Chicago: University of Chicago Press, 1991), 280, 283–84, indicates the promise of such inquiry for the coach. See also T. J. Jackson Lears, *No Place of Grace: Antimodernism and the Transformation of American Culture, 1880–1920* (New York: Pantheon, 1981).

29. *Chicago American*, Jan. 4, 1903; Camp quoted in the *Chicago Journal*, Dec. 4, 1903.

30. *Chicago Chronicle*, Dec. 21, 1902; *Chicago Daily News*, Sept. 26, 1900. Research in English-language newspapers published in Chicago when Stagg lived in the city—1892–1933—indicates that his name was noted more often in the news columns during the entire forty-year period than any other.

31. Stagg and H. L. Williams, *A Scientific and Practical Treatise on American Football for Schools and Colleges* (Hartford, Conn.: Case, Lockwood & Brainard, 1893); Henry L. Williams to Stagg, May 7, 1927, box 7, folder 8, Stagg Papers. The book's publication was announced by *New York World*, Oct. 21, 1894, *New York Times*, Oct. 27, 1894, and *New York Tribune*, Oct. 28, 1894; also, *Hartford Courant*, Nov. 16, 1894, *Philadelphia Press*, Nov. 17, 1894, and *Boston Advertiser*, Nov. 21, 1894; *Chicago Tribune*, *Chicago Journal*, *Chicago Post*, *Chicago Daily News*, and *Chicago Chronicle*, all March 19, 1904; *Touchdown!* 209.

32. Durant and Etter, *Highlights of College Football*, 81, 79–81. Pennsylvania won, 23-11. On Herschberger, see Christy Walsh, ed., *Intercollegiate Football* (New York: Doubleday, Doran, 1934), 17. Chicago beat Texas, 68-0, *Chicago News*, *Chicago Inter-Ocean*, and *Chicago Record-Herald*, Nov. 6, 1904. Texas had played Kansas in 1901, see Walsh, ed., *Intercollegiate Football*, 463.

33. *Chicago Inter-Ocean*, Nov. 13, 1904; *Chicago American*, Oct. 31, 1905; *Chicago Tribune*, Nov. 5, 1905.

34. *Chicago Record-Herald*, *Chicago Journal*, *Chicago Tribune*, and *Chicago Chronicle*, all Nov. 3, 1903. Stagg's statement appeared in *Touchdown!* 301–2.

35. *Chicago Times-Herald*, Oct. 15, 1897; *Harper's Weekly*, Dec. 2 1905, 1731.

36. *Chicago Chronicle*, Aug. 19, 1900; *Chicago Tribune*, Aug. 26, 1900; *Literary Digest*, Nov. 30, 1895, 128.

37. *Chicago Tribune*, Dec. 18, 1902; Stagg, *Touchdown!* 290–93.

38. Stagg, *Touchdown!* 238, 248; *Chicago Chronicle*, Nov. 18, 1896, *Chicago Journal*, Nov. 29, 1905, and *Chicago Tribune*, Nov. 21, 1897, all in box 38, 1898; Football Practice folder, Stagg Papers; *Chicago Times-Herald*, Nov. 29, 1900; *Chicago Record-Herald*, Nov. 27, 1902; *Chicago Inter-Ocean*, Nov. 12, 1904; *Chicago Journal*, Nov. 16, 1905; *Chicago Tribune*, Dec. 3, 7, 1902; *Chicago American*, Dec. 4, 5, 1902.

39. Minutes, Board of Physical Culture and Athletics, Stagg Papers (hereafter cited as BPC&A), Nov. 2, 1901; see also May 24, May 30, 1902.

40. Minutes, BPC&A, May 30, 1902; *Annual Register*, 1901–1902 1 (July 1902): 166–77; *Chicago Tribune*, Nov. 26, 1902.

41. Minutes, BPC&A, May 30, 1902; *Chicago Daily News, Chicago Tribune*,

June 3, 1902; *Chicago Inter-Ocean*, June 2, 1902; *Chicago American*, June 6, 1902. On the meet itself, see *Chicago American* and *Chicago Record-Herald*, June 7, 1902, and *Chicago American, Chicago Record-Herald*, and *Chicago Tribune*, June 8, 1902.

42. *Chicago Record*, Sept. 3, 1900; *Chicago American, Chicago Inter-Ocean, Chicago Record-Herald*, and *Chicago Tribune*, Nov. 26, 1902; Stagg, *Touchdown!* 180–81.

43. *Chicago Inter-Ocean*, Sept. 27, Oct. 8, 1902; *Chicago Tribune*, Oct. 12, 1902; *Cap and Gown*, 1903, 8 (1903): 191; *Chicago Tribune* and *Chicago Inter-Ocean*, Sept. 22, 1902; *Chicago Record-Herald*, Oct. 1, 1902, Aug. 23, 1903; *Chicago American*, Sept. 29, 1902, July 31, Aug. 17, Aug. 24, 1903; *Chicago Examiner*, Sept. 11, 1903; *Chicago Daily News*, Aug. 31, Sept. 1, 1903, July 9, 1904.

44. *Chicago Post, Chicago Record-Herald, Chicago American, Chicago Inter-Ocean*, and *Chicago Examiner*, July 12, 1904; *Chicago Journal, Chicago Inter-Ocean*, July 13, 1904.

45. Harper quoted in *Chicago Examiner*, Jan. 30, 1904.

46. *Chicago Examiner, Chicago Tribune*, June 1, 1903; *Chicago Daily News*, June 2, 1903.

47. *Chicago Daily News*, July 21, 1903; *Chicago Chronicle*, July 22, Nov. 26, 1903; *Chicago Daily News, Chicago Post*, Sept. 1, 1903; *Chicago Tribune*, Sept. 13, 1903, Nov. 30, 1905; *Chicago Journal*, Sept. 15, 1903; *Chicago Record-Herald*, Nov. 26, 1903; Robin Lester, "Fielding Harris Yost," *Dictionary of American Biography*, Supplement 4 (New York: Charles Scribner's Sons, 1974), 917–18. Jordan's speech is in *Proceedings of the Eighth Annual Meeting of the North Central Association of Colleges and Secondary Schools* (Ann Arbor, 1903), 150–51.

48. Henry M. Bates in *Chicago Record-Herald*, Dec. 28, 1902. The player drawing idea was in *Chicago Inter-Ocean*, Sept. 26, 1902. For a discussion of the problems of eligibility and common standards among schools in Boston, see Stephen Hardy, *How Boston Played: Sport, Recreation, and Community* (Boston: Northeastern University Press, 1982), 113–23; for the national scene, M. K. Gordon, "Reform of School Athletics," *Century* 57 (Jan. 1910): 469–71, and A. E. Stearns, "Athletics and the School," *Atlantic Monthly* 113 (Feb. 1914): 145–48.

49. *Alumni Directory of the University of Chicago*, 1861–1906 (Chicago: University of Chicago Press, 1906), 75; Cooley to Harper, May 31, 1901, box 9, folder 5, UPP, 1889–1925. The two met for lunch almost monthly, see Harper to Cooley, Aug. 8, 1902, Sept. 22, 30, 1903, box 9, folder 5, UPP, 1889–1925. Cooley quoted in *Chicago Inter-Ocean*, Nov. 19, 1903. Cf. *Chicago Record-Herald*, Nov. 18, 1903.

50. Cooley et al., letter, Nov. 25, 1903, Athletics 6 folder, UPP, 1889–1925; *Chicago Record-Herald*, Nov. 28, 1903. The *Chicago Chronicle, Chicago Examiner, Chicago Tribune*, and *Chicago Daily News* all noted on Nov. 28, 1903, that the faculty representatives admitted privately that the complaints were well founded.

51. Edwin G. Cooley et al. to the President and Faculty, the University of Chicago, Jan. 27, 1904, Athletics 6 folder, *UPP*, 1889–1925. The letter took note of the "interest taken by the University of Wisconsin, which has sent a committee from its faculty for conference; and the University of Illinois, which has expressed its sympathy with the movement," p. 5. William Rainey Harper to Edwin G. Cooley, April 6, 1904, Athletics 6 folder, *UPP*, 1889–1925.

52. Charles R. Van Hise to William Rainey Harper, Sept. 27, Oct. 11, 1904, Ath-

letics 6 folder, *UPP*, 1889–1925; Harper to Van Hise, Oct. 11, 14, 1904, Athletics 2 folder, *UPP*, 1889–1925.

53. Minutes, BPC&A, Oct. 29, Nov. 23, 1904.

54. *Chicago Tribune, Chicago Daily News,* and *Chicago Record-Herald,* Sept. 18, 1902; *Chicago Inter-Ocean, Chicago American, Chicago Record-Herald,* and *Chicago Tribune,* Sept. 22, 1902; *Chicago Inter-Ocean,* Sept. 25, 26, 1902; *Chicago Journal, Chicago Tribune,* Sept. 14, 1904; *Chicago American, Chicago Examiner, Chicago Tribune,* and *Chicago Daily News,* Sept. 15, 1904.

55. *Chicago Record-Herald,* Dec. 6, 1903; *Chicago Daily News,* Sept. 13, 1904; *Chicago Journal,* Sept. 26, 1905; *Chicago Chronicle, Chicago Record-Herald,* and *Chicago Inter-Ocean,* Oct. 6, 1905. Steffen was named captain of the Maroon freshman team of 1905, *Cap and Gown,* 1906, 11 (906): 249; Steffen's father was quoted in *Chicago Tribune,* Oct. 10, 1905; Steffen and Vanderboom quoted in *Chicago Tribune,* Oct. 11, 1905; *Chicago Record-Herald* and *Chicago Examiner,* Oct. 10, 1905. For the day-by-day account of the "kidnapped Maroon," see *Chicago Chronicle, Chicago Tribune, Chicago Record-Herald, Chicago Daily News,* and *Chicago American,* Oct. 9, 1905; *Chicago Post, Chicago Tribune, Chicago Inter-Ocean, Chicago Examiner, Chicago Record-Herald, Chicago Journal,* and *Chicago Chronicle,* Oct. 10, 1905; *Chicago Tribune* and *Chicago Inter-Ocean,* Oct. 11, 1905; and *Chicago Record-Herald,* Oct. 12, 1905.

56. For example, ranking by grades alone did not occur at Harvard until 1869; see Rudolph, *The American College and University,* 329–48. David Riesman first suggested to me that the twentieth century's athletic meritocracy was simply the latest in a series of such meritocracies in American higher education history.

57. Goodspeed quoted in *Chicago Record,* Nov. 28, 1896, after a victory over Michigan. Stagg later termed Goodspeed "perhaps our most enthusiastic rooter," *Touchdown!* 226.

58. *Chicago Record,* July 19, 1900; *Chicago Tribune,* July 29, Sept. 8, 1900; *Chicago Times-Herald,* Aug. 6, 1900; *Chicago Chronicle,* Aug. 13, 30, 1900; *Chicago Record* and *Chicago Tribune,* Sept. 11, 1900. On Thatcher, see Stagg, *Touchdown!* 277; *Annual Register,* 1892–1893 (Chicago: University Press of Chicago, 1893), 14, 36, 43; *Chicago Times-Herald,* Sept. 7, 1900. Thatcher's self-congratulatory letter to Stagg, Oct. 29, 1913, is in box 104, folder 2, Stagg Papers.

59. *Chicago Record-Herald,* Nov. 12, 1903; Telegram, George E. Vincent to A. A. Stagg, Nov. 13, 1903, Scrapbook, vol. 33, Stagg Papers.

60. Minutes, BPC&A, Oct. 3, Dec. 5, 1896, Oct. 23, 1902, Oct. 9, 1901; *Chicago Inter-Ocean,* Oct. 3, 1902; *Chicago Record-Herald,* Nov. 21, 1902.

61. See the report of James Hayden Tufts, dean of the Senior Colleges, in *The President's Report,* 1892–1902, 75–77; Minutes, BPC&A, Nov. 28, 1903, report attached, 1–2; "Autumn Quarter, 1903; Records of Members of the Football Team," report filed by Alonzo K. Parker, university recorder, ibid., Jan. 21, 1904.

62. Wallace, *Unending Journey,* 83.

63. Stagg to Harper, Jan. 3, 1898, box 9, folder 3, Stagg Papers.

64. Stagg, *Touchdown!* 214–15; the extended quotation is from Stagg to Harper, Nov. 30, 1904, Gifts file, UPP, 1889–1925; cf. Minutes, Board of Trustees, May 18, 1908, and *University Record* 9 (Jan. 1905): 292.

65. The earliest training table hardly stirred the salivary glands of the team: oatmeal and water were included at every meal, and eggs were eaten twice each day. *University of Chicago Weekly,* Oct. 5, 1893, 2; *Chicago Tribune,* Oct. 18, 1894; *Chicago Chronicle,* Sept. 17, 1896, Sept. 5, 1897, Nov. 25, 1902; *Chicago*

Tribune, Sept. 6, 1897; *Chicago Record* and *Chicago Times-Herald,* Sept. 10, 1897; *Monthly Maroon* 1 (Nov. 1903): 1–8; *Chicago American,* Sept. 29, 1902; *Chicago Chronicle* and *Chicago Inter-Ocean,* Sept. 22, 1902; *Chicago Record-Herald,* Oct. 1, 1902. The Training folder, Department Historical File, Stagg Papers, and the *Chicago Times-Herald* and *Chicago Tribune,* May 31, 1897, tell of Stagg's strict enforcement of the rules banning tobacco.

66. Note the lack of any critical discussion regarding the training quarters in Minutes, BPC&A, Oct. 3, 1896. Advisory Committee of the Men's Commons to the Athletic Department of the University of Chicago and the Faculty Committee on the Men's Commons, Nov. 23, 1904, p. 2, box 15, folder 7, *UPP,* 1889–1925.

67. *Chicago American,* Sept. 4, 1903; Minutes, BPC&A, Nov. 14, 1901; Harper to Stagg, Oct. 14, 1902, A. A. Stagg folder, WRHP; Harper to "Mr Allen" (Philip S. Allen), Oct. 23, 1902, Athletics 1 folder, *UPP,* 1889–1925. The emotional diagnosis was headlined by the *Chicago Examiner,* Oct. 24, 1905, and *Chicago Record-Herald,* Oct. 24, 1905. *Chicago Tribune,* Nov. 27, 1905.

68. *Chicago Post,* Dec. 8, 1902; *Chicago American,* Dec. 9, 1902; *Chicago Tribune,* Dec. 10, 1902; *Chicago Record-Herald, Chicago American, Chicago Chronicle, Chicago Tribune,* and *Chicago Inter-Ocean,* Dec. 11, 1902; box 38, Football Practice 1898 folder, Stagg Papers. See the *Cap and Gown,* 1907, 229, for the list of captains and the University of Chicago convocation programs, Convocations 19, 29, 34, 38, 51, and 55, University of Chicago Archives. Harper's statement is in Minutes, University Council, 1903–1908.

69. *Chicago Tribune,* Dec. 2, 1902; *Chicago Post,* Dec. 3, 1902. A theater visit by the team in 1905 was responsible for selling out Louis Sullivan's Auditorium Theatre, *Chicago Record-Herald,* Oct. 29, 1905. Professor Thatcher, "Chicago rooter extraordinary," was a frequent chaperone, *Chicago Tribune,* Dec. 1, 1905. *Chicago Record-Herald,* Oct. 29, 1905; *Chicago Tribune* and *Chicago Record-Herald,* Nov. 2, 1905; *Monthly Maroon* 2 (Nov. 1903): 5.

70. *Chicago Inter-Ocean,* Feb. 24, 1904; *Chicago Tribune* and *Chicago Record-Herald,* March 8, 1903; *Chicago Inter-Ocean* and *Chicago Examiner,* March 9, 1903; *Chicago Tribune,* March 10, 1903; *Chicago Examiner, Chicago Chronicle, Chicago Inter-Ocean,* and *Chicago American,* Feb. 27, 1904. President Theodore Roosevelt complained over a similar matter to President Eliot of Harvard on July 10, 1908: "The action of the faculty has convinced the students that it was because a member of the crew committed the misdeed that the punishment was made heavy." In *The Letters of Theodore Roosevelt,* ed. Elting Morison (Cambridge, Mass.: Harvard University Press, 1951), 5:1, 119.

71. The list of "All-Time All-Americans" selected by the Football Writers Association of America in honor of the centennial of American football in 1969 included Eckersall at quarterback. Durant and Etter, *Highlights of College Football,* 207; John McCallum and Charles H. Pearson, *College Football U.S.A.: 1869–1972* (New York: McGraw-Hill, 1972), 539–43.

72. *Chicago American,* Nov. 23, 1906.

73. Walter Eckersall, "My Twenty-Five Years of Football," *Liberty,* Oct. 23, 1926, 59–62; Jerry Brondfield, *Rockne, the Coach, the Man, the Legend* (New York: Random House, 1976), 40. Cf. the undocumented, unpaginated panegyric by James Peterson, *Eckersall of Chicago* (Chicago: Hinckley and Schmitt, 1957).

74. *Chicago American,* June 3, 1903, Nov. 23, 1906; Eckersall, "My Twenty-Five Years of Football," 59–62. William V. Morgenstern, long-time University of Chicago sports information and public affairs officer, recalled that Stagg admitted

literally taking Eckersall from the Englewood station platform in Chicago as he was waiting for the Ann Arbor train. Oral interview, Aug. 3, 1972. Less than three years later the A.A.U. abrogated its suspension of Eckersall without comment, see *Chicago Tribune*, Nov. 21, 1905; also see box 78, folder 1, Stagg Papers, for undated newspaper clippings and a denial by Stagg that Eckersall received tuition, room, board, and a clerical job for choosing Chicago over Michigan. Cf. Stagg to M. W. Sampson, June 30, 1904, and notorized denials by Eckersall and his parents, Walter and Minnie Eckersall, box 78, folder 1, Stagg Papers. An earlier eligibility controversy in 1898 included the use of Pinkerton detectives to check on athletes, see box 78, folder 4, Stagg Papers.

75. *Chicago American*, Aug. 25, 1904.

76. T. W. Linn, "The Football Season of 1904," *Cap and Gown*, 1905 10 (1905): 177. Eckersall's response to the new play is in box 16, folder 10, and box 24, folder 3, Stagg Papers. The 1904 Michigan game was significant for its injuries. Of the starting Chicago backfield, Eckersall alone remained on the field after twenty minutes of play. Stagg, *Touchdown!* 243–44. Vincent quoted in *The Daily Maroon*, Nov. 24, 1906, 4; Stagg's testimony is in Memorandum, March 25, 1930, box 16, folder 10, Stagg Papers.

77. Walsh, ed., *Intercollegiate Football*, 191. Cf. these headlines from Nov. 1, 1903: 'Eckersall Wins for Stagg's Men," *Milwaukee Sentinel*; "Eckersall Wins for Stagg," *Chicago Chronicle*; "Eckersall Gives Chicago Victory," *Chicago Record-Herald*; and "Eckersall Kicks Himself into Glory," *Chicago American*, Nov. 1903. And Eckersall continued to haunt Wisconsin; his 105–yard kickoff return against Wisconsin in 1904, as related by teammate Leo DeTray, is in box 24, folder 3, Stagg Papers.

78. *Chicago Tribune*, Dec. 1, 1905.

79. *Collier's*, Nov. 11, 1905. In his first quarter he was given no academic credit for his two courses, both of them introductory: Political Science I (civil government in the United States) and English I (rhetoric and English composition), although the former could be taken over in order to obtain credit. Eckersall tied for the lowest-ranking student and led in absences, with fifteen in his class of thirty students in civil government. *Instructors' Reports [IR]*, autumn quarter 1903, University of Chicago Archives, report of Charles E. Merriam, Civil Government, no. 1. Eckersall was the lowest-ranking student of forty-nine and led in absences (twenty) in his class of rhetoric and English composition. Report of Percy H. Boynton, English Composition, no. 1, *IR*, autumn quarter 1903. Cf. the unusual inclusion of the report, "Autumn Quarter, 1903. Records of the Football Team," filed by Alonzo K. Parker, University Recorder, Minutes BPC&A, Jan. 21, 1904. Merriam quoted in *IR*, winter quarter, 1904, Report of C. E. Merriam, Municipal Government, no. 23. Cf. the course description in *Annual Register*, 1903–1904, 227; *IR*, winter quarter, 1904, Report of Percy H. Boynton, English Composition, no. 1. Cf. the course description in *Annual Register*, 1903–4, 305. *Chicago Tribune, Chicago Inter-Ocean*. Jan. 31, 1904, *Cap and Gown*, 1904, 224, 228, for records of the freshman meet participation; Minutes, BPC&A, Feb. 27, 1904; for the University Council inquiry, Minutes, University Council, 1903–1908, Feb. 6, April 2, 1904.

80. *Annual Register*, 1903–04, 228–30; report of Oliver J. Thatcher, The Renaissance Age, no. 9, *IR*, spring quarter, 1904. Eckersall found it possible, during his years at the university, to take all four of the courses that were taught most frequently by the understanding Professor Thatcher. One is tempted to wonder

if the "gentleman's C" at Harvard had been translated into an "athlete's C" at Chicago. Of the eight grades Eckersall received from Thatcher, all were C. Record of College Work, Walter Herbert Eckersall, Registrar's Office, University of Chicago; reports of Oliver J. Thatcher, Medieval Europe, no. 1, and The Dark Ages, no. 7, *IR*, summer quarter, 1905; report of Oliver J. Thatcher, The Feudal Period, no. 8, *IR*, spring quarter, 1906; report of Francis W. Shepardson, History of the U.S., Later Const. Period, no. 18, *IR*, spring quarter, 1904. For the course description and level, see *Annual Register, 1903–04*, 229–32. Shepardson served on the athletic control board as dean of the senior colleges, *Annual Register, 1905–06*, 13, and *Annual Register, 1906–07*, 43. Eckersall took another course from Shepardson in 1906 and, of eighty students, none flunked. Report of Francis W. Shepardson, U.S. History-Colonial Period, no. 83, *IR*, winter quarter, 1906.

81. During the season of 1904, he was absent nine times and received a B minus for class work and a C plus for the final examination in Shepardson's American History: The Colonial Period, report of Francis W. Shepardson, United States—Colonial Period, no. 83, *IR*, autumn quarter, 1904. Cf. *Annual Register, 1904–05*, 200. During the season of 1905 he was absent eleven times and received a B and a C in Principles of Political Economy and was absent eight times and received two Cs in Modern Industries; report of William Hill, Principles of Political Economy, no. 1, and report of Robert Morris, Modern Industries, no. 6, *IR*, autumn quarter, 1905. During the season of 1906, he was absent five times and received a D and a C in Tariffs, Reciprocity, and Shipping and was absent seven times and received a C and a D in Financial History of the United States; report of John Cummings, Tariffs, Reciprocity, and Shipping, no. 23, report of John Cummings, Financial History of the United States, no. 24, *IR*, autumn quarter, 1906. On Eckersall's lower-division status after three and two-thirds years, see *Annual Register, 1903–4*, 532, *Annual Register, 1904–5*, 434, *Annual Register, 1905–6*, 388 (which notes his summer registration), *Annual Register, 1906–7*, 392, and *Annual Register, 1906–7*, 62, 104.

82. *Chicago Post*, Dec. 1, 1905. A Chicago graduate honored "Eckie" with "Eckersall, Eckersall, limber up your leg / . . . Eckie, quick! do the trick! That was slick! Wow!" Scrapbook, vol. 45, inside front cover, Stagg Papers. The *Chicago Record-Herald*, Nov. 26, 1905, carried "The Man with the Toe."

83. *Chicago Journal*, Nov. 28, 1905; *St. Louis Post-Dispatch*, Nov. 23, 1905; *Collier's*, quoted in *Chicago Inter-Ocean*, Jan. 8, 1907; cf. *Chicago Chronicle*, Jan. 8, 1907; *New York Globe*, Nov. 24, 1906. A typical appraisal of Eckersall's place in intercollegiate football history was written during the mid-1930s: "Almost a universal choice for All Time, All-American Quarter. His skill, tenacity, speed and headwork combined to make of this man a marvel." Walsh, ed., *Intercollegiate Football*, 191. Glenn "Pop" Warner chose Eckersall as his all-time, all-American quarterback in 1931, *Collier's*, Nov. 21, 1931, as did Grantland Rice in 1951 for the football Hall of Fame, see Peterson, *Eckersall of Chicago*.

84. *Daily Maroon*, Nov. 24, 1906, 1, 2, 4. Cf. the offering of an "Eckie postal card," *Daily Maroon*, Nov. 28, 1906, 2.

85. *Daily Maroon*, Nov. 24, 1906, 4; D. A. Robertson (secretary to the president) to Walter H. Eckersall, Dec. 1, 1906, box 15, folder 7, UPP, 1889–1925: Charles T. B. Goodspeed to George W. Taft, Oct. 4, 1928, "Reminiscences of Thomas Wakefield Goodspeed," inside the front cover, University of Chicago Archives; Charles T. B. Goodspeed, *Thomas Wakefield Goodspeed* (Chicago: University of Chicago Press, 1932), 57. Edgar Goodspeed recalled that his father, Thomas

Goodspeed, was deeply pleased to be chosen to present the watch to Eckersall. Edgar J. Goodspeed, *As I Remember* (New York: 1953), 56–59. Eckersall to Judson, Nov. 27, 1906, box 15, folder 7, UPP, 1889–1925.

86. *Annual Register,* 1906–07, 392; IR, winter quarter, 1907.

87. *Daily Maroon,* Feb. 1, 1907, 2.

88. Record of College Work, Walter Herbert Eckersall, Registrar's Office, University of Chicago. The emphasis appears on the transcript. The last entry reads, "Died Mar. 24, 1930." No further record was made of Eckersall's expulsion in the records of the junior college faculty, the University Council or Senate, or the Board of Physical Culture and Athletics.

89. George D. Buckley to Judson, March 14, 1907, box 15, folder 7, UPP, 1889–1925. There is no record of the Eckersall letter to Judson.

90. Ibid. Judson to Buckley, March 15, 1907, box 15, folder 7, UPP, 1889–1925. There is no record of such a conference between Judson and Buckley.

91. Murray Sperber, *Shake Down the Thunder: The Creation of Notre Dame Football* (New York: Henry Holt, 1993), 44, 128, 259–60.

92. Dean George E. Vincent to Stagg, Nov. 10, 1908, box 10, Stagg Papers; Stagg to Stella Stagg, Jan. 19, 1924, and Stagg memorandum, Aug. 26, 1931, A. A. Stagg Collection, Amos Alonzo Stagg High School, Palos Hills, Ill.; Knute Rockne to A. P. Ames, March 22, 1929, Notre Dame Director of Athletics Records, box 7: folder 85, Notre Dame University Archives; Stagg, "Walter Eckersall at St. Luke's Hospital," undated memorandum, Walter Eckersall folder, Stagg Papers.

93. Adam's column, "Today's Talk," *Richmond Palladium and Sun-Telegram,* Nov. 12, 1921. Football writer Francis J. Powers stated in the 1940s much of what has become accepted biography: "After graduating from Chicago, Eckersall won new fame as a referee and a sports writer for the *Chicago Tribune.*" Francis J. Powers, "Life Story of Amos Alonzo Stagg," *Official Pro Rules* (St. Louis: C. C. Spink and Son, 1946), 19.

94. Poem by Matthew S. Kelley, Eckersall folder, Stagg Papers; also, the tributes by *Tribune* sports section colleague Edward Burns, *Chicago Tribune,* Nov. 24, 1946, and by 1905 teammate Merrill C. "Babe" Meigs, *American Weekly,* Oct. 26, 1947.

95. See Burton Bledstein, *The Culture of Professionalism: The Middle Class and the Development of Higher Education in America* (New York: Norton, 1978), 289.

Chicago at the turn of the century was one of the leading locations of semiprofessional baseball in terms of numbers of players, quality of play, and size of audiences. The top clubs, whose rosters included former major leaguers, and young men bound for the majors, even had their own ballparks. Among the finest of these teams were African American squads, whose men played year-round and were really professionals and not semiprofessionals. Some of them were good enough to play in the majors, but racist customs barred them from any level of organized baseball. Michael Lomax analyzes the development of the local black teams in the context of the Chicago black community's changing demography, the emergence of a new corps of black leaders whose interests, unlike those of the older black elite, were largely within the community, and the role of black entrepreneurs, especially star hurler Rube Foster, in promoting baseball as a black enterprise.

In 1920, a year after the devastating Chicago race riots, Foster organized the Negro National League (NNL) as an African American parallel to Major League Baseball. The NNL soon had a rival, the Eastern Colored League, that resulted in the Negro World Series. Such public displays of black athletic abilities fueled controversial national debates over the next two decades that questioned the segregation policy of MLB and the validity of American democracy, culminating in Jackie Robinson's entry into the National League in 1947.

Black Entrepreneurship in the National Pastime

The Rise of Semiprofessional Baseball in Black Chicago, 1890–1915

5

MICHAEL E. LOMAX

During the 1980s and 1990s, popular and professional historians of baseball gave increased attention to the black experience in the national pastime. They have examined the game's relationship to white society, analyzed the trials and triumphs of black ball players, and extolled the competency of black ball players as they confronted racist America. Their research has also examined the connection between black baseball and the black community, emphasizing in particular how the game served as a unifying element to communities in transition and how it helped to bridge class distinctions.[1]

These efforts have dramatically expanded our knowledge, but the writings on black baseball have been somewhat narrow and limited. Most of the emphasis has been on the experience of players and the game on the field. While writers have noted the connection between black baseball and the black community, most of the research, especially in popular works, has neglected to analyze this linkage. Part and parcel of these limitations is the virtual absence of any analysis that examines the intersection of the role of local businessmen, communal patterns, and the development of black baseball.

Baseball in black Chicago exemplifies the efforts of black businessmen to pursue sport as an entrepreneurial endeavor. Their attempt to establish baseball as a profitable business illustrates the efforts of black businessmen to counter both discrimination and the exclusion of African Americans from places of amusement. It also illustrates how these African American entrepreneurs responded to obstacles, such as the inability to secure credit, that adversely impacted economic development. These entrepreneurs operated a segregated enterprise within the fabric of the national economy. In other words, the segregated enterprise— black independent teams—operated within the framework of the national economy—white semiprofessional baseball. African American baseball owners did not seek to promote their ball clubs exclusively to a black clientele. But with the expansion of the African American community in Chicago in the 1890s, due to northern migration, black owners began catering to this growing market.[2]

Andrew "Rube" Foster was to emerge as Chicago's most prominent black baseball entrepreneur. He became the first black owner to transform a weekend enterprise into a full-time operation, and he also developed a barnstorming tour in both the West and South in the pre–World War I years. While his Chicago American Giants was a race-based enterprise, Foster recognized the need to maintain business contacts with white baseball owners. This paper will explore the forces that shaped black baseball in Chicago from 1890 to 1915. Four themes will serve to guide the narrative: the changing demographics of Chicago's black community; the emergence of Chicago's new black leadership; the origins of semi-professional baseball; and the internal division among the enterprise's organizers leading to Rube Foster emerging as Chicago's most prominent black baseball entrepreneur.

Ghettoization and the Rise of Semiprofessional Baseball

The black population of Chicago expanded significantly between 1890 and 1915. During the first ten years of this period, Chicago experienced a dramatic increase in its black population, from 14,852 to 30,150, an increase of 103 percent. From 1900 to 1910, while the city's black population continued to climb steadily, its rate of increase declined; the Windy City's black population rose to 44,603, an increase of 46.3 percent. African Americans remained a minority in the Windy City, but their growing numbers made them far more conspicuous, and the large numbers of recent arrivals were pushed to reside in certain areas. In the late 1890s, most Chicago blacks lived in primarily integrated neighbor-hoods, with only a little more than a quarter residing in precincts in which they were a majority. By 1915, the roots of ghettoization became firmly planted as African American enclaves emerged primarily on the south and near west sides. Few white neighborhoods had ever accepted with equanimity the purchase of homes by African American families.

As the black population increased, whites became less tolerant towards black neighbors and actively resisted black settlement in their areas.[3]

Eight or nine neighborhoods made up the core of Chicago's black community. The "black belt" extended from the downtown business district as far south as Thirty-ninth Street. It was slowly expanding to accommodate the growing population. Not only did blacks move steadily southward, but the black belt began to widen as blacks moved into comfortable homes east of State Street. By 1910, blacks were as far east as Cottage Grove Avenue.[4]

Simultaneous with and emerging from these demographic and residential changes was the creation of black institutions that contributed to the growing vitality and selfconsciousness of the black community. The oldest and most stable African American institution was the church. Quinn Chapel A.M.E. was the first black church in the city; it was established in 1847, fourteen years after Chicago was incorporated. By the end of the century, Chicago had more than a dozen black churches, and between 1900 and 1915 this number doubled. These institutions were attractive to African Americans who preferred to avoid white people and their prejudices. They were also important for establishing a sense of racial pride and community spirit. Historian David Katzman states that the "push of discrimination" and the "pull of ethnocentrism" combined to impel black newcomers toward the ghetto. Many migrants sought homes in areas populated by blacks, where they could find familiar people and institutions.[5]

While this dynamic of choice and constraint, which was heavily influenced by economic factors, was similar to the experiences of Chicago's European immigrants at this time, there were significant differences. For example, unfamiliarity with English made the ethnic neighborhood essential for many Europeans. Blacks, on the other hand, had no comparable imperative. White immigrants tended to live near workplaces; blacks, scattered in service occupations, could not. Even when African Americans obtained industrial employment, they were excluded from neighborhoods adjoining Chicago's major industries. European immigrants lived near others of their nationality but usually in ethnically diverse neighborhoods that could hardly be described as ghettos. Whether middle or working class, black Chicagoans were less likely to share public space across ethnic boundaries. More than any other group, blacks in Chicago occupied neighborhoods defined by permanent characteristics.[6]

The sting of segregation affected more than choice of residence. Although state legislation prohibited racial discrimination in municipal services, public accommodations, and places of amusement, these laws were seldom enforced. Numerous incidents testified to a persistent pattern of discrimination in these areas. Blacks could never be certain of the kind of treatment they would receive when entering a restaurant, saloon, theater, or dance hall outside of the black belt. The LaSalle Hotel, for example, turned away a luncheon meeting of one thousand clubwomen because their number included several black members. Most proprietors would accommodate an African American if they thought refusal would create a major controversy. Booker T. Washington stayed regularly at the Palmer House when he visited Chicago. But less prominent blacks were generally harassed or simply refused service in downtown establishments.[7]

It was within this context that a new black leadership began making their imprint on community development. These African American entrepreneurs, also referred to as "Race men," were business leaders who deemphasized the fight for integration and dealt with discrimination by creating black institutions. The growing discrimination in Chicago and other northern cities resulted in the emergence of the physical ghetto. It prohibited African Americans from a host of social and economic institutions. Yet increased separation opened new opportunities for entrepreneurship. Between 1890 and 1915, Chicago's African Americans established a bank, a hospital, and professional baseball teams.[8]

Many of Chicago's new black leadership embraced a business concept known as cooperative business enterprises. This notion of cooperative enterprises had its roots in the black community in the late eighteenth century. Early black entrepreneurs recognized that if they were to attain any success in developing black businesses to an appreciable level in the black community, it would come only through economic cooperation. It was evident to them that no concrete help in obtaining capital and credit could be expected from white America. By the early twentieth century, cooperative business enterprises were more an outgrowth of the ideology of self-help and racial solidarity that developed in response to white discrimination. With blacks being excluded from many commercialized amusements, Chicago's black leaders sought to counter this discrimination by organizing their own commercial enterprises. For instance, by 1910 blacks found themselves completely shut out of the white YMCA, and as a result, the all-black Wabash Avenue YMCA was opened in 1913. Although certainly wanting to make a profit, Chicago's black leaders were genuinely motivated by a desire to provide services and facilities that were otherwise unavailable to blacks.[9]

At the same time, a development outside the African American community occurred that would significantly impact baseball in black Chicago—the rise of semiprofessional baseball. The emergence of semiprofessional baseball teams can be traced back to the 1870s. Commonly referred to as semipros, these teams could be classified into three categories: local teams or "stay-at-homes," traveling teams, and touring teams. Local teams usually played games within proximity of their home base. These teams developed a close-knit network with other semipro teams within, say, a hundred-mile radius, as a means of decreasing travel and overhead expenses. Traveling teams had no home base and would barnstorm the nation for gate receipts. Touring teams fell under both classifications and were the elite of the semipro teams. Possessing their own grounds, and the reputations as "crack" teams, these clubs could expand their travel itinerary and establish rivalries with teams in more lucrative markets, like New York City. Independent touring teams generally did not belong to a league, but they paid their players and charged admission. They commonly discharged their players in the winter, unless they toured the South. Independents often signed their players to one-year contracts, which only rarely contained a reserve clause for the following season. At the beginning of each season, players had to make new arrangements. During the season, independents either paid players a weekly salary or by a "co-op" plan, a method in which a team's share of the gate receipts was divided among the players and owners.[10]

Semiprofessional teams utilized the same business practices as organized baseball did in terms of generating and distributing revenues. A home team would share a percentage of the gate receipts—normally 40 percent—or pay a guarantee, a fixed amount usually set at $250, commonly referred to as a "heavy guarantee," to the visiting team. This guarantee was essential to attract the top clubs to their home grounds.[11]

By the early 1900s, semiprofessional clubs in Chicago began forming leagues and associations. The Chicago City League featured some of the top semipro clubs of the era. Two clubs—Cap Anson's Colts and Mike Donlin's All-Stars—were formed by former major league players. The other clubs that constituted this league included the Logan Squares, the Gunthers, Donohue's Red Sox, the West Ends, the Spaldings, and Rogers Park.[12]

Essentially two factors were significant in the rise of white semipro teams in Chicago. The first was the nature of Chicago's sophisticated park system. In 1901, the Illinois legislature appropriated a $7.7 million bond for the construction of thirty-one small parks and playgrounds equipped with outdoor gymnasiums, athletic fields, swimming pools, and spacious fieldhouses, which became community centers. Parks with baseball diamonds were leased by many of the top semipro clubs, who thus established both a home base and fan constituency. These clubs were able to promote, schedule, and book their own games, thus alleviating the need for a booking agent.[13]

Finally, Chicago City League clubs, in conjunction with semipro clubs without home grounds, were members of the Parks Owners Association (POA). The POA was a governing body that sanctioned league membership and scheduled games for both black and white semipro teams throughout Chicago's park system. There were 22 teams in the City League in 1910, eight of which had their own parks. The POA was a loose association that in the early years was not a promoter but a booking agent primarily for teams that did not possess their own grounds.[14]

The white semiprofessional clubs in Chicago established a symbiotic business relationship with black clubs. As black clubs rose to prominence and developed a winning reputation, white clubs found them to be good gate attractions. As we shall see later, two black clubs were members of the Chicago City League. This symbiotic business relationship illustrated the efforts of black entrepreneurs operating a segregated enterprise within the framework of the white semipro scene. Early black promoters did not seek to market their clubs exclusively to a black clientele. While black migration increased Chicago's black population in the pre–World War I era, it was not substantial enough to support professional black teams. More important, black entrepreneurs did not seek to create a black counterculture. In other words, black businessmen were not to isolate themselves from the larger society, selling only to blacks, nor were black fans to patronize black baseball games only because they were black. African Americans were to advance themselves by free competition on the open market. Black businessmen's economic philosophy was essentially a laissez faire formula for black advancement through individual commitment by individual blacks "to the gospel of work and wealth." The purpose of self-help and racial solidarity was to encourage black unity and self-assertion on a political level, while encouraging cultural and economic assimilation. This would, theoretically, result in the integration of blacks into mainstream American society. In the case of black baseball clubs, this meant white semiprofessional baseball.[15]

It was within the context of ghettoization and the rise of white semiprofessional baseball that Frank Leland emerged as black Chicago's first baseball entrepreneur. Leland was emblematic of the new black leadership that became actively involved in the ownership of black teams. He also exhibited an uncanny ability to establish contacts with local businessmen. Leland was born in 1869, graduated from Fisk University, and was on the roster of the Washington Capital City club of the National League of Colored Base Ball Clubs in 1887. This league was the only attempt to organize a black major league, patterned after the white National League in the late nineteenth century. When the colored league disbanded in May 1887, Leland moved to Chicago, and along with local businessman Henry "Teenan" Jones and two ballplayers, Abe Jones and William S. Peters, formed the Union Base Ball Club. The club was renamed the Chicago Unions the following year, and by 1896, both Leland and Peters transformed it into a stay-at-home club. The Unions toured Indiana, Wisconsin, and Iowa from Thursday to Saturday and played local teams in the Windy City on Sundays. In addition to his business interests, Leland was also a member of the Republican party and was elected Cook County Commissioner.[16]

The Chicago Unions typified the early black independent clubs that began as weekend enterprises. Lucrative Sunday games were vital to the team's economic survival. One Sunday game with a total attendance of 5,000 fans, charging twenty-five cents admission, could amass a gross revenue of $1,250. After paying the visiting team their share of the gate receipts ($500), the Unions would make a profit of $750. The Unions had a significant advantage in residing in the Midwest's largest city. Moreover, according to Sol White—a top black player of the era and later chronicler of the black game—the Unions played 731 games in its existence as both amateurs and professionals, winning 613, losing 118, and tying 12. Clearly the Unions had established themselves as a "crack" team.[17]

The Unions' rise to prominence in the Midwest was instrumental in the emergence of a territorial rivalry referred to as the "World's Colored Championship." The colored championship series was a promotional tool to stimulate fan interest and generate revenue. This series of games possessed an unstructured yet logical format. Beating all the top black clubs within a particular territorial region gave a club the right to proclaim itself as colored champion. The Cuban X Giants, one of the great black teams from the East and reigning colored champions, played a series of fifteen games with the Unions. But Leland's club was no match for the eastern power, and the Cubans won nine out of fourteen games.[18]

While it was not evident at the time, the Unions' loss to the Cuban X Giants marked the start of black entrepreneurs making concerted efforts to exploit Chicago's growing black market. Despite losing the series, Leland had exhibited the ability to attract a top black independent competitor. Clearly either the gate receipts or the guarantee was substantial enough to make it economically feasible for the Cubans to travel to Chicago. Evidently the series caught the eye of other prospective black entrepreneurs, who recognized the market potential and sought to organize a club to challenge the Cubans.

In 1899, under the direction of John W. Patterson, a group known as the Columbia club organized the Columbia Giants. Patterson started out with the Cuban Giants in 1893 as a substitute second baseman, playing behind Sol White, but won a starting position in left field the following year. In 1896, he played for the Page Fence Giants, who went on to defeat the Cuban X Giants for the colored championship. When the Page club disbanded in 1898, Patterson and many of his teammates formed the nucleus of the Columbia Giants. Patterson also signed Chicago Unions pitcher Harry Buckner. Patterson then entered into an agreement with Chicago White Sox owner Charles Comiskey to lease his park on Thirty-ninth and Wentworth, an area within walking distance of the emerging black belt. With the Unions located a few blocks away on Thirty-seventh and Butler, both clubs now competed for the same patronage. This was an obvious conflict of interest for both clubs if they happened to schedule home games on the same Sunday afternoon. Chicago's black community was not large enough to support two teams.[19]

In 1899, while the Cuban X Giants and the Unions were playing their series, the Columbia Giants issued challenges to both clubs. The Cubans accepted, but Leland wanted to avoid the upstarts. He was apparently outraged by their territorial invasion and losing his top pitcher. However, Sol White asserted that out of consideration for the public the Unions agreed to a five-game series. The Unions were completely outclassed by the Columbia club, losing the series in five straight games. Patterson's Giants now turned their attention to the Cuban X Giants. A series of games were scheduled in Chicago and towns in Michigan, with the Cubans defeating the Columbia club seven games to four.[20]

After the championship series, it became evident that two clubs could not develop a lucrative operation within such a close proximity of each other. By 1900, despite their success on the diamond, both the Columbia Giants and the Chicago Unions were in a state of chaos. The Unions defeated the Cuban X Giants for the first and only time. At the same time, the Columbia Giants defeated J. M. Bright's Genuine Cuban Giants of New York. But a disputed championship for local supremacy between the Columbia Giants and the Unions intensified the resentment between the clubs. The following year, financial setbacks caused the collapse of the Columbia Giants. Peters split with Leland and formed Peters's Union Giants. Leland signed several players from the disbanded Columbia club, formed the Chicago Unions Giants, and leased a park on Sixty-first and St. Lawrence, on the outskirts of the black belt.[21]

Leland's Union Giants continued to be a success on the field, but the club was still a financial failure. His split with Peters brought the East–West colored championship to a halt, and thirteen years passed before another series of this nature took place. The Union Giants were recognized as the top club in the Midwest, despite losing a local championship series to the Algona (Iowa) Brownies in 1903. Two years later, the Union Giants reportedly won 112 of 122 games. But success on the field did not necessarily result in financial rewards. By the winter of 1906, the Union Giants, renamed the Leland Giants, were a debt-ridden team.

Recognizing a need for a financial fix, Leland would once again exhibit his ability to form a business coalition.[22]

The Leland Giants Baseball and Amusement Association

In 1907, Frank Leland moved his club to Auburn Park on Seventy-ninth and Wentworth Avenue and sought a business alliance with black Chicago's emerging leadership. Leland's association with the new black leadership resulted in an effort by these "Race" men to gain control of Chicago's growing black consumer market and establish a black professional league on a national scale. The creation of a commercial amusement enterprise, under the auspices of economic cooperation, became the means of achieving these goals.

Two important figures in the consolidation of Leland's ball club into a commercialized amusement and recreation enterprise were Robert R. Jackson and Beauregard Moseley. Jackson, born in 1870, was a Chicago native. He left school in the eighth grade to successfully work as a newsboy, bootblack, postal employee, and finally he established his own printing and publishing business. Moseley was active in politics at an early age. Born in Georgia, he came to Chicago just after 1890. Moseley was a lawyer and businessman and a strong advocate of cooperative business ventures. He lived in a predominantly white section of town, but his law practice drew heavily on the black community. He was also chief counsel of the Olivet Baptist Church, Chicago's largest African American congregation.[23]

Leland, Moseley, and Jackson combined to form the Leland Giants Baseball and Amusement Association (LGBAA). Incorporated in 1907, the LGBAA was more than just a baseball team; it was also a summer resort, skating rink, and restaurant. In 1908, the black-owned newspaper *Broad Ax* carried an advertisement offering stock options to the public. The objective of the advertisement was to raise funds for the club's new ballpark at Sixty-ninth and Halstead. The language employed typified the race rhetoric and racial solidarity that black Chicagoans advocated during the Progressive Era. It asked, "Are You In Favor Of The Race Owning and Operating This Immense And Well Paying Plant, Where More Than 1,100 Persons Will Be Employed, between May and October each year, where you can come without fear and Enjoy The Life and Freedom of a citizen unmolested or annoyed? The Answer can only be effectively given by subscribing for stock in this Corporation."[24]

These "Race" men sought to establish an enterprise that would become a means of racial pride through self-help. The association also aided other institutions in the black community. It contributed annually to Provident Hospital, founded by Daniel Hale Williams, the country's best-known African American physician and one of the outstanding surgeons of his day. On August 26, 1910, the Leland Giants played a benefit game for the hospital at Comiskey Park. The LGBAA became a venture that offered jobs to the black community, even as Moseley, Leland, and Jackson were turning a profit.[25]

At the same time, Leland made his only attempt to organize a black professional league. On November 9, 1907, the *Indianapolis Freeman* reported that a movement was put forth to form the National Colored League of Professional Ball Clubs. The effort to form this league was a clear exposition of the cooperative business philosophy. Under the direction of Leland, Elwood C. Knox, editor of the *Freeman*, and Ran Butler, the owner of the Indianapolis ABC's, these promoters encouraged Race men in the leading midwestern and southern cities to form a stock company as a means of consolidation. The circuit was to be an eight team league with prospective cities to include Cincinnati, Cleveland, Louisville, Pittsburgh, Chicago, Indianapolis, Kansas City, Toledo, Detroit, Milwaukee, Memphis, Nashville, and Columbus, Ohio. In a series of meetings that took place from December 28, 1907, to January 25, 1908, the league directors elected officers and established guidelines for league entry. Leland was elected president and was the driving force behind the movement. For a club to be considered for admission it had to (1) be represented by a stock company fully organized and incorporated under state law; (2) secure a bond (the amount was not specified) determined by the league's board of directors; (3) pay $50 into the league treasury to cover the expenses for league operations; and (4) secure a suitable ballpark and have full support of the black press. In addition, a small percentage of the gate receipts from each city would be placed in the treasury. The season would run from May to September.[26]

Despite these organizers' efforts, the league died without throwing a pitch. Essentially, three factors led to its failure. First and foremost, there was a total lack of commitment by black baseball entrepreneurs in the aforementioned cities. According to the *Freeman*, only Chicago and Indianapolis made commitments to the enterprise. The *Freeman* also indicated that several black baseball magnates were totally against league formation, fearing it would damage their business. It appears that these black baseball entrepreneurs were reluctant to travel outside the regional format they had created for themselves. Prior to 1907, only the Cuban X Giants had ever made an extended barnstorming tour, and they were under white management. If, for example, clubs from Pittsburgh and Nashville were members of the league, it would increase the overhead expenses of the midwestern club to travel there. It would also create an unworkable format due to the majority of the prospective cities being in the Midwest.[27]

Finally, there was no clear-cut plan as to how this league would operate. In other words, there was no attempt to create a business system that would place the black game on a sound economic footing. Many of the proposals, including conditions for league entry, were only suggestions. Nothing was agreed upon that indicated how the league would function. Ultimately, the failure of the league injured Frank Leland's credibility with the LGBAA's leadership. Throughout the remainder of the LGBAA's brief history, Leland would operate primarily as a figurehead within the organization. His effort to regain control of his ball club resulted in dissension within the LGBAA's organizers that would cause the association to crumble at its foundation.

Internal Division and a Second Failed League

Internal division among the LGBAA organizers occurred because the multiple enterprises of the members of the association diverted their attention. This disharmony among the association's organizers was the direct result of several interacting influences: the Leland Giants emerging as the top touring team of the Midwest; Frank Leland's attempt to wrest control of the ball club away from Beauregard Moseley, and a formal ban on black traveling teams by Chicago's Park Owners Association. Although this internal dissension placed black baseball on shaky ground, it was instrumental in forming the structure of the black game in the Windy City in the Progressive Era.

The emergence of the Leland Giants as one of the country's top touring teams was due primarily to one man, Andrew "Rube" Foster. His emergence as their manager and booking agent marked the beginning of his dominance of midwestern black baseball. Foster was born in Calvert, Texas, in 1879, the son of a presiding elder of Calvert's Methodist Church. Devoutly religious, Foster neither drank nor allowed anyone to consume spirits in his household, although he was tolerant of it from others. Foster exhibited his organizational skills at a young age, operating a baseball team while in grade school. He left school in the eighth grade to pursue a career in baseball. By 1897, Foster was pitching for the Waco Yellow Jackets, a traveling team that toured Texas and the bordering states. In the spring of 1902, William S. Peters invited him to join his team, but as he sent no travel money the pitcher remained in Texas. Simultaneously, Leland had also invited Foster to join his club, initiating a stormy relationship between the two men. By mid-spring, Foster quit the Union Giants to join a white semipro team in Michigan. When its season ended, he headed east to play for the Cuban X Giants.[28]

From 1903 to 1906, Foster played for the Philadelphia Giants. Despite their success on the field, the Giants did not reap economic benefits for their exploits. As a result, Foster induced several of the players to jump their contracts at the end of the 1906 season. The player revolt led by Foster coincided with Leland's efforts to persuade the African American flame-thrower to manage his team. Foster accepted Leland's offer, and his first move was to release the players of the previous year despite Leland's opposition. It was evident that Foster wanted his own players, and he had just brought seven of them from the greatest team ever assembled. Next, due to Leland's failing health and his responsibilities as the newly elected Cook County Commissioner, Foster assumed the responsibilities of booking the team's games. From that time on, Foster established a business arrangement whereby gate receipts would be either divided in half or a substantial guarantee would be paid to attract the top teams.[29]

The Giants' revised managerial structure was integrated into the LGBAA's corporate configuration. On January 21, 1909, the association elected the following offiers: Frank Leland, president; Robert Jackson, vice president; Beauregard Moseley, secretary and treasurer; and Rube Foster, manager and captain of the team. With Leland, Moseley, and Jackson supervising the LGBAA's other businesses and Foster booking the baseball games, enough capital was generated to run an adequate operation. The LGBAA finished the year with a post-season series against the National League Chicago Cubs. Although the Cubs swept the Giants in three games, both the series and the revised organizational structure elevated the Leland Giants from the ranks of a stay-at-home to the Midwest's top touring team.[30]

From 1907 to 1910, Foster perfected the barnstorming schedule that would be his trademark for the next decade. On February 20, 1907, the *Indianapolis Freeman* reported that the Leland Giants would embark on a spring training tour. It marked the first time that a semiprofessional club that was both black owned and operated had accomplished this feat. Two years later, the *Freeman* reported that the Leland Giants had traveled 4,465 miles playing both black and white teams in Memphis, Birmingham, Fort Worth, Austin, San Antonio, Prairie View State, and Houston. The Leland Giants traveled in their own private Pullman car, as a means of upholding their reputation as an elite black independent club. In October 1910, after winning twenty straight games in the East and West, the Leland Giants made their first trip to Cuba. More important, the Lelands' trip to the Cuban island served as a means of promoting the LGBAA. Along with the American League Detroit Tigers, the Lelands played the top Cuban clubs including the Havannas—an aggregate of black stars that included John Henry Lloyd and Grant "Home Run" Johnson—and the Alemendares. While the Lelands won the majority of their games, they lost a tough series to the Alemendares.[31]

By 1909, the Leland Giants' success produced a conflict of interest among the team's management. With Moseley supervising the LGBAA's other businesses and Foster managing the ball club, Leland recognized his diminished role within the organization. As a result, he attempted to regain control of the Giants, but the association's investors thought it was in the corporation's best interests to retain Foster as manager. Therefore, in a hostile takeover, Moseley and Foster united to force Leland out. Foster's alliance with Moseley made the split inevitable. In 1910, Leland went to court to prevent Foster and Moseley using the name Leland Giants, but he was unsuccessful. Not only did Leland lose his team, but he lost his interests in the LGBAA's other businesses as well.[32]

In response to being forced out, Leland created in 1910 the Chicago Giants in partnership with Robert Jackson and A. H. Garrett. His goal was to make his Giants a top touring team to compete against the Leland Giants, and he also sought to have them play the top semipro clubs in the area. To accomplish this, Leland raided his old club for players, signing stars like Walter Ball and Pete Booker. Unfortunately for him the Park Owners Association thwarted his aspirations when it prohibited the scheduling of games between black traveling teams from outside the Chicago area. Its reason for this ban was that local patrons complained about the lack of contests being scheduled between some of the regional clubs. The *New York Age* speculated that the prohibition could have emerged as a result of top Cuban teams invading the area for the past two years. In addition, the Philadelphia Giants had also made a couple of barnstorming tours, playing both the top black and white semipro clubs in the Windy City. Race was assuredly an issue in the POA's decision. The POA believed that the rise of both the Leland and Chicago Giants to the status of touring teams, coupled with the arrival of Cuban clubs and the Philadelphia Giants, was a threat to its autonomy. Traveling teams touring the Windy City meant a big payday for both black and white semipro squads, but only clubs that had their own parks could enjoy this luxury. Consequently, both the POA and local teams with no park had a vested interest in keeping the black traveling teams out.[33]

The color ban on traveling teams appears to have directly impacted the Chicago Giants. To remain in the City League, the Giants' management had to refrain from scheduling games with both the black touring and traveling teams. The conservative Leland yielded to the demand. In 1911, his Giants did not touch the South, playing only a local schedule, but the following year, it dropped out of the Chicago City League. Three factors were instrumental in the Giants departure. First, Jackson left the club to pursue a successful career in politics. He was a significant investor in the enterprise, and his loss crippled the club. Second the absence of this capital made it difficult for Leland to compete against the Leland Giants, and the court settlement forced him to vacate Auburn Park. Finally Leland's failing health became a serious concern, and within two years he died at the age of forty-five. In 1913, the Chicago Giants disbanded; two years later, Joe Green, the club's shortstop, reorganized the team as a weekend enterprise, passing the hat to meet expenses.[34]

Moseley had higher aspirations in mind, and neither the POA's ban nor Leland's efforts to put his former club out of business hindered them. As early as 1909, the young black lawyer advocated the need for blacks to organize their own professional league. He also recognized that the continual territorial invasion and the raiding of player rosters were destructive forces and had to be eliminated. In addition, Moseley recognized that the color line drawn by the POA would also adversely impact the LGBAA's ability to generate revenue. But the proliferation of black teams from the South and Midwest made it feasible, in Moseley's view, to form a black professional league.[35]

In 1910, Moseley called together a group of black baseball men from throughout the Midwest and the South. The proposed league was more than just a response to the color line, it was another exposition of the doctrine of self-help. In his statement of purpose, Moseley indicated that blacks "are already forced out of the game from a national standpoint" and find it increasingly difficult to play white semiprofessional teams at the local level. This "presages the day when there will be [no opportunities for black baseball players], except the Negro come to his own rescue by organizing and patronizing the game successfully, which would of itself force recognition from white minor leagues to play us and share in the receipts." Moseley added, "let those who would serve the Race assist it in holding its back up . . . organizing an effort to secure . . . the best club of ball players possible."[36]

The prospective owners first met on December 30, 1910. Moseley was elected temporary chairman and Felix H. Payne of Kansas City temporary secretary. Eight cities were represented: Chicago, New Orleans, Mobile, Louisville, St. Louis, Columbus, Ohio, Kansas City, Missouri, and Kansas City, Kansas. Moseley devised a twenty-point plan explaining how the league should operate. Utilizing the cooperative business philosophy, Moseley suggested that eight race men in each city pool their resources and form a stock company. The league projected an operating capital of $2,500 with each club paying roughly $300. Half the league's umpires would be black and paid five dollars per game. A reserve list would be developed, and players who jumped their contracts would be banned from the league. Finally, an effort would be made to limit the league to one franchise per city.[37]

The league generated a lot of enthusiasm the following year, and rumors persisted of other cities joining the loop, but it still died stillborn. As in the previous organizational effort, there was an unwillingness of investors to come forth. At its inaugural meeting, only Chicago, New Orleans, and Kansas City, Kansas, were represented by investors, with the remaining five being represented by fans. Second, these entrepreneurs were not willing to follow the Leland Giants' lead in embarking on extended barnstorming tours. The majority of these clubs would not venture too far outside their established regions. Finally, migration had significantly expanded the black populations in midwestern cities, but it was still insufficient to create a market to establish both territorial regions and set population requirements for a prospective city for league entry. Even in Chicago, the black community was not large enough to support three teams—the Lelands, Chicago Giants, and Union Giants—not to mention becoming a viable territory in a league. It would have required maintaining the symbiotic business relationship with white semipro clubs, and the POA's ban on traveling teams made this problematic.

In 1911, Foster split with Moseley and formed the Chicago American Giants. It is not clear what led Foster to make a break with the LGBAA, but what is evident is that both the color ban and two attempts to form a league ending in failure were instrumental in him making this decision. The oversaturation of Chicago's black baseball market would become more of a factor when instead of having three teams vying for Chicago's black community's disposable income, now the were four: the American Giants, the Leland Giants, the Chicago Giants, and the Union Giants.

From Player-Manager to Dominant Promoter

Internal division within the LGBAA resulted in Rube Foster becoming an unpopular man in black Chicago. The actions of Leland organizing the Chicago Giants and Moseley forming a coalition of black business professionals were efforts to compete against Foster and put him out of business. The black press also took jabs at Foster, providing negative coverage and turning public opinion against him. In an effort to win over both the press and the black community, Foster made a series of moves that included forming a partnership with John Schorling, a white tavern owner; expanding his barnstorming tour both during the winter and the local season; reviving the East–West colored championship; and fostering good press and community relations as a means of changing his public image.

Following the break with Foster, Moseley organized a booster coalition from the black community. The Leland Giant Booster Club (LGBC) was an aggregate of black middle-class businessmen and professionals. For example, LGBC president, Jesse Bolling, was a restaurant owner who donated his Burlington Buffet as the club's official headquarters. T. W. Allen, the club's secretary, was a city inspector. Other members of the coalition included the editors of Chicago's two leading black newspapers, Robert Abbott of the Chicago *Defender* and Julius Taylor of the *Broad Ax*.[38]

The formation of the LGBC exemplified the cooperative business philosophy prevalent among the new leadership. The venture could serve as a means of promoting one another's businesses. One of the booster club's functions was to organize activities surrounding the Leland Giants' local season that had become ritualized in the prewar years. For example, at the opening of each season, the Giants had what was known as "Flag Raising Day." It was equivalent to throwing out the first ball on opening day of the major league baseball season. Another event the LGBC staged consisted of a touring car, known as the Red Devil, parading through the streets to the ballpark. But the booster club's main objective was to provide a united front against both Leland's Chicago Giants and Foster's American Giants.[39]

Despite the LGBC's enthusiasm, the venture failed, as it lacked the financial and political resources to be effective. This rather conservative coalition lacked allies in the local government. Although a black political machine was being organized at this time, it did not become instrumental in black community affairs until after World War I. By 1912, the LGBC ceased to exist.[40]

Moseley had other obstacles confronting him. He was engaged in several business ventures at once besides organizing a baseball league and booking games for the Lelands, and he probably did not delegate authority to booster club members or have an adequate management team to supervise his many operations. While Moseley attempted to reach the black patrons, his facilities were located outside the black belt, where increased white hostility made venturing unpleasant for Chicago's African Americans. The African American working class could not afford these amusements and the middle class was not large enough to sustain them. To make matters worse, Moseley had just moved into and renovated the ballpark on Sixty-ninth and Halsted, no doubt at large expense. The obstacles were more than the LGBAA could bear. By 1912, the skating rink closed for good and the Leland Giants were relegated to a local club.[41]

While the LGBAA was in a state of decline, Foster still faced opposition from the black press. Julius Taylor was disgusted by the baseball
situation. In a 1912 editorial he expressed his disenchantment with the
unwillingness of blacks to organize themselves as well as commit to this
venture. The *Broad Ax* editor further noted that the Leland Giants' success proved to be its misfortune. Rivalry and a desire for control led to
fragmentation in an effort to "compete for patronage and prowess of the
Leland Giants." The issue that most upset Taylor was that the revenues
baseball generated went into the coffers of white men. That same year,
the *Defender* began to take jabs at Foster because it was also upset over
the revenue "going over to the other race." The black newspaper insisted
that this was "why so many are pulling against Rube." In addition, it was
critical of the lack of support the American Giants gave black institutions
in the community, primarily the *Chicago Defender*.[42]

In spite of this opposition, Foster made a series of moves that enabled
his rise as dominant promoter. First was his partnership with John M.
Schorling. Schorling had operated a sandlot club in Chicago for several
years. He leased the grounds of the old White Sox park on Thirty-ninth
and Shields after the American League team moved into their new stadium. The White Sox had torn down the old grandstand, and Schorling
built a new one with a seating capacity of 9,000. He approached Foster
with an offer of a partnership. Foster now had a ballpark to operate in
and Schorling had the best booking agent and field manager outside of
organized baseball. Over the next fifteen years they became the best
management team at the semipro level.[43]

Several factors led to Foster's success. Unlike the LGBAA, whose
facilities were outside the black belt, the Chicago American Giants' park
was accessible to the majority of the black population. The better location
facilitated gate receipts instrumental to the attraction of the top touring
and traveling teams to the Midwest. More significantly, the relocation
allowed Foster to accomplish what Moseley failed to achieve: corner
the black market. Foster also focused his promotion solely on baseball,
and he knew everything about the game. His objective was to present
the best product possible to Chicago's black community, which meant
securing the best talent available and developing a winning reputation. To
achieve such standards, a management team committed to baseball had
to be in place. Schorling had prior baseball experience and shared Foster's
objectives. His involvement was an unpopular decision as it required that
Foster go outside the black community to achieve his goals.

Even more significant, Foster's business approach became the model
for future black baseball entrepreneurs to emulate. He was a businessman first and a race man second. At no time did Foster show any indica-

tions of severing any business relations with white semipros; in fact he attempted to strengthen them. Yet because these business connections increased his profits, Foster could help serve Chicago's black community by conducting several benefit games to raise funds for civic institutions. In essence, Foster had achieved the objectives spelled out in the compilation of ideologies commonly attributed to Booker T. Washington, building a segregated enterprise within the framework of a national economy. In other words, the segregated enterprise—the Chicago American Giants—through the creation of annual booking arrangements with both black and white semipros, operated successfully within the framework of the national economy–semiprofessional baseball.

From 1912 to 1915, Foster established a barnstorming tour on the West Coast during the winter months, and the Chicago American Giants became the first black semipro team to regularly play weekly games. The American Giants played in the California Winter League, a conglomerate of teams comprising former and current major and minor league players and teams from the Pacific Coast, Southern, and Northwest leagues. The American Giants won the California League Championship in its first season. On July 5, 1913, the *Defender* reported that the American Giants celebrated winning the championship with a parade, unfurling a banner and displaying their new uniforms. In addition, Foster's alliance with Schorling enabled him to schedule games with white semipro teams during the week. Foster had now established the structure that ensured a successful operation of a black semiprofessional team.[44]

Foster's work on reviving the East–West Colored Championship was also instrumental to his success. On July 5, 1913, the *Defender* reported an upcoming championship series between the Chicago American Giants and the Lincoln Giants of New York. A series of thirteen games was scheduled in Chicago and New York. After nine games the series was tied at four victories apiece and one tie. But the Lincoln Giants won the final four games in New York earning the right to be crowned "World's Colored Champions." Although Foster's American Giants had lost the series, he had won the hearts and minds of Chicago's black community.[45]

Finally, Foster and Schorling had learned their lesson well regarding press and community relations. In the prewar years they set a precedent that became a constant throughout the war years. In addition to raising funds for civic institutions, Schorling donated the use of the ballpark for local community activities, like the Chicago Church League championship game. Foster also developed positive press relations. He began by granting an interview with the *Defender* providing readers with insights about his early career in baseball. Throughout the war years, he granted many interviews and become a local patron as well.[46]

The California Winter League championship and the East–West colored championship brought Foster accolades from a prominent member of Chicago's black middle class and on the sport pages of the *Defender*. Julius Avendorph, the "Ward McAllister of the South Side," was an assistant to the president of the Pullman company. He became "personally acquainted with more millionaires than any other colored man in Chicago." From 1886 up until 1910, Avendorph was considered "Chicago's undisputed social leader." Writing in the *Defender* on April 5, 1913, Avendorph extolled the American Giants for "their high class baseball playing . . . [and] for their gentlemanly conduct on the ball field." Avendorph added that the American Giants were "an example that lots of white clubs can take pattern from." When some of Chicago's black patrons berated Foster for raising his ticket prices, the *Defender* came to his defense for the first time. Chicago's black fans would "have to pay for quality and they [the fans] have certainly got their money's worth lately, referring to the colored championship. Moreover, the *Defender* reminded its readers that many of the Windy City's black fans "never knew what it was to see a game among those of their race unless forced to go to 79th Street. . . . Now it is a stone's throw from their homes."[47]

Epilogue

Rube Foster's American Giants operated as a segregated enterprise while maintaining a symbiotic business relationship with white semi-professional teams. He sustained a booking pattern with the top black and white semipros on a consistent basis. In spite of the obstacles that confronted him, Foster had managed to integrate his operation within a segregated market and a national one. Because of the press coverage in Chicago and Indianapolis, Foster's American Giants had become a source of racial pride and solidarity among African American people in the Midwest.

Despite Foster's rise as a dominant promoter, Chicago's market was still a saturated one. Joe Green continued to operate the Chicago Giants, while William S. Peters managed the Union Giants until 1923. Robert Gilkerson, a former ballplayer, assumed control of the club and renamed it Gilkerson's Union Giants. But Green, Peters, and Gilkerson were not as ambitious as Foster, choosing to remain weekend operators and passing the hat to cover expenses. During the years of the Great Migration, Foster would absorb these clubs under his booking control, marking the beginning of his autonomy in the Midwest. In addition, Foster would make rental agreements with major league owners, like Frank Navin in

Detroit, and would finance clubs like the Detroit Stars, to gain controlling interest. This midwestern alliance would form the foundation for the Negro National League in 1920. More importantly, at the community level, Foster accomplished what previous black baseball entrepreneurs sought to achieve in creating an institution that served as a source of racial pride and solidarity through self-help.[48]

Notes

"Black Entrepreneurship in the National Pastime: The Rise of Semiprofessional Baseball in Black Chicago, 1890–1915" by Michael Lomax, published by the *Journal of Sport History* 25 (1998): 43–64. Copyright by the 1998 North American Society of Sport History and Michael Lomax. Reprinted with permission.

1. General histories on black baseball from the 1980s and 1990s include Sol White, *History of Colored Base Ball, with Other Documents on the Early Black Game 1886–1936* (Lincoln: University of Nebraska Press, 1995); Richard Bak, *Turkey Stearnes and the Detroit Stars: The Negro Leagues in Detroit, 1919–1933* (Detroit: Wayne State University Press, 1994); Phil Dixon and Patrick J. Hannigan, *The Negro Baseball Leagues 1867–1955: A Photographic History* (Mattituck, NY: Ameron House, 1992); Janet Bruce, *Kansas City Monarchs: Champions of Black Baseball* (Lawrence: University of Kansas Press, 1985); Donn Rogosin, *Invisible Men: Life in Baseball's Negro Leagues* (New York: Atheneum, 1983); Linda Zeimer, "Chicago's Negro Leagues," *Chicago History* 23 (Winter 1994–1995): 36–51. The most comprehensive community study examining black baseball is Rob Ruck's *Sandlot Seasons: Sport in Black Pittsburgh* (Urbana: University of Illinois Press, 1987). Neil Lanctot provides an excellent account on the business practices of early black baseball entrepreneurs, as well as the origins of white semiprofessional baseball in *Fair Dealing and Clean Playing: The Hilldale Club and the Development of Black Professional Baseball, 1920–1932* (1994, rep., Syracuse: Syracuse University Press, 2007). On the origins of white semiprofessional baseball, see also Harold Seymour, *Baseball: The People's Game* (New York: Oxford University Press, 1990). For a discussion of where the recent works on black baseball's place in the broader baseball history, see Larry R. Gerlach, "Not Quite Ready for Prime Time: Baseball History, 1983–1993," *Journal of Sport History* 21 (1994): 121–29.

2. For an account on the notion of operating a segregated enterprise within the fabric of a national economy, see Vishnu V. Oak, *The Negro's Adventure in General Business* (Yellow Springs, OH: Antioch Press, 1949).

3. *Abstract of the Eleventh Census: 1890* (Washington, DC: Government Printing Office, 1894), 34; *Abstract of the Twelfth Census of the United States* (Washington, DC: Government Printing Office, 1902), 103–4; *Thirteenth Census of the United States: Taken in the Year 1910* (Washington, DC: Government Printing Office, 1913), 95; Allan H. Spear, *Black Chicago: The Making of a Negro Ghetto* (Chicago: University of Chicago Press, 1967), 11–27; Thomas L. Philpott, *The Slum and the Ghetto: Neighborhood Deterioration and Middle Class Reform, Chicago 1880–1930* (New York: Oxford University Press, 1978), 119, 147–48.

4. Spear, *Black Chicago*, 11–17.

5. David M. Katzman, *Before the Ghetto: Black Detroit in the Nineteenth Cen-*

tury (Urbana: University of Illinois Press, 1973), 67–80; Spear, *Black Chicago*, 91–110; James R. Grossman, *Land of Hope: Chicago, Black Southerners, and the Great Migration* (Chicago: University of Chicago Press, 1989), 127.

6. Spear, *Black Chicago*, 91–110; Grossman, *Land of Hope*, 127; Herbert S. Nelli, *Italians in Chicago 1880–1930: A Study in Ethnic Mobility* (New York: Oxford University Press, 1970), 23–25.

7. On Illinois state law and treatment of African Americans outside the black belt, see Spear, *Black Chicago*, 41–42.

8. The rise of the new black leadership illustrates the diverse, and often divisive, class structure at the turn of the century. Between 1865 and 1900, black leaders' primary focus was on securing equal rights for African Americans. They were absorbed in campaigns to secure the ballot, assure an integrated school system, pass and then broaden the Civil Rights Act, and finally bring suits under the act. Any attempt to organize a separate black institution was met with stiff opposition from those who regarded it as a form of self-segregation. One reason why the new black leadership was attracted to recreation and amusement enterprises was the funds required to start such an endeavor were both short and long term in character. In other words, they did not require a substantial financial investment. See Abram L. Harris, *The Negro As Capitalist: A Study of Banking and Business among American Negroes* (Philadelphia: American Academy of Political and Social Service, 1936), 53–56. For accounts on black middle class formation, see E. Franklin Frazier, *Black Bourgeoisie* (Glencoe, IL: Free Press, 1957); Bart Landry, *The New Black Middle Class (*Berkeley: University of California Press, 1987). For accounts on the old black leadership in Chicago, see Spear, *Black Chicago*, 51–70; Grossman, *Land of Hope*, 123–60.

9. Earl Ofari, *The Myth of Black Capitalism* (New York: Monthly Review Press, 1970), 11–48. For the cooperative business philosophy as an outgrowth of the ideology of self-help, see Louis Harlan, *Booker T. Washington: The Making of a Black Leader* (New York: Oxford University Press, 1972), 204–71. For a detailed discussion on the Wabash Avenue YMCA, see Spear, *Black Chicago*, 100–101.

10. Seymour, *Baseball*, 258–75.

11. For an account on the early business practices of professional baseball, see Gerald W. Scully, *The Business of Major League Baseball* (Chicago: University of Chicago Press, 1989), 1–12. In the 1880s, the Cuban Giants attracted clubs from either National League or American Association with a substantial guarantee. See for example, "The Browns Strike," *Sporting Life*, September 21, 1887, 4.

12. Seymour, *Baseball*, 265–70.

13. For an account on Chicago's sophisticated park system, see Michael P. McCarthy, "Politics and the Parks: Chicago Businessmen and the Recreation Movement," *Journal of Illinois State Historical Society* 65 (1972): 158–72; see also Steven A. Riess, *City Games: The Evolution of American Urban Society and the Rise of Sports* (Urbana: University of Illinois Press, 1989), 128–39.

14. "No Color Line," *Indianapolis Freeman*, September 21, 1907, 7; "Park Owners Association," *Chicago Defender* June 4, 1910, 4.

15. Wilson Jeremiah Moses, *The Golden Age of Black Nationalism 1850–1925* (Hamden, CT: Archon Books, 1978), 83–102. On the gospel of work and wealth, see Samuel R. Spencer, *Booker T Washington and the Negro's Place in America* (Boston: Little, Brown, 1955), 108–24.

16. James A. Riley, *The Biographical Encyclopedia of the Negro Baseball Leagues* (New York: Carroll & Graf, 1994), 474–75; Dixon and Hannigan, *Ne-*

gro Baseball, 96–97; Robert Peterson, *Only the Ball Was White: A History of Legendary Black Players and All-Black Professional Teams* (Englewood Cliffs, NJ: Prentice-Hall, 1970), 63–64; White, *History,* 29; "Frank Leland Laid to Rest, *Defender,* November 21, 1914, 5; "The Chicago Giants Base Ball Club," *Defender,* January 22, 1910, 1.

17. The estimated attendance figures for black baseball was derived from examining several newspaper accounts from both the *Broad Ax* and the *Defender* from 1907 to 1915. White, *History,* 26. See, for example, "Leland Giants Making a Record," *Freeman,* August 1, 1908, 7; "Lelands," *Freeman,* August 3, 1909, 4; "The Chicago Giants Show Class," *Defender,* October 29, 1910, 3.

18. While the notion of a colored championship could be traced back to the Philadelphia Pythians of the late 1860s, this series as a commercial endeavor coincided with the rise of black semiprofessional teams in the 1880s. For a detailed account on this phenomenon, see Michael E. Lomax, "Black Baseball, Black Community, Black Entrepreneurs: The History of the Negro National and Eastern Colored Leagues, 1880–1930," (Ph.D. diss., Ohio State University, 1996), 68–77.

19. It should be noted that in 1896 the ballplayers with the Cuban Giants broke with John M. Bright and signed with Edward B. Lamarant and became the Cuban X Giants. Bright continued to operate a ball club, and as a means of averting confusion, renamed it the Genuine Cuban Giants. For an account on the origins of the Page Fence Giants, see Thomas Powers, "The Page Fence Giants Play Ball," *Chronicle: The Quarterly Magazine of the Historical Society of Michigan* 19 (Spring 1983): 14–18. For accounts regarding the origins of the Columbia Giants, see White, *History,* 28–31, 38–40; Dixon and Hannigan, *Negro Baseball,* 96–97. Patterson's background is in Riley, *Encyclopedia,* 609–10.

20. White, *History,* 28–31, 38–40. White had stated that the Unions and the Columbia Giants were at "loggerheads" with each other.

21. Ibid., 38; Lanctot, *Fair Dealing,* 32.

22. Zeimer, "Chicago's Negro Leagues," 37; White, *History,* 39; Dixon and Hannigan, *Negro Baseball,* 97.

23. Harold F. Gosnell, *Negro Politicians: The Rise of Negro Politics in Chicago* (Chicago: University of Chicago Press, 1935), 67–68; "Major General R. R. Jackson, Assistant Supt. Armour Station Financial Secretary Appomattox Club," *Broad Ax,* December 27, 1902, 1; "Col. B. F. Moseley," *Broad Ax,* March 30, 1901, 1; "Col. Beauregard F. Moseley, Lawyer, Orator, and Property Holder," *Broad Ax,* December 29, 1906, 1, 5.

24. "Opening of the Chateau de la Plaisance," *Broad Ax,* November 2, 1907, 1; "The Chateau de la Plaisance," *Broad Ax,* November 16, 1907, 1. For the advertisement offering stock options to the public, see any issue of the *Broad Ax* in 1908. For a discussion on race rhetoric and racial solidarity advocated during the Progressive Era, see Moses, *The Golden Age,* 83–102.

25. For their yearly contributions to Provident Hospital, see "Honor to Whom Honor Is Due," *Defender,* May 14, 1910, 4; for the benefit game for the hospital, see "Giants Take Benefit Game," *Defender,* August 27, 1910, 5.

26. "A National League of Professional Negro Baseball Clubs for Next Season," *Freeman,* November 9, 1907, 6; "Growing Interest Taken in Proposed League," *Freeman,* November 16, 1907, 6; "To Organize Colored League," *Freeman,* November 23, 1907, 6; "League Meeting a Successful One," *Freeman,* December 28, 1907, 6; "A Successful Meeting Is Sighted," *Freeman,* January 25, 1908, 6.

27. While the evidence is limited, one newspaper account suggests that William S. Peters attempted to block league formation by building a park "in the colored center of the population on the South Side, which would affect the Leland Giants materially." See "Make War on Leland Giants," *Freeman*, February 1, 1908, 6. For an account regarding club owners against league formation, see "League Does Not Fear Outlaws," *Freeman*, December 28, 1907, 6; "An Understanding about the League," *Freeman*, February 15, 1908, 6.

28. "A Great Historical Account of a Great Game of Ball," *Freeman*, September 14, 1907, 6; "Baseball's Greatest Figure Dead," *Defender*, December 13, 1930, 1, 14; John B. Holway, *Blackball Stars: Negro League Pioneers* (New York: Carroll & Graf, 1988), 9–10; Charles E. Whitehead, *A Man and His Diamonds: A Story of the Great Andrew (Rube) Foster* (New York: Vantage Press, 1980), 3, 18–19; Peterson, *Only the Ball*, 104–5; George E. Mason, "Rube Foster Chats about His Career," *Defender*, February 20, 1915, 10.

29. Mason, "Rube Foster," 10; Holway, *Blackball Stars*, 13; Whitehead, *A Man*, 22–23; Peterson, *Only the Ball*, 107–8.

30. "Chateau Rink Notes," *Broad Ax*, January 30, 1909, 2. Cubs series in Zeimer, "Chicago's Negro Leagues," 39. In the following years Foster would issue challenges for post-season series with the Cubs; none were ever accepted. See for example, "Rube Foster Challenges the Cubs," *Defender*, October 18, 1913, 8.

31. "Champion Leland Giants to Go South for Spring Training," *Freeman*, February 20, 1907, 7; "Leland Giants Complete a Successful Southern Trip," *Freeman*, May 15, 1909, 7; "Chateau Rink Notes," *Broad Ax*, October 8, 1910, 2; "Leland Giants to Play Baseball in Cuba," *Defender* October 8, 1910, 3; Lester Walton, "Baseball Flourishing in Cuba," *New York Age*, December 8, 1910, 6.

32. Andrew Foster, "Negro Base Ball," *Freeman*, December 23, 1911, 16; Peterson, Only the Ball, 108; "Frank C. Leland Enjoined from Using the Name Leland Giants," *Broad Ax*, April 23, 1910, 2.

33. In 1906, the National Association of Colored Professional Base Ball Clubs was formed. This association served as means for eastern black clubs, primarily from New York, to play Chicago City League clubs. In other words, this association formalized scheduling commitments between eastern and western black clubs, while at the same time curb the destructive practice of player raiding. It was through this organization that Cuban clubs from Gotham and the Philadelphia Giants played in Chicago. For a discussion regarding this organization see Lomax, "Black Baseball," 207–51. "The Chicago Giants Baseball Club," *Defender*, January 22, 1910, 1; Jack Pot, "Bars Alien Colored Clubs," *Defender*, July 23, 1910, 3; "Fans Objects to Color Line," *Defender*, July 23, 1910, 1; Lester Walton, "Colored Teams Barred in Chicago," *New York Age*, July 21, 1910, 6; for the barnstorming tours of the Philadelphia Giants to the Midwest, see "ABC'S Easy for Giants," *Freeman*, August 1, 1908, 7; Lester Walton, "Philadelphia Giants Defeat Leland Giants," *New York Age*, August 19, 1909, 6; idem., "Philadelphia Giants Win in Tenth," *New York Age*, June 30, 1910, 6.

34. Lester Walton, "No Colored Team in Chicago League," *New York Age*, April 18, 1912, 6; "Frank Leland Laid to Rest," *Defender*, November 21, 1914, 5. For Leland vacating Auburn Park, see "The Chicago Giants in Their New Home," *Defender*, June 25, 1910, 1.

35. For Moseley's efforts to form a black professional league, see "Attorney B. F. Moseley Favors the Formation of National Negro Baseball League," *Broad Ax*,

November 26, 1910, 2; "Call for a Conference for Persons Interested in the Formation of a National Negro Baseball League," *Broad Ax*, December 17, 1910, 2.

36. "Big Negro National Baseball League Formed," *Defender*, December 31,
1910, 1; "Big Negro National Baseball League Formed," *Broad Ax*, December 31,
1910, 1; "A Baseball Appeal of a Worthy Undertaking by a Worthy Men; Read and
Respond," *Broad Ax*, January 21, 1911, 2.

37. Ibid.

38. For the activities and membership of the booster coalition, see any issue
in either the *Defender* or the *Broad Ax* from May to June 1911.

39. "Diamond Dust," *Defender*, May 20, 1911, 4; "'Boosters' Ukase from the
President," *Defender*, May 27, 1911, 4.

40. For a discussion of black Chicago's political situation in the prewar years,
see Gosnell, *Negro Politicians*, 65–67, 81–83; see also Spear, *Black Chicago*,
118–26.

41. For the closing of the skating rink, see "The Chateau Rink," *Defender* Feb-
ruary 25, 1911, 3. The Leland Giants moved into the ballpark on Sixty-ninth and
Halstead in 1910. See "Moseley's Leland Giants to Have New Park," *Defender*,
March 12, 1910, 1.

42. "Baseball," *Broad Ax*, May 18, 1912, 1; "Here and There," *Defender*, July
12, 1913, 5; "Sporting," *Defender*, August 2, 1913, 3.

43. Peterson, *Only the Ball*, 108.

44. "Rube Foster's Review on Baseball," *Freeman*, December 28, 1912, 7; Frank
Young, "Local Sports," *Defender*, March 22, 1913, 3; idem., "American Giants
Lose," *Defender*, July 5, 1913, 8. As the *Defender* grew, the American Giants
received better coverage.

45. "American Giants Lose," 8; "Sporting," *Defender*, August 9, 1913, 7; Lester
Walton, "American Giants in New York," *New York Age*, July 10, 1913, 6; idem.,
"Lincoln Win Series," *New York Age*, July 24, 1913, 6.

46. "Benefit for the Old Folks Home," *Defender*, August 16, 1913, 8; Mason,
"Foster Chats about his Career," 10.

47. For Julius Avendorph's background, see Spear, *Black Chicago*, 65–66; Julius
Avendorph, "Rube Foster and His American Giants," *Defender*, April 5, 1913, 7;
"Here and There," *Defender*, August 9, 1913, 7.

48. For an account on Rube Foster's midwestern alliance during the years of
the Great Migration, see Lomax, "Black Baseball," 290–325.

In 1919 the Chicago White Sox lost the World Series in eight games to the Cincinnati Reds. There was some speculation at the time that the highly favored American Leaguers had not played their best. There had been rumors in the past of fixed games, but few people took it seriously. What big leaguer would not play his best? Baseball was motherhood, apple pie, and the Model T all rolled up in one. Charles Comiskey responded to the negative rumors by offering $10,000 to anyone who could prove the series had been fixed, but no one came forward. Then late in the 1920 season, a Chicago Cubs game was said to have been prearranged by the nefarious Hal Chase, the Cubs' first baseman. This led to a grand jury investigation, which broadened its scope to consider the 1919 World Series. Three players were called to testify before the grand jury: pitchers Eddie Cicotte and Lefty Williams and left fielder Joe Jackson. They were advised by Comiskey's attorney Alfred Austrian to speak freely to the grand jury, but he neglected to recommend they seek immunity beforehand. While Cicotte and Williams played a prominent role in the fix, losing all five games between them, Jackson batted .375 in the series. No one has ever claimed that Jackson actively participated in the fix, although he did accept $5,000 in the course of the affair.

The Black Sox scandal, coming on the heels of the devastation of World War I, shook Americans' idealistic beliefs in their own social and moral superiority. Children had been brought up with the belief that the "national game" exemplified all that was good about America. Baseball players were idolized as heroes, but the scandal threatened that stature. Baseball soon had a new hero in Babe Ruth, however, and he changed the way the game was played with his powerful home runs. The Black Sox represented the old "scientific game" of hit and run, bunts, and stolen bases to manufacture runs. Babe Ruth, the great new prowess hero, scored runs with one swing of the bat and his excessive lifestyle ushered in a new celebrity culture. The Black Sox scandal marked the end of innocence in America.

6 News, Narratives, and the Black Sox Scandal
History's First Draft

DANIEL A. NATHAN

Hugh Fullerton and Harbingers of Scandal

In October 9, 1919, shortly after the White Sox outfielder Joe Jackson grounded out to the Reds second baseman Morrie Rath to end the World Series, Hugh Fullerton—a diligent, inquisitive, widely respected reporter—set about making his deadline for the *Chicago Herald and Examiner*. First, however, Fullerton apparently met briefly with the White Sox owner, Charles A. Comiskey, and the White Sox manager, William "Kid" Gleason, in Comiskey's office. "Some years before," writes Eliot Asinof in *Eight Men Out: The Black Sox and the 1919 World Series* (1963), "Comiskey had given Fullerton his first job and he felt a great loyalty to him. So it was not just to get a story that he went to the Old Roman's office after the final game: he wanted to share Comiskey's grief."[1] Fullerton had predicted that the White Sox would beat the Reds, five games to three; that he was wrong was no doubt irksome, since he had a reputation as a knowledgeable sports prognosticator. Not long after he had made his prediction, but before the games began, Fullerton and his fellow scribes heard rumors that the series was fixed. Agitated and fearful, Fullerton enlisted the assistance of the former New York Giants pitching great Christy Mathewson, who was covering the series for the *New York World*. "They arranged to sit together in the press box and go over every doubtful play," notes Asinof. "And just for the record, Fullerton decided he would pencil a circle on his score card around every play that was really suspect."[2] By the end of the series, Fullerton had idenified seven question-able plays. It is unclear what exactly was said in Comiskey's office that October afternoon. The following day Fullerton warned in his column: "There will be a great deal written and talked about this world's series. There will be a lot of inside stuff that never will be printed, but the truth will remain that the team which was the hardest working, which fought hardest, and which stuck together to the end won. The team which ex-celled in mechanical skill, which had the ability, individually, to win, was beaten." Superb teamwork and effort had overcome the odds (which were unusually volatile just before the series began) and a seemingly superior opponent. The White Sox played so poorly, Fullerton wrote, "that an evil minded person might believe the stories that have been circulated during the series. The fact is that this series was lost in the first game, and lost through over confidence. Forget the suspicious and evil minded yarns that may be circulated." The Reds were not really the better team, Fullerton stressed, but "they play ball together, fight together and hustle together, and remember that a flivver that keeps running beats a Rolls Royce that is missing several cylinders." Despite these attempts to explain the Reds' victory, Fullerton did hint that something was amiss with the series. "Yesterday's game in all probability is the last that ever will be played in any world's series," wrote Fullerton cryptically. "If the club owners and those who have the interests of the game at heart have listened during this series they will call off the annual inter-league contests." Finally, Fullerton assured his readers that, despite a strong nucleus, the White Sox would field a significantly different team in 1920: "There are seven men on the team who will not be there when the gong sounds next Spring and some of them will not be in either major league." Fullerton did not elaborate or explain, but added that the "unbeaten faction of the beaten White Sox did not quit."[3] Purposefully oblique, Fullerton stopped short of suggesting that another faction had conspired to lose the series.

Months passed, the baseball establishment did not take Fullerton's warnings seriously, and nothing was done to quell the rumors. Fullerton persisted.[4] He wrote an impassioned series of articles charging that Major League Baseball was in the throes of a crisis. Unable to convince the *Chicago Herald and Examiner* to publish his articles—they were apparently deemed too risky to publish, in part due to libel laws and in part because upending baseball's image as a hallowed national institution might hinder the sale of newspapers—Fullerton eventually convinced editors at Joseph Pulitzer's *New York Evening World* to run them. On December 15, as the baseball magnates conducted their winter meetings, page three of the *New York Evening World* blared: "Is Big League Baseball Being Run for Gamblers, with the Players in the Deal?" Fullerton declared:

Professional baseball has reached a crisis. The major leagues, both owners and players, are on trial. Charges of crookedness among the owners, accusations of cheating, of tampering with each other's teams, with attempting to syndicate and control baseball, are bandied about openly. Charges that gamblers have succeeded in bribing ballplayers, that games have been bought and sold, that players are in the pay of professional gamblers and that even the World's Series was tampered with are made without attempt at refutation by the men who have their fortunes invested in baseball.

Fullerton put the matter bluntly: "The time has come for straight talk. How can club owners expect writers, editors and fans to have any faith in them or their game if they make no effort to clean up the scandal?" Although he noted that numerous problems plagued professional baseball, Fullerton maintained that the "most serious assaults on the good name of the game have been made during and since the World's Series between the Reds and the White Sox. In Chicago, St. Louis and other cities the stories have been discussed, names used, alleged facts stated until half the people believe there was something wrong with the series." Certainly Fullerton took such talk seriously. He noted that the "public has for years had little faith and much disgust in the officials and club owners of the major league clubs. But never before have players been so freely charged with cheating." Rather than lend credence to the allegations of malfeasance on the part of the ballplayers, Fullerton argued that the "fault for this condition lies primarily with the owners. Their commercialism is directly responsible for the same spirit among the athletes and their failure to punish even the appearance of evil has led to the present situation, for the entire scandal could have been prevented and the future of the game made safe by drastic action in the Hal Chase case."[5] (In 1918, Chase, a talented but notoriously corrupt first baseman, was suspended for allegedly betting on a game and attempting to bribe a teammate. During the off-season, National League president John Heydler acquitted and reinstated Chase due to a lack of evidence.)[6]

Careful not to directly accuse anyone of wrongdoing, Fullerton wrote that others had charged "that several members of the Chicago White Sox team entered into a conspiracy with certain gamblers to throw the series. I have steadfastly refused to believe this possible. Some of the men whose names are used are my friends and men I would trust anywhere, yet the story is told openly, with so much circumstantial evidence and with so many names, places and dates, that one is bewildered." Bewildered though he may have been, Fullerton concluded quite reasonably: "If these men are guilty, they should be expelled as Patrick expelled the snakes and [William] Hulbert [the former president of the National

League] expelled the baseball crooks of years ago. If they are innocent, they should be allowed to prove it, and the persons who are responsible for the charges should be driven out of the sport forever."[7] Despite Fullerton's challenge and despite how "widely read" were the articles, notes the historian David Q. Voigt, the pieces "were discounted as improbable muckraking. One critic objected that Fullerton was 'always scoffing at the honesty of an institution, no matter how sacred.'"[8] This response is relatively mild compared with how some people reacted to Fullerton's articles. In fact, his stories provoked a firestorm of rebuttals from the baseball establishment.[9]

In retrospect, it is clear that no one wrote more prescient and influential articles about the 1919 World Series and the Black Sox scandal than Hugh Fullerton. For one thing, he was correct: something was amiss with the World Series and a great deal would be written about it, probably more than he could have imagined. Furthermore, Fullerton's stories remind us that it matters who writes our news. More than just observers or go-betweens for a reading public or cogs in the bureaucracy that manufactures news, reporters are often implicated—sometimes subtly, sometimes more explicitly—in the construction of the events they cover. Like other storytellers, reporters are often an integral part of the narratives they tell. In addition, a reporter's authority frequently endures and inevitably shapes the ways in which events are later understood. In this way reporters are actively involved in the production of history. As one critic argues: "The popular historians of baseball are the journalists, figures of such power that it can be said, fairly, that the history of baseball is more their story than the story of those who played the game."[10] If this is the case, perhaps Fullerton deserves even more credit than he is usually given for his role in exposing the Big Fix. Not only did Fullerton's stories anticipate the game-fixing revelations—indeed, his stories helped bring the conspiracy to the public—but they also position us to examine how the event was narrated by the media at the time. His stories began the process of crafting the scandal as a tragic morality play (as opposed to a comedy or an inconsequential human interest story), as an unfolding drama that mattered to much of the nation. Regardless of how improbable they may have seemed to some people, Fullerton's stories were auspicious harbingers of things to come.[11]

Seeing the Scandal

In many ways the Black Sox scandal provides us with a fine example of an ideal news story, for it combined "celebrity with scandal in an action that can be simply stated but provides the possibility of endless speculation."[12] The World Series game-fixing affair had all of the above, which explains why from late September 1920 to early August 1921 millions of words were written about it in newspapers all over the country. Yet when reports about the alleged game fixing first broke in late September 1920, people did not actually need to read the stories to understand its importance: they could immediately see its significance. In the beginning, accounts of the thrown games and the clandestine meetings between the ballplayers and gamblers were not relegated to the sports section—they were printed on the front page, often in conjunction with bold, banner headlines. For approximately a week in late September and early October, the size of the headlines—one of the most obvious ways the hierarchy of news is expressed—proclaimed the event's significance, at least within the context of the newspaper. There is, of course, some truth to the old adage that "a headline is not an act of journalism, it is an act of marketing."[13] But that does not really matter here. What is important is that daily newspapers made it clear—visually—that the baseball scandal mattered.

One way this was conveyed was by giving the game-fixing stories the most prominent space in the newspaper. On September 29, 1920, the day after Cicotte and Jackson testified before the Cook County grand jury, many newspapers used headline sizes usually reserved for the outbreak of war or the assassination of a prominent political leader. (In this way the press coverage of the World Series scandal can be viewed as part of a continuum of spectacular coverage rather than as a singular phenomenon.) The *New York Times*, "the closest thing America had to a national newspaper," proclaimed across its three far-right columns: "EIGHT WHITE SOX PLAYERS ARE INDICTED ON CHARGE OF FIXING 1919 WORLD SERIES; CICOTTE GOT $10,000 AND JACKSON $5,000."[14] That same day, the *New York Tribune* ran the following headline across the right half of its front page: "EIGHT WHITE SOX ARE INDICTED; CICOTTE AND JACKSON CONFESS GAMBLERS PAID THEM $15,000." The *New York World*, which Joseph Pulitzer had made hugely successful, printed "CICOTTE AND JACKSON BARE SALE OF GAMES; 8 WHITE SOX INDICTED" on top of its two far-right columns. Not to be outdone, the upstart *New York Daily News*, which proclaimed itself to be "New York's Picture Newspaper," ran the headline "EDDIE CICOTTE ADMITS BRIBE" all the way across its front page; it also printed individual photographs of the eight implicated ballplayers.

Of course, the scandal was big news in places besides New York City. The *Boston Daily Globe* provided photographs of the "Eight Alleged Baseball Crooks" while its headline—"TWO WHITE SOX STARS ADMIT THROWING BIG 1919 SERIES"—ran across two-thirds of its front page. The *Baltimore Sun* announced in bold, capital letters: "TWO WHITE SOX PLAY-

ERS CONFESS; 8 ARE INDICTED; COMISKEY CLEANS OUT TEAM." The front page of the September 28, 1920, evening edition of the *Atlanta Journal* proclaimed: "8 WHITE SOX PLAYERS INDICTED." The *New Orleans Times-Picayune* headline the following day declared: "EDDIE CICOTTE AND JOE JACKSON CONFESS GREATEST SCANDAL IN BASEBALL HISTORY." (It should be noted that in some cities the game-fixing news was regarded more coolly. The *Washington Post* resisted some of the hype; its September 29 headline occupied only one column and simply read "SOX STARS ARE HELD." Three thousand miles to the west, the *Los Angeles Times* merely reported, "WHITE SOX INDICTED.")

But in Chicago, as one would expect considering that thousands of local readers had a partisan interest, the headlines on September 29 were extraordinary. The front page of the *Chicago Tribune*, which immodestly referred to itself as "The World's Greatest Newspaper," screamed "TWO SOX CONFESS" in huge letters; to the right, a subheading read, "Eight Indicted; Inquiry Goes On." The *Chicago Herald and Examiner*, owned by William Randolph Hearst and one of the *Chicago Tribune's* leading rivals, matched the *Tribune* headline for headline. In enormous letters across the entire front page, the *Herald and Examiner* headline exclaimed: "EIGHT SOX INDICTED CICOTTE AND JACKSON CONFESS COMISKEY SUSPENDS 7 STAR PLAYERS." That same day, the *Chicago Daily News*, another of Chicago's well-established papers, proclaimed in its late edition, all the way across the front page, "FELSCH, WILLIAMS CONFESS; INDICT FIXERS." To further impress upon its readers the significance of the indictments, the *Chicago Daily News* published a cartoon entitled "The Harvest Moon" in the middle of its front page. The cartoon depicts approximately a dozen shadowy figures ("gamblers" and "crooks") carrying sacks (with dollar signs on them) over their shoulders; surveying the scene, with surprise and dismay, is an anthropomorphized moon marked with baseball seams.

Not surprisingly, newspaper headlines emphasized local connections to the scandal whenever possible. The *Cleveland Plain Dealer* viewed the affair in terms of its effect on the Indians, who were in a tight race with the White Sox for the 1920 pennant. "JACKSON AND CICOTTE ADMIT GUILT," exclaimed its September 29, 1920, headline, "CLEVELAND ALMOST SURE OF PENNANT." Elsewhere, community newspapers noted roles their native sons may have played in the game fixing. The *Boston Daily Globe* announced on its front page, "JURY INDICTS BOSTON MAN," a reference to the gambler Joseph "Sport" Sullivan. The day before, the *Des Moines Register* had reported, "DES MOINES GAMBLERS IN SOX RAID," a reference to David Zelcer (sometimes spelled Zelser), who was apparently an associate of some of the men who allegedly carried out the conspiracy.[15]

These examples suggest that for people who only had time to glance at their morning newspaper over breakfast or who hurriedly passed by newsstands, there was no uncertainty about the day's lead story. The Black Sox scandal was literally bigger news than the upcoming presidential election or the political violence in Ireland. Newspaper headlines, in other words, signified that the game-fixing revelations were scandalous and that the unfolding events were a major civic spectacle and catastrophe.

In addition to dramatic, attention-grabbing headlines, most newspapers underlined the importance of the scandal via other visual signifiers. At first, newspapers were littered with photographs and cartoons about the affair. For most of the week leading up to the indictments, the *Chicago Tribune* published photographs of Charles Comiskey, American League president Ban Johnson, many of the players alleged to have participated in the fix, and the Cook County grand jury.[16] The populist-minded *Chicago Herald and Examiner* printed even more photographs than its cross-town rival. The day after Cicotte's confession, the *New York Tribune* published individual portraits of all the implicated players.[17] That same day, the *Cincinnati Enquirer*, the *New Orleans Times-Picayune*, the *Cleveland Plain Dealer*, and the *Boston Daily Globe* featured a cluster of players' portraits on their front pages. While these (and other) photos certainly augmented the written texts they accompanied, they should be viewed as another category of news that further promoted the Big Fix as a singular and sensational moment.

Many cartoons devoted to the episode performed a similar function in late September and early October. The *Chicago Tribune*, for example, printed a "before-and-after" cartoon on its front page. In its first panel (subtitled "Our National Sport as It Has Been Regarded"), two men, obviously enjoying themselves, are at a baseball game. One says to the other: "The beauty about baseball is that it's always been kept straight and clean." In the second panel ("It Now Joins the 'Black Eye Club'") a bruised and battered anthropomorphized baseball is being introduced to other social outcasts: a black-eyed boxer, a jockey, a politician, and a financier. The same paper has another notable illustration. "It May Sicken Him of That Dish" portrays a nervous-looking fan preparing to spoon a hard-boiled egg (labeled "Organized Baseball") whose foul smell (the words gambling and scandal emanate from the cracked egg) gives him nervous pause.[18] The *Chicago Herald and Examiner* published a cartoon featuring a fan gasping as a baseball headed figure falls off the pedestal of clean sport.[19] The *New York Tribune* printed an elaborate four-paneled cartoon featuring a man wearing glasses reading his newspaper at a breakfast table. Unperturbed by headlines of "fixes" in government and finance, the bespectacled man is outraged by the rumors that baseball games were fixed.[20] The *St. Louis Star* ran a cartoon with a cigar-chomping gambler digging a grave for baseball's coffin. In the background, head-stones for boxing and horse racing loom prominently.[21] Like the photos, these cartoons alerted readers that the baseball scandal was important and deserved their attention.

The Color of Scandal

The World Series game-fixing scandal also owed some of its promi-nence to the poetry of its sobriquet: the Black Sox scandal. Even people who had only a dim sense of baseball or the World Series affair could (and still do) sense the ignominy of the phrase. Though it is difficult to pinpoint the precise origin of the expression, the phrase merits consid-eration. One of the first times it appeared was on October 1, 1920, in the *Chicago Herald and Examiner*, where it was used in the headline to Charles Dryden's sports column: "Here's Hope for Black Sox. Let 'Em Grow Beards and Change Names."[22] Dryden, it is worth noting, did not use the expression in his column, which suggests that it was probably the creation of an editor or a production worker at the newspaper.

The expression gained currency as the scandal dragged on. In the fall of 1920 it was used sporadically, but by the spring and summer of 1921 newspapers nationwide used it regularly. From the outset, how-ever, nearly every journalist, editorialist, and cartoonist who reported or commented on the story represented the implicated players and the scandal in terms of blackness. Newspapers consistently referred to the implicated ballplayers as "black sheep" and to the day that Cicotte and Jackson testified as "baseball's black day."[23] "Any kind of gambling on baseball is bad," said the noted Broadway celebrity George M. Cohan (who reportedly lost money on the series), "and this affair has given the game a mighty bad black eye.[24] A few days later, the *Chicago Daily News* ran a cartoon on its front page entitled "Contrast in Black and White" in which a batter (labeled an "Honest Ballplayer") is at home plate with a giant black splotch (labeled "Scandal Blot") behind him.[25] The semiotics of the word *black* are not difficult to perceive in these examples. In its long-standing Western cultural tradition, the word *black* has unmistak-ably pejorative connotations: it signifies corruption, immorality, and guilt. It is a readily available cultural marker and metaphor for depravity.[26] Furthermore, the consistent use of blackness to describe the scandal and those implicated in it drew upon (and reproduced) racist uses of language, despite the fact that colored and Negro were the words most commonly used to describe African American people at the time. Dependent upon conventional tropes and characterizations, the press certainly used them when reporting on the scandal.

Cleanliness and Contamination

Since the implicated White Sox players supposedly "blackened" baseball's reputation, it is not surprising that there were so many allusions in the media to "cleaning up" the game. At one point or another, virtually every commentator used this idea. Neither a cliché nor a dead metaphor, the cleanliness trope was one of the primary ways people— reporters, participants, and readers—made sense of the episode. These calls to cleanse baseball need to be understood within the broader context of the "cleanliness craze" led by progressive reformers, who inherited the impulse from their Victorian forebears. Today, Upton Sinclair's famous muckraking novel *The Jungle* (1906), which exposed the horrors of the Chicago meat-packing industry and spurred its reform, is one of the best-known examples of this impulse. By the beginning of the twentieth century, writes Suellen Hoy in *Chasing Dirt: The American Pursuit of Cleanliness* (1995), "middle-class Americans idealized cleanliness as their 'great virtue.'"[27] Twenty years later, by the time of the Black Sox scandal, Hoy maintains that "public and private cleanliness were the American norm, ubiquitously honored if not everywhere faithfully practiced."[28] Certainly those concerned with the well-being of baseball evoked the rhetoric of cleanliness, even before the scandal was revealed.

On September 19, 1920, the *Chicago Tribune* published a letter written by Fred Loomis, a respected local businessman and "one of Chicago's most enthusiastic baseball followers." Loomis, like many baseball fans, wanted to know if there was any substance to the widespread and persistent rumors that the White Sox had deliberately lost the series. Startled by the rumors, Loomis wrote: "Up to this time baseball has been accepted by the public as the one clean sport above reproach in every particular and engaged in by men, both owners and players, whose honesty and integrity have been beyond suspicion or reproach." To protect baseball's sanctity, Loomis argued, "the game must be cleaned up and it must be cleaned up at once."[29] On the same page was an article that complemented Loomis's letter. "During the last few months," the *Chicago Tribune* reported, "a number of [White Sox] players, feeling the sting of this distrust of their faith and integrity, have expressed a desire to have the entire affair cleaned up so that the innocent ones may be restored to good standing and the guilty, if any, be expelled."[30] In many ways, these responses—and many of those to follow—were appropriate. For as the anthropologist Mary Douglas argues: "Dirt offends against order. Eliminating it is not a negative movement, but a positive effort to organise the environment."[31] The implicated ballplayers, in other words, had so stained the national pastime that the lords of the game, the press, and some of the public supported their expulsion.

During September and October 1920, newspapers all over the country consistently used the metaphor of "cleaning up" the national pastime. Two days before Cicotte and Jackson testified before the Cook County grand jury, Harvey Woodruff, the sports editor of the *Chicago Tribune*, wrote: "Seldom has a grand jury been intrusted with a greater responsibility. Baseball, as the national sport, is worth all this effort to keep it clean and wholesome—free from all crookedness."[32] The following day, both the *New York Times* and the *New York Tribune* followed suit. "The game itself will suffer temporarily as a result of the public's confidence being shaken," the *New York Times* editors observed, "but the sport will thrive under cleaner conditions."[33] The sports columnist W. O. M'Geehan of the *New York Tribune* maintained: "All sportsmen, all lovers of clean sport, hope that the investigation will be thorough and carried through until it is settled for once and all as to whether or not the series" was fixed. M'Geehan was forthright about the matter: "The game must be cleaned up," he insisted.[34] Two days later, the *New York World* contended that the public "had always believed that baseball was a clean sport. It will not return to that belief until it knows that the last taint has been removed."[35] This was abundantly clear to the baseball magnates.

The baseball establishment repeatedly expressed concern for cleanliness within its ranks. Hard hit by the game-fixing revelations, Comiskey announced: "I would rather close my ball-park than send nine men on the field with one of them holding a dishonest thought toward clean baseball."[36] "I am willing to do anything I can to clean up the game," insisted John McGraw, the fiery manager of the New York Giants. "I think it is the duty of managers to clean up their own clubs."[37] John Heydler, president of the National League and the man who, just the year before, had cleared the corrupt first baseman Hal Chase to play for the New York Giants, avowed: "Baseball must be cleaned at any cost."[38] Ban Johnson, president of the American League and a Comiskey nemesis, said of the scandal: "I'm glad it's all cleaned up."[39] (Johnson spoke wishfully and prematurely, for the resolution would not come for almost a year.) Some in the press viewed this indignation and righteousness with circumspection. The *Cincinnati Enquirer*, for instance, printed a cartoon in which a Cook County grand juror is sweeping "gambling filth" out of a doorway marked "Organized Baseball." To the left, Heydler (who is holding "The Old [Hal] Chase White Wash Brush") and Johnson look on in surprise as Johnson says, "Oh, dear, oh, dear, I never dreamt of it!"[40] Later, as the legal system continued to pursue the allegations, the syndicated columnist Damon Runyon wryly observed, "As long as the affair is out of baseball hands there is hope that it will eventually be thoroughly cleaned up."[41] (At the time, judge Kenesaw Mountain Landis had not yet been given baseball's reins.)

Several men associated with the Cook County baseball investigation also employed the cleanliness trope. Henry Brigham, the grand jury foreman, declared: "I hope the cleaning process of this investigation will extend to all the sore spots in the sporting world."[42] Less than a week later, judge Charles McDonald, who presided over the investigation, intoned: "I believe you men [the grand jurors and prosecutors] are doing a patriotic duty in cleaning up the baseball situation."[43] In fact, the discourse of cleanliness was so pervasive that some ballplayers used it. Eddie Cicotte testified that taking "that dirty, crooked money" caused him "hours of mental torture" and left him "with an unclean mind." Keeping his secret, deceiving "the boys who had stayed straight and clean and honest," was excruciating, said Cicotte. Possibly speaking metaphorically, Joe Jackson testified that the $5,000 he received was given to him in a "dirty envelope."[44]

The conventional wisdom of the day was that a dirty, unkempt house was an affront to decency and bred vice and that baseball demanded better, cleaner accommodations. The *Washington Post* editors were hopeful that a "drastic housecleaning throughout the baseball world would quickly follow any proof of wrongdoing."[45] In the Queen City of the West, the *Cincinnati Enquirer* reported that the "grand jury has shown that baseball needs a thorough house cleaning from top to bottom."[46] Similar sentiment was expressed elsewhere in Ohio. The *Cleveland Plain Dealer*, which noted that the scandal "puts no stain upon Cleveland's achievement of winning this year's league pennant," further editorialized: "Unless the national game be given a house-cleaning from top to bottom, unless every crooked influence is rooted out and kept out, baseball, popular as it is today, will not long survive the shock of these disclosures."[47] Frightened by the media and public outcry, team owners accelerated their reorganization of the game's governing structure. An opponent of any plan that would limit his authority, Ban Johnson sought delays: "I believe in a thorough housecleaning before starting to remodel the house."[48] Despite his protestations and warnings—Johnson apparently described Judge Landis as a "pompous fraud"—the team owners remodeled their house anyway and installed Landis as its sole commissioner, thereby effectively leaving Johnson out in the cold.[49]

For almost a year, the press reiterated these metaphors and images. In June 1921, a few weeks before the trial began, Landis proclaimed: "Honesty in baseball is necessary for its continuance as the great American game and it must be kept clean at all hazards."[50] During the trial, one prosecutor argued that "Comiskey wants to keep the game clean for the American public and I tell you now that if the owners don't get busy when rottenness crops out baseball won't last long." Like many others, he contended that the indicted ballplayers had "dragged the game through the mire and in their blindness deliberately fouled their own nest."[51] Clearly, for many Americans in the early twenties, cleanliness and "whiteness" equaled virtue.

Since the implicated ballplayers had allegedly soiled themselves and their profession, the authorities believed they had to be laundered to cleanse the national pastime. One defense attorney noted: "This trial is a laundry for the American League and it wants the jury to run the washing machine."[52] To the prosecution's consternation, the jury did not cooperate: on August 2, 1921, the indicted ballplayers and gamblers were acquitted of all charges. The *New York Daily News* headline blared "BLACK SOX WASHED WHITE" all the way across its front page.[53] The Associated Press declared that the Black Sox had been "laundered officially."[54] The *Atlanta Journal* sports columnist Morgan Blake insisted that, rather than being truly laundered, "the Dirty Sox were only dry cleaned. The perfume remains."[55] Two days after the trial, the *Chicago Daily News* printed a cartoon on its front page entitled "A Difference of Opinion." A heavy-set woman (whose back has the lettering "Jury Verdict") attempts to bring "Clean and White" laundry (also labeled the "Ex-Sox") into a house. Blocking her entry to the door is Landis, who proclaims: "They look just th' same to me as they did before."[56] The *New York Times* editors responded to the acquittal with sarcasm: "The Chicago Sox are once more whiter than snow. A jury has said that they are not guilty, so that settles that."[57] Despite being acquitted, the Black Sox were widely considered polluters. Moreover, they were doubly depraved, for they not only crossed the line that demarcated propriety and sportsmanship from illegitimacy and corruption but also endangered the integrity of others via guilt by association.

For many in the press and the baseball establishment, the threat of contamination was palpable. Gambling and corruption (as opposed to an exploitative labor arrangement and poor working conditions) were the dreaded diseases plaguing professional baseball and contaminating an otherwise healthy and admirable national institution. (This, of course, was a convenient fiction.) Nearly a year before the World Series game-fixing rumors were substantiated, one noted baseball writer, John B. Sheridan, argued that any ballplayer who would throw a game would "infect the entire fabric of baseball."[58] Crooked ballplayers and gamblers, the *Sporting News* editorialized (almost three months before the scandal broke), were poisoning baseball's system.[59] After the game fixing was made public, the *Brooklyn Eagle* simply described the scandal as "a nauseous mess that for a moment beclouds the greatest professional sport in the world."[60]

That "moment" would last for over a year and the press continued to use contamination metaphors, as if professional baseball were a sick organism in need of dramatic, life-saving treatment. The *New York Times*, for example, remarked: "Let whatever rottenness that has infested the game be brought into public view that it may be the better eradicated."[61] Once the source of baseball's contamination was identified—and there was virtually unanimous agreement that it was gambling—pundits promptly set about offering remedies. The consensus was that baseball needed to be purged and purified. Editors at the *Chicago Tribune* maintained that if the Cook County grand jurors and prosecutors "can purge the game of any taint of scandal they will have accomplished a great deal."[62] For its part, the *Chicago Herald and Examiner* tried to reassure its readers: "The courage and prompt action of baseball owners will, let us hope, save the game from the cancerous blight of professional gambling."[63] Ever the moralist, Ban Johnson insisted: "Baseball must be cleaned of all the poison that was injected into its system by a few petty gamblers and several easily tempted players, and I will not rest content until the general public says of the national game that the wound has been thoroughly healed and the guilty have been sufficiently punished."[64] Baseball, "infected with fraud," according to the *Detroit Free Press*, could not sustain its hold on the national imagination, and thus its profitability, unless it underwent some type of purification.[65] To reconstitute its status as a symbolically significant national institution, Major League Baseball had to excise the "dangerous lesion" afflicting it.[66]

The Great Double Cross

One of the most influential ways the media conveyed the Black Sox scandal to readers was as a crime story of seemingly epic proportions. Narrating the event in this manner brought the principals and issues into dramatic focus and effectively simplified a complicated episode. Nonfiction crime stories (to say nothing of detective and mystery stories) had already been selling well in the United States for more than a hundred years.[67] According to Andie Tucher, crime news was a staple of the penny press in the 1830s because "it was easy and inexpensive to gather; it was pleasant and familiar to readers already conversant with street literature; it provided New Yorkers [and others] with useful and important information about the way their *city* worked; and it would meet no serious competition from the established press."[68] Soon thereafter the established press began in earnest to publish crime stories, which no doubt contributed to mounting circulation rates. By the twenties, two veteran journalists agreed that crime "is the most interesting of all news themes—judged by circulation gains and popular interest."[69] In this way, as in many others, the media's treatment of the World Series scandal should be viewed as part of a continuum rather than as a break from tradition. Still, the Big Fix was an exemplary crime narrative. It had all the necessary components of the conventional crime story formula: calculating villains (the implicated ballplayers and the professional gamblers), unsuspecting victims (Comiskey, boys, and the nation), and virtuous heroes (the journalists, the prosecutors, the baseball officials and players who were trying to get to the bottom of the scandal); it had a dastardly deed (the manipulation of a nearly sacred national institution), a tearful confession (Eddie Cicotte apparently wept on the stand), and an uncertain conclusion (it was unclear if the game-fixing and conspiracy allegations could be proven in court).

First and foremost, the language the press used to tell the "story of the most gigantic sporting swindle in the history of America," as the *New York Tribune* put it, made it clear that the Black Sox affair was *the* crime story of the moment.[70] The *Chicago Tribune* described the tale told by one of the fix's many bit players as "a drama that a scenario writer might well name 'The Great Double Cross.'"[71] Cliff Abbo of the *New Orleans Times-Picayune* wrote that the affair was "one of the most colossal attempts at wholesale burglary perpetrated by any clique of gamblers or dishonest participants."[72] The nationally syndicated sportswriter Grantland Rice, who exerted a great deal of influence in shaping preferred ways of understanding American sport, opined that the individuals "mixed up in this crookedness are worse than thieves and burglars. They are the ultimate scum of the universe, and even the spotted civilization of the present time has no place for them outside of a penitentiary."[73] Clearly beyond the pale of respectable society, the indicted ballplayers and gamblers were quickly vilified and transformed into national objects of disgrace. "Some degree of respect can be entertained for a thief in the night when compared with this collection of so-called humans," continued Abbo. "It is like the comparison of the sweet-scented lilac with the fetid, decomposed carcass of a skunk."[74] The men caught up in the Big Fix were thought to be so heinous, so despicable, that many journalists were compelled to evoke historical analogies to convey their presumed treachery.

More than any other historical figure, Benedict Arnold was invoked to describe the perpetrators. A notable story carried all over the country reported that a coterie of newsboys in Boston had condemned "the Chicago baseball players whose corruption in the last world series, they said, struck a 'murderous blow at the kids' game.'" The newsboys, who probably expressed the sentiment of many others, referred to the implicated players as "the Benedict Arnolds of baseball."[75] Morgan Blake of the *Atlanta Journal* added: "Every ball player who is honest, every fan who loves the game for the game's sake will always despise them. In the history of the game they will be likened to Judas and Benedict Arnold. The most contemptible character on earth is the man who betrays his friends."[76] The next day, Charles Dryden, the sports columnist of the *Chicago Herald and Examiner*, "handpicked [a] Benedict Arnold All-Star team" comprised mostly of the accused White Sox players, and the *Pittsburgh Post* ran a story entitled "'Benedict Arnolds' of Baseball Slink from View of Oldtimers, Who Can't Believe Disclosures."[77] Months later, during the criminal trial, the *Chicago Herald and Examiner* ran a photograph of men and boys in the courtroom listening to testimony that portrayed "their heroes of the diamond as worse than Benedict Arnold or Judas Iscariot."[78] Like Benedict Arnold and Judas, the Black Sox were loathed (arguably inordinately) in part because they had been trusted and admired by those they had betrayed.

Because crime stories call for justice, the Black Sox scandal ended up in a courtroom, even though State's Attorney Maclay Hoyne admitted from the beginning that he was "uncertain whether any crime has been committed."[79] Legal action was taken largely because of the perception that the public demanded it. After months of delay, and after weeks of exasperating jury selection, the Black Sox trial finally commenced in mid-July 1921.[80] Many months before, George Phair of the *Chicago Herald and Examiner* penned a poem in anticipation of the trial:

> The game of ball will soon be heard
> Throughout the favored land.
> The umpire soon will raise his voice
> And issue his command.
> The batter soon will amble up
> And take the witness stand.[81]

On the last point at least, Phair was wrong: none of the accused men testified on his own behalf. And despite the confessions and waivers of immunity proffered by three indicted players before the grand jury the previous fall—which had mysteriously disappeared by the time the case came to trial—the prosecution had difficulty establishing that a criminal conspiracy had occurred.[82] As one defense attorney argued: "It is true there has been some evidence of transactions with gamblers, but to find the defendants guilty the state had to establish there was a conspiracy, as the indictments charged. And this they have signally failed to do."[83] The presiding judge, Hugo M. Friend, instructed the jury that the law required proof of intent to defraud the public and the alleged victims identified in the indictments, not just of intent to throw baseball games. After the jury acquitted all the charged ballplayers and gamblers, the *Chicago Tribune* reported that "the verdict was greeted with cheers" and that the courtroom "was like a love feast" due to all the handshaking, back slapping, and other public displays of affection."[84] The celebration, it would turn out, was premature.

Since the press constructed the fixed World Series as a crime story—even if technically a crime had not been committed—it made perfect sense that a federal judge was given the last word. Immediately after the verdict was announced, Landis declared: "Regardless of the verdict of juries, no player who throws a ball game, no player that undertakes or promises to throw a ball game, no player that sits in a conference with a bunch of crooked players and gamblers where the ways and means of throwing a game are discussed, and does not promptly tell his club about it, will ever play professional baseball."[85] That said, Landis eliminated the affair's irksome loose ends and gave the incident some closure. Although he did not investigate the alleged crime or preside over the case, Landis effectively "solved" the problem the acquittals presented the baseball establishment. Through his action the verdict became an acquittal only in a technical sense. Not surprisingly, Landis was widely hailed for his decisive action. "Judge Landis took his position to give organized baseball a character bath," the *Chicago Tribune* editors observed. "With the Black Sox back in the game the bath would have looked worse than if it had been drawn from the Missouri river in flood time."[86] That same day, the *Cleveland Plain Dealer* noted that the "thanks of the baseball world are due judge Landis for his prompt declaration."[87] In a similar vein, the *Cincinnati Enquirer* printed a cartoon with the eight Black Sox, dripping with "Legal Whitewash," huddled on a rock in the middle of the ocean. Landis, on a ship named *Organized Baseball*, is sailing away in the distance and says, "Not a chance."[88]

Writing in a different context, the literary critic Peter Huhm notes that most "detective stories start out with a community in a state of stable order. Soon a crime (usually a murder) occurs, which the police are unable to clear up. The insoluble crime acts as a destabilizing event, because the system of norms and rules regulating life in the community has proved powerless in one crucial instance and is therefore discredited."[89] It is not difficult to transpose this schema onto the Black Sox scandal. Professional baseball had been trying hard to promote itself as a stable, virtuous national institution reflecting all that was good in American society. Then, seemingly from nowhere, a heinous and apparently aberrant development was revealed. Try as they might, the legal authorities could not effectively solve the credibility problems this "destabilizing event" produced. In this way the Big Fix, like many formulaic crime stories Huhm discusses, became an occasion to reconstitute order and power, and it provided openings for various ideological reaffirmations.

Finally, Huhm argues that after the authorities admit that the crime (and the criminal) has stumped them, "the detective takes over the case, embarks on a course of thorough investigations, and finally identifies the criminal, explaining his solution at length," and in the process "restores the disrupted social order and reaffirms the validity of the system of norms.[90] At first glance, it might appear that Hugh Fullerton played this role, but in the end Fullerton did not have much power to exert. Furthermore, most of Fullerton's colleagues were not interested in giving him his fair share of credit for bringing the affair to light. Instead, for many in the media, Judge Landis was a far more convenient and attractive hero, particularly as the scandal approached its uncertain conclusion. When the episode was in need of closure, Landis provided it with a dramatic flourish—thus ending what a Chicago journalist described as "one of the most startling and tangled tales of graft and interlocking double-crossing ever unfolded in the Criminal courts building."[91] It was quite a claim considering Chicago's reputation for corruption.

Lean-Faced and Long-Nosed Gamblers

The media's portrayal of some of the scandal's "calculating villains" deserves more attention. Usually, loss and disappointment precipitate a search for objects of blame. Moreover, in moments of crisis it is common for the powerless or the unpopular to be scapegoated. In some such moments in this country, even though anti-Semitism has not led to pogroms, Jewish conspirators have been found behind problems.[92] Given the nation's nativist temperament during the early twentieth century and the conspicuous presence of professional gamblers from Jewish backgrounds at the 1919 World Series, it is not surprising that an undercurrent of anti-Semitism is detectable in the media's Black Sox scandal coverage.[93]

At the outset, rather than hastily vilify and accuse gamblers of tampering with the series, the press essentially ignored the rumors that implicated them. There were, however, some notable exceptions. As early as October 1919, the *Sporting News* editorialized: "There are no lengths to which the crop of lean-faced and long-nosed gamblers of these degenerate days will go.[94] A short time later, after Hugh Fullerton wrote critically of some players' performances, the *Sporting News* responded that just "because a lot of dirty, long-nosed, thick-lipped, and strong-smelling gamblers butted into the World Series—an American event, by the way—and some of said gentlemen got crossed, stories were peddled that there was something wrong with the way the games were played."[95] This often-cited passage is notable for its stonewalling the possibility of a fix, its reactionary tone, its use of stereotypical anti-Semitic imagery, and its insinuation that Jewish gamblers were somehow less, or even un-American because they may have meddled with a virtually sacred national institution. It is also worth mentioning that as the scandal took shape the *Sporting News*'s response became more evenhanded, though no less bigoted. Surveying the implicated gamblers, the *Sporting News* reminded its readers that "it does look like most of the [Abe] Attell gang—but then we're all American born, and don't forget that a [Joseph 'Sport'] Sullivan is involved as well as a[n] [Arnold] Rothstein."[96]

Later, when the story finally broke, many newspapers not so subtly implied that Jewish outsiders were responsible for despoiling the national pastime. Although there were few explicit references to their Jewish backgrounds, the noted underworld figures Arnold Rothstein and Abe Attell (aka "The Big Bankroll" and "The Little Champ," respectively) figured prominently in the coverage. More specifically, they were commonly personified as a dual threat: not only had they allegedly assaulted the integrity of organized baseball with gambling and commercialism but they also had threatened some of the traditional American values for which the game stood, such as meritocracy, equality, and openness.

It is now generally agreed upon that Arnold Rothstein—one of the best-known and most powerful New York gangsters and the inspiration for Meyer Wolfsheim in E. Scott Fitzgerald's *The Great Gatsby* (1925)—did *not* fix the 1919 World Series. "Rothstein's name, his reputation, and his reputed wealth were all used to influence the crooked baseball players," writes his biographer Leo Katcher. "But Rothstein, knowing this, kept apart from the actual fix. He just let it happen."[97] Nevertheless, like virtually everyone associated with the affair, Rothstein was no innocent. He knew of the fix early on and profited greatly from it. Katcher speculates that Rothstein won at least $350,000 on the series.[98] Whether he deserved it or not, Rothstein was (and remains) closely associated with the scandal. As F. Scott Fitzgerald famously suggested, he was widely believed to have been "the man who fixed the World Series" and played "with the faith of fifty million people—with the single-mindedness of a burglar blowing a safe."[99] After being consistently mentioned in the early Black Sox scandal narratives as a possible "fixer," Rothstein publicly denied being involved. When he voluntarily presented himself before the Cook County grand jury—in part because the rumors linking him to the scandal brought his illicit businesses unwanted attention—Rothstein deflected the media glare by implicating his sometime associate Abe Attell.[100] "My friends know that I have never been connected with a crooked deal in my life," Rothstein said. "I have been victimized more than once and have been forced to bear the burden as best I could."[101] But as Katcher notes: "No one really believed in his innocence, only in his cleverness."[102]

Few believed in Abe Attell's innocence, either. The featherweight boxing champion of the world between 1904 and 1912, Attell was instrumental in fixing the series. An associate and occasional bodyguard for Rothstein, Attell apparently deceived several small-time gamblers and White Sox players into believing that Rothstein was backing their venture. When the scandal was exposed, Attell's name was, like Rothstein's, constantly coupled with the plot and his whereabouts were newsworthy throughout the affair. As one would expect, Attell at first denied being involved. "I never handed any money to the White Sox players," Attell claimed. "I never acted as a fixer."[103] Years later, though, Attell seemed to be proud of his association with the Black Sox scandal. In 1926, he bragged to sportswriters, "I was the payoff man."[104] In spite of his complicity, Attell, like almost all the gamblers, escaped prosecution, in no small part due to Rothstein's assistance. Although he was indicted by the grand jury, attempts to extradite the New Yorker were unsuccessful.[105] It was Attell who succinctly observed that the episode "was a game of cheaters cheating cheaters."[106]

Perhaps the press's most virulently anti-Semitic stories emanated from Henry Ford's *Dearborn Independent*. One of the best-known and wealthiest men in the United States, Ford helped to revolutionize mass industrial production and to popularize the country's consumer culture. But by the twenties Ford was also "America's best known anti-Semite."[107] During most of the twenties, Ford's newspaper published articles (reprints were quickly collected in book form) that revealed obviously far-fetched Jewish conspiracies and accused "Jews of utilizing communism, banking, labor unions, alcohol, gambling, jazz music, newspapers, and the movies to attack and weaken America, its culture and people."[108] The combination of the Black Sox scandal's cast of prominent Jewish characters and Ford's awareness that baseball's popularity was at least partially rooted in its embodiment of traditional American values simply added fuel to his anti-Semitic fire.

In September 1921, Ford's newspaper published two long articles that addressed the Big Fix, "Jewish Gamblers Corrupt American Baseball" and "The Jewish Degradation of American Baseball."[109] The anonymous writer put the matter bluntly: "If fans wish to know the trouble with American baseball, they have it in three words—too much Jew." Noting that the World Series scandal "was curiously notable for its Jewish character," the writer suggested that the implicated ballplayers were simply "Gentile boobs" and "Jewish dupes" who were only involved in the game fixing because they "had listened to the suggestions of a Jew." In this bigoted diatribe the author also argued that baseball had passed into the hands of an assortment of Jews (those in the upper levels of baseball management, as well as professional gamblers) who were conspiring to turn the national pastime into a commercial, rather than a sporting, enterprise. "If baseball is to be saved," Ford's writer instructed, "it must be taken out of their hands until they have shown themselves capable of promoting sport for sports' sake."[110] The historian Peter Levine correctly notes that the articles displayed "little knowledge of the history of the game but an unfortunately good grasp of racist stereotyping and anti-Semitism."[111]

Of course Rothstein and Attell drew much of the *Dearborn Independent*'s wrath. Described as "a slick Jew" and "the man higher up" in the scandal, Rothstein was "either the vilest crook or the most abused man in America." As for Attell, the articles alternately described him as a "Jew gambler" and as the "king bee" of the scandal. Expressing the conventional wisdom of the day, the anonymous writer added: "Attell is of such a character that he ought to be barred from the grounds of any sport."[112] Levine judiciously points out that "Ford was wrong to interpret Attell and Rothstein's involvement in the Black Sox scandal as evidence of an international Jewish conspiracy to corrupt Anglo-Saxon institutions. Wrong about the responsibility of Jews for turning baseball into commercial enterprise, Ford was correct in noting that America's national pastime was big business."[113]

There is little argument about whether Rothstein and Attell were involved in the Black Sox scandal: they most certainly were, though possibly to a lesser extent than is generally believed. Rothstein's role in the fix was probably limited to damage control, while Attell's role is often expediently minimized or exaggerated. Still, despite their involvement, Rothstein and Attell (along with several other lesser Jewish gamblers) were portrayed by the media as the Big Fix's driving force in large part because their ethnicity fit the popular cultural stereotype of the deceitful, dishonest, and money-hungry Jew. Rather than unduly castigate the players (who probably initiated the scheme) or the labor conditions and relations that engendered the game fixing, the media focused on the menace that professional gamblers (often code for Jewish gamblers) posed. By using Rothstein and Attell to reinforce a potent ethnic stereotype, the media were able to personify the pair as the source of baseball's tragedy and moral disorder.

Notes

1. Eliot Asinof, *Eight Men Out: The Black Sox and the 1919 World Series* (1963, rep., New York: Henry Holt, 1987), 123.

2. Ibid., 47.

3. Hugh Fullerton, "Fullerton Says Seven Members of the White Sox Will Be Missing Next Spring," *Chicago Herald and Examiner*, October 10, 1919, 9.

4. Asinof casts Fullerton in the role of the muckraking, ethical hero: "His love for the game permitted no whitewashing. He insisted on a cleanup. With a sense of outrage, he began a series of articles to jolt the executive world of baseball into action. He would expose, finally, what every decent baseball writer knew, but never had the courage to write. He would break down the hypocritical wall of silence behind which baseball pretended to be holy. He would quote gamblers he had spoken with, recount experiences that indicated dirty work, and above all, name names, lots of names." Asinof, *Eight Men Out*, 132.

5. Hugh Fullerton, "Is Big League Baseball Being Run for Gamblers, with the Players in the Deal?" *New York Evening World*, December 15, 1919, "sporting page."

6. Harold Seymour, *Baseball: The Golden Age* (New York: Oxford University Press, 1971), 288–90.

7. Fullerton, "Is Big League Baseball Being Run for Gamblers?"

8. David Q. Voigt, *American Baseball: From the Commissioners to Continental Expansion* (University Park: Pennsylvania State University Press, 1970), 126

9. For instance, an editorial in the November 1919 issue of *Baseball Magazine* ripped Fullerton: "If a man really knows so little about baseball that he believes the game is or can be fixed, he should keep his mouth shut when in the presence of intelligent people." Immediately after the series, editors of the *Sporting News*, without mentioning Fullerton by name, ridiculed any thought that the games were fixed and disparaged those who suspected corruption. Later, after Fullerton's articles appeared in the *New York Evening World*, a writer at *Baseball Magazine* noted that the "sport world was recently greeted with a giddy screed from the facile pen of Hugh Fullerton," who was described as a "visionary and erratic writer." Even after the game-fixing charges were confirmed—by ballplayer confessions—late in the 1920 season, the editors at *Baseball Magazine* were unrelenting in their criticism of Fullerton: "Mr. Fullerton picked up an ugly story that was kicking around the gutter, a story that most reputable writers refused to handle. His articles were constructed out of gamblers' rumors and bar-room conversation. His attack was vicious, premature, unfounded. Under the circumstances the *Baseball Magazine* could do nothing but defend the game from such a tirade of abuse. At that time it could not know whether the investigation of baseball would disclose crooked work. No one knew. The fact that events have proved those ugly rumors true is beside the point. Mere empty suspicion offers no just ground for wholesale mudslinging. Mr. Fullerton merely made a wild, hazardous guess and for once in his life he guessed right." "Editorial Comment," *Baseball Magazine*, November 1919, 458; "Editorial Comment," *Baseball Magazine*, February 1920, 519; "Editorial Comment," *Baseball Magazine*, December 1920, 316.

10. Peter Williams, "When Chipmunks Became Wolves: The Scapegoating of Sportswriter Joe Williams by His Peers," *Nine: A Journal of Baseball History and Social Policy Perspectives* 4 (Fall 1995): 51.

11. For more on Fullerton, see Steve Klein, "The Lone Horseman of Baseball's Apocalypse," *Blue Ear* (November 1, 1999), in author's possession; Steve Klein,

"Hugh Fullerton, the Black Sox Scandal, and the Ethical Impulse in Sports Writing (M.A. thesis, Michigan State University, 1997).

12. Peter Andrews, "The Press," *American Heritage*, October 1994, 60.

13. Kevin Barnhurst, *Seeing the Newspaper* (New York: St. Martin's Press, 1994), 196.

14. Bruce J. Evensen, *When Dempsey Fought Tunney: Heroes, Hokum, and Storytelling in the Jazz Age* (Knoxville: University of Tennessee Press, 1996), 65.

15. *Des Moines Register*, September 29, 1920, 1.

16. *Chicago Tribune*, September 19, 1920, pt. 2, p. 1, September 23, 1920, 3, September 24, 1920, 3.

17. *New York Tribune*, September 29, 1920, 2.

18. *Chicago Tribune*, September 24, 19203 I, 8.

19. *Chicago Herald and Examiner*, September 27, 1920, 6.

20 *New York Tribune*, September 30, 1910, 10.

21. *St. Louis Star* quoted in *Literary Digest*, October 9, 1920, 12.

22. Charles Dryden, "Here's Hope for Black Sox," *Chicago Herald and Examiner*, October 1, 1920, 9.

23. *Chicago Tribune*, September 24, 1920, 2, September 29, 1920, 15.

24. *Chicago Tribune*, September 26, 1920, 10.

25. *Chicago Daily News*, September 30, 1921, 1.

26. For a cultural history of the color black, see John Harvey, *Men in Black* (Chicago: University of Chicago Press, 1995).

27. Suellen Hoy, *Chasing Dirt: The American Pursuit of Cleanliness* (New York: Oxford University Press, 1995), 88.

28. Ibid., 86.

29. *Chicago Tribune*, September 19, 1920, II: 1. The Loomis letter is also notable because Loomis probably did not write it. In his history of the *Chicago Tribune*, Lloyd Wendt writes: "In July, 1920, [James] Crusinberry [a *Chicago Tribune* sportswriter] prepared a story about an impending baseball scandal, based in part upon a conversation he had overheard between two gamblers about the fix of the 1919 Series, but [Harvey] Woodruff [the *Tribune*'s sports editor] held the story, feeling there were not enough facts available. By late August, although no new information had surfaced, there was talk of initiating a grand jury investigation. In early September, Crusinberry, convinced that matters were moving too slowly, persuaded Fred M. Loomis, a Chicago businessman and baseball fan, to sign a letter to the *Tribune* that he, Crusinberry, had written." Since Loomis was willing to put his name to the letter, it is fair to assume that he shared its sentiments. Lloyd Wendt, *Chicago Tribune: The Rise of a Great American Newspaper* (Chicago: Rand McNally, 1979), 452.

30. *Chicago Tribune*, September 19, 1920, II: 1.

31. Mary Douglas, *Purity and Danger: An Analysis of the Concepts of Pollution and Taboo* (New York: Routledge, 1991), 2.

32. *Chicago Tribune*, September 26, 1920, II: 1.

33. *New York Times*, September 27, 1920, 11.

34. *New York Tribune*, September 27, 1920, 11.

35. *New York World*, September 29, 1920, 14.

36. *Chicago Tribune*, September 29, 1920, 3.

37. *New York World*, September 29, 1920, 2.

38. *Cincinnati Enquirer*, September 29, 1920, 2.

39. Ibid.

40. *Cincinnati Enquirer*, September 30, 1920, 7.

41. Damon Runyon, "The Grand Jury Resume," *Chicago Herald and Examiner*, October 21, 1920, 9.

42. *Chicago Tribune*, September 29, 1920, 2.

43. *Chicago Herald and Examiner*, October 3, 1920, 3.

44. *Chicago Tribune*, September 29, 1920, 1.

45. *Washington Post*, September 29, 1920, 6.

46. *Cincinnati Enquirer*, October 3, 19 2 0, 38.

47. *Cleveland Plain Dealer*, September 30, 1920, 14.

48. I. E. Sanborn, "Johnson Hints New Baseball," *Chicago Tribune*, October 15, 1920, 22.

49. Voigt, *American Baseball*, 133.

50. *Chicago Herald and Examiner*, June 22, 1921, 10.

51. *Chicago Tribune*, August 3, 1921, 2.

52. *Chicago Herald and Examiner*, August 3, 1921, 1.

53. *New York Daily News*, August 3, 1921, 1

54. *New York Daily News* quoted in *Literary Digest*, August 20, 1921, 13.

55. Morgan Blake, "Dirty Sox Only Dry Cleaned," *Atlanta Journal*, August 3, 1921, 17.

56. *Chicago Daily News*, August 4, 1922, 1.

57. *New York Times*, August 4, 1921, 14.

58. John B. Sheridan, "Back of the Home Plate," *Sporting News*, October 23, 1919, 6.

59. *Sporting News*, June 17, 1920, 4.

60. *Brooklyn Eagle* quoted in *Literary Digest*, October 9, 1920, 12.

61. *New York Times*, September 27, 1920, 11.

62. *Chicago Tribune*, September 23, 1920, 2.

63. *Chicago Herald and Examiner*, November 12, 1920, 6.

64. *Chicago Herald and Examiner*, March 31, 1920, 8.

65. *Detroit Free Press*, September 30, 1920, 6.

66. *Literary Digest*, August 20, 1921, 14. Other writers used different metaphors to convey the same message. For example: "Whitewash alone will not remedy a bad smell. The public does not distrust the players, but it distrusts the management; and as sure as God made little apples the owners must provide a management above suspicion of carelessness and inefficiency, or professional baseball will go over Niagara in a broken barrel." *Chicago Herald and Examiner*, October 18, 1920, 6.

67. Andie Tucher, *Froth and Scum,: Truth, Beauty, Goodness, and the Ax Murder in America's First Mass Medium* (Chapel Hill: University of North Carolina Press, 1994), 199.

68. Ibid., 11.

69. Harper Leech and John C. Carroll, *What's the News?* (Chicago: Pascal, 1926), 13.

70. *New York Tribune*, September 28, 1920, 1.

71. *Chicago Tribune*, September 28, 1920, 1.

72. Cliff Abbo, "The Gambling Mess," *New Orleans Times-Picayune*, September 29, 1920, 14.

73. Grantland Rice, "The Sportlight," *New York Tribune*, September 30, 1910, 12.

74. Abbo, "The Gambling Mess," 14.

75. *New York Times*, October 1, 1920, 2.

76. Morgan Blake, "Baseball Traitors and Crooks Are Uncovered," *Atlanta Journal*, September 29, 1920, 11.

77. Charles Dryden, "Benedict Arnold's Team," *Chicago Herald and Examiner*, September 30, 1920, 9; Alexander E. Jones, "'Benedict Arnolds' of Baseball Slink from View of Oldtimers, Who Can't Believe Disclosures," *Pittsburgh Post*, September 30, 1920, 8.

78. *Chicago Herald and Examiner*, July 21, 1921, 4.

79. *Pittsburgh Post*, September 30, 1920, 8.

80. The jury was all male, all but two jurors were married, and their ages ranged from thirty to forty-seven. The *Washington Post* reported that "none is a student of the game or of the tin-fan type." *Washington Post*, July 16, 1921.

81. George Phair, "Breakfast Food," *Chicago Herald and Examiner*, February 8, 1921, 8.

82. The mysterious disappearance of the original confessions and waivers of immunity is often noted to suggest that corruption was widespread. It was. But as a purely legal matter, it was not significant, for Judge Hugo M. Friend ruled that in place of the original confessions, the state could have the court stenographers from the grand jury inquiry read from their shorthand notes the testimony of the three players. The judge also granted permission for Judge Charles McDonald (who presided over the grand jury investigation) and others to whom the players told their stories before appearing before the grand jury to testify about these conversations. According to the *Washington Post*: "The actual transcripts of the confessions varied but little from the frequently published reports of them." *Washington Post*, July 27, 1921, 10.

83. *Chicago Herald and Examiner*, August 1, 1921, 5.

84. *Chicago Tribune*, August 3, 1921, 1.

85. *Chicago Herald and Examiner*, August 4, 1921, 1.

86. *Chicago Tribune*, August 4, 1921, 8.

87. *Cleveland Plain Dealer*, August 4, 1921, 8.

88. *Cincinnati Enquirer*, August 4, 1921, 8.

89. Peter Huhm, "The Detective as Reader: Narrativity and Reading Concepts in Detective Fiction," *Modern Fiction Studies* 33 (Autumn 1987): 452.

90. Ibid.

91. *Chicago Tribune*, July 21, 1921, 1.

92. See Leonard Dinnerstein, *Uneasy at Home: Antisemitism and the American Experience* (New York: Columbia University Press, 1987); David A. Gerber, ed., *Anti-Semitism in American History* (Urbana: University of Illinois Press, 1986); John Higham, "American Anti-Semitism Historically Reconsidered," in *Jews in the Mind of America*, ed. George Salomon (New York: Basic Books, 1966); Harold E. Quinley and Charles Y. Glock, *Anti-Semitism in America* (New York: Free Press, 1979); and Frederic Cople Jaher, *A Scapegoat in the Wilderness: The Origins and Rise of Anti-Semitism in America* (Cambridge, Mass.: Harvard University Press, 1994).

93. Although Peter Levine observes that the Black Sox scandal "did not include any Jewish athletes," he notes that "Erskine Mayer, a Jewish boy of German descent born in Atlanta, and the first Jewish hurler to win 20 games in two consecutive seasons, appeared in one inning of the fifth game of the series for Chicago." Mayer, however, was not involved in the conspiracy. His name does

not appear in the *Baseball Encyclopedia's* White Sox team roster for the 1919 season nor was he mentioned in contemporary accounts of the "fix" or in studies of the scandal. Peter Levine, *Ellis Island to Ebbets Field: Sport and the American Jewish Experience* (New York: Oxford University Press, 1992), 84, 103.

94. *Sporting News*, October 9, 1919, 4.

95. *Sporting News*, October 16, 1919, 4.

96. *Sporting News* quoted in Richard C. Crepeau, *Baseball: America's Diamond Mind, 1919–1941* (Gainesville: University Presses of Florida, 1980), 14.

97. Leo Katcher, *The Big Bankroll: The Life and Times of Arnold Rothstein* (New York: Harper and Brothers, 1974), 139.

98. Ibid., 148.

99. F. Scott Fitzgerald, *The Great Gatsby* (1925, rep., New York: Collier Books, 1986), 74.

100. Asinof, *Eight Men Out*, 218–19.

101. *New York World*, October 1, 1920, 1.

102. Katcher, *The Big Bankroll*, 148.

103. *Chicago Tribune*, October 1, 1920, 1.

104. George Barton, "Weaver's Role in Fixed World Series," *Baseball Digest*, April 1956, 49.

105. Asinof, *Eight Men Out*, 231–33.

106. Eliot Asinof, *Bleeding between the Lines* (New York: Holt, Rinehart, and Winston, 1979), 105.

107. Levine, *Ellis Island to Ebbets Field*, 106.

108. Deborah Lipstadt, *Denying the Holocaust: The Growing Assault on Truth and Memory* (New York: Free Press, 1993), 37.

109. See "Jewish Gamblers Corrupt American Baseball" and "The Jewish Degradation of American Baseball," in *Jewish Influences in American Life*, volume 3 of *The International Jew: The World's Foremost Problem* (Dearborn, Mich.: Dearborn Independent, 1921).

110. "Jewish Gamblers Corrupt American Baseball," 49 (first quote), 37 (second quote), 50 (sixth quote); "Jewish Degradation of American Baseball," 53 (third and fifth quotes), 54 (fourth quote).

111. Levine, *Ellis Island to Ebbets Field*, 106.

112. "Jewish Gamblers Corrupt American Baseball," 43 (first and second quotes), 44 (third quote), 46 (fourth and fifth quotes), 47 (sixth quote).

113. Levine, *Ellis Island to Ebbets Field*, 108.

Harold "Red" Grange was as responsible as anyone for putting professional football on the map. During the "Golden Age of Sports" in the 1920s, he was the most famous intercollegiate athlete in the United States, making all-American from 1923 to 1925. His greatest moment occurred in a 1924 game against Michigan when he scored four touchdowns on a total of 262 yards just in the first period. Grange gained the nickname of the "Galloping Ghost of the Illini" and was considered the greatest football player of the day, a national sports hero like Babe Ruth and Jack Dempsey.

College stars at this time shunned professional football, which did not pay well and had very little status. But Grange took the unheralded step of hiring an agent, C. C. Pyle, and right after his final college game in 1925, he signed an unprecedented contract with Chicago Bears owner George Halas. The contract guaranteed Grange a share of the gate for the remainder of the season and a subsequent national tour that made him one of the highest-paid athletes in the world. His presence brought out huge crowds and gave the National Football League the recognition it had previously lacked.

7 | Red Grange and the Chicago Bears

JOHN M. CARROLL

As Grange prepared to play his final game at Memorial Stadium against Wabash College on November 14, he continued to be the object of national attention. Chicago admirers began to circulate petitions to nominate him as a Republican candidate for a special at-large congressional seat. They argued that he would be within six months of the legal age to serve when the Congress elected in 1926 was first scheduled to meet in December 1927 and defied politicians to object that he would be underage. The day after the petition campaign began, rumors circulating in Chicago held that Grange had been offered $40,000 to play three games for the New York Giants of the NFL after his last college game. He refused to deny or confirm the report, and Harry March of the Giants dismissed the rumors at the time. Yet it is clear that Tim Mara, the Giant's owner, did travel to Illinois to make some sort of offer to Grange. The *Chicago Tribune* maintained that he had been "besieged with offers of every description" since the 1924 Michigan game and that more had been piling up since the Penn game, including "contracts to appear in motion pictures, play professional football, and also write for a newspaper syndicate." The *Tribune* also stated that it was understood that University of Illinois officials opposed him playing pro football "but would probably not oppose a career in athletic motion pictures or newspaper writing."[1]

Amid the swirl of publicity, Grange made only a token appearance in the Wabash game, which Illinois won easily, 21-0. The following day, Miami newspapers alleged that Grange had signed a contract to play football in that city on Christmas Day for a syndicate headed by C. C. Pyle and had accepted $5,000 as part of a $25,000 guarantee. When asked about the stories, Grange said, "I know nothing about it." Reporters then descended on Wheaton to seek out Lyle Grange's opinions about his famous son's activities. Lyle maintained that he would not object to Red accepting any of the other numerous offers made to him, but he did not approve of commercialized football. "Every time I read in the paper that Harold has accepted a contract from this or that team, it gives me a shock." The senior Grange added, "I think he's entitled to 'cash in' on the long runs his gridiron fame has brought him. It has been expensive for me to send Harold and his brother Garland through the University. We are not rolling in wealth and I think the public would approve of anything Harold does." At the end of its report on the interview, the *New York Times* noted perceptively that "there probably will break out the most intense argument that sports has ever listened to on amateurism and professionalism" when Grange ended his college career.[2]

Early in the week before his final game with Ohio State at Columbus, the *Champaign News-Gazette* summoned Grange for an interview and accused him of having signed a pro football contract. Grange recalled, "I replied that I had not affixed my signature to any contract and defied them to produce evidence to the contrary. At this point I put on my hat and walked out." Throughout the week he repeatedly denied having signed a professional contract. His purported denial also extended to Coach Zuppke, who had reportedly commanded Grange and Earl Britton (also accused of having signed to play for Pyle in Florida), "If you are ineligible, turn in your suits." Grange did confirm, however, that Pyle, with his consent, had taken action against an automobile company that had used Grange's name in advertising. Reached in Tampa, Florida, where he was negotiating a contract for another game in his proposed postseason pro tour, Pyle stated, "If Grange denies having signed a contract, then he must have some reason for doing so."[3]

During the week, University of Illinois president David Kinley met with Grange and urged him not to accept any offers to play professional football. He later told reporters, "I talked to Harold last week and he told me he was not tied up with anybody and I believe him." After the meeting, athletic director George Huff excused Grange from football practice for two days and advised him to go home to Wheaton and talk matters over with his father. Although Lyle had little to say about his discussions with his son, reporters who questioned him surmised that he had given his consent for Red to play pro football after his last college game. When he returned to campus looking haggard from what he might have supposed was a modern version of the Spanish Inquisition, Grange received the first good news he had heard in days. Ohio State athletic director L. W. St. John announced that he would not challenge Grange's eligibility or ask for an investigation of rumors concerning a pro contract. Meanwhile, Big Ten commissioner John L. Griffith, who had been waffling on the question of whether signing a professional football contract violated any conference regulation, proclaimed that any athlete signing such a contract forfeited amateur standing. He added, however, that he had investigated reports to this effect concerning Grange and "was positive that Grange had signed no contract."[4]

If he thought his week of torment was almost over, Grange was mistaken. He remained in seclusion on the Wednesday evening before the team's last practice for the Ohio State game, admonishing his fraternity brothers not to answer either questions or the telephone. After evading reporters and hurrying to the practice field on Thursday, Grange was confronted outside the locker room by an Associated Press correspondent who held an affidavit sworn by E. P. Albertson of Kokomo, Indiana. Albertson attested that he had seen Grange's signature on a contract with C. C. Pyle making Pyle Grange's agent. The contract with Pyle stipulated that Grange was to receive 45 percent of all income in connection with the use of his name. Albertson further claimed that four other businessmen he named knew of the existence of the contract. In desperation, Grange blurted out his final public denial of professionalism: "They have nothing on me. I have not received a penny. I have not signed a contract. If Pyle were asked the same question he would give the same answer." After Grange abruptly broke off the interview he participated in a short practice with his teammates before preparing to depart with the team for Columbus that evening. On the train, Zuppke asked him for the first time about his future plans, Grange remembered "hedg[ing] by saying I would tell him anything he wanted to know after the game."[5]

As the train carrying the University of Illinois team pulled into Union Station in Columbus just after noon on Friday, it became apparent that the impending game was the sideshow and that Grange and his future plans were the main attraction. The *New York Times* reported that if the train from Champaign "had been bearing the President, Jack Dempsey and Douglas Fairbanks, it is doubtful if the awaiting crowd would have been any larger." Grange had to squirm and dodge through the crowd to a taxi that passed thousands of spectators lined up along the route to the Great Southern Hotel to catch a glimpse of him. Earl Britton led the interference, which allowed Grange to make the fifteen-yard dash into the lobby. Throughout the day Grange remained in seclusion. That evening Zuppke sent a substitute player to impersonate Grange at a large parade he was scheduled to lead through the city streets and spared his star player the excitement and aggravation of doing so. Grange remained locked in his room, refusing to be photographed or to issue a statement concerning his future plans.[6]

More than a hundred newspapers, press associations, and other news-gathering agencies sent correspondents to cover the Saturday game. A record college football crowd of 85,500 jammed Ohio State's massive stadium to watch Red Grange play his final collegiate game; an estimated twenty thousand were turned away. The game itself was unremarkable, with the Illini overpowering an injury-plagued Buckeye team in the first half and hanging on for a 14-9 victory. Grange carried the ball twenty-one times from scrimmage for a respectable 113 yards and threw nine passes for forty-two yards, including a seventeen-yard touchdown completion in the second period that provided the eventual margin of victory. Despite failing to make a touchdown, Grange played a solid game, especially on defense, where he intercepted two passes, one of which halted a Buckeye comeback bid near the end of the game.[7]

Five minutes after the final whistle blew and he had reached the safety of the Illinois locker room, Grange announced to a horde of reporters that he would drop out of college and play professional football. In a muddled statement apparently designed to divert the media from his intention to travel to Chicago and sign contracts with Pyle and the Chicago Bears, he declared that he was leaving that evening for his home in Wheaton and planned to organize and manage his own pro team, which would play its first game on Thanksgiving Day probably in Chicago. After Grange showered and dressed, Zuppke, visibly shaken by the announcement, accompanied his star player back to the hotel in a taxi. The trip lasted more than an hour because Zuppke ordered the cab driver to keep circling as he attempted to change Red's mind. At one point, according to Grange, Zuppke said, "Keep away from professionalism and you'll be another Walter Camp. Football isn't a game to play for money." Grange replied that Zuppke made a living out of teaching and coaching football, "so what's the difference if I make a living playing football?" When the taxi finally reached the hotel the two men had made their cases but parted in disagreement.[8]

Reflecting on the incident many years later, Grange pointed out that "all the college coaches and athletic directors, they were 100 per cent against professional football. They thought anybody connected with it was going to hell, you might say. When I joined the Chicago Bears, as far as the University of Illinois was concerned, I would have been more popular if I joined the Capone mob." After the encounter with Zuppke, Grange packed his bags, climbed down a hotel fire escape to avoid detection, and took the next train for Chicago, where he checked into the Belmont

Hotel under an assumed name. The next day he signed a contract with Pyle making him his manager; they then both signed a contract with Halas and Sternaman of the Bears. Grange was now officially a professional, but it is unclear whether he fully comprehended the firestorm of controversy his signing those contracts would evoke or the rigors that Pyle's deal with the Bears would entail.[9]

The Great Debate

The same day that Grange signed contracts with Pyle and with Halas and Sternaman in Chicago that made him a professional, he attended the Bears game against Green Bay at Cubs Park. Accompanied by Pyle and attired in a sumptuous raccoon coat, Grange entered the field through the baseball dugout and took a seat on the Bears' bench. When the fans saw him, they stood and roared a deafening tribute. Police had to be summoned to prevent a boisterous crowd from mobbing their idol. After the half-time interval, Red remained in the Bears' locker room a full five minutes after the kickoff to prevent further disturbances, but a throng of three thousand fans refused to return to their seats and blocked the runway from the clubhouse to the field until he emerged. When he did appear, it required a squad of police to get him through the frenzied mob and safely back to the bench. The *Milwaukee Sentinel* remarked that "Babe Ruth or Jack Dempsey, in their palmiest days, never were accorded a nosier or more enthusiastic tribute than that which Grange achieved in his first appearance as a professional, even though it was strictly an appearance."[10]

Given the massive and intrusive publicity he had endured during his senior year and the near certainty that it would continue after signing contracts with Pyle and the Bears' owners, why did Grange decide to play professional football? After all, he was a shy, humble, self-effacing small-town midwesterner who disliked publicity and on occasion hinted that he did not like football all that much.[11] The most obvious reason for launching a career in pro football was the money: $100,000 in hard cash. That amount was the equivalent of several million dollars in terms of the 1990s. But Grange could have made substantial sums of money, although possibly not $100,000, in any number of business ventures offered him without subjecting himself to the intense public scrutiny he knew pro football would bring. In addition to the lure of $100,000, Grange's decision to turn professional was based on several factors: his desire for long-term security, his hard-nosed midwestern practicality, his innate honesty, and the influence of Charlie Pyle.

As a boy, Grange had been shunted around from one household to another and later struggled with domestic chores and responsibilities in order to help provide a decent home life for Gardie, his father, and himself. He wanted what he had not had as a youth except on those occasions when the Dollinger family helped provide it—security. The money he could amass, presumably quickly, in pro football would allow him to have the material things denied him as a youth as well as, and more important, the security he craved.

Grange also chose pro football over other business options for a very practical reason. He believed Charlie Pyle's projection that he could make a small fortune in a relatively short time by casting his fate with Pyle and the pro game. For Grange, that meant being able to pay back his father for funding his education, providing for his and his family's future security, being free from the intrusive media and hysterical public in short order, and returning to a normal life. In New Orleans during Pyle's 1926 winter football tour, Grange estimated that his drawing power in professional football and the movies would be over in two years, "but by then" he added, "I'll have enough so I can say when I'll work and where I'll work, and work at what I want." He pointed out confidently that officers of a Champaign bank were investing his earnings in Liberty Bonds and first mortgages on real estate. Already the return on the investments "was several hundred dollars a month."[12]

Grange further believed that when the time came to cash in on his fame, which he never denied doing or regretted, integrity required that he do so by continuing to play football. After signing the professional contracts, he explained one reason for deciding to play pro football: "I have received many alluring offers to enter fields of enterprise in which I have had no training or experience. I believe the public will be better satisfied with my honesty and good motives if I turn my efforts to that field in which I have been most useful in order to reap a reward which will keep the home fires burning."[13]

Although he appreciated the opportunities afforded him at Illinois, Grange was unimpressed by allegations that were already abroad and that would escalate in the coming months: He was said to be betraying his coach, college, and the public by entering the "corrupt world" of pro football. Critics charged that he was making a mockery of higher education and "amateur" college football by dropping out of school and cashing in on the fame he had achieved by attending the University of Illinois. In a statement to reporters shortly after he turned pro, Grange duly thanked his coach and athletic director, the university, the public, and even the press, but he had few illusions about the purity of college sport. The University of Illinois and its athletic officials had provided an education, coaching, and an arena in which to display his enormous talents—but nothing more. Grange was keenly aware of the vast commercial enterprise that college football had become. He pointed out on several occasions that few people would have complained had he signed a contract to play professional baseball. He was, he realized, the victim of a class bias against pro football shared by many associated with the collegiate game. Accusations that he was betraying the college game did not ring true and sometimes angered him. A short time after signing with the Bears, Grange returned to Champaign for a football banquet honoring the Illini team. During the evening, Coach Zuppke gave a speech berating Grange for turning pro and at one point proclaimed that he did not want any more $100,000 football players at Illinois. "I'm somewhat of a bullheaded guy, I guess," Grange recalled, "and that kind of talk riled me up, and I walked out of the banquet (while Zuppke was speaking), and Zuppke and I didn't talk to each other for a couple of years."[14]

Despite his determination to cash in on his fame, Grange might not have summoned the courage to become a pro football player had it not been for Charlie Pyle. The Champaign theater owner had a profound effect on him. Grange had never met a man more articulate, suave, or persuasive. At the time they met, Pyle was everything Grange was not. When asked why Grange, a shy, small-town youth who detested the spotlight, might opt for a career in pro football, his friend Richard Crabb replied that Pyle had "put it in his head. He kicked him in his head. He changed Grange. There isn't any question about that."[15]

Pyle's influence appears to have been an important factor in prompting the retiring young man to challenge the advice of university officials and also conventional wisdom and play professional football. How he accomplished that is not altogether clear. Perhaps Grange saw in him the stylish sophistication and adroitness that was so lacking in his boyhood Wheaton and subconsciously aspired to be part of that world. In later years, when Pyle came to be regarded more and more as a shill and a huckster, Grange went out of his way to defend his former manager and agent. Although he seldom spoke critically about anyone, Grange was particularly protective of Pyle. When sportswriter Myron Cope good-naturedly poked fun at the Bunion Derby, for example, Grange became testy and defensive describing the transcontinental foot race as "the greatest feat ever put on in this country, from an athletic standpoint."[16]

A firestorm of controversy erupted over Grange's decision to quit college before graduating to play professional football. The "great debate" on the merits of his decision and its impact on public perception of higher education in general—and intercollegiate and professional football in particular—would be far-reaching. The controversy concerning the "amateur ethic" associated with college football and the corrupting influences of commercialism and professionalism on the sport was as old as intercollegiate football itself. As a result of the nation's participation in World War I and the role athletics apparently played in training and motivating American soldiers, however, the controversy had been muted for a number of years. During the early fall of 1925, at least in part because of the attention Grange's notoriety was focusing on intercollegiate football, the presidents of some small colleges leveled a blistering attack on the game and emphasized the familiar charges of commercialism and professionalism. A number of sportswriters, notably Grantland Rice, deflected the assault by claiming that the intercollegiate game had largely reformed itself since the turn of the century's lack of regulation. Grange's defection to the professional ranks ignited a new, more intense dispute.[17]

Newspaper opinion to Grange's signing was mixed. The *New York Times*, like many urban eastern newspapers, generally supported his decision, but with a note of sarcasm. In an editorial on November 24, the *Times* expressed "a note of regret" that Red had turned professional but added that when "Grange accepts $10,000 for participating in a single game of football, he is doing well not only for himself but for the community at large. It would have been a distinct social waste if the greatest football genius of the year had set out to make himself a doctor or a lawyer or a real estate agent." The editorial concluded that "there is no reason in morals or esthetics why the rewards should be withheld from the most famous name in the American ice industry since Eliza crossed the Ohio in front of the bloodhounds" in Harriet Beecher Stowe's *Uncle Tom's Cabin*.[18]

The *Peoria Journal*, like many midwestern newspapers, assumed a more serious tone in likening Grange to U.S. Army colonel Billy Mitchell, who testified in his presidential court-martial that he was "ashamed of the cloth he wore as an aviator. Referring to the opportunity the University of Illinois provided Grange, the journal maintained that his turning professional before graduation "must be distinctly harmful to any institution that it confirms critics who contend colleges have gone daft on interscholastic athletic contests and that education has been lost in the shuffle." The editorial pointed out that "without the 'cloth,' we probably never should have heard of 'Red' Grange or Colonel Mitchell." Along a similar line, a *Cleveland Plain Dealer* editorial chastised Grange for quitting school because he had "undoubtedly harmed college football, and has done a disservice to the institution which he has represented on the athletic field."[19]

During the weeks after Grange joined the Bears, college administrators, athletic directors, football coaches, and their allies lashed out at

Grange, professional football, and promoters like Pyle, who, they claimed, sullied the good names of higher education and intercollegiate football. Many college presidents, such as Kinley of Illinois, chose to remain publicly silent, confident that the storm would pass and the prestige of American universities would endure. Kinley and his colleagues must have been vexed, however, if they read a *Christian Science Monitor* editorial on November 6 that concluded with the mocking words, "James Russell Lowell once wrote that a university was a place where nothing useful was taught. How admirably Illinois has answered this slur by so instructing an undergraduate that he could earn a million dollars without even the formality of graduating!"[20] College football officials and their confederates were neither as secure about their institution nor restrained in their responses to the controversy as were most college presidents.

The Great Eastern Tour

As the renewed and intensified debate over the role of intercollegiate football in American life began in late November 1925, the eyes of much of the nation were focused on Grange and his debut as a professional football player. After only three days of practice, Grange was scheduled to play his first NFL game for the Bears on Thanksgiving Day against the league-leading Chicago Cardinals. Interest was so great that the twenty thousand tickets the Bears had printed were sold in three hours on the Monday before the game. George Halas had more tickets printed, and a standing-room-only crowd of thirty-six thousand fans jammed Cubs Park to witness one of the most publicized football games in history. Outside the park, police battled with an estimated twenty thousand would-be spectators who had been denied admission. Before the game got underway, a number of outcast fans broke down a gate in the left-field section of the park in effort to gain entrance, but Chicago police drove them off. The game itself, played in damp and chilling weather on a muddy field, was an anti-climax.[21]

Cardinal tailback and punter Paddy Driscoll, until that time the highest paid pro football player, made a reported $500 per game and was determined to neutralize Grange and achieve victory over the cross-town rival Bears by punting away from him. The strategy, aided by the soggy field, worked well; Grange returned only three of Driscoll's numerous punts. Grange, with "77" sewn on his Bears' jersey, returned those errant punts for fifty-six yards, marking his best offensive performance of the day. From scrimmage, he ran the ball sixteen times for a mere thirty-six yards and failed to complete any of his six forward passes. His most noteworthy feat of the day was intercepting a pass under his own goalposts, which foiled the Cardinal's best scoring opportunity of the game in the third period. For a good part of the afternoon the frigid fans amused themselves by booing and hissing Driscoll for his reluctance to loft punts in Grange's direction. Driscoll later explained, "It was a question of which of us would look bad—Grange or Driscoll. I decided it wouldn't be Paddy." When the game ended in a scoreless tie, thousands of fans swarmed onto the field and tried to reach Grange, but police rescued him and escorted him to safety. George Halas, who reputedly cried while counting the record gate receipts, later remarked on Grange's impact, "There had never been such evidence of public interest since our professional league began in 1920. I knew then and there that pro football was destined to be a big-time sport."[22]

Halas had good reason to weep for joy at the gate receipts, as well as at the knowledge that the Bears' upcoming home game that Sunday with the little-known Columbus Tigers, strictly a road team in the NFL, was already a sell-out. The Bears, like other NFL teams during the early 1920s, had struggled for their very survival. Pro football began as a regional sport that was mainly confined to small cities in the Midwest. When the American Professional Football Association (renamed the NFL at the suggestion of Halas two years later) was organized in 1920, Buffalo and Rochester were the only eastern teams in the fourteen-team league. Franchises were cheap (only $100 when the league was founded, although few owners actually paid), and that led many "tank towns" such as Rock Island, Duluth, and Racine to join the NFL. The pro game was not very profitable, drew crowds that averaged only a few thousand, and was generally not much respected as a sport. John Underwood exaggerated only slightly when he wrote, "People who patronized professional football were thought to be of a caliber you now associate with Roller Derby."[23]

By 1925 football had spread into the East, and a team was reestablished in New York City when Tim Mara, a Tammanyite politician and bookmaker, bought the Giant franchise at the behest of NFL president Joe Carr for $2,500, stating that a franchise on anything in New York must be worth at least that much. Even the Bears, one of the best teams in the early 1920s, averaged about five thousand fans for home games and were a shoestring operation. Grange recalled that Halas "would sell tickets and then go to the locker room to tape the players' ankles. After the game, he personally would go around to the Chicago papers to get a little story on the sports pages."[24]

Halas was ecstatic when twenty-eight thousand hardy Chicagoans braved a heavy snowstorm on November 29 to watch the Bears play the winless Columbus team in a game that without Grange might have drawn a few thousand fans at best. Halas had been advertising "see the Chicago

Bears with Red Grange," but the ads read "see Red Grange with the Chicago Bears" after the Columbus game. Grange played a much better game than in his pro debut despite an icy field, running for seventy-nine yards from scrimmage and accounting for nearly 140 yards in total offense in the Bears' unimpressive 14-13 victory.[25]

After the game, Halas and Sternaman announced the signing of Earl Britton, Grange's college teammate and premier blocker, to play in the Bears' remaining games. Chicago also added two former Illinois linemen and Johnny Bryan, a former University of Chicago back, to its roster. One of the enduring myths about Grange was that he was the first important college player to play pro football. In fact, dozens of all-American college players had played in the NFL before Grange, and the overwhelming majority of pro players were college men. Grange and Britton, however, were among a lesser number of players who had dropped out of college to join the pro ranks before their class graduated. It was the professionals' practice of raiding intercollegiate or even high school teams for players that particularly infuriated college officials.[26]

After the Columbus game, the Bears embarked on the first of two tours that were to become the highlight of the 1925–26 professional football season, the first from mid-November to approximately December 13, 1925, and the second from approximately December 26, 1925 to January 30, 1926. Chicago had five scheduled games remaining with NFL opponents. To use the term *scheduled games* in the early NFL, however, is misleading. The NFL schedule that team owners determined before the season was often amended as the season progressed. Teams contending for the league championship (decided on the basis of the best winning percentage) routinely added or dropped games toward the end of a season based on their projection of how they might gain the best winning percentage. Halas and Sternaman, most likely with input from Pyle, had road games scheduled with Frankford (Philadelphia), New York, Providence, and Detroit as well as a final game against the Giants at Cubs Park.[27]

Beyond this formidable NFL schedule, Pyle, whom Chicago sportswriter Westbrook Pegler had dubbed "Cash and Carry," added non-league games against makeshift pro teams in St. Louis, Washington, and Pittsburgh. In just twelve days, between December 2 and 13 the Chicago Bears were going to play eight football games. Such a murderous schedule meant that Pyle clearly knew very little about pro football, but Halas and Sternaman should have known better. Early NFL teams generally carried from fifteen to eighteen players, and the starting eleven played all or most of the game, in part from pride and also because of the substitution rules. Grange was only required to play thirty minutes per game under his contract, but he would likely be a special target for opposition tacklers. The tour was suicidal. It had nothing to do with good football or competing for an NFL championship and everything to do with making money by exploiting the Grange phenomenon to its fullest.[28]

The tour began in St. Louis on a bitterly cold day against a hastily assembled team called the Donnelly Stars that was sponsored by a mortician. With the temperature hovering at twelve degrees, a midweek crowd of only eight thousand braved the elements to watch Grange play one of his best games of the tour. He scored four touchdowns on short rushes, ran for eighty-four yards from scrimmage, accounted for seventy-three yards throwing and receiving passes, and made the longest gain of the day on a thirty-three-yard punt return. The Bears easily defeated the over-matched Stars 39-6. Jimmy Conzelman, on temporary leave from the NFL Detroit Panthers, made the only St. Louis touchdown. When Grange sat out most of the second and third periods, the crowd put up several yells for his return. A deputy sheriff briefly interrupted the game when he served garnishment papers on Grange, the result of a lawsuit against the Pyle Motor Service Company, allegedly owned by Charlie Pyle. The game was typical of the tour in that it was played in bad weather, Grange's teammates allowed him to make touchdowns whenever possible, he sat on the bench for long stretches of time, and fans became restless during his absences and demanded his return to action.[29]

After the St. Louis game, Grange and the Bears enjoyed the first tour's longest period of rest between games, two days, although one was spent on a train bound for the East. In Philadelphia, some of the major sportswriters of the day, including Grantland Rice, Damon Runyon, and Ford Frick from New York newspapers and Westbrook Pegler of Chicago, covered the Bears' game with the Frankford Yellow Jackets and remained with the Bears for most of the remaining eastern games. "I knew pretty well after that that pro football had come a long way," Grange remembered, when prominent sportswriters began to follow the tour. The game at Shibe Park, which attracted thirty-five thousand fans, reminded Grange of his first appearance in Philadelphia a few weeks earlier in that it was played on a cold, rainy day that turned the field into a quagmire. He turned in what the *New York Times* described as "a worthy performance under the conditions" by scoring both Chicago touchdowns on short runs after setting up the first score on a twenty-yard pass reception and the second on a twenty-yard pass to halfback Johnny Mohardt. Chicago defeated the stubborn Yellow Jackets 14-7 in a game shortened by darkness. Although Grange only played one full period and part of two others, the fans were satisfied with what they saw. After the game, the Chicago players, still in muddy uniforms, rushed to the train station to catch the last train for New York, where they were scheduled to play the Giants the following afternoon. As they changed out of their mud-soaked equipment, the players realized they would have to wear the same soggy gear the next day. The ever-present Pyle turned to Halas, who also played end for the team, and assured him, "This tour will make you so wealthy, Halas, that next year you'll be able to afford two sets of uniforms."[30]

The invasion of New York by Grange and the Bears proved to be both the highlight and the undoing of the first tour. Because the game had been announced two weeks earlier, the New York media had publicized the coming of Red Grange as only they knew how. Allison Danzig of the *New York Times*, emphasizing the rural-urban division that was a prominent issue during the 1920s, described Grange as "the youth who has arisen from the obscurity of a Middle Western village to the position of the most advertised athlete the world probably has ever known." He further tried to account for the mass appeal of athletic celebrities such as Grange by suggesting that his many admirers were "victims in common of that fetish for hero worship which is inspired by the man of might on the baseball diamond, in the boxing ring or on the football gridiron. They were attracted to Red Grange because he is the living symbol of the power and the glory that all aspire to and dream of and which only the chosen few attain.[31]

Because of the intense publicity and extraordinary interest in Grange, the city, under its new mayor James J. Walker, assigned a special detail of fifty police to escort the famous redhead to his dressing room. Two hundred and fifty other patrolmen were disbursed to handle the expected record crowd at the Polo Grounds. To further heighten interest, Pyle issued a statement assuring fans that Grange, barring injury, would play the entire game. Although estimates of the official attendance vary, based on the net gate receipts of $142,000 it seems likely that between seventy and seventy-two thousand fans jammed every nook and cranny of the Polo Grounds, which seated sixty-five thousand, to watch Grange play. It was the largest gathering ever to see a football game in New York and by far the biggest crowd in pro football history. The game likely saved the NFL franchise in New York. Giant owner Tim Mara, who had rolled up a debt of $35,000 in his first season in the league with no relief in sight, recalled, "When I saw that crowd and knew that half the cash in the house was mine, I said to myself, 'Timothy, how long has this gravy train been running.'"[32]

Grange responded to the massive crowd by playing his best all-around game of the two tours. Despite a muddy field he rushed for fifty-three yards from scrimmage in eleven attempts, completed two passes for thirty-two yards, caught one pass for twenty-three yards, and ran back two kicks for thirteen yards. Beyond that, he threw the key block that allowed quarterback Joey Sternaman, the star of the game, to score one of his two touchdowns. In the final period Grange secured Chicago's 19-7 victory when he intercepted a Giant pass and sprinted thirty-five yards for a touchdown. He accomplished all this in about thirty-five minutes, a little more than half the time that Pyle had promised New York fans they could expect to see his client on the field.[33]

During that time, the Giants appeared intent on roughing up Grange, who later described the game as "one of the most bruising battles I had ever been in." In the second period after Grange knocked down a Giant pass, Westbrook Pegler described how "Red was slugged with a Firpoesque slam on the back of the headgear by [Joe] Williams of the Giants, who had been sent out to receive the throw." The *Chicago Tribune* sportswriter related that "Red stumbled unsteadily but did nothing about it, and neither did the officials who were about as hostile to fist fighting as Tex Rickard is, all afternoon." When Grange returned to action in the final period, Pegler continued, "Red was kicked on the forearm by [Tommy] Tomlin of the Giants' front line and it wasn't long after that till Joe Alexander, the Giants' center, stopped him in a line play and squatted on the ground with Grange in his lap, trying to twist his head off to see what kind of sawdust he's stuffed with. The officials told Alexander he oughtn't to do that but didn't charge him anything for it."[34]

After the game, Grange, battered and bruised and suffering from a head cold as a result of his afternoon's work, gave a radio address in support of Near East Relief, a talk heard in a dozen cities from Washington, D.C., to St. Paul, Minnesota. Although reporters speculated that he had earned $30,000 for his thirty-five minutes of play against the Giants, Grange assured listeners that football's "rewards are spiritual rather than material, but they are certain." The following morning, while the rest of the Bears enjoyed a rare day off, Pyle, with Grange at his side, set up shop in Grange's suite at the Aster Hotel to welcome all endorsement proposals. According to George Halas, Pyle, who was shaving, pointed his straight-edge razor at Grange and said, "Son, this is the blade that knows no brother. We are going to take a deep cut at the dough on Old Broadway, let the [chips] fall where they may." Grange remembered that "the only thing I needed to do was just meet the people. I never had any part in the discussions or anything." To heighten interest in the endorsement auction, Pyle wrote out a check for $300,000 and flashed it around to the press, claiming it was payment for a movie contract Grange had signed. Grange remembered it as "strictly a friendly promotion, and we didn't receive anything near that amount, but he had a lot of people believing it." The *New York Times* reported the next day that Grange would receive the $300,000 from the Arrow Production Company to make one movie in March. His only comment was that "he had refused to be a 'sheik.'" From that point on during the two tours, Grange's teammates called him "Rudy" in reference to Rudolph Valentino, who had played the romantic role of a sheik in a recent film.[35]

Pyle and Grange secured endorsement contracts totaling an estimated $40,000, excluding the bogus movie check. Grange remembered that Pyle "wasn't afraid to talk money. When the average guy would say $5,000, Pyle would say twenty-five or thirty thousand. He got mostly cash. Cash or check. He didn't fool around." In New York, Grange agreed to endorse a sweater ($12,000), a football doll ($10,000), shoes ($5,000), ginger ale ($5,000), a cap ($2,500), and even a meat loaf. He balked at a $10,000 offer to say he smoked a certain brand of cigarettes but accepted $1,000 from the tobacco firm to use his name in advertising with the stipulation that no insinuation would be made that he smoked. During the course of the next year, Grange would add another dozen or more endorsements to those obtained in New York. As he later observed, "I guess I was the first football player to have a manager or business partner like that." In fact, Grange's endorsements and their commercial success would pave the way for future football stars to cash in on their fame, as Honus Wagner, Ty Cobb, Babe Ruth, and others had earlier done in baseball.[36]

Despite his athletic and commercial triumphs in New York, Grange, apparently still tormented by the controversy that surrounded him, departed the city on a defensive note. "I have been criticized for leaving college and turning professional," he told reporters. "If I were a baseball player and joined the Chicago Cubs or the White Sox there would be no criticism, but because I happen to be a football player there seems to be some question of the ethics of my decision."[37] When Grange and his teammates boarded the train en route to their next game in Washington, they were exhausted and bruised, the cumulative result of playing five games in the eleven days since Thanksgiving. What was worse, the Bears were scheduled to play three games in the next three days. By the time he reached the nation's capital, Grange's left arm was beginning to swell, most likely as a result of a bruise he had sustained in St. Louis and aggravated by a blow from Tommy Tomlin at the Polo Grounds.

At the American League Park before a disappointing crowd of seven thousand, the Bears played the Washington All-Stars, "a tough bunch of sandlot players who mauled and roughed us up at every opportunity" in Grange's description. Chicago prevailed over Washington 19-0 in a game marred by a fistfight, but Grange did little except appear on the field for his contracted thirty minutes and drop-kick an extra point. He carried the ball eleven times for a net gain of only eight yards. For Grange, the highlight of the day was meeting President Calvin Coolidge at the White House.

George Halas may be the source of an anecdote that Grange frequently recalled over the years: After Grange was introduced to the president as "Red Grange, who plays with the Chicago Bears" the tight-lipped Coolidge shook his hand and said, "Nice to meet you, young man, I've always liked animal acts." The *New York Times* reported that after Senator William McKinley of Illinois introduced Grange to Coolidge, "The President shook hands, asked him where he lived and wished him luck."[38]

Before leaving Washington for New England, Grange admitted to a correspondent for the *New York Evening Post*, "Gee, I'm tired. I'm played out, pipped." Sporting two blackened eyes and a bruised nose in addition to his injured arm, he admitted, "It's not all as easy as I thought. And the criticism—whew!" "I went into this thing for all I could get," he stated. "I'm getting it—in the neck." The midweek game against the NFL Providence Steam Roller, which had been shifted to Boston's Braves Field to maximize attendance, could not have been played under worse conditions as far as the battered Bears were concerned. At kickoff time the temperature was six degrees below zero and the field was frozen solid. Whenever possible, runners headed for the sidelines rather than risk being tackled on the hard turf. To boost the gate, Steam Roller general manager Charles Coppen had hired a group of former college stars, including Don Miller and Jim Crowley, who were two of Notre Dame's famed Four Horsemen, and Fritz Pollard, a former Brown all-American halfback who had played the 1925 season with the Akron Pros. This became a common practice for Bears' opponents during their second tour, as former college players tried to cash in on the Grange phenomenon. Despite the promotional efforts, severe weather conditions and high ticket prices for the Wednesday game restricted the crowd to about fifteen thousand.[39]

Boston fans gave Grange an enthusiastic reception. Three thousand mobbed him before the game and forced him to warm up in an area the size of a clothes closet. But their adulation did not last long. Grange played his obligatory two periods but with limited results. He carried the ball five times for eighteen yards, threw three passes with no completions, and had another pass intercepted. "My arm was in such pain I couldn't do anything right," he remembered. The climax of the game came in the third period when Steam Roller punter Red Maloney intentionally booted the ball directly at Grange, who stood dead in his tracks and deliberately allowed the ball to sail over his head and out of bounds. A *Providence Journal* reporter recounted that "the freezing fans, with the fickleness of a mob, rose as one man at the end of the third quarter when a substitute left halfback trotted on to the field and booed and hissed and jeered with cries of 'get the ice tongs'" as Number Seventy-seven left the game. When the final whistle blew, Providence had upset Chicago 9-6, ending the Bears' unbeaten string since Grange had joined the team on Thanksgiving Day. "As Grange went down the hole to his dressing room and the mob pressed in on him, mocking the fellow whose name was something of a national boast a few weeks ago," Pegler reported, "one of the civilian handlers of the Bears took a smack at the nearest of Red's tormentors and a brawl began that surged over a full acre and needed lots of cops." Grange remembered being booed for the first time in his career in Boston and learned that "a pro must deliver, or else."[40]

After an all-night journey to Pittsburgh, the Bears played the next day on the icy turf at Forbes Field against the local All-Stars. The Bears were so desperate for able-bodied players, Grange recalled, that "we suited up our trainer, Andy Lotshaw, who was a big guy, but he had never played football and we put him in as tackle. He played about half a game before they killed him. Not literally, of course." Grange himself lasted for only ten plays into the first period before being struck on his injured arm, forcing him to retire for the afternoon. Many in the crowd of 4,111 booed as he walked sluggishly to the dressing room. The All-Stars went on to overwhelm the listless Bears by a score of 24-0.[41]

Gustav Berg, team physician for the Pittsburgh Pirates baseball club, diagnosed Grange's injury as a torn ligament and a broken blood vessel in the arm and recommended that he rest for two weeks or more. George Halas, who had earlier predicted that his star player would be able to play in three or four days, promptly ordered a second opinion. Charlie Pyle, whom the press and some of the Bears would blame for the foolhardy schedule of games that led to Grange's injury, was on the West Coast making arrangements for a second tour. The following day in Detroit, where Chicago had a game with the NFL Panthers, a second physician confirmed the diagnosis and warned that a blot clot that had formed in Grange's arm could prove fatal if it reached his heart. He put Grange's arm in a sling and ordered an extended rest. Grange watched from the sideline as the Panthers decisively defeated the weary Bears 21-0. Despite his obvious pain, Grange was introduced to the sparse crowd at half-time. After it had been announced that he would not play, nine thousand fans exchanged their tickets for a refund at the gate. Detroit coach Jimmy Conzelman was irate because, he claimed, Chicago had not contracted the games in Washington, Boston, and Pittsburgh when the Detroit game had been arranged. The Panthers folded after the 1926 season, and NFL football did not return to the Motor City until the Lions entered the league in 1934. Conzelman was convinced that the struggling Panther franchise would have survived if only Grange had played that day.[42]

Even before Grange's injury in Pittsburgh, a Champaign newspaper reported that Lyman "Beans" DeWolf, Grange's friend and former

Wheaton schoolmate, would join him on the tour in the capacity of personal adviser, confidant, and secretary. The story related that the addition of DeWolf to Grange's retinue "was urged by Grange's father." Red was already receiving personal advice and assistance on the tour from Marion "Doc" Cooley and Dinty Moore, two pals from the University of Illinois. The addition of DeWolf to his entourage indicates that Grange was beginning to feel more like a victim than the feature performer in the Pyle-Halas traveling show. Despite the concerns he and his father had about the effect of the tour on Red's reputation and physical well-being, the younger Grange was determined to see it through so he would be "set for life."[43]

Chicago played its final game of the first tour against the New York Giants at Cubs Park on December 13. Grange, without the sling, was on the bench and wrapped in his raccoon coat. With him out of action, the Bears made refunds at the gate to thousands of ticket-holders, but still fifteen thousand fans attended the game. The Giants subdued the stubborn but sluggish Bears 9-0. James Crusinberry reported in the *Chicago Tribune* that "when the combat was over the weary Bears dragged themselves off the field as if they wished to go to bed for the rest of the season. Undoubtedly they are convinced that one must be a superman to play football five times a week." After the game, a dozen policemen escorted Grange out of the park and into a waiting taxi to protect him from the admiring throng. The following day Halas announced that a game with the NFL Cleveland Bulldogs scheduled for the next Sunday had been canceled. The most arduous tour in football history was over.[44]

A number of commentators have asserted that Grange's debut in pro football was the making of the professional sport. George Halas was closer to the mark when he stated during the eastern tour, "We have been doing well in professional football and making money for several seasons. We were gaining ground steadily but slowly." That was not true for all NFL teams, but the pro game by the mid-1920s had already emerged from the chaotic dark age of the zeros and early 1920s. Grange's first eight games as a pro, however, did bring pro football to the attention of sports fans as never before. In those games he played before more than 175,000 fans, many of them viewing a professional football game for the first time. Millions of others read extensive newspaper accounts about Grange and the tour. How many spectators or readers became converts to pro football as a result of that experience remains in doubt. Michael Oriard has argued convincingly that fans came out to see Grange rather than professional football and that few became loyal followers of the pro game. He maintains that pro football, like other sports of the 1920s, was rooted locally and "could not connect with fans outside the relatively few cities where franchises were located."[45] Football fans could identify with Red Grange, but their interest did not carry over to the NFL in this pretelevision era. Although Oriard's observations are correct, the game made substantial short-term incremental progress before television exposure made it the national sport. As a result of Grange's tour, major sportswriters watched and wrote about pro football for the first time, and many continued to follow the game after interest in Grange diminished. The expanded coverage was a small but important step forward for professional football.

The fact that Grange turned pro also helped the NFL evolve from a distinctly small-time operation in 1925 to a more firmly established league by the early 1930s. Given the history of major league baseball, it seems that the NFL of the mid-1920s was changing from a league burdened with too many marginal franchises in small cities to one that was beginning to recognize that success and prosperity were linked to promoting teams in larger cities. When Grange arrived on the scene, Joe Carr was already moving cautiously in that direction. In terms of weeding out some of the tank town franchises that made up the NFL, however, he was impeded by the facts that they had been the core of the league when it was founded in 1920 and their owners remained a considerable force in NFL affairs. After Grange demonstrated that pro football could potentially attract crowds of thirty, forty, and even seventy thousand to a single game, it was difficult to resist the process of transforming the NFL from an organization based on small franchises primarily surrounding the Ohio Valley to one grounded in larger cities. Such a transformation was inevitable if the league were to prosper, but Grange's impact on pro football speeded the transition.[46]

Grange did not play up to his college standard in his first eight pro games. He scored seven touchdowns (four against the makeshift team in St. Louis), kicked one extra point, and gained about 655 yards. After his superb performance and injury in New York, he could do little more than go through the motions on the field. A few observers both then and later claimed that the public became disillusioned with Grange and pro football as a result of the tour. Frankford Yellow Jacket player-coach Guy Chamberlin maintained that "Grange broke down mentally and physically, because more was asked of him than any human being could perform. The pro players on other teams were affected by the Grange splurge, and the public is disillusioned." That might be partially true. The problem, however, was not Grange but the tour itself. It was an ill-conceived and murderous series of games played at the end of a hard season that eventually maimed not only Grange but also most of the Chicago team. Playing ten games in seventeen days and mainly sleeping on trains on off-days was, Grange remembered, "a killing pace under any circumstances, but especially so when considering the team carried only eighteen men." Most of the games, moreover, were played in abysmal weather. Grange maintained in 1953 that "no other team before or since has ever attempted such a grueling schedule as the 1925 Bears—and I'm sure never will." As disenchanted as he was with the tour and pro football by mid-December 1925, however, Grange was determined to make his fortune while the opportunity existed and prepared himself for the second installment of the Pyle-Halas traveling football show.[47]

Barnstorming, Hollywood, and the AFL

After the Bears' final game in Chicago, Grange left for Danville, Illinois, to be examined by Dr. E. B. Cooley, the father of one of his personal advisers. The elder Cooley made an X-ray examination of the injured left arm and pronounced that with rest Grange would be able to resume play by Christmas. Three days later he felt fit enough to appear in a benefit show at the Studebaker Theater in Chicago along with numerous vaudeville stars. Meanwhile in New York, the Motion Picture Theater Owners of America threatened to boycott any film in which Grange might appear because his alleged $300,000 deal with the Arrow Picture Corporation was "bunk publicity." Grange refused to discuss the $300,000 film contract at the time, but a few weeks later admitted that it was phony. Pro football received another black eye as the Bears, reinforced with four additional players, prepared to embark for Florida the week before Christmas on the first leg of their second tour. A Chicago newspaper reported that the Milwaukee Badgers had used four high school players in a December 10 game against the Chicago Cardinals.[48]

Unlike the hastily arranged first tour, the Bears traveled in style to Florida and on to the West Coast. Pyle arranged for the players to ride in their own Pullman car ("Bethulla") and have a personal porter to handle their luggage. He also had them outfitted in sweaters imprinted with the word *Bears*, matching knickers, and knee socks. Earl Britton remembered that the players called the Pullman car the "Dog House" and "everybody learned to bark like a dog." Barnstorming teams traveling from town to town during the off-season to play exhibition games for profit was an established practice in professional baseball but relatively new to pro football. Fritz Pollard and the American Professional Football Association champion Akron Pros had conducted one of the first pro football barnstorming tours in California after the 1920 season but without much success. Pyle and the Bears had scheduled a much more extensive trip that would begin in South Florida, end in Seattle, and eventually cover more than seven thousand miles.[49]

When the team arrived in Miami for a game against the Coral Gables Collegians, scheduled for Christmas Day in that Miami suburb, Florida was in the midst of a building boom. Advertised as "America's Most Beautiful Suburb," Coral Gables had more than a thousand houses and other structures under construction. William Jennings Bryan had once been engaged by the community's principal landowner to sit under an umbrella on a raft in a lagoon to help sell lots to a crowd assembled on the shore. Three days before the game, however, there was no place to play a football game except for an open field where the Bears had been directed to practice. The following day, two hundred carpenters went to work and built a wooden stadium seating twenty-five thousand. "They sold tickets, ranging up to $20 apiece," Grange recollected, "and the next day they took down the stadium. You'd never know a ball game had taken place there."[50]

George Halas was shocked by the miserable condition of the playing field. He immediately telephoned New York and ordered new shoes with long spikes that would improve footing, including a pair with a hard toe for his kicker, Earl Britton. Britton protested that the hard toe wouldn't be "worth a damn for punting," but Halas ordered him to wear the shoe in the game anyway. After Britton booted two mammoth punts, nearly fifty yards up and fifty yards straight down, Halas relented and allowed his punter to change shoes. Britton would later redeem himself as the Bears defeated the Collegians, most of them pro players who had attended Pennsylvania colleges, 7-0. Sporting a black eye he had received in a practice scrimmage, Grange was the outstanding player of the game, making two long runs and scoring the winning touchdown on a short plunge. Financially the game was a disappointment. Fewer than eight thousand attended, primarily because of ticket prices more than five times higher than normal NFL rates. As was the case with a number of games on the second tour, Pyle's contract called for a sizable guarantee and allowed local promoters to set ticket prices. The promoters set the prices too high, which helped account for smaller crowds than anticipated.[51]

At the Bears' next stop in Tampa, Grange would face football legend Jim Thorpe and a team composed primarily of his teammates from the Rock Island Independents. Grange recalled that Thorpe, thirty-seven, was pathetically out of shape, fumbled several times, and had lost his former speed. "I never saw him in his prime," Grange declared, "but Halas did and said he lived up to his clippings." Pyle had arranged a more reasonable schedule for the second tour, and the players had a week to bask in the Florida sunshine before the New Year's Day game against Thorpe's team, which local promoters had named the Tampa Cardinals. Although he had good friends on the Bears' team, half of whom were University of Illinois alumni, Grange also fraternized with the rich and famous. When he was arrested for driving sixty-five miles an hour in Tampa on the eve of the game, Grange was accompanied by Jim Barnes, the British golf champion; Helen Wainwright, an Olympic swimming champion; and Johnny Farrell, a golf professional from New York. With a game scheduled the following day in Jacksonville and the temperature around 80 degrees, Grange played only thirty minutes against the Cardinals. He was ineffective until the final period, when he broke away on a seventy-yard touchdown run that elated the crowd. The touchdown broke a 3-3 tie, and the Bears went on to win 17-3. Despite another small crowd of eight thousand, Pyle collected a $10,000 guarantee from local promoters. Before leaving Tampa, Grange and Pyle each invested $17,000 in local real estate, an unfortunate decision because a devastating hurricane later that year ended the Florida land boom of the 1920s.[52]

The Bears' game against the Jacksonville All-Stars was the most highly publicized of the Florida exhibitions because of the presence of Stanford's triple-threat all-American Ernie Nevers in the local team's lineup. Next to Grange, Nevers was the most publicized football player of the mid-1920s. Stanford coach Glenn "Pop" Warner, who had also coached Thorpe in college, considered Nevers a better all-around player than his former Carlisle star. Shortly before Christmas, promoter John O'Brien had signed Nevers for a reported $50,000 to play five exhibition games in Florida, of which the Bears' game was the first. Nevers would play in a second game against the New York Giants before an injury forced him to abandon the exhibition tour. O'Brien was so excited about the impending game with the Bears that he announced to Pyle, "I aim to cover the South with an anouncement that no red-blooded man should miss the titanic struggle between the Galloping Ghost and the Lion of the Sierras—Red and Ernie. It will be a sell-out with lamentable numbers turned away at the gate." With ticket prices ranging from $5.50 to $8.50 (four times the normal NFL rate), however, only 6,700 turned out for the heralded contest. Pyle was not overly disturbed by the sparse crowd because he had already collected a $20,000 guarantee and shared in 65 percent of the net receipts.[53]

The game did not live up to advance publicity because neither of the highly touted stars performed any spectacular feats. Grange threw a twenty-six-yard touchdown pass to end Vern Mullen for the Bears' first score, but gained little yardage in only five carries. Nevers showed some of his triple-threat potential by completing eight passes, doing some excellent punting, and scoring a late touchdown on a five-yard plunge, but his repeated fumbles helped Chicago register a 9-6 victory. Halas remembered the contest as "a dirty game" that at one point resulted in some of the Bears chasing an offending All-Star player into the stands. O'Brien and the Jacksonville promoters reportedly lost nearly $12,500 on the game. With their game with the New Orleans All-Southerners not scheduled for more than a week, the Chicago contingent enjoyed a leisurely junket along the Gulf Coast to the Crescent City.[54]

In New Orleans, Halas had the Pullman parked in a remote part of the railroad yard and put lineman Ed Healy in charge of the players while he, Ed "Dutch" Sternaman, Pyle, and Grange moved into the Roosevelt hotel. Before he had much time to enjoy the easy pace of life in New Orleans, however, Grange was engulfed in another controversy. In Chicago, Archie Schatz, known in the theatrical world as Johnny Small, sued him for $50,000 damages for breach of contract. Schatz, who was from Wheaton, claimed that Grange had entered into a thirty-two-week vaudeville contract with him the previous August. Grange was to receive $2,000 a week to perform on stage. He immediately denied the charges but made a $750 out-of-court settlement with Schatz in April. The settlement further indicated that Grange had not been forthright in revealing the extent of his commercial interests while still a college player.[55]

Before the game, the Bears were guests at Fair Grounds Racetrack to watch the feature race, the Red Grange Handicap. Prickly Heat was the winner, and Grange appeared in the winner's circle to present the jockey with a massive pink floral football. The publicity stunt did not do much to generate interest in the football game, however, because only six thousand fans attended the contest at Heinemann Park. Chicago easily subdued the local team led by Tulane star Lester Lautenschlager 14-0, its fourth straight victory on the tour. The team's success was not unexpected. The Bears' opponents, despite some exceptional individual stars, were of dubious quality and did not enjoy the advantage of having played together before. Grange scored one of the Bears' touchdowns in New Orleans on a short plunge and electrified the crowd with a fifty-one-yard punt return that was reduced by thirty yards because of a holding penalty.[56]

After the game and before leaving for the Bears' next stop on the West Coast, Grange gave an interview to local reporters and attempted to counter some of the criticism leveled against him. He might have been motivated by the Schatz affair or by the steady stream of what he considered to be misleading stories written about him. According to one version of the interview, Grange began by saying, "I'm tired of being a target. I want to do a little shooting myself. I've got a few things I want to get off my chest." He commented on a number of subjects, ranging from the number of his alleged girlfriends (none, although he reportedly received two hundred thousand fan letters from women in 1925) to his now familiar justification for joining the Bears. Newspaper reports of the interview, however, focused on what he had to say about his former coach Bob Zuppke. Grange criticized Zuppke for saying that Red owed it to Illinois not to become a professional player. "What's Zuppke but a professional?" Red asked. "Does he feel that he owes so much to the University of Illinois that he wouldn't leave them at the end of his contract if some other university offered him $5,000 a year more to coach for them?" After the interview was published, Grange wrote to Jimmy Corcoran of the *Chicago American* and denied having said anything derogatory about Zuppke or the University of Illinois.[57]

While the Bears were en route to Los Angeles for their next game, John N. Kennedy published an article in *Collier's* that called Grange "the saddest young man in America." The author, who had earlier interviewed Grange, compared him to Rudolph Valentino, whom he described as the last word in unhappiness. Whatever his mental outlook, Los Angeles could not wait to welcome Grange. Damon Runyon reported that the commotion surrounding Grange's arrival was astonishing. He noted that the Bears would face a worthy opponent in the Los Angeles Tigers, led by George "Wildcat" Wilson, a former University of Washington all-American halfback and recent Rose Bowl star, but drolly remarked, "I doubt that many persons understand this. The popular impression seems to be that only Mr. Red Harold Grange will play for his side against the Los Angeles Tigers. The game is referred to as 'the Grange game.'" Pyle was in his element in the motion picture capital and had Grange and his teammates posing for photographs with everyone from Harold Lloyd and Mary Pickford to Luther Burbank. He even concocted a stunt in which some Chicago players threw footballs from the roof of the Biltmore Hotel to an awaiting crowd of five thousand who hoped to catch a ball and reap the $25 in prize money Pyle offered. Considering that the building was thirteen stories high, it was a wonder no one was seriously hurt.[58]

The publicity and hoopla paid off, and an estimated seventy-five thousand fans, the largest number ever to attend a pro football game, turned out at the Los Angeles Coliseum to watch Grange. Total gate receipts were nearly $135,000, and Grange later estimated that he and Pyle shared nearly $50,000 after paying players on both teams from $100 to $200 a man and covering other incidentals, including a substantial share for the promoter. Wildcat Wilson lived up to advance billing by rushing for 118 yards to Grange's 33, but Red, playing almost the entire game, set up two Chicago touchdowns on pass plays and scored two himself on short runs. The Bears easily defeated the Tigers, who had future movie star Andy Devine in the lineup, 17-7. Bob Zuppke attended the game, the first time he had seen a pro football event, and pronounced Grange still brilliant but his skills dimmed by the nature of the pro game, which, Zuppke maintained, had no real blocking and little team play. The University of Illinois student newspaper had reported that Zuppke and Grange were scheduled to dine together in Los Angeles and speculated that if they did "they must be going to eat swordfish." When they did attend a dinner sponsored by Illinois alumni, the *Los Angeles Times* reported that the tenseness of the situation was defused when Grange walked across the room and shook Zuppke's hand. Grange invited his former coach to sit on the Bears' bench, but Zuppke declined, saying, "I've sat on enough benches for some time to come."[59]

After the exciting spectacle at the Coliseum, the following day's game at a San Diego high school stadium against a group of local players called the California All-Stars generated little excitement. Only ten thousand watched Grange perform listlessly during his thirty minutes of play. He scored one touchdown late in the final period but otherwise, a newspaper reported, "his notable effort was the run he made from the field to the dressing room, [Larry] Walnuts running interference for him." Fatigued by the back-to-back games, the Bears went through the motions in defeating the All-Stars 14-0 in a shortened game. After a week's rest, the Bears again faced Wildcat Wilson's Tigers at Kezar Stadium in San Francisco before twenty-three thousand fans, who witnessed Chicago's only loss on the second tour by a score of 14-9. Before he left the game because of an injury in the fourth period, Wilson decisively outplayed Grange, who gained only forty-one yards in seven carries. In recalling the San Francisco game, Grange noted that although Chicago players generally got along well together they could occasionally become volatile. "I've seen more doggone fights by football players," he said. "They didn't have anything else to do, they'd fight." At the hotel in San Francisco before the game, Dutch Sternaman informed the Bears' massive center George Trafton that he wasn't starting. In that era, it was an insult for regular players not to be in the starting lineup or to be taken out of the game. Trafton promptly slugged Sternaman, knocking him through a window and out onto the lawn. The next winter in Chicago, Grange remembered, the diminutive Sternaman and Trafton decided to finish the fight. "Sternaman told Trafton to take his overcoat off and when Trafton had his overcoat about half way off, Sternaman started in on him and gave Trafton a good wailing."[60]

Chicago played its last two games of the tour and the season in late January in Portland and Seattle. Most of the Bears' opponents, the Portland Longshoremen and the Washington All-Stars, were semipro players who were badly outclassed. Wildcat Wilson, who played in both games, could do little to spark either team. With only six thousand fans attending at the minor league baseball park in Portland, Grange scored two touchdowns and gained more than a hundred yards from scrimmage before sitting out the second half with a minor injury. "The Bears loafed through most of the game," the Associated Press reported, while piling up a 60-3 final score against the local team. The following day in Seattle before another sparse crowd (five thousand), Grange ended the tour on a high note by running for two thirty-yard touchdowns and throwing a sixty-yard touchdown pass before sitting out the second half. Chicago won easily, 34-0.[61]

The Bears finished the second tour with an 8-1 record and played before approximately 150,000 fans. It is estimated that Grange and Pyle cleared about $150,000 from gate receipts on the second tour, which, in addition to their $100,000 (including endorsements) from the pre-Christmas tour, totaled an impressive $250,000. The newspapers and promoters of the two tours tended to overstate attendance, however, as well as Grange's share of gate receipts; the actual amount he collected is unknown. The Bears' organization netted about $100,000 from both tours, which George Halas described as "the first financial cushion we'd managed to accumulate." Chicago players who participated in both tours earned on average a little over $3,000 for playing in seventeen football games. Red Grange did not save pro football—or, for that matter, make it a respectable game as some commentators have claimed. Other pioneers of the game had already accomplished that. He did, however, provide the pro game with much-needed publicity. Many years later, Halas summarized Grange's initial impact on what some NFL officials euphemistically called postgraduate football: "I believe that as a result of our Grange tour, pro football for the first time took on true national stature." Michael Oriard has pointed out, however, that Grange and the much-publicized tours could not transform pro football into a sport that had a large national following during the 1920s.[62]

During the long trip home from Seattle to Chicago, Pyle huddled with Halas and Dutch Sternaman to discuss the financial arrangements it would take to keep Grange in a Chicago uniform for the 1926 NFL season. The Bears' owners believed that the 1925 deal had heavily favored Grange and Pyle but were willing to accept the same arrangement for another year in order to retain the services of Grange, later described by Halas as "the golden lad." Pyle was amenable to the fifty-fifty split of gate receipts, but only if he and Grange also received a one-third ownership in the Bears. Halas and Sternaman rejected the proposal unequivocally. Several more days of discussions among the three men failed to produce an agreement. Finally, Pyle boldly announced that without the one-third ownership he would be forced to organize his own team built around Grange. Halas and Sternaman refused to budge, and Grange and Pyle parted company with the Bears' owners.[63]

Pyle had to act quickly if he hoped to secure an NFL franchise for the 1926 season; league owners were scheduled to conduct their winter business meeting in Detroit in early February. He and Grange hurried to the Motor City to make an application for an NFL franchise in New York City, which they would jointly own. By telephone, Pyle was able to obtain from New York Yankee business manager Edward Barrow a five-year lease of Yankee Stadium. The men had less success in Detroit. After being put off for a day while the owners discussed a resolution that eventually became the Grange Rule, they received word that New York Giants owner Tim Mara would not grant permission for a rival NFL team to operate in New York City. Mara disliked Pyle personally, but his objection to another New York team was more practical. His franchise might be devastated if Grange played for another NFL team across the Harlem River. League president Joe Carr, who had recently suspended the Pottsville franchise for playing an unauthorized game in Frankford Yellow Jacket territory (Philadelphia) during the 1925 season, upheld Mara's veto. Pyle was infuriated by the Giants' veto and, according to Halas, told Grange, "No blasted Irishman going to keep me out of New York!" He promptly announced that he would organize a new league at a February 17 meeting in Chicago that mould compete with the NFL. In other business related to the Chicago Bears' recent tours, NFL owners voted to raise the team roster limit from sixteen to eighteen players and restrict teams from playing more than two league games per week.[64]

The American League of Professional Football Clubs (AFL) was formally organized in mid-February in Chicago. In a meeting at the Morrison Hotel, Pyle announced the formation of the league's flagship team, the New York Yankees, who would play at Yankee Stadium and feature Red Grange. He and Pyle were co-owners of the team. The ownership and location of the other proposed eight or nine teams were less certain as Pyle and other organizers frantically entertained and evaluated propositions from potential owners at the meeting and via long-distance telephone.[65]

Eventually, the AFL would be composed of nine teams ranging from the Boston Bulldogs in the East to the Los Angeles Wildcats in the West, the Wildcats playing strictly as a road team. In five cities there would be head-to-head competition with NFL franchises. After Walter Eckersall declined the position as league president, William "Big Bill" Edwards, a former Princeton football captain and well-known football referee, accepted the job at an annual salary of $25,000. It was reported that he would have broad powers akin to those of Kenesaw Mountain Landis, the major league baseball commissioner, but few doubted that Pyle actually would be in control. Edwards's first action was to uphold the integrity of the AFL by adopting the recently established NFL rule that no college player would be eligible to play until his class graduated. He pronounced that "the good qualities of the game and the tremendous public interest in it combine to make it now the property of the public, and it must be played by others than college men and schoolboys."[66]

After assisting Pyle in establishing the framework for the AFL, which the press referred to as the "Grange League," Red returned to Wheaton, where he bought his father a new home. The large, three-story house on the outskirts of town, complete with an automobile repair shop, cost Grange the then substantial sum of $25,000. With his pockets bulging from the recently completed tours, Grange developed a fondness for the good life and enjoyed spending his money.[67]

Notes

From Red *Grange and the Rise of Modern Football.* Copyright 1999 by the Board of Trustees of the University of Illinois. Used with permission of the University of Illinois Press.

1. *New York Times*, Nov. 11, 12, 1925; *New York World*, Nov. 12, 1925; Joe Williams, "Tim Mara Quits Suckers Long Enough to See His Giants," newspaper clipping, Aug. 31, 1939, Pro Football Hall of Fame, Canton, Ohio; Robert W. Peterson, *Pigskin: The Early Years of Pro Football* (New York: Oxford University Press, 1997), 98; *Chicago Tribune*, Nov. 12, 1925.

2. Harold E. Grange, as told to Ira Morton, *The Red Grange Story: An Autobiography* (Urbana: University of Illinois Press, 1993), 79; "Red Denies Signing Large Contract to Play in Miami, Fla.," Nov. 15, 1925, newspaper clipping, University of Illinois Archives, Urbana (first quotation); *New York Times*, Nov. 15 (second quotation) and 17, 1925; *Chicago Tribune*, Nov. 17, 1925 (third quotation).

3. Grange, *Red Grange Story*, 93; Gallagher, "Galloping Ghost," 94; *New York Times*, Nov. 18, 1925.

4. *New York Times*, Nov. 19 (first quotation) and 20, 1925; Grange, *Red Grange Story*, 93–94; *Chicago Tribune*, Nov. 20, 1915 (second quotation).

5. *Chicago Tribune*, Nov. 20, 1925; *New York Times*, Nov. 20, 1915 (first quotation); Grange, *Red Grange Story*, 94–95 (second quotation). Grange also wrote that "a lot of hogwash has been written that almost everyone, including George Huff, Bob Zuppke, and my father, tried to discourage me from casting my lot with the pros. The plain fact is that no one except the newspapers ever brought up the subject until Zup questioned me about my future plans as we traveled on the train to Columbus for the Ohio State encounter" (94–95). Grange is more critical of Illinois officials in Gallagher, "Galloping Ghost," 94.

6. William D. Richardson, "Grange Plays Last Game Today," *New York Times*, Nov. 21, 1925; Grange, *Red Grange Story*, 95; Al Stump, "The Ghost Still Gallops," *Pageant* (Dec. 1952): 148.

7. Richardson, "Grange Plays Last Game"; "Grange Turns Pro; Illinois Wins, 14–9," *New York Times*, Nov. 22, 1925.

8. *New York Times*, Nov. 22, 1915; Grange, *Red Grange Story*, 96 (first quotation); Gallagher, "Galloping Ghost," 94 (second quotation).

9. Gallagher, "Galloping Ghost," 94; Whittingham, *What a Game They Played*, 19.

10. *Milwaukee Sentinel*, Nov. 23, 1925.

11. "What, Ho Grange Says He Doesn't Like Football," undated newspaper clipping, 1924, Wheaton College Archives, Wheaton, Ill.

12. "Grange Turns on Those Who Have Criticized Him," *Milwaukee Sentinel*, Jan. 7, 1926.

13. *New York Times*, Nov. 23, 1925.

14. Ibid.; Gallagher, "Galloping Ghost," 94–95; Grange, *Red Grange Story*, 96; Michael Oriard, "Home Teams," *South Atlantic Quarterly* 95 (Spring 1996): 477–78. Although he may have walked out of the banquet, Grange spoke with Zuppke a few months later in Los Angeles.

15. Author interview with Richard Crabb, June 15, 1992.

16. Myron Cope, interview with Red Grange, 1974, Pro Football Hall of Fame, 8. "Shall Intercollegiate Football Be Abolished?" *Literary Digest*, Oct. 10, 1925, 68–76; "How Football Fosters Fair Play and Clean Living," *Literary Digest*, Jan. 15, 1927, 80–81.

17. *New York Times*, Nov. 24, 1925.

18. *Peoria Journal*, Nov. 24, 1925; *Cleveland Plain Dealer*, Nov. 23, 1925.

19. David Kinley to Edward Keator, Dec. 10, 1925, box 129, David Kinley Papers, University of Illinois Archives, Urbana; "A Tribute to Higher Education," *Christian Science Monitor*, Nov. 23, 1925.

20. John Underwood, "Was He the Greatest?" *Sports Illustrated*, Sept. 4, 1985, 117; Stagg, *Touchdown!* 293.

21. Richard Whittingham, *The Chicago Bears: From George Halas to Super Bowl XX* (New York: Simon and Schuster, 1986), 43, 45; "Red Grange Collects $12,000, Teams Tie," newspaper clipping, Nov. 27, 1925, Pro Football Hall of Fame; Jim Muzzy, interview with Red Grange, 1984, Pro Football Hall of Fame.

22. Neft and Cohen, *Pro Football* 114; Whittingham, *Chicago Bears*, 45 (first quotation), 43 (second quotation); *New York Times* Nov. 27, 1925; "Red Grange Collects $12,000"; Underwood, "Was He the Greatest?" 118.

23. Whittingham, *Chicago Bears*, 43; Riess, *City Games*, 233; Underwood, "Was He the Greatest?" 117.

24. Henry McLemore, "Tim Mara a Cool Hand at Horses, but Football Makes Him Wild Man," *Milwaukee Journal*, Sept. 7, 1938; "George 'Papa Bear' Halas Was Mr. NFL," Dec. 1983, unidentified newspaper article, University of Illinois Archives, Urbana.

25. *New York Times*, Nov. 30, 1925; Whittingham, *Chicago Bears*, 46; *Chicago Tribune*, Jan. 28, 1991.

26. *Chicago Tribune*, Dec. 1, 1925; Oriard, "Home Teams."

27. Neft and Cohen, *Pro Football* 13–14; Dan Daly and Bob O'Donnell, *The Pro Football Chronicle* (New York: Collier Books, 1990), 16–18.

28. Daly and O'Donnell, *Pro Football Chronicle*, 16–18; Grange, *Red Grange Story*, 105.

29. *New York Times*, Dec. 3, 1925; Whittingham, *Chicago Bears*, 47–48; Daly and O'Donnell, *Pro Football Chronicle*, 18, 22; Champaign News-Gazette, Dec. 4, 1925.

30. Whittingham, *Chicago Bears*, 48–49; Myron Cope, interview with Red Grange, 1974, Pro Football Hall of Fame; *New York Times*, Dec. 6, 1925; Grange, *Red Grange Story*, 101; Daly and O'Donnell, *Pro Football Chronicle*, 22. John

Hennessy, the referee that day at Shibe Park, claimed that Grange scored only one touchdown. According to his account, after a Chicago player plunged over for a second touchdown that resulted in a muddy pile-up near the goal line, a newspaper photographer asked him who had made the score. Before Hennessy could answer, Bears' center George Trafton winked at the official and shouted, "Grange." Hennessy looked around and spotted Grange standing up about ten yards away from the play. The referee was convinced that Trafton believed that a two-touchdown game for Grange would help increase attendance for the game at the Polo Grounds the following day. John Hennessy to the College of Agriculture, University of Illinois, Sept. 21, 1960, University of Illinois Archives, Urbana.

31. Allison Danzig, "Hero Worship Urge Brings Out Throng," *New York Times*, Dec. 7, 1925.

32. "Seventy Thousand May Watch Grange Here Today," *New York Times*, Oct. 6, 1925; McLemore, "Tim Mara a Cool Hand at Horses."

33. Daly and O'Donnell, *Pro Football Chronicle*, 22; Richards Vidmer, "Seventy Thousand See Grange in Pro Debut Here," *New York Times*, Dec. 7, 1925.

34. Grange, *Red Grange Story*, 101, Westbrook Pegler, "Red Intercepts Pass, Races Thirty Yards to Score," *Chicago Tribune*, Dec. 7, 1925.

35. "Grange Gets $30,000; Says It's Secondary," *New York Times*, Dec. 7, 1925 (first and fifth quotations); Condon, "Galloping Ghost Rambles toward Seventy-seven," *Chicago Tribune*, June 11, 1980 (second quotation); Gallagher, "Galloping Ghost," 95 (third and fourth quotations); Grange, *Red Grange Story*, 52.

36. Myron Cope, interview with Red Grange, 1974, Pro Football Hall of Fame, (first quotation); "Grange's Two Days Here Yield $370,000," *New York Times*, Dec. 8, 1915; Gallagher, "Galloping Ghost," 95 (second quotation); Whittingham, *Chicago Bears*, 52.

37. *New York Times*, Dec. 8, 1925.

38. Daly and O'Donnell, *Pro Football Chronicle*, 18 (first quotation); Richard Whittingham, *What a Game They Played: An Inside Look at the Golden Age of Pro Football* (London: Simon and Schuster, 1987), 20 (second quotation); Peterson, *Pigskin*, 39; *New York Times*, Dec. 9, 1925 (third quotation).

39. "Football History as Made by the Illinois Iceman," *Literary Digest*, Dec. 26, 1925, 29 (quotation); Earl Loftquist, "Inside-Out," *Providence Journal*, undated newspaper clipping provided by Pearce Johnson; *Providence Journal*, Dec. 1925.

40. Grange, *Red Grange Story*, 103–4 (first quotation); *Providence Journal*, Dec. 10, 1925 (second quotation); Westbrook Pegler, "Boston Jeers As Red Fails to Scintillate," *Chicago Tribune*, Dec. 10, 1925 (third quotation).

41. Transcript of an interview with Red Grange, undated, Wheaton College Archives, Wheaton, Ill.; *New York Times*, Dec. 11, 1925; Daly and O'Donnell, *Pro Football Chronicle*, 22.

42. *New York Times*, Dec. 12, 13, 1925; Daly and O'Donnell, *Pro Football Chronicle*, 22; Grange, *Red Grange Story*, 106.

43. *Champaign News-Gazette*, Dec. 8, 1915; "Football History as Made by the Illinois Iceman," 32.

44. James Crusinberry, "Tired Bears Drop Contest to N.Y. Team," *Chicago Tribune*, Dec. 14, 1925; Daly and O'Donnell, *Pro Football Chronicle*, 18. The Cleveland Bulldogs later sued Grange and the Bears for breach of contract.

45. For an example of two writers who equate Grange's first pro tour with the rise of professional football, see Heinz, "The Ghost of the Gridiron," 56, and Underwood, "Was He the Greatest?" 118. See also Daly and O'Donnell, *Pro Football*

Chronicle, 16 (first quotation); and Oriard, "Home Teams," 471–500 (quotation on 483).

46. James Quirk and Rodney D. Fort have argued that the struggle between the NFL and Grange and Pyle's American Football League in 1926 convinced Joe Carr that his league's future lay in large metropolitan franchises. Although the war with the AFL may have expedited that transition, it seems more likely that Grange drawing huge crowds in New York, Chicago, and Philadelphia in 1925 convinced Carr to concentrate on large urban franchises. James Quirk and Rodney D. Fort, *Pay Dirt: The Business of Professional Team Sports* (Princeton, N.J.: Princeton University Press, 1992), 337.

47. *New York Times*, Dec. 17, 1925; Daly and O'Donnell, *Pro Football Chronicle*, 21 (first quotation); Grange, *Red Grange Story*, 107 (second and third quotations).

48. *Chicago Tribune*, Dec. 16, 1925; *Illinois Alumni News*, Jan. 1926, 142, University of Illinois Archives, Urbana; *New York Times*, Dec. 16, 1925, Jan. 12, 1926; *Daily Illini*, Dec. 24, 1925.

49. Whittingham, *Chicago Bears*, 52; George Halas, with Gwen Morgan and Arthur Veysey, *Halas by Halas: The Autobiography of George Halas* (New York: McGraw-Hill, 1979), 111–12; Earl T. Britton to Dan T. Desmond, undated letter, Wheaton College Archives, Wheaton, Ill.; John M. Carroll, *Fritz Pollard: Pioneer in Racial Advancement* (Urbana: University of Illinois Press, 1992), 144.

50. Frederick Lewis Allen, *Only Yesterday: An Informal History of the 1920s* (New York: Harper and Row, 1964), 228–29; Cope, "The Game That Was," 103 (quotation).

51. Earl T. Britton to Dan T. Desmond, undated letter, Wheaton College Archives, Wheaton, Ill.; *New York Times*, Dec. 25, 1925; "Only Eight Thousand See Bears Win," Dec. 27, 1925, newspaper clipping, University of Illinois Archives, Urbana.

52. Grange, *Red Grange Story*, 110; Underwood, "Was He the Greatest?" 134; Daly and O'Donnell, *Pro Football Chronicle*, 23; *New York Times*, Jan. 1, 1926; "Grange Wins, Fails at Gate," Jan. 2, 1926, newspaper clipping, Pro Football Hall of Fame; Richard O. Compton to the editor of the Illinois Alumni News, Feb. 9, 1926, University of Illinois Archives, Urbana.

53. Richard Whittingham, *Saturday Afternoon: College Football and the Men Who Made the Day* (New York: Workman Pub., 1985), 78; Billy Evans, "Football's Young Frenzied Financiers," Dec. 21, 1915, newspaper clipping, University of Illinois Archives, Urbana; Whittingham, *Chicago Bears*, 53 (quotation); *Daily Illini*, Jan. 12, 1926.

54. "Nevers Fumbles Often, Grange's Team Wins," Jan. 3, 1926, newspaper clipping, Pro Football Hall of Fame; Daly and O'Donnell, *Pro Football Chronicle*, 23 (quotation).

55. Halas, *Halas by Halas*, 112–13; *New York Times*, Jan. 8, April 16, 1926; *Chicago Tribune*, Jan. 8, 1926.

56. Whittingham, *Chicago Bears*, 52–54; Daly and O'Donnell, *Pro Football Chronicle*, 23; Halas, *Halas by Halas*, 113; "Grange Is Great Show Down South," Jan. 11, 1926, newspaper clipping, University of Illinois Archives, Urbana; Oriard, "Home Teams," 480.

57. "Grange Turns on Those Who Have Criticized Him"; "College Game Will Always Be Greatest Says Harold Grange," Jan. 12, 1926, and "'Red' Denies All

Manner of Things Papers Say He Said," Jan, 11, 1926, newspaper clippings, University of Illinois Archives, Urbana; Stump, "The Ghost still Gallops," 144.

58. John B. Kennedy, "The Saddest Young Man in America: An Interview with Red Grange," *Collier's*, Jan. 16, 1926, 15; Illinois Alumni News, Feb. 1926, 184. University of Illinois Archives, Urbana; Damon Runyon, "L.A. to Welcome Red Grange," Jan. 14, 1926, newspaper clipping, Pro Football Hall of Fame; Halas, *Halas by Halas*, 113; Whittingham, *Chicago Bears*, 54.

59. *New York Times*, Jan. 18, 1926; Charles Chamberlain, "Red Made $50,000 in One Game," *Urbana-Champaign Courier*, Jan. 17, 1947; Whittingham, *Chicago Bears*, 54; Daily Illini, Jan. 13 (first quotation), 19, 1926. Zuppke quoted in Daly and O'Donnell, *Pro Football Chronicle*, 20–21 (second quotation). Michael Oriard has suggested that the attendance at the L.A. Coliseum may have been close to sixty-two thousand and that many newspapers tended to overstate Grange's share of the profits in this and other games on both tours. See "Home Teams." 487–89.

60. "Grange Loafs As Bears Win," Jan. 18, 1926 (first quotation), and "Frisco Tigers Beat Grange," Jan. 25, 1926, newspaper clippings, Pro Football Hall of Fame; Daly and O'Donnell, *Pro Football Chronicle*, 23; Myron Cope, interview with Red Grange, 1974, Pro Football Hall of Fame (subsequent quotations).

61. "Red Grange Bears Defeat All-Stars by 54–3 Score," Jan. 31, 1926, newspaper clipping, University of Illinois Archives, Urbana; "Grange Stars in Victory." Feb. 1, 1926, newspaper clipping, Pro Football Hall of Fame.

62. Daly and O'Donnell, *Pro Football Chronicle*, 24; Whittingham, *Chicago Bears*, 54 (quotations), 56; Oriard, "Home Teams," 471–500, esp. 481–82.

63. Whittingham, *Chicago Bears*, 57; Halas, *Halas by Halas*, 121.

64. Irving Vaughtn, Grange, the Capitalist," in *The Greatest Sports Stories from the Chicago* Tribune, ed. Arch Ward (New York: A.S. Barnes, 1953), 218–19; "The Grange League," *Coffin Corner* 19 no. 2 (1997): 6–8; *New York Times*, Feb. 7, 8, 1926; Neft and Cohen, *Pro Football*, 54; Halas, *Halas by Halas*, 121.

65. James Cusinberry, "Pyle's New Pro Grid League Is Officially Born," *Chicago Tribune*, Feb. 18, 1926.

66. "Edwards Named President of Grange League," March 8, 1926, newspaper clipping, University of Illinois Archives, Urbana (quotation); "Pro Football's New Czar: 'Big Bill' Edwards," *Literary Digest*, Mar. 27, 1926, 54; "Grange League," 8–9.

67. Grange, *Red Grang Story*, 122; *Peoria Journal*, March 17, 1926.

Chicago was an important center of prize fighting in the late nineteenth century until the sport was halted by the municipality in 1905. Thereafter the city had only amateur boxing until 1926, when a new state law was passed to legalize prize fighting, which had gained status from a 1920 New York law legitimizing the sport under its state athletic commission. The purpose of such laws was to raise revenue by taxing admissions at professional fights. The first pro match under the new Illinois law was held at Comiskey Park before 20,000 on July 2, 1926. In the match, Sammy Mandell of Rockford took the light heavyweight crown from Rocky Kansas. On September 23, 1926, heavyweight champion Jack Dempsey was upset in Philadelphia by former marine Gene Tunney, and a wide clamor immediately arose for Chicago to secure the rematch. Supporters of prize fighting, like President William Veeck Sr. of the Cubs and Mayor William H. Thompson—a prominent sportsman of his day—believed that staging a rematch for the heavyweight championship would put Chicago on the map as the sporting capital of the country. Promoter Tex Rickard scheduled the rematch for September 22, 1927, at Soldier Field. Tunney was paid $990,000 to defend his title before the largest sports crowd in American history up to then—104,000—and the biggest gate in boxing, $2.6 million. The bout, which became known as the "long-count fight," became one of the most controversial in history: In round seven, Dempsey knocked Tunney down, but referee Dave Barry did not begin to count the champion out until five seconds later because Dempsey did not go to a neutral corner until then. Tunney arose on the count of nine and went on to win the fight.

Chicago and Soldier Field took their place alongside New York as a major site for American sport spectacles. Chicago began not only to host major prize fights but became even more important than ever before as the training grounds for amateur boxers, especially through the emergence of the Catholic Youth Organization in the 1930s and high-level competition in events like the Golden Gloves tournament, which began in 1928.

8 | The Dempsey-Tunney Fight

BRUCE J. EVENSEN

Behind Tunney's arms-length relationship with the press and the public was his "intense anxiety with crowds." The star status that went with celebrity in jazz-age America wearied him. His cool and calculated preparation for Dempsey in the ring was quite useless outside it. It was the "unknown quantity" that truly frightened him. He didn't doubt that he could beat Dempsey again. What he did doubt was his "ability to get up and face that mob of people without trembling." In his infrequent meetings with reporters, he expressed the certainty that "fate" was directing him "to an ending pre-ordained before birth." But as the night for the Chicago fight approached, it was apparent that the new champion remained very much in the shadow of the old one. Damon Runyon found reporters who gathered for prefight predictions at Chicago's Morrison Hotel hoping almost to a man that "one good swat from Dempsey would knock Tunney bowlegged." Fans felt the same way. Chicagoans, Gene Fowler wrote, were a lot like most Americans, except more so. They would welcome a little "fistic crotchkicking" in which "nothing less than homicide" would do.[1]

The promotional skill of Tex Rickard, the personality of Jack Dempsey, and the self-interest of sports writers and editors had helped transform boxing from illegal sideshow to civic spectacle and lucrative business. Paul Gallico of the *New York Daily News* was among those noting how much things had changed. "In the old days there was a purse for the winner and a frightful beating for the loser," he observed. "Hunger and need drove men to struggle long after exhaustion and humanity demanded that they stop." Now boxing was a business in which everyone, losers included, stood to make a mighty profit. Tunney would be making a million dollars for the Chicago fight, simply because it was Dempsey he was fighting. Before he fought in Philadelphia, the most Tunney had ever earned for a single fight was $12,000. Now he prepared to join Dempsey as the sport's second millionaire fighter. Like Dempsey he strove to become a corporate fighting legend.

Dempsey could remember when he and Doc Kearns had played poker with reporters covering training camp to fill free time. Now reporters needed to navigate through social secretaries, accountants, bankers, lawyers, publicists, real estate developers, representatives of advertising agencies, mayors, civil servants, and the professionally civic-minded to find out where Dempsey was. The assiduous cultivation and projection of his personality had brought celebrity status and the responsibilities of running his own corporation. Training now took its place with conferences, business luncheons, and small receptions with various intimate and interested parties. A reporter, frustrated with his inability to see the great one, asked for a photo of Dempsey instead. He took it with him to his typewriter, gave it a long look, and wired his editor, "Saw Dempsey today. He looks great."[2]

Not all Chicagoans shared his enthusiasm. Four members of the Chicago City Council, heeding the call of the American Legion and other veterans groups, opposed staging the Dempsey-Tunney return match in Chicago's war memorial stadium. Fortieth Ward Alderman John Chapman thought it a "travesty" for a draft dodger to profit in a stadium dedicated to servicemen. But Chapman's argument was met by Fifth Ward Alderman Bert A. Cronson, an ally of Chicago Mayor "Big Bill" Thompson. Cronson noted that "if Dempsey ain't an ex-serviceman, Tunney is." The "Fighting Marine" had been a dollar-a-day man while in uniform. For a night's work in Chicago he would be earning $25,000 a minute, $1 million for a maximum thirty minutes work, making him the country's 208th million dollar man.[3] *Chicago Tribune* publisher Col. Robert McCormick argued proceeds from the stadium's rental could go to fund "a fitting memorial to our soldier dead." Editorial writers agreed. Dempsey had "come clean" with his war record. He'd admitted he'd "made a mistake" and "taken the heat for it." Now it was time to "get on with the show." Rickard put the matter to rest by noting "that war stuff about Dempsey is old news anyways."[4]

Civic reformers and evangelical Protestants, who received an eager hearing from Mayor William Dever a year before when they opposed Rickard's flirtation with the city, received a deaf ear from Thompson. The Boston-born wheeler dealer was a bootlegger's dream, a "political

Barnum" who campaigned on doing "big things" for Chicago, even if newspaper attacks proved "experts" were paid many times the cost of construction. To allies in the Hearst press, his win over Dever was "a victory for the people." For Al Capone and other hoods who had fled to neighboring Cicero until the heat lifted, it meant business would now return to normal. To critics he was a caricature of "arrested development," a symbol of twenties rapacity, a "striking example of Chicago's moral amnesia" and "the potency of demagoguery."[5]

Thompson recruited George Fulmer Getz, a man who made his millions as a coal dealer, to head a three-hundred-member businessmen's committee to "do something big for Chicago." Getz fancied himself a big game collector and liked sailing to Africa to stock his private zoo in Holland, Michigan. His first catch as chairman was Tex Rickard and the Dempsey-Tunney rematch.[6] The deal had been cut before Jack Sharkey had been carted from Yankee Stadium [after Dempsey had knocked him out in round seven on July 21, 1927]. Rickard would be able to charge $40 as a top ticket price to Chicago's 100,000–seat lake front stadium. In exchange, Rickard would be responsible for certain "incidental" expenses. This included contributions to the mayor's favorite "charities," Westbrook Pegler playfully wrote, particularly "the fund for aged and indigent building inspectors, the fund for the relief of starving aldermen, and, most importantly, the precinct committeemen's Christmas fund."[7]

The city's surrender to the flare, blare, and hokum it had ambivalently resisted the year before, when boxing was first legalized in the state, was all but complete. The *Chicago Defender*, the city's black-owned newspaper, which in true Chicago immodesty advertised itself as "the world's greatest weekly," railed against Rickard's failure to release a diagram of stadium seating. The paper reported that some "ringside seats" would be five blocks or more from the fighters. Cultural critics noted Chicago's staging of the spectacle reminded one of "the decadent days of Rome," where "citizens clamored for bread and circuses." Nowadays, the *New Republic* noted, "we seem willing to omit the bread." Witnesses to the September 22 walloping, the *New York Evening Post* reported, were "playing the world's greatest lottery" by not knowing where they'd be seated with no hope of refund. "The democracy of fandom," one critic wrote, now "exalted to an idolatrous rite" the "release of pent up emotions of the cave man type."

A changing world had taken boxing to its bosom, with "the sedulous art of publicity" boosting a bit of barbarity to the level of a "stabilized and standardized industry."[8] Fights once fought at remote sites for fear they'd be stopped by the law were now held under bright klieg lights before a vast team of reporters and broadcasters intimately connected to a promotional apparatus that helped make such extravaganzas civic statements as hyperbolic as storytelling and public passion permitted. Cities that once shunned such a spotlight now vied for the privilege. New York's boxing commission, in what struck Chicago civic planners and sports writers as a fit of "comic opera," were now telling Rickard that "all was forgiven." He could hold the fight in New York after all. Philadelphia, Rickard told reporters, felt the same way. The sesquicentennial was over but the need to pay for it wasn't. As usual, Rickard made the most of the situation. In separate "exclusives" with the Chicago press, the newly remarried Rickard showed off his much younger bride, and admitted "promoting is a funny racket" while promising his heart and the fight to Chicago.[9]

The second Dempsey-Tunney fight grew to become larger than the cumulative reputations and efforts of those absorbed in selling it, from the fighters and Chicago city fathers to the promoters, reporters, broadcasters, and advertisers who stylized the event as social tableau and media tome. Anyone associated or thought to be associated with the spectacle became embedded in the narrative of its daily chronicling. A man calling himself "Tom Rickard" from Champaign, Illinois, made the wire services when he came to Chicago seeking tickets to the fight from his "long lost cousin." Tex Rickard's ticket manager Walter Fields made the papers when he received a scratch in a traffic accident between two taxis north of the city's Loop. Carolyn Bishop arrived in the Windy City, "ash blonde, eighteen, and as pretty as any girl has a right to be." The press reported that "Dame Rumor has it" that Tunney was "absolutely crazy over the flapper's "patrician carriage," despite what went unreported—they had never met.[10]

One could be somebody by being bound up in the mythology of the fight. A twenty-year-old bride of four months, Margaret Coale, made the wire services when she drank poison rather than accompany her husband to Chicago for the fight. Canton, Ohio, Police Chief Jiggs Wise made the national wire when, on his way to the fight, his car overturned north of Lima and he was killed. Salt Lake City newlyweds R. R. Scott and Janet McMurrin made headlines when they received two tickets to the fight as a wedding present. Minnie and Anna Cook of Bloomingdale, New Jersey, were postponing their double wedding at Rev. Charles Waldron's Methodist Episcopal Church to hear the radio call of the contest. Mary Lozzi from South Chicago went into labor with twins just before the big battle and promised to name her boys Jack and Gene. Thirteen-year-old Frankie Barone of 4015 Lowerre Place in the Bronx made the papers when he stole $120 his father Pasquale had hidden in the closet and made his way to Chicago for the fight. Twenty-two-year-old John Brennan tried to make a similar escape from Sing Sing but was captured "smelling fear-fully" in a garbage can of coffee grounds, potato peelings, and decaying cabbage leaves. Even death could not separate some Americans from the spectacle. Two condemned murderers at San Quentin received permis-sion and publicity when they asked to hear the fight hours before their scheduled executions.[11]

One hundred forty-five thousand miles of Associated Press–leased wires were brought on line to transmit the fight to twelve hundred newspapers, the most for any event in the organization's history. Every available printer was trucked in to composing rooms of member papers to save a few seconds of transmission time in getting the story from edi-tors to Linotype operators. Sixty newspapers prepared to broadcast the progress of the fight through radio stations they owned or leased. This was in addition to the nationwide network NBC had arranged for the fight and a still unspecified number of stations being organized by the infant Columbia Broadcasting System.[12] CBS had hired J. Andrew White away from NBC to broadcast fight coverage and bolster its lofty claims that it was the nation's newly emerging radio network. White's flight to Chicago was a stunt designed to publicize the broadcasting upstart and left Rickard fuming. CBS was claiming rights to the broadcast through its Chicago affiliate WMAQ, the station owned by the *Chicago Daily News.* Rickard's threat to bar WMAQ's transmission of the fight bemused CBS representative Stuart Rogers, who argued the air waves belonged to the public not any individual.[13]

CBS's self-promoting strategy was a dose of Rickard's own medicine. He had become a millionaire by cultivating the power of public imagina-tion and the ability of mass media to shape and stylize events to nourish that imagination. Now he told reporters the Chicago fight was to be his "crowning achievement." The thirty-two-year-old Dempsey could not go on forever, he admitted, and with his passing, the ring would be reduced to men who lacked his "color" and "passion."[14] Rickard's musings may have been part promotion and part merchandising, but also an equal part nostalgia. On the twenty-first anniversary of when he placed $30,000 in $20 gold pieces in his Goldfield saloon front to boost the lightweight championship between Battling Nelson and Joe Gans, he placed two gold-embossed, seven-color ducats, bigger than a dollar bill, in the shiny Fifth Avenue showfront of Thomas Cook & Son, the company conducting the airline tours to Chicago for the big bout. Twenty large passenger planes left New York, Boston, and Philadelphia the day before the fight, with each patron paying $575 for hotel accommodations, meals, a ringside seat, and a pep talk from Rickard. The lobby of Chicago's grandest hotel, the Palmer House, became ticket headquarters for the big event. High rollers seeking seats in the glass-enclosed, partially heated Soldier Field press box dealt directly with Rickard. To the last, he reported a "spirited bidding" for the privilege. Rickard's Madison Square Garden shareholders mightily approved of the show, sending the corporation's stock to an all-time high.[15]

There was no doubt that the draw was Dempsey. When George Getz introduced him at home plate at Wrigley Field, a capacity crowd stood and cheered. Police chief Michael Hughes made him an honorary cop. According to Dempsey publicist James De Tarr, one fanatical fan "cut his hand to pieces" by thrusting it through a car window in hopes of shaking the former champ's hand. Another begged Dempsey to "give him a lump" he could show all his friends, while another wrote he had bet his home Dempsey would win. Dempsey's training sessions were now covered live by WLS, a Sears Roebuck, *Chicago Evening Post* [radio] station. Special editions gave blow-by-blow summaries of Dempsey's sparring.[16] Veteran sports writer John Kieran noted that Dempsey's resurrection from fallen hero to cultural icon was facilitated by the way Tunney held the title. America knew Dempsey as the fellow who "crawled out from under a freight car and became a millionaire by knocking over every one who got in his way." But all the boosting in the world "couldn't color Tunney. It came out in the wash." Kieran observed how "no riotous mob of well-wishers" clung to Tunney and perhaps in his reticence he preferred it that way. Tunney "would never get across" to most Americans, Warren Brown wrote on the eve of Tunney's title defense, and what was worse he didn't seem to care if he did. Dempsey "loved the approval of the crowd" as much as he did the fame that went with the crown, several veteran sports writers observed at a testimonial dinner to Dempsey at the Morrison Hotel on the eve of the battle.

Dempsey's suggestion he might retire from the ring following the fight created a sense of urgency within the nostalgia. A *New York Times* reporter thought the end of Dempsey's career would likely make the upcoming contest "the greatest sports spectacle of all time." Ralph Gannon of the *Chicago Daily Journal* saw the drama's central irony. More than 100 million men and women worldwide would witness an event staged in a field memorializing America's war dead in which the generation's most notorious shirker and one of its better-known war heroes would fight to the finish. Yet it was the slacker, the "mixed breed enigma," whom "everyone wanted to win" with an intensity formerly found only in the Great War itself.[17]

Garage men estimated that $250,000,000 in cars descended on Chicago, its lakefront, and sports stadium the day before and of the fight. There were accommodations for fifty thousand of them, barely a third of the number of people planning to come to the city. Chicago's thirty thousand hotel rooms had been booked weeks before. All that remained through the Chicago Hotel Men's Association was routing to private rooms that went for five dollars a night. The Pullman Company reported that for the first time in its history every private car in its service had been placed in operation. People accustomed to drawing rooms and compartments were happy to get an upper berth. The same was being reported by the Twentieth Century, the Broadway Limited, and the Baltimore and Ohio. Specials were being run by nearly every railroad in America—the New York Central, the Illinois Central, the Rock Island, the Michigan Central, and the Northwestern. Officials at local and regional airdromes and landing fields were reported in a panic. Planes were arriving in unprecedented numbers, but pilots were not wiring ahead their plans.[18]

Fight fans clogged Michigan Avenue, spilled out into Grant Park, and trod underfoot Burnham Gardens, named in honor of the architect who had fashioned the Great White City for the Columbian Exposition. Along the lakefront looking north, they could see the gargoyles and grotesques of Tribune Tower rising above the Chicago River where Marquette and Joliet began their inquiry into the upper Mississippi. A visitor standing here would have his back turned to the Doric columns of the war memorial stadium within which a twenty-foot squared ring waited for its "knuckle-dusting spectacle" with a security detail of twenty-eight hundred police officers and an undisclosed number of Prohibition agents to keep order. It was all fight talk now. Nest eggs and fortunes were won and lost in the most heavily wagered event in American history. It was estimated that between ten and fifty million dollars would change hands, with bookies admitting they had "never seen anything like it." A last minute surge in smart money, buoyed by reports of Dempsey's determined training, made him a slight favorite. It was the first time many could remember a heavyweight champion entering the ring as an underdog.[19]

Although crowds gathered in municipal parks, storefronts, taverns, hotel lobbies, athletic clubs, and before newspaper offices to witness the fight, many went home to listen privately. At the Radio World's Fair, which opened in Madison Square Garden on the eve of the fight, Gov. Al Smith observed that radio more than any other technology was "bringing the peoples of the world together." But when Dempsey fought Tunney a second time, this was certainly not true. Communal witnessing of the fight now competed with spectatorship in the privacy of one's home. Consumers had two thousand receiving sets to choose from. Thirty percent of them could be plugged into a light socket, and in 1928 the number would rise to 50 percent. The signal they received was more certain, the work of the Federal Radio Commission in minimizing interference and the work of patents developed under the Radio Corporation of America to improve transmission. Ads taken out in most metropolitan dailies argued the big fight was the perfect reason to buy a radio. Even Dempsey seemed to approve. A full-page ad taken out by Wurlitzer showed the former champ looking natty in a three-piece suit with sweater vest, argyle socks, and spats seated next to his "Wurlitzer Championship Radio."[20]

When everyone was assembled, Dempsey came out from among them, cutting his way to the ring and appearing to Grantland Rice "lean, hard, ready" and determined "to get the man who got him" in Philadelphia. All James Dawson sitting beside him could see was "a solid sea of faces" rising in serried rows into the darkness, "yelling themselves hoarse" as the saddle-colored Dempsey in a white bathrobe entered the battle platform and its "pool of white light." For the $5 patrons, who sat beneath American flags rippling at the top rim of the stadium, the ring was more than seven hundred feet away. Some brought binoculars, others opera glasses, and a few had telescopes. Many could be seen gathered around their radios. Just before ten, the voice of Graham McNamee, the nation's best-known baritone, was heard to say, "Good evening, ladies and gentlemen of the radio audience. This is the night."[21]

At six minutes past ten local time, W. O. McGeehan of the *New York Herald-Tribune* looked down at his watch. Both fighters were in the ring, had taken their gloves from an incongruous box tied with "pretty blue ribbon," and were waiting for the bell. It was then Damon Runyon sensed that the crowd became "strangely silent." Tunney seemed to be smiling slightly, a confidence that infuriated Dempsey as much as his ploy to keep the former champion waiting before climbing through the ropes.

The action was duly noted by the country's most famous cousins, Robert McCormick and Joseph Medill Patterson, who sat side by side at ringside, and William Randolph Hearst, who sat with his entourage several rows away. The artists colony included Charlie Chaplin, John Barrymore, Douglas Fairbanks, Mary Pickford, Harold Lloyd, Gloria Swanson, Buster Keaton, Fatty Arbuckle, and film czar Will Hays, pulling for fellow thespian, Jack Dempsey. Dempsey was also the choice of Broadway envoys George M. Cohan, Al Jolson, Florenz Ziegfeld, and David Belasco, who had backed the former champ in a play. Ringside watchers wanted to know how financier Bernard Baruch had bet the action, or how David Sarnoff felt watching a fight that would seal the reputation of his newly emerging radio network, or what Albert Lasker and John Ringling thought of the spectacle as a promotion. Tex Rickard sat taking it all in under a gray fedora and brought a cigar to his mouth as the uncertain sound of the opening gong was struck. As near to Dempsey's corner as he could get, Doc Kearns set aside a green beard he wore to the fight as both gag and disguise. He was going to "pull hard" for Dempsey and "bet big" that way.

John Kieran of the *New York Times* remembers that the bout began with a burst of "several thousand flashbulbs" from three photographers' nests sixteen feet above the action. Fight films clearly capture Dempsey rushing out and leading with a long left. Tunney clinched and circled left. Dempsey bore into the body. Tunney counterpunched and circled left away from Dempsey's hook. His pre-fight publicity predicted Dempsey would tire if forced to chase and that Dempsey "would be beaten by his own legs." For the first six rounds that seemed to be the case. Rice saw Tunney "run and dance away" from Dempsey's "wild and flailing fists." Edward Niel of Associated Press reported Dempsey "worked furiously" with little sustained effect and took two blows for every one he gave. In the "bowl of the battered noses," Gene Fowler wrote in the Hearst press, the crowd clamored for Dempsey for every blow he struck and with every blow by which he was struck. By Paul Gallico's count Tunney had won the last three rounds and five of the first six, but Dempsey had won the crowd with his determination to "keep stalking" regardless of cost. Just before the end of the sixth round, McNamee thought he saw something. A right-left combination fired at close range got through Tunney's guard and made "the ring tremble" above McNamee's head. At the bell, veteran ring reporter Nat Fleischer saw it too. For the first time Tunney was "bothered" and "breathing heavily." Frank Getty of United Press wired he had glimpsed "a vision of the Dempsey of old."[22]

The seventh round of the Chicago fight, the most famous in the history of the ring, began not with the old Dempsey but the new Tunney forcing the action. Tunney's tendency to attack when attacked led him to uncharacteristically force the fight as the round opened. With Dempsey bobbing and weaving and circling right in a low crouch, Tunney stood bolt upright at the center of the ring, abandoning the movement that had him the fight's prohibitive leader in points. Tunney launched a left, a right, and a left that Dempsey easily avoided before clinching. Dempsey ducked a right-hand lead to the head that exposed Tunney's chin and followed with three light lefts to the face. Dempsey feinted with a right that Tunney blocked.

And then it happened, the most famous moment in the history of sports. Dempsey connected with a looping left-hand lead and fired a right that took Tunney to the ropes. A left caught Tunney on the chin as he sprang from the ropes and a right on the button had him going down. He crumpled under a right-left-right barrage, his left arm dangling helplessly against the middle rope, his seat on the canvas, his eyes glazed over, as Dempsey circled behind him. "Tunney is down," McNamee seemed to be saying. "Tunney is down," he appeared to be repeating, as a hundred thousand throats filled the uncertain space that followed. Referee Dave

Barry was pushing Dempsey toward a neutral corner and Dempsey, not understanding or not wanting to, stood in the corner nearest his fallen foe. Robert Edgren looked at his watch. Timekeeper Paul Beeler was on his feet counting Tunney out and Hype Igoe of the *New York Journal* was counting with him. McNamee's voice fell silent. There was confusion in the ring and pandemonium around it. Fleischer had picked up Beeler's count at four, but Barry hadn't. "The fight is going on," was all McNamee could think to say, "and they are counting," as Dempsey scurried to a neutral corner and Barry turned to face Tunney. It was 10:34 Chicago time. "Six . . . seven . . . eight . . .," McNamee seemed to be saying, but whose count he was recounting remained obscure. Barry began the count at one. Beeler's call as photographers flashed the image of Dempsey standing with his massive arms on the corner ropes and Tunney seated across the ring beneath Barry, dazed and down.[23] At the count of three, Tunney lifted his head and looked at Barry. At the count of six he looked at his corner. At nine he was on his feet.

"Tunney is up," McNamee was heard by some to say, "and now they are at it again." But ten fight fans in six states never heard the outcome. They died of heart attacks during the "long count" and two more died just after it; one of them, fifty-four-year-old factory worker James J. Dempsey, was stricken while defending his namesake in a heated argument. Publicizing their passing became, like the long count itself, an inextricable part of the civic spectacle scrupulously cultivated and carefully chronicled in Chicago on that day and for many years afterwards.[24]

The confusion over the count had given Tunney time to clear his head and consider his options. He had no recollection of the final combination that sent him to the canvas for the first time in his ring career. Instead, he noticed the distance between his eyes and the canvas seemed short and realized reluctantly that he must be sitting. "It felt good," he thought, as his cornermen "wild-eyed" pleaded with him to get up again. He calculated that he could clinch when he rose but Tunney had seen Dempsey paralyze men with a close-in chop to the back of the neck. Tunney considered launching a haymaker with Dempsey carelessly coming in, but in seventeen rounds, Dempsey had shown he could take whatever Tunney dished out. That left escape the only survival strategy, so Tunney decided to backpedal. Dempsey launched two looping lefts and Tunney danced to the left evading them. Dempsey bore in but Tunney retreated diagonally away. The brush with defeat seemed to energize Tunney as much as the nearness of victory appeared to exhaust Dempsey. Later in the round he fired a left-right-left combination and had Tunney on the ropes but couldn't finish him. Tunney backpedaled out of harm's way and Dempsey appeared spent."[25]

That was when the coda for the long count fight occurred, a moment as rich in simple symbolic significance in its first telling as in its many retellings. It was near the end of the seventh round. Tunney was back on his bicycle, retreating to the left. Dempsey attempted to cut off his escape, but Tunney avoided his left again. Dempsey stopped in the middle of the ring, motioned to Tunney, and reportedly said, "Come on and fight." But Tunney was too sensible for that. In so doing, he escaped the fate that befell Sharkey. Tunney retrieved the situation in the eighth when an exchange with Dempsey had the former champion down for the count of one. Just as characteristically, Dempsey refused to take the nine count that had saved Tunney in the seventh, later telling reporters "I wanted to kill the bum." The result was that Dempsey took a beating in the ninth and took matters into his own hands when he wrestled Tunney to the canvas at the start of the tenth. At the bell it was apparent Tunney would win the fight by decision, but that was not the decision sports writers and their readers and the fight's 100 million worldwide witnesses had come to.[26]

"We was robbed," said Dempsey's manager Leo P. Flynn, a sentiment shared by Dempsey's previous manager Doc Kearns, who blamed Flynn for not taking Dempsey from the ring as he had done in the first round of the Willard fight. "The Chicago count," Paul Gallico wrote, had saved "King Gene the First" even if public opinion made Dempsey his conqueror. The romance of sports writers and readers with Dempsey, Damon Runyon wrote, soured them to a successor as "serenely colorless" as Tunney. He appeared a new kind of champion, the first to emerge from a business culture that brought marketing and merchandising "to the manly art of busting beezers." Tunney's trouble with the fight mob had always been that he wasn't Dempsey. Now he had defeated their beloved Dempsey for a second time while admittedly on the deck for more than fourteen seconds. For the "sluggish human stream that flowed glacierlike slowness" from Soldier Field down Michigan Avenue in the direction of Chicago's honeycombed skyline, the experience of the fight had been an exercise in nostalgia, pitting "marionettes," as one writer put it, against one another in a passion play linked in the cultural imagination to "when the world was young again" and "we lived for a brief moment in the valley near the cliffs." If it was true, as Kearns later claimed, that "they don't come back," no one had given it a better show than Jack Dempsey, nor left his fans with more garish memories.[27]

The Chicago fight showed the power of tall-tale telling in creating civic spectacles that stylized the uncertainties of a nervous generation. The publicity apparatus that united the daily press and newly emerging radio networks in the promotion of sports and the creation of celebrity had "put Chicago on the map," in the words of Big Bill Thompson. It had stimulated the circulation of the city's many newspapers to record levels, served as a windfall for area hotels and restaurants, and contributed to the campaign coffers of Thompson and his fund for overaged aldermen. The implication seemed clear. Similar rewards would come to those cities smart enough to claim their slice of the consumption culture. The *Christian Century* thought it time to admit the fact that the pyramiding interest in prize fights was not the result of a few men who admired seeing other men "pummeled into pulp." Rather, hosting and promoting a prize fight had become as socially sanctioned and infinitely more profitable than "hosting an Elks convention." Indeed, no sooner had the fight ended than the controversy surrounding it began to build. Rickard doctored the films of the Chicago fight, extended Tunney's time on the canvas, and inserted a training-camp picture of an unmarked Dempsey. This message seemed a certain winner. Dempsey had been had. Rickard saw a $4 million rematch on his horizon with many cities bidding on it and launched a distribution company to put the fixed film of the Chicago fight into every home in America.[28]

The historic irony of the Chicago fight was that it was as much an end as it was a beginning. The civic spectacles carefully crafted for public consumption by Kearns and Rickard and Dempsey and a cooperating mass media during a prosperous decade would soon be finished. Dempsey, fearing blindness, resisted Rickard's angling and the public/press clamor for an immediate rematch. He had made nearly a million dollars in his last two fights and knew he would never be the fighter he once was, nor the noble savage the press and an adoring public had imagined him to be. Tunney told reporters he would never retire undefeated and then proceeded to do precisely that after a title defense against the equally colorless Tom Heeney in 1928 cost Rickard a fortune. There were few calls for his return. Rickard was suddenly left without a heavyweight worth promoting. As he huddled with Dempsey to "figure it all out," time was about to run out on the wily promoter and the golden decade he had helped to create.

When Dempsey fought Tunney at Soldier Field on the evening of September 22, 1927, memories were made for many of the nearly 102,460 people present, and a great many more who were not there, that would last a lifetime. Lieutenant Carl Ekman of the Evanston police department locked up his friend, brick maker Rudy La Bohn, when La Bohn announced he was going to wager his $10,000 bond on a Tunney triumph. Ekman, a Dempsey diehard, "couldn't bear" to see his friend lose the money and only released him when the bout was over. La Bohn, enraged, got drunk, and was arrested for driving under the influence. Associated Press did not note whether Ekman was also the arresting officer.

Thirty-four-year-old Duff Lewis, of 935 Sunnyside Avenue in Chicago, was arrested by police when he got to seat twenty-five in the eighteenth row of the thirtieth section of Soldier Field. His ticket had been stolen from an insurance office safe in Davenport, Iowa. Police were checking his story that he had purchased the ticket from a sidewalk scalper. Warden County jailer Edward J. Fogarty had such a poor seat he "didn't see a blow struck." That didn't stop him from saying Dempsey was the "clear winner" and from wishing he had "stayed at home and gotten the returns over the radio." The "five dollar boys" sitting at the rim of the stadium had a better view of a fight between "a bum in a brown hat" and "a bum who wasn't wearing one" who insisted on standing on their seats to see the ring. But as the "binocular brigade" left the stadium and crossed Grant Park on their way home, they could be heard to wonder aloud "how one fellow could knock the other fellow flat and still lose the fight.[29]

Pittsburgh's Bridget O'Brien wired Dempsey that she had bet her house and only son on him and was certain he had won. So was a Montana rancher who remained convinced the Manassa Mauler could tame Tunney and his wildest horse on the same evening. The 750 citizens of Salt Lake City who signed a twenty-two-foot telegram reminded Dempsey he would always be their champ. Four young men who had been living in Soldier Field's Doric columns for four days prior to the fight to assure a "good view" of their man Dempsey missed their chance when security found them but claimed "it was worth it anyway." A fan who carried a .45 Colt on his hip to the fight "just in case they said Tunney won" was relieved of his firearm and left powerless to reverse the result he had feared. Gene Fowler, who had begun his career as sports writer when Jack Dempsey had begun his as a fighter, observed that the open end of the emptying stadium faced the Field Museum of Natural History with its plaster casts of Neanderthal and Piltdown. These were the "patron saints of primitive fighting" just as Dempsey and Tunney and Tex Rickard and Doc Kearns were the founding fathers of boxing as big business, mass spectacle, and civic celebration.[30]

Rickard's wife of only a year had worn a white fox fur to an occasion that drew together the Vanderbilts and Harrimans, the Morgans and the Mellons, and the Insulls and the Chryslers in the socially approved event of the season. They sat beside more than one hundred governors, mayors, cabinet officers, and congressmen in a gathering of America's first families at the height of their powers in the nation's prosperity decade. The press, however, played their presence as a part of the country's ultimate democratizing event. Nowhere else, reporters noted, "had so many cross sections of America been assembled in one place at one time. Culture and "commonality" rubbed shoulders. And if their dress gave social class away, their cheering did not. The "veneer of civilization" fell before "the tumult and the shouting," the event uniting "highbrow" and "roughneck," cosmopolitan, sophisticate, and prodigal in an enduring public memory of jazz-age America. It wasn't enough that the nation had listened in and witnessed the event. Now much was being made of the dictaphone technique developed by Westinghouse to preserve "for all time" Graham McNamee's call of the historic contest.[31]

The long count lingered as the sustaining image of the Chicago fight, while Rickard and sports writers worked assiduously to keep it that way, hoping for another big payday. Pseudo-scientific explanations were given for Dempsey's refusal to go to a neutral corner when the championship appeared his. "Autointoxication, caused by Dempsey's frenzied, venomous rage," one ring judge told reporters, produced a chemical reaction called "toxine poisoning" that made it impossible for him to move when the referee ordered it. Furthermore, Dempsey's "wild fury" left him almost as weak as "the man he had just floored" and prevented him from finishing Tunney off. It was reasoned that while it only took ten pounds of pressure behind a punch to floor a man, Dempsey hit with fifty. That meant "in his mad desire to annihilate his opponent," Dempsey burned up "unnecessary energy." Experts could be found to argue that Dempsey remained Tunney's "physical master" and that only the long count by a "Tunney leaning referee" was responsible for the result. In short, it was hard to imagine and even more difficult to accept that Dempsey was through and with him the spectacular saga of the squared ring that had been meticulously built up around him.[32]

The class with which Dempsey handled defeat in the Philadelphia rain and the Chicago long count further endeared him to his generation. After abandoning plans to appeal the decision, Dempsey told reporters it was simply "the breaks of the game." Dempsey no longer needed to fight to make money. In an era of personal publicity he had helped to launch, Dempsey was a celebrity simply by appearing. He starred with wife Estelle in *The Big Fight*, produced by David Belasco, and premiered to enthusiastic audiences during the summer of 1928 in Philadelphia.[33]

Denied another million dollar payday, Tunney faced New Zealand heavyweight Tom Heeney in a July 1928 title defense staged by Rickard in New York which was remarkable for the lack of interest it generated. Soon after that sluggish victory, Tunney announced plans to retire from the ring and marry Mary Josephine (Polly) Lauder of Connecticut, heir to the Carnegie estate. He had become a millionaire through boxing Jack Dempsey and would make a second fortune as a corporate executive. He traveled extensively, made friends with George Bernard Shaw, Thornton Wilder, and other members of the literary community and even lectured on Shakespeare at Yale. He had lost but one of sixty-three recorded bouts, but when he retired from the ring, there was little of the nostalgia and gloom that marked Dempsey's passing. His ascendancy had briefly been interpreted as a Horatio Alger success story, but his "unspectacular efficiency" inside the ring and "bookish social climbing" outside it failed to touch, as Heywood Broun put it, "the heart of America" as Dempsey had and did.[34]

• • •

When Jack Dempsey fought Gene Tunney, the largest crowds to ever gather on the North American continent could be found before radio receivers and men who spoke through megaphones in public squares across the country. Many had gotten out of work early, eaten dinner quickly, dressed for the occasion, and hurried to the place where fight returns would be read or broadcast. It was as important to get a good spot as it was to be present. As the hour-long fights went on, no one minded standing. The announced rally of either fighter was a cause for celebration or desolation, depending on one's point of view. When the two men had finished fighting and the decision was read, there were few anxious to rush home. One's tendency was to linger at the spectacle and extend the shared experience. Differing points of view were passionately argued for a fight all had witnessed but none had seen. Mass communication had connected these communities, if only for the evening.

The Dempsey-Tunney fights, however, were an end as much as a beginning. The time was fast approaching when one could follow a favorite fighter through a radio receiver in the privacy of one's own home. When that time came, there was no lack of appetite for heroes. Mass media would cultivate celebrity as anxiously for Depression-era audiences as jazz-age writers had when Dempsey fought Tunney. But future personalities would never be witnessed in precisely the same public way. A consumption culture's early and eager embrace of leisure was above all a public romance in America's jazz age, made possible through a newly emerging communication network that tied the country's disparate communities together in civic spectacles that helped define and shape the era.

Notes

Reprinted by permission from Bruce Evensen, *When Dempsey Fought Tunney: Heroes, Hokum, and Storytelling in the Jazz Age*. Copyright 1996 by the University of Tennessee Press.

1. *Chicago Evening American*, September 21, 1927, 26; *Chicago Herald and Examiner*, July 8, 1927, 17, September 20, 1927, 18, September 21, 1927, 24.

2. The frustrated reporter was George Barry of the *Minneapolis Daily Star*. His story appears in *Minneapolis Daily Star*, September 13, 1927, 11. See also *New*

York Times, August 27, 1927, 11; *New York Daily News,* July 22, 1927, 32; *Chicago Evening Post,* September 1, 1927, 9; *Hyde Park Herald,* September 16, 1927, 1, 12; *Daily Calumet,* September 21, 1927, 1.

3. *Chicago Tribune,* July 26, 1927, 15; *Chicago Evening American,* July 26, 1927, 1, 4; *Chicago Herald and Examiner,* July 26, 1927, 13, 16; *St. Paul Pioneer Press,* September 14, 1927, 6, September 18, 1927, V: 1.

4. *Chicago Tribune,* July 29, 1927, 8, September 1, 1927, 10. *New York Daily News,* July 27, 1927, 28; *Chicago Evening Post,* September 1, 1927, 9; *Chicago Eagle,* September 17, 1927, 1.

5. Lloyd Wendt and Herman Kogan, *Big Bill of Chicago* (Indianapolis: Bobbs-Merrill, 1953), 274–75; John Bright, *Hizzoner Big Bill Thompson* (New York: Jonathan Cape & Harrison Smith, 1930), 177–82; Paul M. Green and Melvin G. Holli, *The Mayors: The Chicago Political Tradition* (Carbondale: Southern Illinois University Press, 1987), 71–77; June Skinner Sawyers, *Chicago Portraits: Biographies of 250 Famous Chicagoans* (Chicago: Loyola University Press, 1991), 251–52; Laurence J. McCaffrey, Ellen Skerrett, Michael F. Funchion, and Chris Fanning, *The Irish in Chicago* (Urbana: University of Illinois Press, 1987), 79–88.

6. The Getz scrapbook at the Chicago Historical Society shows Getz to have been a wheeler dealer in more than coal. He sailed to Africa to stock his private zoo in Holland, Mich., which was run by a staff of thirty-five, and seen, if one is to believe Getz's own publicity, by 800,000 visitors a year. See also *Christian Science Monitor,* September 19, 1927, 1; *Chicago Herald and Examiner,* July 26, 1927, 13; *Chicago Evening American,* July 29, 1927, 19; *New York Times,* July 26, 1927, 12.

7. *New York Daily News,* July 28, 1927, 33; *Chicago Herald and Examiner,* August 2, 1927, 1. *Chicago Tribune,* July 26, 1927, 15; Green and Holli, *The Mayors,* 76–77; Robert Cromie, *A Short History of Chicago* (San Francisco: Lexikos, 1984), 116–18.

8. *Chicago Defender,* September 10, 1927, 8; *The New Republic,* September 21, 1927, 109. *Literary Digest,* September 17, 1927, 36, 41; *New York Evening Post,* September 11, 1927, 11; *New York Herald-Tribune,* September 13, 1927, 12.

9. *New York Daily News,* July 29, 1927, 36, July 30, 1927, 24, 25, August 2, 1927, 26; *New York Times,* July 27, 1927, 19. July 28, 1927, 11. July 29, 1927, 12. July 30, 1927, 9, July 31, 1927, IX: 6; *Chicago Daily News,* September 16, 1927, 32; *Southtown (Chicago) Economist,* August 31, 1927, 1; *Chicago Daily Journal,* August 29, 1927, 11; Mrs. Tex Rickard and Arch Obeler, *Everything Happened to Him: The Story of Tex Rickard* (New York: Frederick Stokes, 1936), 328–29.

10. *St. Paul Pioneer Press,* September 16, 1927, 11; *Chicago Evening American,* September 22 1927, 1, 3. *Chicago Tribune,* September 18, 1927, II: 5.

11. *Chicago Tribune,* September 20, 1927, 22, September 23, 1927, 4, 6; *New York Times,* September 22, 1927, 20, 21, September 23, 1927, 19, 20; *Deseret News,* September 23, 1927, 4; *St. Louis Post-Dispatch,* September 22, 1927, 14; *New York Herald-Tribune,* September 22, 1927, 11.

12. *New York Times,* September 22, 1927, 21; *Problems of Journalism,* 6 (1928): 12–19, 7 (1929): 25–29, 91. See also Kent Cooper, *Kent Cooper and the Associated Press* (New York: Random House, 1959), 212–22; Victor Rosewater, *History of Cooperative News-Gathering in the United States* (New York: D. Appleton, 1930), 242–47; Oliver Grambling, *AP.— The Story of News* (New York: Farrar and Rinehart, 1940), 262–73; "Editors Set 1928 Goals for Journalism" *Editor and Publisher,* December 31, 1927, 7, 42. NBC's efforts to promote itself as the "fight network" are described in NBC Papers (1927), correspondence, box 2, folder 61, State Historical Society of Wisconsin.

13. *New York Times*, September 22, 1927, 21; *Chicago Daily News*, September 17, 1927, 1, September 20, 1927, 23, September 22, 1927, 27. See also William Ray Mofield, "Broadcasting Comes of Age, 1900–1945," in *The Media in America: A History*, ed. Wm. David Sloan and James G. Stovall (Worthington, Ohio: Publishing Horizons, 1989), 313–21; Lewis J. Paper, *William S. Paley and the Making of CBS* (New York: St. Martin's Press, 1987), 117–32; J. Fred MacDonald, *Don't Touch That Dial: Radio Programming in American Life from 1920 to 1960* (Chicago: Nelson-Hall, 1979), 89–101; Erik Barnouw, *A Tower in Babel: A History of Broadcasting in the United States to 1933* (New York: Oxford University Press, 1966), 125–52; Reynold Wik, "The Radio in Rural America during the 1920's," *Agricultural History* 55 (1981): 339–50; Francis Chase, Jr., *Sound and Fury* (New York: Harper, 1942), 67–83; Philip Collins, *Radio: The Golden Age* (New York: Chronicle Books, 1988), 34–45.

14. *New York Times*, August 27, 1927, 11; *Chicago Evening Post*, September 1, 1927, 9; *Denver Post*, September 24, 1927, 29, 31; *Minneapolis Star Tribune*, September 15, 1927, 10.

15. *Christian Century*, September 22, 1927, 1091–92; Getz Scrapbook, Chicago Historical Society. *Chicago Eagle*, September 3, 1927, 5; *New York Times*, August 14, 1927, S: 6, August 22, 1927, 13, September 15, 1927, 27; *Chicago Tribune*, August 23, 1927, 17, September 18, 1927, II: 4.

16. Getz Scrapbook, Chicago Historical Society; *New York Times*, July 25, 1927, 17, August 21, 1927, IX: 7; *Chicago Evening Post*, August 31, 1927, 11, September 3, 1927, 7, September 22, 1927, 11; *Chicago Herald and Examiner*, September 17, 1927, 13; *Chicago Evening American*, September 16, 1927, 1, 37; *Kansas City Times*, September 21, 1927, 26.

17. *New York Times*, August 26, 1927, 13, September 18, 1927, 9; *Chicago Herald and Examiner*, August 5, 1927, 15; *Chicago Evening Post*, September 20, 1927, 20; *Chicago Daily Journal*, September 22, 1927, 15.

18. *New York Times*, September 22, 1927, 20; *Chicago Daily News*, September 21, 1927, 1, 27; *Chicago Evening Post*, September 21, 1927, 1; *Hyde Park Herald*, September 23, 1927, 1;. *Daily Calumet*, September 21, 1927, 1.

19. A. T. Andreas, *History of Chicago* (New York: Arno Press, 1975), I: 13–21; Bessie Louise Pierce, *A History of Chicago* (New York: Knopf, 1937), I: 5–13; Emmett Dedmon, *Fabulous Chicago* (New York: Atheneum, 1981), 271–73; Harold Mayer and Richard Wade, *Chicago: Growth of a Metropolis* (Chicago: University of Chicago Press, 1969), 87–102; Reid Badger, *The Great American Fair: The World's Columbian Exposition and American Culture* (Chicago: Nelson-Hall, 1979), 126–30; David F. Burg, *Chicago's White City of 1893* (Lexington: University of Kentucky Press, 1976), 277–91; *Chicago Herald and Examiner*, September 3, 1927, 4; *Chicago Evening American*, September 21, 1927, 5; *New York Times*, September 18, 1927, S: 5, September 22, 1927, 21; *New York Daily News*, September 23, 1927, 60.

20. *St. Paul Pioneer Press*, September 19, 1927, II: 3; *New York Times*, September 23, 1927, 1, 18; *Denver Post*, September 23, 1927, 3; *Time*, October 3, 1927, 29.

21. *New York Herald-Tribune*, September 23, 1927, 1; *Chicago Herald and Examiner*, September 23, 1927, 1, 2; Jack Dempsey and Barbara Dempsey, *Dempsey* (New York: Harper & Row), 210–15; Tunney, *A Man Must Fight*, 262–63; *Chicago Evening American*, September 23, 1927, 3; *Chicago Evening Post*, September 23, 1927, 10; *New York Times*, September 18, 1927, S: 5; *Chicago Tribune*, September 22, 1927, 1.

22. *New York Times*, September 23, 1927, 20, 21; *Chicago Evening American*, September 16, 1927, 39, September 19, 1927, 20; *St. Paul Pioneer Press*, September 23, 1927, 9; *Denver Post*, September 23, 1927, 1; *Chicago Herald and Examiner*,

September 23, 1927, 3; *New York Daily News*, September 23, 1927, 2; Nat Fleischer, *Jack Dempsey* (New Rochelle, N.Y.: Arlington House, 1972), 168–69; *Rocky Mountain News*, September 23, 1927, 1, 13.

23. "Jack Dempsey vs. Gene Tunney, September 22, 1927, Chicago, Ill.," *Fantastic Fights of the Century* (n.p.: TM Productions, 1980), vol. 1; Fleischer, *Jack Dempsey*, 172; Gene Tunney, *A Man Must Fight* (Boston: Houghton Mifflin, 1932), 268–69; *New York Journal*, September 23, 1927, 1; *Chicago Daily News*, September 23, 1927, 1; *New York Times*, September 23, 1927, 21, September 24, 1927, 10; *Chicago Evening American*, September 23, 1927, 3; *New York Daily News*, September 23, 1927, 1.

24. "Jack Dempsey vs. Gene Tunney"; *New York Times*, September 23, 1927, 21, September 24, 1927, 10; *Chicago Evening American*, September 23, 1927, 17, 55; *Chicago Tribune*, September 23, 1927, 1, September 24, 1927, 4; *Chicago Herald and Examiner*, September 24, 1927, 1; *Chicago Daily Journal*, September 23, 1927, 1.

25. "Jack Dempsey vs. Gene Tunney"; Tunney, *A Man Must Fight*, 269–73; Mel Heimer, *The Long Count* (New York: Atheneum, 1969), 247–51; Randy Roberts, *Jack Dempsey, the Manassa Mauler* (Baton Rouge: Louisiana State University Press, 1979), 259–62; Gene Tunney, "My Fights with Jack Dempsey," in *The Aspirin Age*, ed. Isabel Leighton (New York: Simon & Schuster, 1949), 163–68.

26. "Jack Dempsey vs. Gene Tunney"; *New York Times*, September 23, 1927, 21; Gene Tunney, *Arms for Living* (New York: W. Funk, 1941), 135–38; John Durant and Edward Rice, *Come Out Fighting* (New York: Essential Books, 1946), 105; Tim Cohane, *Bypaths of Glory: A Sportswriter Looks Back* (New York: Harper & Row, 1963), 90–92; *Chicago Tribune*, September 24, 1927, 8.

27. *Chicago Herald and Examiner*, September 22, 1927, 23, 24, September 23, 1927, 1, 2; *New York Daily News*, September 23, 1927, 2; *Chicago Evening Post*, September 23, 1927. 10.

28. *Chicago Daily News*, September 23, 1927, 52; *Chicago Evening Post*, September 23, 1927, 8; *Chicago Tribune*, September 24, 1927, 8; Cohane, *Bypaths of Glory*, 91–92. *New York Times*, September 29, 1927, 20; *Chicago Evening Journal*, September 23, 1927, 4; *Christian Century*, September 22, 1927, 1091–92.

29. *Chicago Daily Journal*, September 23, 1927, 4, 11; *Chicago Evening Post*, September 23, 1927, 3; *Chicago Daily News*, September 23, 1927, 5; *Chicago Evening American*, September 23, 1927, 9; *Daily Calumet*, September 23, 1927, 1.

30. *Chicago Herald and Examiner*, September 23, 1927, 5; *Chicago Eagle*, September 24, 1927, 1; *Salt Lake Tribune*, September 23, 1927, 5; *Deseret News*, September 22, 1927, 3; *Chicago Tribune*, September 23, 1927, 2; *Chicago Evening American*, September 23, 1927, 11. That Piltdown was a fake was a fact that lay hidden from Fowler in his metaphor making.

31. *Chicago Herald and Examiner*, September 23, 1927, 4, 6; *Chicago Evening American*, September 23, 1927, 18; NBC Papers (1927), correspondence, box 2, folder 61, State Historical Society of Wisconsin, Madison; *Minneapolis Daily Star*, September 24, 1927, 16.

32. *Chicago Herald and Examiner*, September 24, 1927, 2; *Chicago Evening American*, September 23, 1927, 55; *New York Daily News*, September 25, 1927, 59; *New York Times*, September 25, 1927, 17; *The Nation*, September 28, 1927, 305; *Christian Century*, September 22, 1927, 1091–92.

33. *New York Times*, September 24, 1927, 9, 10; *Philadelphia Inquirer*, August 23, 1928, 21; *Philadelphia Public-Ledger*, August 31, 1928, 12.

34. *New York Times*, July 27, 1928, 1, 14, July 28, 1940, 20; *New York Daily*

News, July 27, 1928, 2, 32; *New York Herald-Tribune,* July 27, 1928, 16. See also Gene Tunney, preface to *Ten and Out: The Complete Story of the Prize Ring in America* by Alexander Johnston (New York: Ives Washburn, 1927); Cohane, *Bypaths of Glory,* 91–92; Tunney, *Arms for Living,* 228–43; Tunney, *A Man Must Fight,* 282–83; Benny Green, *Shaw's Champions: G. B. S. and Prize Fighting from Cashel Byron to Gene Tunney* (London: Elm Tree Books, 1978), 137–46, 176–85; *The Nation,* August 8, 1928, 125; Gene Tunney, "The Blow That Hurts," *Atlantic Monthly,* June 1939, 839–41.

The critical moment in the Dempsey-Tunney world heavyweight championship fight of 1927 at Soldier Field occurred after the seventh round knockdown, when referee Jack Berry directed Dempsey to a neutral corner before beginning his count. Photo courtesy of the Chicago History Museum (SDN-066912).

The elated Black Sox with their attorney, following their acquittal by a Chicago jury of the charge of throwing the 1919 World Series. From *Chicago Daily News*, 1921. Photo courtesy of the Chicago History Museum (IChi-32253).

Coach Amos Alonzo Stagg shown diagramming plays for his University of Chicago football team. He made the school a national athletic power and established the model for coaches as faculty members on college campuses. Photo courtesy of the Chicago History Museum (IChi-51374).

Thoroughbreds thunder down the track at Washington Park, where the American Derby was a premium event in American horse racing. The well-dressed spectators and elaborate clubhouse give evidence of its social status. Photo courtesy of the Chicago History Museum (IChi-51375).

Chicago, once a center of bicycle riding, featured a West Side velodrome. This 1901 race included an African American cyclist, possibly Major Taylor, the American sprint champion. Photo courtesy of the Chicago History Museum (SDN-000525).

Rube Foster, star pitcher for the Leland Giants and the American Giants, top Chicago semiprofessional teams composed entirely of African Americans. Foster established the Negro National League in 1920, since the major leagues continued to deny contracts to black players. Photo courtesy of the Chicago History Museum (SDN-055355).

Chicago was the site of the first automobile race in the United States in 1895. The Automobile Association of America sponsored open wheel races at Speedway Park, a two-mile board track in Maywood, Illinois, beginning in 1915 with a 500–mile event. Photo courtesy of the Chicago History Museum (SDN-060341).

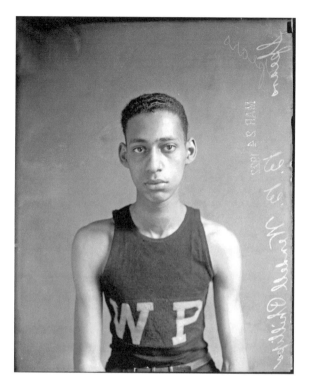

Reuben Spears, the center for the Wendell Phillips High School basketball team, led the school to glory from 1922 to 1923, shortly before the emergence of the Harlem Globetrotters, a barnstorming professional team from the South Side. Photo courtesy of the Chicago History Museum (SDN-063207).

Red Grange of the University of Illinois running around left end against the University of Chicago in 1924. Grange gained 300 yards and scored all three touchdowns in the 21-21 tie. The Maroons won their last Big Ten title in that same year. Grange led the Illini to second place. The Galloping Ghost of the Illini was the greatest football player of the Golden Age of sport. *The 1926 Illio* (n.p., 1925), p. 183.

The National Hockey League was founded in 1917 by five Canadian professional teams, including the Montreal Canadiens and the Toronto Arenas (later the Maple Leafs). Seven years later the NHL expanded into the United States with the Boston Bruins. Two years later, after adding two more U.S. teams, the league added the New York Rangers, the Detroit Cougars (now the Red Wings), and the Chicago Black Hawks (now spelled Blackhawks), producing a ten-team league. The negative effects of the Depression and World War II led to a six-team league in 1942 with what are now considered the original six NHL teams: the Black Hawks, Boston Bruins, Montreal Canadiens, Toronto Maple Leafs, New York Rangers, and Detroit Red Wings. This essay, specifically commissioned for this book, examines how Chicago secured a franchise in the young National Hockey League, how the owners tried to build the franchise into a competitive team, and how management tried to make the Blackhawks a profitable venture in a major sporting city despite the lack of a local hockey heritage.

9 Entrepreneurship and the Rise of the Chicago Blackhawks

JOHN CHI-KIT WONG

At 10:08 in the morning of 17 December 1944, Major Frederic McLaughlin passed away in Lake Forest hospital in Chicago. His obituary the next day described the deceased as a son of a wealthy coffee merchant who had inherited the family business when his brother George D. McLaughlin died in an automobile accident in 1933. According to the notice, McLaughlin was also "prominent in Chicago society as a sportsman and clubmen" but "was known to the sports world principally for his connection with the Blackhawks hockey team, of which he was chairman of the board, his title since he yielded the presidency to (William J.) Tobin in 1939."[1] If McLaughlin's fortunes seem to have been handed down to him by his family, there is no denying his accomplishment as a sports entrepreneur and as the owner of the Chicago Blackhawks of the National Hockey League (NHL).

McLaughlin is well known, at least in the hockey circles, as the owner who ruled the Blackhawks with an iron hand, firing and hiring thirteen coaches in his first ten years, more than even George Steinbrenner of the present-day New York Yankees.[2] However, few hockey enthusiasts have heard of another equally important character in the Chicago franchise history, one Huntington R. (Tack) Hardwick, who led the successful bid for an NHL franchise in Chicago. By the time McLaughlin took over, before the Blackhawks' first season, Hardwick had already had the players and playing facility in place. Hardwick was as important an entrepreneur as McLaughlin and made the Chicago franchise possible.

An entrepreneur, according to the renowned economist Joseph Schumpeter, can affect the marketplace by introducing a product or service innovation, a different mode of production, an alternative organizational structure, new means of acquiring resources, or new markets.[3] Hardwick and McLaughlin played equally significant parts in opening a hockey market in Chicago. While the former initiated the franchise, the latter guided it in the formative years. Ice hockey had not been a prominent local institution before the Blackhawks arrived. By the time McLaughlin passed away, the team had won two Stanley Cup championships and "enjoyed the largest attendance of all teams in the United States and Canada."[4]

An entrepreneur is a decision maker who sees opportunities when others do not or choose not to take action. An entrepreneur is an innovator, who profits (or loses) by taking the uncertainty of introducing an innovation into the marketplace, making him or her an agent of social or economic change. Yet innovations are impermanent. Once they enter the marketplace and the market receives them favorably, others will move in. Good management must exist to maintain the entrepreneur's advantage of being the first in the marketplace. Management and entrepreneurship are not mutually exclusive endeavors: Entrepreneurship comes not only in new ventures, but also exists in established business enterprises. The Chicago franchise embodied two entrepreneur types: a speculative initiator and a managerial/entrepreneurial overseer.[5]

Since the emergence of the study of sport history, much exciting work has been published on the significance of sport in our society. Focusing on "long-term *social forces* that have nudged sporting practices in certain directions" and on "the *social functions* of sport within this context" [emphasis original], the study of sport history has blossomed into a "Glorious Disarray" of diverse investigations on the relationships between sport and social class, race, gender, and ethnicity. Until recently, little research has been done on the structures of production and the minute elements of decision-making of entrepreneurs in the sport industry who had helped organize, shape, and deliver the sport product. This chapter seeks to address this gap in the field of study by examining the actions and decisions of these two entrepreneurs, Huntington Hardwick and Major Frederic McLaughlin.[6]

Sport in Chicago in the Early Twentieth Century

By the 1920s, a mass consumer market had emerged in the United States, of which sport was an integral element. Spectator sports had begun to boom in the late nineteenth century, especially baseball, college football, horse racing, and boxing, when middle-class reformers employed modern sports as part of their social engineering schemes in the late nineteenth and early twentieth centuries. After World War I, when the standard of living rose markedly across all social classes, spectator sports were mainly perceived as a way to have fun. The growing populace in major urban centers, and not just the middle class, but increasingly the working class as well, flocked to sporting events for excitement and entertainment. Opportunistic entrepreneurs promoted sporting events and spectacles to the emerging consumer market. Athletes like Babe Ruth, Red Grange, and Jack Dempsey became national heroes in the "Golden Age of Sports." Given the economic prosperity of the 1920s, the growing urban middle class consumed sporting entertainment just as it did mass-produced goods such as automobiles, furniture, and phonographs. The increasingly sophisticated advertising industry equated the good life with material possession and urged the people to acquire it through affordable credit buying. In fact, participation in mass consumption, at least in Chicago, spread beyond the middle class by the late 1920s. Chicago, like other major industrial and commercial centers in the United States, was a prime market for commercial sports.[7]

At the beginning of the 1920s, Chicago was a well-established commercial, transportation, industrial, and trade center of the country. It was second only to New York as a major money market.[8] The demands of businesses and industries in cities across the nation fostered the growth of a middle class and the nature of that middle class had shifted from the traditional small entrepreneurs and self-employed professionals to mostly white-collar, salaried employees. This development of an expanding group of white-collar employees was no different in Chicago, where the number of clerical workers increased from 120,000 to 210,000 between 1910 and 1920.[9] Despite the increased possession of material goods, however, many in the middle class toiled in large corporations where "routinization, standardization, and bureaucracy with a decline in individuality and autonomy" were the order of their daily work lives.[10]

Although enjoying a life of material possession made possible by technological advances and creative financing that their grandparents and parents did not have, the growing middle class, especially urban males, found that opportunities for fulfillment, such as independence and advancement through initiatives and hard work, were seemingly unreachable in the corporate world. Moreover, many of them felt threatened by the "new woman" of the decade. Men perceived the entry of more and more women into the public sphere as a challenge to long-held gender roles and their own masculinity. Increasingly, they looked to other avenues where dreams of masculine achievement and recognition were still possible. One beneficiary of the middle class's psychic discontent was the young motion picture industry, which immersed customers, for a relatively cheap price, in the adventures and successes of performers such as Harold Lloyd, Douglas Fairbanks, and Rudolf Valentino. Ticket sales grew from $40 million to $100 million during the 1920s.[11] Between 1916 and 1923, the seating capacity of Chicago theaters, for example, rose from 224,403 to 275,446.[12] Another arena in which to witness success through pluck and talent was the commercialized sport industry.

By the end of World War I, Chicago already had a vibrant sporting culture that included some of the previously marginalized groups, such as the ethnic immigrants. Unlike the consumption of other material goods, the sporting calendar in Chicago, from boxing bouts to professional football to polo matches, offered up a variety of sporting dramas that catered to consumers of different means.[13] More than cathartic substitutes for unfulfilled ambitions like the movie-going experiences and grounded in solid masculinity in the exhibition of physical prowess, commercialized sports also provided a sense of identity based on place and community to Chicagoans, as in other cities and towns, via intercity competitions. For growing urban centers that had a significant migrant population, sport could and did provide a sense of belonging and pride of place. Indeed, long before the development of a mass consumer culture, cities had been using sport to promote themselves by creating rivalries with other localities. Greg Lee Carter argues that the competitive, salient, and simple nature of sport made it a favorite tool in civic boosterism, especially after the emergence of modern sports and a structure of league competition. Winners and losers were there for all to see.[14] Moreover, the hierarchical structure of sport competition demonstrated the prowess of a city's athletic team, and civic boosters and sport promoters often trumpeted team successes and equated them with the city's status within the nation, no matter how questionable that relationship was. To show the world its importance, a major metropolis must be represented in major league sport. It was under this atmosphere of economic prosperity, changing middle-class work life, gender role anxiety, and civic boosterism that ushered in the Chicago franchise in the NHL.

The Founding of the Chicago Blackhawks

Chicago's professional hockey franchise came about during the expansion fever of the NHL in the middle third of the 1920s. Sport promoter Thomas Duggan of Montreal jump-started professional hockey's expansion when he sought permission from the league to peddle NHL franchise rights in 1923. Although Chicago had the first full-size (54' x 208') artificially refrigerated ice rink in the country when it hosted the 1893 World's Columbian Exposition, a fire destroyed the building before it was completely finished. Hockey, however, had never been a significant feature on the Chicago sporting menu prior to the 1920s "[e]xcept for a few scattered amateur teams of more or less ability."[15] Since Chicago did not have much of a hockey tradition, Duggan astutely looked to New York and Boston, which did have a history of hockey, for possible buyers of his franchise options.[16] From four Canadian-based franchises in 1923, the NHL had grown to seven at the beginning of 1925 with the Boston Bruins, Pittsburgh Pirates, and New York Americans.[17] During the NHL's governors' meeting in January 1926, Chicago, along with Detroit and a second New York application backed by Madison Square Garden, submitted requests for franchises, and in February, Cleveland, Buffalo, and Philadelphia also sought membership in the league. The idea that professional hockey could be a viable business enterprise, even for a city without a hockey culture, prompted not one but two groups in Chicago to forward their applications in April when the NHL considered admitting new members. Huntington Hardwick headed one of these groups, and the other was headed by Chicago sports promoter Paddy Harmon.[18]

A Bostonian, Huntington R. (Tack) Hardwick, was an exceptional athlete at Harvard, excelling in tennis, rowing, track, basketball, baseball, and football: he was a multipurpose All-American end who also punted and played quarterback and halfback. Under Coach Percy Haughton, Hardwick's team never lost to their bitter rival Yale. Yet Hardwick had no apparent association with hockey or connection with Chicago that would encourage him to spearhead a Chicago bid for an NHL franchise. His employment, in the investment firm Hayden, Stone and Company of Boston after graduation, may in part help explain Hardwick's interest in sport for its investment and speculative opportunities.[19] Hardwick was the major stockholder of the successful Chicago bid in the beginning, owning $105,000 of the original $200,000 capitalization when the club was first incorporated.[20] Hardwick's interest in hockey might well have been spurred by Charles Adams, the owner of the Boston Bruins and proprietor of one of the leading grocery store chains in the United States. It is entirely possible that Hardwick's achievements at Harvard connected him with the New England social elite. In fact, the relationship between Adams and Hardwick was strong enough that the former endorsed Hardwick's check to the NHL.[21]

Equally unclear is why Major Frederick McLaughlin wanted to be involved with a hockey franchise. McLaughlin had no prior experience or connection with the hockey world. He was better known in the Chicago sporting circle as a polo player. It was McLaughlin who gave the team its name. McLaughlin was a veteran of World War I and named the club after the nickname of his 333d Machine Gun Battalion, the 86th (Black-hawk) Division. His wife, Irene Castle, the famous dancer who married McLaughlin after the death of her husband Vernon Castle, supposedly designed the team jersey.[22]

At the height of the expansion fever, the NHL began to worry that it could not accommodate all the applicants it received and was afraid that rejections might trigger the failed franchise bidders to start a rival league. Consequently, the current team owners agreed to bind themselves for the next fifteen years and demanded any new entry do the same.[23] There were also rumors that boxing impresario Tex Rickard, president of Madison Square Garden, was behind the Hardwick bid because Rickard was going to build a facility in Chicago "and lease it to somebody else to operate."[24] The New York Americans, owned by bootlegger Bill Dwyer, was a tenant at the new Madison Square Garden, and in 1926 Rickard got his own New York franchise, the Rangers, which worried the other owners about the possibility that Rickard might control the league if he was involved in the Hardwick bid. Indeed, Hardwick had to give assurance that those associated "in this application are . . . in no way interested in any other franchise or team."[25] After the Hardwick bid was accepted, Hardwick informed NHL president Frank Calder on 1 June that a "Chicago man will shortly be elected President, and the Board of Directors will be composed largely of Chicago men."[26] The next day, McLaughlin filed papers to incorporate the Chicago National Hockey Team, Inc., under Delaware laws and received permission to operate in Illinois on 21 June. The Illinois application listed McLaughlin as the principal agent of the company.[27] In August, Hardwick confirmed to Calder that McLaughlin had assumed the presidency of the new Chicago franchise.[28]

The Owner's Guide to an NHL Franchise

As far as the league was concerned, the two pillars of its success and that of its new franchises were an excellent facility and player talent. The NHL formally approved the Hardwick group's bid during a special meeting on 15 May. Two days later, Calder advised Hardwick of the news and gave him four required conditions with which to comply. Among them, Hardwick must "give assurance by September 1st that you will be equipped with a team of a caliber suited to the requirements of the National Hockey League, and that at the same time the construction of your rink has advanced to such a stage as may reasonably insure its completion by November 10th, 1926."[29] For a city with little hockey tradition, the new franchise holder must start from scratch searching for player talent and erecting a playing facility. In these two endeavors, the Chicago club was not without help.

A driving force contributing to the increasing commercialization of sports—and, more specifically, the NHL expansion—was the trend since the turn of the century to build modern, massive sporting venues that could accommodate large crowds. Prompted by large crowds in intercollegiate football matches, colleges first began building new stadiums made of concrete and steel. During the "golden age of sport," an increase in the size and number of entertainment venues accompanied the increasing number of consumers of popular culture. Not only did the venues need to accommodate the greater consumer demand, there was also a movement toward building facilities that catered to the creature comfort in hopes of luring a more affluent clientele.[30] Comparing the professional and college football games, the *Chicago Tribune* pointed out that the "spectator at the pro game is there to see finished football; not to cheer for a team . . . [and because] of this quiescent attitude the pro customer won't suffer physical inconvenience to see a game."[31] Deeming the old Madison Square Garden inadequate, Tex Rickard, for example, built a new Madison Square Garden in 1925 to house the New York Americans. On the night of the first home game, New York society flocked to the new facility even though most of them knew little to nothing about the game. "Park Avenue mingled with Broadway . . . [and] the spacious lobby looked like the foyer at the opera. Fashionably gowned women were there in furs and jewels. It was a hockey crowd de luxe."[32]

As a boxing promoter and facility provider, Rickard was not interested in hockey at the beginning. Hockey was only one of the calendar fillers for the new Madison Square Garden. When his tenant, the New York Americans, began drawing large crowds to the Garden, the entrepreneurial Rickard dreamt of a string of Madison Square Gardens in major metropolises across the country. While the rumor that Rickard was behind Hardwick's bid might have been untrue, there was no doubt that Rickard was planning a Chicago Madison Square Garden with Hardwick's bid in mind. He had been negotiating with the Phipps Estate, which owned properties at the southwest corner of Franklin and Monroe, to locate an indoor sport arena near the Loop even before the NHL considered the application.[33]

In response to the league's demand for a suitable facility, Hardwick confirmed that there was a connection between his bid and Rickard's arena plan. Although there were "one or two technicalities" that had to be approved by the Chicago City Council, Hardwick assured Calder that he "had left no stone unturned" in getting the facility ready; but he could not tell "the Phipps' corporation when and how they [sic] are to spend some $5,000,000." Furthermore, since the idea of erecting a sport arena apparently came from the Phipps estate, "there is absolutely no reason to believe that they are not definitely committed to it."[34]

Hardwick, however, was wrong about Rickard's effort. By early August, it became questionable whether the Chicago Madison Square Garden was going to be ready for the coming season, since the city still had not approved the project. Even as Rickard continued to push his idea of a Madison Square Garden in Chicago, Hardwick proceeded to secure the Chicago Coliseum as a temporary solution and began installing ice-making machinery in the Coliseum.[35] Like the series of Madison Square Gardens in New York, the Chicago Coliseum in 1926 was the second iteration of the one built in 1893 at 63d and Woodlawn Avenue. The second Coliseum was built in 1899 at 1513 South Wabash Avenue by candy manufacturer Charles Gunther after the stockholders increased the capital stock from $300,000 to $400,000.[36] By 1925, the Coliseum Company had changed its name to the Coliseum Building Corporation and was now run by Charles R. Hall, who, along with Patrick T. Harmon, was behind the other Chicago bid for an NHL franchise. The Coliseum's capacity, only around 7,000, and its lack of an ice-making plant may well have been why the NHL chose the Hardwick syndicate with its promise of a new facility.[37]

In regard to the other demand from the league that the new franchise secure major-league-caliber players, the Chicago club was more fortunate. When Boston, the first U.S. franchise, entered the league in 1924, it had to scrounge for players. Even though manager Art Ross was able to sign players through his longtime friendship with Lester and Frank Patrick, the influential hockey moguls on the West Coast, Boston came dead last in its first season, winning only six games during the thirty-game season.[38] By the end of the 1925–26 season, the Patricks had determined that major league hockey in the West could not compete with an expanded NHL. They anticipated that new NHL franchises, with their heavy capitalization, brand-new facilities, and large population base, would ultimately disregard the agreement between the two major leagues and raid the western league's players. Hence, they convinced a majority of the Western Hockey League owners to appoint them as representatives to sell their players to the new franchises so that they could at least receive something in return. Hardwick seized the opportunity and bought the Portland Rosebuds team from the Patricks for $100,000 and also hired the Portland coach, Pete Muldoon, as the first coach of the team.[39]

Major league hockey in Portland made its first appearance in the 1914–15 season in the Pacific Coast Hockey Association (PCHA), a Patrick family enterprise. The Portland team actually won the league title in the next season and challenged for the Stanley Cup, in which it lost the series to the Montreal Canadiens in five games. It dropped out of the league after the 1917–18 season but rejoined the new Western Hockey League in the 1925–26 season, finishing fourth in the six-team league. In terms of player talent, Dick Irvin of the team was second in league scoring. Its goalkeeper, however, had the worst goals-against average at the end of the 1925–26 season. Still, it was an advantage for a new franchise to purchase a whole team rather than separate players who had not played with each other before.[40]

As an entrepreneur, Hardwick was quick to seize the opportunity in major league hockey. His inexperience in the industry, however, put the franchise in a disadvantageous position. Boston, which had been out of the playoffs for its first two seasons, used Ross's connections to the Patricks to secure the best picks of the WHL players. The injection of the western players helped them get to the Stanley Cup in the 1926–27 season and win it all two years later. After Chicago's purchase of the players became public, some observers believed that the Blackhawks would end up in last place. When McLaughlin visited Madison Square Garden some time in late summer, Colonel John Hammond and E. Carey of the New York Rangers told him that his team was "nowhere near as strong as [it] should be." Consequently, McLaughlin asked Hammond to phone Calder to repeat their assessment. Calder confirmed what Hardwick and Muldoon had told McLaughlin, that the team would be "all right." Despite assurances from Calder and Muldoon, both of whom had been connected with hockey for a long time, McLaughlin was still unconvinced because he had "met a lot of people who were interested in hockey, and . . . [I] can find no one but you three who think anything at all of our team as having a possible chance of finishing at the top in the National League."[41]

McLaughlin's skepticism came from his own sense of inferiority on matters of hockey, a desire for his team to measure up against the other major metropolises' representatives, namely, New York and Boston, and an anxiety about the financial consequence of a weak team. Revealing his sense of regionalism, he confided to Calder that "Chicago has a lot of civic pride, and, it must be confessed, jealousy of New York and the East in general." Influenced by the pessimistic assessment of his team, McLaughlin was getting anxious as the season drew near. He surmised that if the Chicago team did not have a good showing, especially against teams from the East, it would not be able to draw "more than two thousand." McLaughlin also acknowledged that he was "new and absolutely green at hockey but . . . had a lot of athletic and business experience" and pleaded with Calder that if the team needed strengthening, to say "how and where material can be found."[42]

When the Patricks sold Hardwick the Portland players, only eight players—Albert (Red) McCusker, Dick Irvin, George Hay, Charles (Rabbit) McVeigh, Landis (Duke) Dutkowski, Bob Trapp, Arthur Townsend, and Percy Traub—actually joined the Blackhawks. Hugh Lehman and Jack Connolly of Vancouver, Cully Wilson, Art Duncan, and Gordon MacFarlane of Calgary, and Jocko Anderson of Victoria were added to supplement the Portland players.[43] A problem with the transaction, probably unknown to Hardwick at the time, was that there was no guarantee the players would sign and report to the new owner, since the Western Hockey League had been disbanded, making the players free agents. The probable reason Hardwick hired Muldoon as the Blackhawks coach was his familiarity not only with the Portland players but other western players as well. His relationship with the Portland players and his knowledge of the western talent would be tremendously helpful when it came time to sign these players, as twelve of the fourteen Portland Rosebud players included in the original deal eventually signed with Chicago.[44] Muldoon was also able to sign Ken Doraty of Portland, who was not included as part of the original purchase, over the summer. While Muldoon was busy trying to sign the players on the list, the new Detroit club, at the same time, attempted to lure one of them, Art Duncan, away by offering him the manager position. McLaughlin was livid and immediately complained to Calder.[45]

With the Duncan episode ongoing and his own uncertainty about his team's strength, McLaughlin decided that his team needed reinforcements. On October 5, the Chicago club purchased Duncan McMillan (Mickey) Mackay's contract from the Patricks. As a twenty-year-old, Mackay first entered professional hockey with the Vancouver club of the PCHA in 1914 and promptly led the league in scoring that season. He also came second in scoring when the Vancouver team defeated the powerful Ottawa team in the 1914–15 Stanley Cup challenge series. By 1926, even as his years as a hockey player were fading, Mackay still placed twelfth in western league scoring, and second, behind Frank Boucher, in the Vancouver club.[46]

Still not satisfied, McLaughlin next signed Cecil (Babe) Dye, possibly during the NHL meeting held in Toronto on October 16, from the Toronto St. Patricks. Dye had come up through the Ontario amateur hockey system and began his professional career with the St. Patricks in the 1919–20 season. Other than a one-game stint with Hamilton in 1920, Dye stayed with the Toronto club his whole career until Chicago acquired his services. Dye was also a brilliant scorer, leading the NHL in scoring twice in 1920–21 and 1924–25.[47] At the same meeting, McLaughlin confronted the Detroit owner, Charles Hughes, about the Duncan tampering affair. Both men could not come to an agreement, and the other owners ended up deciding the conflict for them. They awarded Duncan to Detroit, who, in return, had to give up Art Gagne and Gordon Fraser from its roster.[48] With the roster set by mid-October, McLaughlin and his club awaited the opening game.

The Franchise Takes Shape

Hockey was undisputedly Canada's national pastime when the Blackhawks entered the NHL in 1926. Since the end of World War I, the Canadian Amateur Hockey Association had been strengthening the administration of amateur hockey in Canada and began to sponsor junior and intermediate championships, along with the Allan Cup, the senior amateur championship. Professional hockey benefited from this development, for its players were drawn from the cream of the crop in the amateur ranks. Dye was one example of the overwhelming majority of Canadian-born players in the NHL. Knowing that Canada was the cradle of hockey, McLaughlin specifically asked Calder to have either "Ottawa or some Canadian team play our big opening game," and Calder obliged by arranging the Toronto St. Patricks to visit Chicago on 17 November.[49]

As an entrepreneurial endeavor—introducing a Canadian game played by Canadian players in Chicago—the inaugural appearance of the Blackhawks achieved the results that McLaughlin wished for but not before he, following in Rickard's footsteps, made sure that the opening game would be a glamorous event. McLaughlin tried to attract Chicago's social elite by announcing that proceeds from the game would go toward the Junior League. He knew that many if not all of the society crowd could not "distinguish the fouls, penalties, or brilliant plays of the team," so he installed a public address system "to educate the fans rapidly." Finally, to make the event even more than just a hockey game and to perhaps cater to the taste of the more refined, "fancy skaters will entertain the crowd" between periods.[50] On opening night, prominent Chicagoans such as Marshall Field, the Swifts, the Armours, and a total of 6,088 people "pushed their way into the building, and there were cheers from the time the game started until the final whistle."[51] McLaughlin had apparently succeeded in attracting the city's social leaders, since all 348 box seats, at $4.40 per seat, were taken.[52] After the game, a cautious but obviously relieved McLaughlin confessed to Calder, "We still have a lot of rough edges to smooth but it does look as though it we're pretty safe to say already that hockey in Chicago will be a go."[53]

The first game of the new franchise also alleviated somewhat one of McLaughlin's other preseason concerns, the team's caliber, as the Blackhawks defeated Toronto 4-1. But the full season gave a much better picture on the strengths and weaknesses of the Blackhawks' personnel. When the season ended, the team finished third in its division, as well as third in both scoring and giving up the most goals in the league.[54] The incongruous record might have something to do with a relatively young defense, ranging from twenty-one to twenty-seven years of age, and the more experienced forwards, with Irvin and Mackay, both thirty-two years old. After Boston defeated Chicago in the first round of playoffs in March by an aggregate score of ten to five, McLaughlin fired his coach for not finishing first and began a new search for players. Muldoon supposedly retaliated with a curse that the team would never finish in first place. The team ended the next two seasons in last place in its division.[55]

The Chicago Stadium

In 1929 the Blackhawks moved from the Coliseum to the new Chicago Stadium, which would be their home for sixty-five years. The Stadium was the brainchild of Paddy Harmon, a child of the Chicago street culture, who had started out operating ballrooms and then became a promoter of roller skating, six-day bicycle racing, and boxing. Harmon had failed to secure an NHL franchise in 1926, but he recognized the city's need for a world-class indoor arena to replace the Chicago Coliseum, and he pushed for a new 19,500–seat facility, the largest indoor arena in the United States. Harmon invested some of his own money and convinced many of the city's financial elite, especially Canadian transplant James N. Norris, a grain dealer, to help finance a $7 million structure at 1800 W. Madison. It opened on 29 March 1929, with a light heavyweight boxing championship match between titlist Tommy Loughran and Mickey Walker. Then on 16 December 1929, the Blackhawks moved in. They defeated Pittsburgh, 3-1, in front of more than 14,000 fans.[56]

The Americanization of the Chicago Blackhawks

As overseer of the team, McLaughlin's concern about players and his reputation for hiring and firing coaches demonstrated his hands-on style of management. Moreover, his unfamiliarity with the sport made some of his ideas innovative if unconventional within the hockey culture. In 1929, for example, the Blackhawks held their training camp entirely in the United States, instead of somewhere in Canada as was the usual practice for U.S. teams. McLaughlin had the team begin dryland training at the University of Notre Dame, "following methods employed by Knute Rockne and other famous football coaches."[57] Then the team traveled to Tulsa, Oklahoma, for on-ice training. Believing that early condition-ing and games would have the players in stride when the regular season began, he arranged an unprecedented five exhibition matches in Tulsa, Kansas City, and Buffalo.[58]

Just before the start of the 1930–31 season, a more confident McLaugh-lin gave a rare interview outlining his management philosophy and his vision for his club. He told Arch Ward of the *Chicago Tribune* that he believed "a hockey team should be run like a football, baseball, or polo club. There must be cooperation—team play—for success." McLaughlin acknowledged that his managers often complained about his meddling with the team. But he justified his involvement in the details of team operation because he "wanted to know why no effort had been made to improve [the weaknesses] in a player's work" and refused to accept the explanation given to him that "hockey stars, like opera singers, were temperamental . . . [and] suggestions were out of order." As McLaughlin gained more and more experience in the hockey business, he became increasingly convinced of the correctness of his ways. He pointed as evidence to the success of the 1929–30 season, when the Blackhawks finished second in the division and lost to the Canadiens, the eventual Stanley Cup winners, by the aggregate score of three to two in the first round of the playoffs. (See Appendix A for the Blackhawks standings during McLaughlin's reign.) He concluded, "We finally obtained results. There are no players on the club now who spurn helpful hints. . . .We haven't got a ranking star on the club. . . . But we have a group of comers striving hard to work for one another. You can't go wrong with lads like that. If the Blackhawks were to be sold individually they wouldn't bring a great return, but as a team they are worth their weight in gold."[59]

As if McLaughlin were prophetic about his approach to managing a winning hockey team, the Blackhawks finished the 1930–31 season with a run to the finals of the Stanley Cup, losing to the Canadiens in a thrilling five-game series.[60] He must have been pleased when one of the *Chicago Tribune* sports editors, who rarely gave any space to the Blackhawks in his column, congratulated McLaughlin for his "perseverance, or obstinacy, or whatever it was that is now rewarded from the viewpoint of accom-plishment, and seems in a fair way to be rewarded financially."[61] Indeed, if gate receipts were any indication, the Blackhawks began to attract a following after their first three dismal years. Thereafter the team did well in the box office in comparison with the rest of the league. The opening of the Chicago Stadium in 1929 helped make the team a better attrac-tion than the average NHL team in both the 1929 and the 1930 seasons. The team performed below the league average in 1931–32 and 1932–33, but thereafter it was always above the league average in gate receipts on

McLaughlin's watch.[62] (See Appendix B.) While there is no denying that the Chicago Stadium gave the team the hockey palace it needed, McLaughlin still had to produce the kind of team that excited customers.[63]

Perhaps the final proof of McLaughlin's method came when the Black-hawks won the Stanley Cup in the 1933–34 season. After the near miss at the Stanley Cup three years before, the Blackhawks silenced criticism of their owner's interference with team operation by beating the Detroit Red Wings three games to one in the finals. One of the conquering heroes for the hometown fans was center Elwyn (Doc) Romnes, who—together with left wing Louis Trudel, defenseman Clarence (Taffy) Abel, utility player Roger Jenkins, and right wing Leroy—were the rarities in the NHL, since all were U.S. players. There was just a sprinkling of U.S. players in various NHL teams at the time, but McLaughlin would make an entrepreneurial innovation that separated him from other U.S. owners in the later part of the 1936–37 season, when he decided to build a team composed entirely of U.S. players.

McLaughlin's decision came from his resentment toward the NHL as a Canadian-run enterprise, even though there were more U.S.-based than Canadian-based franchises. Rather than introducing a new product—an entire NHL team consisting of U.S. players—to capture a certain segment of the market, there is some evidence that McLaughlin saw the Americanization of his team as a personal crusade against the Canadian dominance of the game. He complained to Calder that his Blackhawks were getting the short end of the stick by Canadian referees "because this was the only team of which an American was the prominent and predominating factor." On the other U.S. clubs, he argued, the owners "stayed in the background while a prominent Canadian ran the Club[,] . . . whereas here nobody has ever run this Club but me." He was also annoyed and perhaps jealous that the Canadian media was friendly toward the Boston and New York franchises because their respective managers spent their summers in Canada and therefore "must necessarily have many mutual friends, whereas I stay here all the year around and as evidenced very clearly by the Canadian press have no friends in Canada."[64]

There was more to the story, however, than that McLaughlin was an eccentric, meddlesome owner with a nationalistic fervor. Given McLaughlin's tendency to run the club as he saw fit, much has been made about his recruitment of U.S. hockey players. Yet, as an owner, McLaughlin's first obligation was to produce a winning team, despite his own feelings about U.S. players. There was never any evidence that McLaughlin favored U.S. over Canadian players. It may very well be that McLaughlin was still learning the hockey business. By 1930, however, the Depression prompted the federal government to harden its policies on immigrant workers while many U.S. workers found it difficult to find employment. Since the majority of the hockey players came from Canada, the NHL tried to work out a deal with the U.S. government to classify players as artists, a category exempt under labor law, thus allowing them to cross the border. In the end, the U.S. government required the league to post bond for all Canadian players in order to ensure their return to Canada once the season was over. Although the process had been smoothed over the course of the decade, it nevertheless added expenses and effort for the owners. Having a team composed entirely of U.S. players would eliminate this headache.[65]

The impetus for McLaughlin to focus on U.S. players came at the end of the 1936–37 season. McLaughlin, through his manager, Bill Tobin, had been negotiating with a number of players during the season as was the practice for all clubs. While many of these players were from the Unites States, the Blackhawks also pursued Canadians.[66] By February 1937, the team had signed a number of U.S.-born players and inserted them into the team's reserve list. The season had been going badly for the Blackhawks. An overtime tie with Toronto on home ice on 7 March and a 10 March victory by the New York Rangers eliminated the Blackhawks from any chance of making the playoffs.[67] McLaughlin decided, once the Blackhawks were out of the playoff hunt, and with a number of regulars injured, that it was time to test his theory about the competency of U.S.-born players in the NHL, and he ordered an all-U.S. starting lineup in the team's game against Boston on 11 March. The Blackhawks already had U.S. players on the roster from their Stanley Cup victory three years ago, many of whom had cut their hockey teeth in Canada. In this latest version, all the newly signed players got their start in U.S. leagues and had no NHL experience.[68]

When word got out about McLaughlin's experiment, others, especially the Rangers and the Red Wings, were furious, since they were jostling for playoff positions. Lester Patrick of the New York Rangers wired Calder to "instruct Chicago to ice their best team in their remaining games."[69] James Norris, owner of the Red Wings, protested Chicago's use of "five amateurs against Boston."[70] With the other clubs complaining, Calder urged McLaughlin not to field "a team below strength . . . [i]n view of the close fight between Rangers and Boston for second place and a possible close finish for first place" so that there would not be any "unfavourable aftermath in New York and Detroit."[71] McLaughlin, however, told Calder that he had already postponed the U.S. players' debut because the team had a shot at the playoffs. Since the Chicago media already had widely publicized their debut, he did not think it was possible to disappoint the fans and the press with a second postponement, and he regretted "exceedingly that your advice did not come earlier."[72] Publicly, however, McLaughlin asserted his right to run the team without interference from outsiders.[73]

Not all entrepreneurial innovations became successful. As a first-time experiment, the all-U.S. lineup was a bust. It probably did not say anything about U.S. talent as much as it did about the players' lack of experience and also playing on a bad team. Boston defeated the Blackhawks 6-2. None of the new players figured in the scoring and the two defensemen, Ernest Klingbeil and Butch Schaeffer, were on the ice for all six Bruins goals. In the aftermath, the local press was, of course, kind to the team and its latest additions. It described the novice forward line as having "distinguished itself by its passing and checking," and the rookie defensemen Klingbeil and Schaeffer as "full of fight."[74] Yet the victorious Boston manager, Art Ross, grumbled. "It's the most farcical thing ever attempted. It's a disgrace to hockey."[75] McLaughlin, however, was undaunted by this result and vowed that "we're going to push the theory of using American born players . . . [because] they did as well as any regulars could have done."[76]

Despite the bravado, McLaughlin was not blind to the fact that these five new players were not of major-league caliber. At the end of the season, the Blackhawks released all of them. Yet the owner had a stubborn streak. Since four of the five came from the amateur rank, he reasoned that the way to a better showing of U.S. talent should come from material in the minor leagues. Hence, he sent his coach to scout the minor league talent after the season was over.[77]

McLaughlin's plan to continue his quest for a team composed of U.S. players did not exactly materialize in the 1937–38 season, when other matters demanded his time. Besides his coffee business, he was preoccupied with a drawn-out divorce that required him to appear in court quite frequently. He readily admitted to Calder that he was not "being very active in hockey this year."[78] Indeed, McLaughlin missed the league's semi-annul meeting in September and the governors' meeting in December. Hence, the management of the team fell on the shoulders of manager Tobin. While Tobin followed McLaughlin's wish to build the Blackhawks with U.S.-born players, he did not pursue them exclusively.[79]

At the start of the season, the team added three new players, Canadian Oscar Hensen and Americans Carl (Cully) Dahlstrom and Vic Heyliger. Dahlstrom was drafted by the Blackhawks from the St. Paul Hockey Club of the minor-league American Hockey Association, while Heyliger was captain of the University of Michigan hockey team and McLaughlin had pursued him during the 1936–37 season. But Heyliger played only seven games and was released. During the season, the Blackhawks added six more players to the roster, including U.S.-born Roger Jenkins, Carl Voss,

and Virgil Johnson. Half the players on the 1937–38 team, which won the
Stanley Cup, were born in the United States.[80] The objective of a second
Stanley Cup superseded any nationalistic sentiment. Media reports of
the series did not even identify the nationality of the players. There
was enough praise for all the players on a team that had earned a losing
season record (14–25–9) and the fewest points (37) among all the teams
in the playoffs and yet won the Stanley Cup. McLaughlin was jubilant
afterward, but even he did not bring up the topic of the nationality of his
players in the celebration.[81]

"Sixth in the National League and First in the World!"

In the aftermath of the Blackhawks' second Stanley Cup victory,
Chicago Tribune hockey reporter George Strickler captured the remarkable achievement of the local champions who had a subpar record during the regular season—"Sixth in the National league and first in the
world!"[82] This celebration, however, was the last one for McLaughlin,
since the Blackhawks did not reach the Stanley Cup again before his
death in 1944. In fact, the team finished last in the league the following
season and McLaughlin relinquished his role as president to Bill Tobin in
1938.[83] Still, through his efforts, McLaughlin had established Chicago as
a hockey city by that time. Its average gate receipt of $12,850.06 for the
1938–39 season was third-best in the league even though the team did
poorly in the standings. Only Toronto and Boston, which finished first
and third, had higher gate averages.[84] While the New York Americans,
the Pittsburgh Pirates, the Montreal Maroons, and the Ottawa Senators,
who all predated the Blackhawks, had dropped out of the NHL by the
end of World War II, the Chicago franchise and five others, popularly
known as the "Original Six," would enjoy a period of unprecedented
stability and prosperity between the end of the war and the 1970s. No
matter how eccentric and obstinate McLaughlin was, he must be given
the credit for the long-term success of the Blackhawks. It may very well
be that McLaughlin's stubborn streak and his unconventional innovations contributed to the club's survival through the first few lean years
and then the Great Depression.

One must not forget the contribution of Hardwick. Entrepreneurs are
opportunists who take action. Hardwick might have been overly optimistic and naïve when he charged into a business that he knew little about
and recruited an equally inexperienced McLaughlin as the president of the
new franchise. His lack of experience in the hockey industry led him to
purchase a group of players who were not necessarily the best available.

There is no doubt, however, that his decision to seize the opportunity of a burgeoning consumer market in Chicago marked the beginning of a solid hockey community in the city. Indeed, Hardwick's involvement in the industry was positive enough that he left the Blackhawks and became a director of the new Boston Garden in 1929.[85]

Hardwick and McLaughlin, then, represented two different types of entrepreneurs in opening a new market. Whereas the former initiated the project with his connections and enthusiasm, the latter provided leadership continuity through thick and thin. One can question McLaughlin's innovations, especially his foray into building a team with U.S. players. But then, entrepreneurs are the type who will accept uncertainties. In this sense, Hardwick and McLaughlin were equally valuable and, indeed, essential to the existence of the Chicago Blackhawks.

Appendix A: Chicago Standings by Season

Season	Regular Season	Playoffs
1927–28	last in division	
1928–29	last in division	
1929–30	2d in division	lost in the 1st round to the Canadiens
1930–31	2d in division	lost in the Cup finals to the Canadiens
1931–32	2d in division	lost in the 1st round to Toronto
1932–33	last in division	
1933–34	2d in division	Stanley Cup Champions
1934–35	2d in division	lost in the 1st round to the Maroons
1935–36	3d in division	lost in the 1st round to the Americans
1936–37	last in division	
1937–38	3d in division	Stanley Cup Champions
1938–39 (a)	last in league	
1939–40	4th in league	lost in the 1st round to Toronto
1940–41	5th in league	lost in the 2d round to Detroit
1941–42	4th in league	lost in the 1st round to Boston
1942–43 (b)	5th in league	
1943–44	4th in league	lost in the Cup finals to the Canadiens

a. In 1939 the NHL eliminated divisions, since the Montreal Maroons dropped out of the league, making it a seven-team league.

b. New York Americans dropped out at the end of the previous season, reducing the league to six teams.

Source: Charles L. Coleman, *The Trail of the Stanley Cup* (Sherbrooke, Que.: Sherbrooke Daily Record,1964), vol. 2.

Appendix B: Chicago Average Gate Receipts and NHL Average Gate Receipts, 1927–1944

Season	Chicago	NHL
1927–28	$4,625.95	$8,348.23
1928–29	$4,383.65	$10,370.73
1929–30	$12,844.29 (a)	$11,048.67
1930–31	$13,800.31	$11,020.20
1931–32	$10,208.45	$11,055.33
1932–33	$5,656.97	$8,475.34
1933–34	$9,627.17	$7,574.41
1934–35	$10,216.42	$7,885.58
1935–36	$12,113.11	$9,092.81
1936–37	$10,097.66	$9,797.99
1937–38	$11,020.35	$10,322.36
1938–39	$12,850.06	$11,231.47
1939–40	$14,018.92	$10,195.08
1940–41	$14,849.05	$10,961.29
1941–42	$15,955.44	$10,460.88
1942–43	$14,630.40	$12,413.42
1943–44	$16,566.91	$13,713.28

a. The first six games were played at the Chicago Coliseum. Beginning with the seventh game, all home games were played at the Chicago Stadium. For the first six games, the average gate was $8,296.86; it was $14,033.88 for the remainder.

Source: Gate receipts reports filed by the Detroit club to the NHL. NHL Average Gate Receipts are taken from John Chi-Kit Wong, *Lords of the Rinks: The Emergence of the National Hockey League, 1875–1936* (Toronto: University of Toronto Press, 2005), Appendix G. For the two seasons (1927–28 and 1928–29) that are not included in the above source, the information is calculated based on gate receipts reports of the NHL. No provisions were given to the differences in exchange rates between the Canadian and U.S. currencies in all league gate receipt reports.

Notes

1. *Chicago Tribune*, 18 December 1944, 3.
2. George Vass, *The Chicago Black Hawks Story* (Chicago: Follett, 1970), 5.
3. Joseph A. Schumpeter, *The Theory of Economic Development* (Cambridge, Mass.: Harvard University Press, 1934), 66, as cited in Stephen Hardy, "Entrepreneurs, Organizations, and the Sport Marketplace: Subjects in Search of Historians," *Journal of Sport History* 13 (Spring 1986): 20–21.
4. *Chicago Tribune*, 18 December 1944, 3.
5. Randall G. Holcombe, *Entrepreneurship and Economic Progress* (London: Routledge, 2007), especially chapters 2 and 3. See also Mark Blaug, "Entrepreneurship Before and After Schumpeter," in *Entrepreneurship: The Social Science View*, ed. Richard Swedberg (New York: Oxford University Press, 2000), 76–88; D. S. Landes, "A Historian Looks at Entrepreneurship," in *Crossroads of Entrepreneurship*, eds. Guido Corbetta, Motron Huse, and Davide Ravasi (Boston: Kluwer Academics, 2004), 75–82; Richard Arena and Paul-Marie Romani, "Schumpeter on Entrepreneurship," in *The Contribution of Joseph Schumpeter to Economics*, eds. Richard Arena and Cécile Dangel-Hagnauer (London: Routledge, 2002), 167–83. 3M is an example of entrepreneurship that exists in a highly complex business organization. See Thomas J. Peters and Robert H. Waterman, Jr., *In Search of Excellence: Lessons from America's Best-Run Companies* (New York: Harper and Row, 1982).
6. Hardy, "Entrepreneurs, Organizations, and the Sport Marketplace," 14. For an assessment of the development of sport history as a study before the 1980s, see Nancy Struna, "In Glorious Disarray: The Literature of Sport History," *Research Quarterly for Exercise and Sport* 56 (1985): 151–60. A more recent historiography of the field can be found in Catriona M. Parratt, "About Turns: Reflections on Sport History in the 1990s," *Sport History Review* 29 (May 1998): 4–17. Two notable exceptions that focused on sport entrepreneurs instead of the dominant focus on social history are Peter Levine, *A. G. Spalding and the Rise of Baseball: The Promise of American Sport* (New York: Oxford University Press, 1985); and James Overmyer, *Effa Manley and the Newark Eagles* (Metuchen, N.J.: Scarecrow Press, 1993).
7. For sport, progressivism, and consumer culture, see Mark Dyreson, "The Emergence of Consumer Culture and the Transformation of Physical Culture: American Sport in the 1920s," *Journal of Sport History* 16 (Winter 1990): 261–81. For advertising and mass consumption, see Roland Marchand, *Advertising the American Dream: Making Way for Modernity, 1920–1940* (Berkeley: University of California Press, 1985); T. J. Jackson Lears, "From Salvation to Self-Realization: Advertising and the Therapeutic Roots of the Consumer Culture, 1880–1930," in *The Culture of Consumption: Critical Essays in American History, 1880–1980*, eds. Richard Wightman Fox and T. J. Jackson Lears (New York: Pantheon Books, 1983), 1–38; and Jennifer Scanlon, *Inarticulate Longings: The Ladies' Home Journal, Gender, and the Promises of Consumer Culture* (New York: Routledge, 1995). See Lizabeth Cohen, *Making a New Deal: Industrial Workers in Chicago, 1919–1939* (New York: Cambridge University Press, 1990), 99–158, for Chicago working-class reaction to the consumption of mass culture. For a synopsis of sport in the context of the 1920s, see Benjamin G. Rader, *American Sports: From the Age of Folk Games to the Age of Televised Sports*, 5th ed. (Upper Saddle River, N.J.: Prentice Hall, 2004), 122–39.
8. For an assessment of Chicago business, see Paul Henry Heidebrecht, *Faith and Economic Practice: Protestant Businessmen in Chicago, 1900–1920* (New York: Garland, 1989), 66–88.

9. Heidebrecht, *Faith and Economic Practice*, 70. It should be noted that the notion of white-collar middle class is much more complex than working conditions. Among other things, gender, ethnicity, and family size played a part in determining the degree and types of participation in the mass consumer culture.

10. For the middle-class work world in the 1920s, see Lynn Dumenil, *The Modern Temper: American Culture and Society in the 1920s* (New York: Hill and Wang, 1995), 71–76, 75 (quote).

11. William E. Leuchtenburg, *The Perils of Prosperity, 1914–32*, 2d ed., (Chicago: University of Chicago Press, 1993), 195. For material consumption as psychic compensation, see Lears, "From Salvation to Self-Realization," 1–38. A history of the motion picture industry can be found on the Art Institute Website, http:// www.filmsite.org/20sintro.html (retrieved 24 November 2006). For women in the 1920s, see Dumenil, *The Modern Temper*, 98–144. For the connection between sport and changing concept of masculinity, see E. Anthony Rotundo, *American Manhood: Transformation in Masculinity from the Revolution to the Modern Era* (New York: Basic Books, 1993), 239–40, 248–52, 257–62.

12. Cohen, *Making a New Deal*, 129–30. Cohen also pointed to the trend of the disappearance of small neighborhood theaters and the consolidation of control of the theaters by a few companies, similar to the merger and consolidation movement in other industries that helped eliminate small, local businesses.

13. Gerald R. Gems, *Windy City Wars: Labor, Leisure, and Sport in the Making of Chicago* (Lanham, MD: Scarecrow Press, 1997),especially chapters 5 and 6.

14. Gregg Lee Carter, "Baseball in Saint Louis, 1867–1875: An Historical Case Study in Civic Pride," *Bulletin—Missouri Historical Society* 31 (1975): 253–63.

15. *Chicago Tribune*, 14 November 1926, II: 5. Although an important figure in the success of the NHL as an international business, Duggan's role was largely ignored by writers of hockey history. See Donald M. Clark, "Early Artificial Ice," in *Total Hockey*, ed. Dan Diamond (Kansas City: Andrews McMeel, 1998), 564–65 for a description of the Chicago rink. For a more detailed discussion of the NHL expansion, see John Chi-Kit Wong, *Lords of the Rinks: The Emergence of the National Hockey League, 1875–1936* (Toronto: University of Toronto Press, 2005), chapters 7 and 8.

16. Hockey had established beachheads in New York and Boston around the beginning of the twentieth century. For early Boston hockey, see Stephen Hardy, "Long before Orr: Placing Hockey in Boston, 1897–1929," in *The Rock, the Curse, and the Hub: A Random History of Boston Sports*, ed. Randy Roberts (Cambridge, Mass.: Harvard University Press, 2005). For New York, see Clark, "Early Artificial Ice," 564–65.

17. During this spurt of growth of the league, one of the four Canadian NHL franchises, Hamilton, was disbanded. In its place, the first New York team, the New York Americans, was admitted into the league. Hence, there were really four new franchises added to the league. Besides the three American franchises, Montreal also received a second team, the Montreal Maroons. The chronological order of their membership is as follows: 1924–25, Boston and Montreal; 1925–26, Pittsburgh and the New York Americans.

18. 1926 NHL Meeting Minutes, 10 January, 14 February, 17 April. National Hockey League Archives (hereafter NHLA). See also *Chicago Tribune*, 17 April 1926, 21.

19. For a brief biography of Huntington, see *New York Times*, 27 June 1949, 28.

20. *Chicago Tribune*, 4 November 1926, 19. See also "Chicago National Hockey Team, Inc.," Dissolved Domestic Corporations, RG 103.112, Corporation file no.

Fo3098818, Illinois State Archives, Springfield, Ill. (hereafter ISA). The original incorporation papers file in Delaware confirmed the $200,000 initial capitalization, but the papers do not show the stockholders or their holdings.

21. Frank Calder, NHL president, to Adams, 3 May 1926, 1925–26 Boston Professional Hockey Association Inc. file, NHLA.

22. For a brief biography of Frederick McLaughlin, see Vass, *Chicago Black Hawks Story*, 11–12, and Morey Holzman and Joseph Nieforth, *Deceptions and Doublecross: How the NHL Conquered Hockey* (Toronto: Dundurn Group, 2002), 274–75.

23. There was a previous binding agreement in 1924. See Wong, *Lords of the Rinks*, 89, and Appendix D. The motion proposing a binding agreement is in 1926 NHL Meeting Minutes, Special General Meeting, 15 May, NHLA.

24. *Chicago Tribune*, 19 April 1926, 21. This report had three Chicago groups submitting bids. Beside the Hardwick application, E. L. Gary of Madison Square Garden and Patrick Harmon of Chicago also submitted bids. But the meeting minutes showed that only Hardwick and Harmon had bid for a Chicago franchise, Gary (spelled Garey in the minutes) was admitted in the meeting when the New York Rangers franchise was approved (1926 NHL Meeting Minutes, 17 April, NHLA). Rickard had gone to Chicago in March "on a hockey mission" (*Toronto Globe*, 24 March 1926, 8).

25. 17 April 1926, 1925–26 Chicago National Hockey Team Inc. file, NHLA. The note was handwritten on Windsor Hotel (Montreal) stationery and was addressed to the directors of the NHL. The Windsor Hotel was where the bidders presented their applications. The impromptu nature of the note suggests it is very possible that Hardwick either was notified or knew such an assurance was necessary. Hardwick also publicly denied Rickard's involvement in the Chicago bid. See *Chicago Tribune*, 23 April 1926, 21.

26. Hardwick to Calder, 1 June 1926, 1925–26 Chicago National Hockey Team Inc. file, NHLA.

27. "Chicago National Hockey Team, Inc.," Dissolved Domestic Corporations, RG 103.112, Corporation file no. Fo3098818, ISA.

28. Hardwick to Calder, 5 August 1926, 1925–26 Chicago National Hockey Team Inc. file, NHLA. Huntington retained the title chairman of the board.

29. Calder to Hardwick, 17 May 1926, 1926–27 Chicago National Hockey Team Inc. file, NHLA. The other two conditions demanded that the Chicago franchise sign the fifteen-year binding agreement and that the new franchise not be eligible for any money derived from the sale of any current or previous franchises. See also *Chicago Tribune*, 16 May, 1926, II: 1.

30. For the football stadium construction boom, see Rader, *American Sports*, 188; Steven A. Riess, *Sport in Industrial America*, 1850–1920 (Wheeling, Ill.: Harlan Davidson, 1995), 130–31. See Douglas Gomery, "The Movie Palace Comes to America's Cities," in *For Fun and Profit: The Transformation of Leisure into Consumption*, ed. Richard Butsch (Philadelphia: Temple University Press, 1990), 136–52, for a discussion of the effort of Chicago's movie entrepreneurs to gentrify the moviegoing experience by improving service, architectural design, and consumer comfort. Cohen also discovered that movie theaters in Chicago had moved from small nickelodeons to large chain-owned theaters. Cohen, *Making a New Deal*, 129–30. More specific to hockey, see Russell Field, "Passive Participation: The Selling of Spectacle and the Construction of Maple Leaf Gardens, 1931," *Sport History Review* 33 (2002): 35–50.

31. *Chicago Tribune*, 3 November 1926, 31.

32. *New York Times*, 16 December 1925, 29. For a list of guests invited to the opening night, see *New York Times*, 13 December 1925, S3.

33. For Rickard's involvement in the Chicago facility, see *Chicago Tribune*, 18 April 1926, II: 1, 20 April 1926, 23, 1 May 1926, 19, 21.

34. Hardwick to Calder, 20 May 1926, 1926–27 Chicago National Hockey Team Inc. file, NHLA.

35. Hardwick to Calder, 5 August 1925–26 Chicago National Hockey Team Inc. file, NHLA. See also *Chicago Tribune*, 2 November 1926, for Rickard's continuing effort to build the arena in Chicago.

36. On the fire of 24 December 1897, see *New York Times*, 26 December 1897, 2. For a brief history of the Coliseum, see Paula Lupkin, "Places of Assembly," *Encyclopedia of Chicago History*, http://www.encyclopedia.chicagohistory.org/pages/333.html, R. Craig Sautter, "Political Conventions," *Encyclopedia of Chicago History*, http://www.encyclopedia.chicagohistory.org/pages/986.html, and "Chicago Coliseum, http://hockey.ballparks.com/NHL/ChicagoBlackhawks/veryoldindex.htm. See "Coliseum Company," Dissolved Domestic Corporations, RG 103.112, Corporation file no. 07900562, ISA for the increase in capital stock of the company. The Coliseum Company was actually formed in 1898 by seven investors. Of those, A. J. Bishop was the majority stockholder, owning 2,993 shares (par value $100).

37. It is also noteworthy that the Rangers and the Bruins both voted for the Hardwick application and against the Hall-Harmon one. In fact, the Boston club seconded the motion to accept the Hardwick bid (1926 NHL Meeting Minutes, 15 May, NHLA).

38. Wong, *Lords of the Rinks*, 93.

39. *Chicago Tribune*, 4 May 1926, 23. Hardwick to Calder, 1 June 1926, 1926–27 Chicago National Hockey Team Inc. file, NHLA. For a more detailed discussion of the sale of the Western Hockey League players, see Wong, *Lords of the Rinks*, 95–97.

40. Charles L. Coleman, *The Trail of the Stanley Cup* (Sherbrooke, QC: Sherbrooke Daily Record Co., 1964), I: 500–501.

41. McLaughlin to Calder, 25 August 1926, 1926–27 Chicago National Hockey Team Inc. file, NHLA. Calder had been the president of the NHL since its founding in 1917 and was the secretary-treasurer of the NHL's forerunner, the National Hockey Association. Muldoon had played elite-level amateur hockey in Canada. In 1911 he led the New Westminster team of the then-new Pacific Coast Hockey Association to a championship. He was the coach of the Portland team in its first season in 1914 and left to coach the new Seattle entry into the PCHA the next season. In the 1916–17 season, he led the Seattle team to its Stanley Cup championship, the first U.S. team ever to do so. For Muldoon's athletic career, see *London Free Press*, 9 December 1926, as cited in Holzman and Nieforth, *Deceptions and Doublecross*, 279–80. See Wong, *Lords of the Rinks*, 96–97, 99, for a discussion on Boston's role in the selling of the Western Hockey League players and its aftermath.

42. McLaughlin to Calder, 25 August 1926, 1926–27 Chicago National Hockey Team Inc. file, NHLA.

43. Memo, 2 May 1926, 1925–26 Western Hockey League file, NHLA. The Portland player roster comes from Coleman, *Trail of the Stanley Cup*, 1:500–502. Three Portland players—Joe McCormick, Ken Doraty, and Bobby Rowe—were not included in the original purchase for reasons unknown.

44. Players signed by Chicago was confirmed in Muldoon to Calder, telegram,

22 October 1926, 1926–27 Chicago National Hockey Team Inc. file, NHLA. Percy Traub did not sign until November 16 when Muldoon had "a little talk" with Traub in Chicago for Traub "to come out of retirement" (Muldoon to Calder, 17 May 1926, 1926–27 Chicago National Hockey Team Inc. file, NHLA).

45. For complaints against Detroit in tempting Duncan, see McLaughlin to Calder, telegram, 9 and 10 September 1926, 1925–26 Chicago National Hockey Team Inc. file, NHLA. Duncan actually served as a player-manager for the Detroit club and played in 34 games, scoring 3 goals and 2 assists. See "Pre-Expansion Player Register," in *Total Hockey*, ed. Dan Diamond (New York: Total Sports, 1998), 696. In Duncan's entry, it is noted that Chicago traded Duncan to Detroit for Art Gagne and Gordon Fraser on 18 October. See also Coleman, *Trail of the Stanley Cup*, II: 20, on Duncan's statistics. Coleman listed Duncan as playing only 33 games.

46. For Mackay's career, see "Pre-Expansion Player Register," 751, and Coleman, *Trail of the Stanley Cup*, I: 276–84, 501. Coleman had listed Mackay as having played 34 games in the 1925–26 season.

47. For Dye's career, see "Pre-Expansion Player Register," 697, and Coleman, *Trail of the Stanley Cup*, I: 381, 472. Dye's biography also appeared in the Hockey Hall of Fame website at http://www.legendsofhockey.net/ (retrieved 23 November 2006). Dye was supposedly an excellent multitalented athlete, and Connie Mack had offered Dye $25,000 to play with the Philadelphia Athletics baseball club in 1921.

48. 1926 NHL Meeting Minutes, 16 October, NHLA. "Pre-Expansion Player Register," 696, suggested a trade between the two clubs had occurred on 18 October. However, there is no record of such a trade in either the Detroit or the Chicago file in the NHLA. While Fraser and Gagne were on the original player list sold to Detroit, only Fraser appeared in Chicago's roster in late October. Gagne played for the Canadiens in the 1926–27 season. It is unclear what happened in the case of Gagne (Coleman, *Trail of the Stanley Cup*, II: 10–11).

49. McLaughlin to Calder, telegram, 28 September 1926, 1925–26 Chicago National Hockey Team Inc. file, NHLA.

50. *Chicago Tribune*, 17 November 1926, 25.

51. Ibid., 18 November 1926, 18. Vass, *Chicago Black Hawks Story*, 9.

52. William Tobin to Calder, 26 November 1926, 1926–27 Chicago National Hockey Team Inc. file, NHLA. There were four price categories for the opening game: $4.40 box seats, $3.30, $2.20, and $1.10 reserved seats. It should be pointed out that of the sold-out box seats, 20 were given as complimentary tickets. It is also interested to note that of the 3,627 $2.20 reserved seats, 1,183 were not sold, making it the largest category in unsold tickets. McLaughlin actually apologized for the delay in sending the first game's gate receipt report. He blamed the delay on the Junior League, "a club composed of Chicago debutantes," who "are charitable and fashionable but not too businesslike." McLaughlin to Calder, 26 November 1926, 1926–27 Chicago National Hockey Team Inc. file, NHLA.

53. McLaughlin to Calder, 19 November 1926, 1926–27 Chicago National Hockey Team Inc. file, NHLA.

54. Coleman, *Trail of the Stanley Cup*, II: 18.

55. Ibid., 22–23. First-round playoffs consisted of two games with the team having the most goals advancing to the next round. Boston defeated Chicago 6-1 in the first game and tied the second game 4-4. The ages of the players were culled from "Pre-Expansion Player Register," 647–822.

56. Vass, *Chicago Black Hawks Story*, 18–19; Don Hayner and Tom McNamee, *The Stadium, 1929–1994: The Official Commemorative History of the Chicago Stadium* (Chicago: Performance Media, 1993); *Chicago Tribune*, 29 March 1929, 29; P. D. Paddock, "World's Greatest Sports Arena," *Popular Mechanics* 53 (March 1930): 451–53; "Chicago's Madison Square Garden, *Scientific American* 144 (April 1931): 250–31; Wong, *Lords of the Ring*, 133–35. For a discussion of the efforts of Harmon to secure another hockey franchise for Chicago, see ibid., 135–41.

57. *Chicago Tribune*, 15 October 1929, 34.

58. For the 1929–30 season training camp news, see *ibid.*, 14 October 1929, 23, 21 October, 1929, 21–22; and 28 October 1929, 27.

59. *Chicago Tribune*, 20 November 1930, 23.

60. Coleman, *Trail of the Stanley Cup*, II: 128–30. See also *Chicago Tribune*, 4 April 1931, 21–22, 6 April 1931, 29, 10 April 1931, 29–30, 12 April 1931, II:1, 15 April 1931, 25–26.

61. *Chicago Tribune*, 9 April 1931, 27. At least until the late 1930s, there were two editorial columns that appeared regular in the sports section of the newspaper. Rarely did these columns pay any attention to the Blackhawks.

62. Gate receipts reports are incomplete for the 1926–27 season for most teams and therefore no calculations are possible. It is, however, difficult to believe that the Blackhawks drew well, in light of the numbers for the next two seasons.

63. McLaughlin's relationship with the Chicago Stadium management was not exactly harmonious. For a discussion on the Chicago Stadium and the Blackhawks, see Wong, *Lords of the Rinks*, 133–35.

64. McLaughlin to Calder, 4 January 1937, 1936–37 Chicago National Hockey Team Inc. file, NHLA.

65. For McLaughlin's effort in fielding an all-American hockey team, see Vass, *Chicago Black Hawks Story*, 36–43; Stan Fischler, "Chicago Blackhawks," in Diamond, *Total Hockey*, 177. For troubles with Chicago and other NHL club players crossing the border, see for example *Chicago Daily Times*, 22 October 1930, 23; *Chicago Tribune*, 21 October 1930, 19. See also 1931 NHL Meeting Minutes, 9 May, NHLA.

66. In fact, one of Chicago's prospective recruits was John Taylor, the second son of the famous hockey player Fred "Cyclone" Taylor. Taylor's son, however, was unavailable because he was studying medicine in Toronto at the time and, besides, another NHL club already had claimed him. Taylor to Tobin, 4 November 1936, 1936–37 Chicago National Hockey Team Inc. file, NHLA.

67. *Chicago Tribune*, 10 March 1937, 23. With five games remaining and a twelve-point gap between the Rangers and the Blackhawks, the Rangers victory mathematically eliminated the Blackhawks. Seven points separated the first-place Detroit and the second-place Bruins, which was separated from the third-place Rangers by three points.

68. The Blackhawks had put five Americans on the reserve list by February. The five and their birthplace were as follows: Milt Brink (Hibbing, Minn.), Ernest Klingbeil (Hancock, Mich.), Bun Laprairie (Hibbing, Minn.), Butch Schaeffer (Hinkley, Minn.), and Al Suomi (Eveleth, Minn.). Except for Laprairie, contracts for the players were sent in on March 4. Tobin to Calder, 4 March 1937, 1936–37 Chicago National Hockey Team Inc. file, NHLA. Laprairie's was sent in early (Tobin to Calder, 13 February 1937, 1936–37 Chicago National Hockey Team Inc. file, NHLA). See *Chicago Tribune*, 10 March 1937, 24, for an injury report of the Blackhawks.

69. Patrick to Calder, telegram, 11 March 1937, New York Rangers Hockey Club file, NHLA.

70. Norris to Calder, telegram, 11 March 1937, Detroit Red Wings Hockey Club file, NHLA.

71. Calder to McLaughlin, telegram 11 March 1937, 1936–37 Chicago National Hockey Team Inc. file, NHLA.

72. McLaughlin to Calder, telegram, 11 March 1937, 1936–37 Chicago National Hockey Team Inc. file, NHLA. It would be foolish to think that McLaughlin did not know the playoff race was tight and that all game results would affect the race.

73. *Chicago Tribune*, 12 March 1937, 27.

74. Ibid. Klingbeil and Bruin Dit Clapper got into a fight in the first period.

75. Vass, *Chicago Black Hawks Story*, 38.

76. *Chicago Tribune*, 12 March 1937, 27.

77. *Chicago Tribune*, 25 March 1937, 21.

78. McLaughlin to Calder, 15 November 1937, 1937–38 Chicago National Hockey Team Inc. file, NHLA. McLaughlin did not tell Calder why he had not been involved to that point. Much of the correspondence about the team came from Bill Tobin, the manager. In fact, McLaughlin was complaining of a lack of promotional material coming from the league office. To protect his investment in the team, he thought it might be time for him to get back in the thick of things because "it means so much to us in dollars and cents that I do not feel justified in overlooking it." His divorce from his second wife, Irene Castle, dragged out in the courts until December 1939, when Castle withdrew her lawsuit. The suit was for the custody of their children. (See *Chicago Tribune*, 18 December 1944, 3.)

79. McLaughlin excused his absence in the December meeting because his daughter would be coming home "from school in the East, and I can't think of anything that would take me away from home during that period. . . . Tobin, whose family is here all year, will have to bat in my place." McLaughlin to Calder, 8 December 1937, 1937–38 Chicago National Hockey Team Inc. file, NHLA.

80. Player information is taken from "Pre-Expansion Player Register."

81. Coleman, *Trail of the Stanley Cup*, II: 326–41. See also *Chicago Tribune*, 13 April 1937, 27–28.

82. *Chicago Tribune*, 13 April 1938, 27.

83. While McLaughlin's obituary said that he delegated the position of president of the club to Tobin in 1939, archival correspondence showed that Tobin became the president some time in the summer of 1938. Tobin to Calder, 1 July 1938, 1937–38 Chicago National Hockey Team Inc. file, NHLA. McLaughlin's obituary is in *Chicago Tribune*, 18 December 1944, 3.

84. Coleman, *Trail of the Stanley Cup*, II: 354. Boston won the Stanley Cup that season. See Appendix B for Chicago's gate receipt average. Toronto and Boston's averages are taken from the 1938–39 gate receipts reports for the respective teams. See 1938–39 Box Office Statements—Boston and 1938–39 Box Office Statements—Toronto, NHLA.

85. "Chicago National Hockey Team, Inc.," Dissolved Domestic Corporations, RG 103.112, Corporation file no. F03098818, ISA. The original Chicago National Hockey Team, Inc., was dissolved in February 1929. In its place, McLaughlin and four of the directors formed Ice Sports, Inc., which changed its name to the Chicago National Hockey Team, Inc., in March 1929. Ice Sports, Inc., was incorporated on November 23, 1928.

Basketball originated at the Springfield, Massachusetts, YMCA in 1891. The game spread rapidly throughout the United States, but historians of the game have largely concentrated on its eastern developments. This essay details the early history of the game in Chicago as the Midwest epicenter and the expansive role of women in the game's popularity. Chicago high school girls had formed a league as early as 1895. Basketball provided particular entrepreneurial and competitive opportunities for the African American community as segregation in other areas of life increased. The Chicago Defender *promoted the values of sport, and black churches, YMCAs, and entrepreneurs fielded teams that brought pride, profit, and a measure of respect to the community. Perhaps more important, black teams developed their own style of play, a much quicker version that featured speed and crisp passing. A barnstorming Chicago team, the Harlem Globetrotters, would become world famous and professional champions by 1940. Their winning performances against the Minneapolis Lakers of the NBA in the late 1940s proved that black athletes could compete with whites, dispelling long-held stereotypes and assumptions of black deficiencies. NBA teams began drafting black players thereafter and the black style of play had national repercussions as it transformed the NBA with deft ballhandling, soaring dunks, and individual brilliance by the latter twentieth century; and Michael Jordan became not only an American, but a global, icon.*

10 | Blocked Shot
The Development of Basketball in the African-American Community of Chicago

GERALD R. GEMS

Despite the scholarly attention focused on sport and the consequent publication of sports-related works over the past two decades, basketball has received relatively little attention. Few books examine the historical development of the game, and those that do focus on its eastern origins. Localities outside of that region are largely ignored. Likewise, the African-American experience in basketball, save more recent biographies of National Basketball Association stars, is almost unknown.[1] This story attempts to shed some light on the development of basketball among African-Americans in the Midwest, its relationship to the black sports network of the East and the larger white society, and the adoption of a particular style of play to the game. In the process, black basketball players won entry into the dominant white circuit when blacks were being excluded from professional baseball and football. They did so while maintaining particular cultural values resistant to subjugation by whites.

The Illinois constitution of 1848 prohibited "Negro immigration" into the state. Although the law proved unenforceable, most freedmen who left the South chose to settle their families on western lands, particularly in Kansas and Oklahoma.[2] Blacks comprised less than 2 percent of Chicago's population throughout the nineteenth century.[3] That pattern changed abruptly when Robert Abbott founded the *Chicago Defender* newspaper in 1906 and began promoting the city as a northern paradise for African-Americans.[4] Relative to black life in the South, Abbott could well substantiate his claims. More than 44,000 blacks resided in at least 24 of Chicago's 35 wards in 1910. Racial harmony seemed to exist as blacks enjoyed voting rights, held jobs, sent their children to integrated public schools, and played alongside whites in athletic leagues.[5]

Following the Civil War, John Jones, Chicago's most prominent African-American, who had been an ardent abolitionist, had been elected to the Cook County Board of Commissioners. The refugees from the South capitalized on their newfound political opportunities by electing two of their own, Louis B. Anderson and Oscar De Priest, to aldermanic positions on the city council after the turn of the century. Further exemplifying the possibilities in Chicago, Jesse Binga, a former railroad porter, opened his own bank in the city, which brought him wealth and prestige. Chicago symbolized the mecca of African-American achievement, and Jack Johnson, newly crowned heavyweight champion of the world in 1908, soon established his residence there.[6]

African-American athletes, in particular, had integrated freely and successfully in the city since 1885. Rube Foster's baseball team prospered in the City League, and Julius Avendorph, founder of the first black baseball league in Chicago, extolled "sports as the means to friendly relations between the races" and "as a means to college scholarships for black men."[7]

While baseball remained the premier sport in the African-American community, football and basketball players also made a name for themselves. Sam Ransom starred in four sports at Hyde Park High School, leading its first basketball team to the Cook County Championship in 1901. As Avendorph had predicted, Ransom's athletic prowess earned acceptance at Beloit College. Fritz Pollard, too, followed his athletic exploits in Chicago, with All-American status at Brown University.[8]

The perception of racial equality proved a myth, however. As rural, southern blacks heeded Abbott's call and headed north, race relations eroded. Over 100,000 blacks flocked to Chicago in search of jobs by 1920, and almost 234,000 African-Americans resided in the city a decade later.[9] As Abbott promised, opportunities in the north far surpassed the restricted socioeconomic structure of the southern states; but the opportunities were hardly equal to those of whites. African-Americans faced what Antonio Gramsci characterized as a hegemonic relationship, in which whites, middle-class males in particular, rested atop an already established social hierarchy. In such positions of power they ordained the cultural norms and values which all subordinate groups were given the choice of accepting, rejecting, adopting or adapting.[10] In fact, the African-American community had little choice in the matter. The white working class saw blacks, who might accept even lower wages, as a threat to their job security, and the white middle class refused to accept even the wealthiest of black entrepreneurs as its equals. While many blacks had hoped to assimilate into the mainstream white society on an equal footing, such actions forced the development of a parallel and alternative culture, one that adapted some white forms but synthesized them with traditional values rooted in the African-American experience to produce a distinct black urban culture.[11]

Allen Spear has asserted, in *Black Chicago*, that one manifestation of such development occurred in the "wide range of social clubs that catered to specific groups in the community."[12] Black athletic clubs, such as Rube Foster's Leland Giants, spearheaded an initial drive for assimilation, based on W. E. B. DuBois's philosophy that "a talented tenth" of African-Americans might compete equally and favorably with whites and win their acceptance.[13] Middle-class blacks thus began to organize their own basketball leagues shortly after the turn of the century. The *Defender* cited a men's league in 1909, and a church league operated within three years.[14] Black women's social clubs organized the first game among females, as the Philomathics defeated the Nonpareils at Ogden Park in 1911.[15]

The *Defender* reported that black youth lacked interest in basketball, favoring indoor baseball instead. The black community became more interested when a basketball game occasioned a racial incident. In 1913 Evanston High School refused to play Lane Tech, whose team was led by a black star, Virgil Blueitt. The referee awarded a forfeit victory to Lane. While other racial incidents had predated the event, the Blueitt case signaled a wholesale change in race relations. Despite the favorable ruling, overt discrimination, segregation, and exclusionary practices became the norm thereafter.[16]

With initial funding supplied by Julius Rosenwald, a Jewish philanthropist, a YMCA was built in the heart of the African-American community in 1913. Thereafter it was supported largely by a consortium of meatpacking companies that had begun using black workers as strikebreakers as early as 1900. With the advent of World War I, southern blacks flocked to Chicago in search of such jobs. As many as 70,000 flooded the metropolis, supplying 25 percent of the stockyards labor force, and congregating in what was rapidly becoming a black ghetto in the area around the Wabash Avenue YMCA on the city's South Side.[17] Ida Wells Barnett, a black civic leader, charged that white YMCAs, the Salvation Army, and the Mills Hotels denied blacks the usage of rooms and their gymnasiums. Likewise, when black neighborhoods encroached upon city parks or playgrounds, an African-American playground director was appointed by city officials, implicitly signaling that the space was suitable only for blacks.[18]

The increasing segregation of the African-American community indicated the exclusionary intent of white society, but the YMCA programs provided continued hope for integration and a boon to the development of basketball. By 1914 the Y had its own league of four men's teams and engaged in competition with white teams throughout the city. Within a year the *Defender* reported that basketball had become "the leading attraction" at the black YMCA in suburban Evanston.[19] The team at the Wabash Y in the city declined a challenge from their counterparts in Louisville because "they were tied up with white teams for the remainder of the season and wished to measure their skills with their white brothers."[20] One local adversary even included Napoleon Blueitt, brother of the Lane Tech basketball star.[21] The next year, the Blueitt brothers and their colleagues formed a black athletic club, the Lincoln A.C., to compete with the whites in football and basketball. Fritz Pollard and other notable black stars later joined the team for important games.[22]

The Y basketball team, known as the Wabash Outlaws, provided a measure of racial pride as blacks began to feel the hurt of segregation and discrimination in other spheres of life. The Outlaws defeated the White Eagles convincingly, 33-24 in 1915. Described as a "rough bunch of Polacks who, if they can't win fair, they rough it," the White Eagles were banned by most teams in the city.[23] With Virgil Blueitt contributing 17 baskets, the Outlaws swamped the white Harrison Maroons, 63-9, and went on to defeat Hull House and several other white teams, often by large scores, during the 1915–16 season.[24]

Such lopsided victories, coupled with whites' growing perception of blacks as job stealers, may have heightened racial tensions. The *Defender* looked inward and began to cover black basketball teams in the East in 1917. Such coverage fostered the sense of a national black sporting culture parallel to that of white society, and goaded by the *Defender*, the team from the Wabash Y embarked on an eastern tour for inter-city contests. When Will Anthony Madden brought his New York Incorporators to Chicago for a return match in 1918, he seemingly violated the growing sense of racial consciousness by using two white players. Despite Chicago's protest, New York prevailed, but fights ensued during the game, and crowds swarmed the court afterward, verbally abusing the New Yorkers.[25]

Despite such mishaps, the middle class board of the YMCA continued to extol the promise of sport, and businessmen and churches avidly supported more basketball teams.[26] Most blacks, however, faced the realities of segregation and discrimination. Parks, playgrounds, and schools became increasingly exclusive, and red-lining real estate agents and fire-bombing campaigns ensured that African-Americans remained within the designated black belt. Escalating social tensions finally erupted in the summer of 1919, when a race riot cost 38 lives.[27]

After World War I, racial boundaries became clearly established in the city. Increasing segregation and race pride led to self-reliant entrepreneurial ventures. The belief that a "talented tenth" could still succeed in white society persisted throughout the 1920s, however.[28] Black entertainers proliferated, particularly in the black and tan cabarets of the black belt. Whites, however, owned the majority of such clubs, just as they continued to control athletic facilities. Rube Foster was the first to seek greater independence, removing his baseball team from the City League and forming the Negro National League in 1920.[29] Black basketball teams soon sought similar freedom. More churches began sponsoring teams that drew large crowds, and one observer claimed that the teams served as a publicity tool to increase attendance. Olivet Baptist Church supported men's and women's teams and eventually claimed 11,000 members, reputedly the largest congregation in the country. Clergymen, the YMCA, the *Defender*, and athletes preached the congruent values of church and sport as a means of hope, salvation, and racial harmony.[30] Cornel West has charged that this black middle class, anxious, insecure, and questing for socioeconomic status, was too willing to be coopted by whites.[31]

If wholesome sports activities, as defined by the middle-class organizers, were meant to induce racial harmony and integration, they also served racial pride, which transcended class lines. In 1921 the Forty Club, an organization of black socialites, sponsored a team of former high school and college stars, including Virgil Blueitt and Sol Butler, the Olympic track star, on an eastern tour and in the AAU tournament. The *Defender* took especial glee in reporting the team's tournament victory over a white American Legion team, which "gave the Fortys the laugh . . . expecting an easy victory."[32] The *Defender* reported that after the black team took a 14-8 halftime lead, an "orgy of fouls" and questionable calls by the referees ensued in the second half to help the white team, but to no avail. In the second game against the white DeSoto A.C., the *Defender* charged, "all fairness and clean sportsmanship were thrown to the winds," as five fouls were called on black players in the closing minutes to allow a white victory.[33] Another black team representing the 8th Regiment, highly esteemed African-American veterans of World War I, finished with a 71-5 record and second place in the City League against white teams.[34]

Sensing profit in black sporting ventures, the *Defender* avidly reported on basketball games, particularly those of eastern teams. Since 1917 it had prodded local teams to challenge their New York counterparts. By 1921 the *Defender* took it upon itself to sponsor the former Forty Club team in intercity competition and initiated its own tournament, in which two black teams defeated whites to gain both the lightweight and the heavyweight championships. The commercial potential of such games attracted interracial crowds and a previously untapped black audience. Such ventures spawned numerous other teams, including one from the Giles Post of the American Legion, which would eventually evolve into the Harlem Globetrotters. Even the YMCA team was forced to defend itself against charges of professionalism in its attempts to win at all costs.[35]

Among the independent teams a strong women's contingent emerged. The Chicago Roamers, managed by Sol Butler, began play in 1921 under women's rules with three offensive and three defensive players. Led by Isadore Channels, a meatpacker and national black women's tennis champion, the team, mostly composed of school teachers, enjoyed great success against other women's and boys' teams.[36]

In 1924 the Roamers stated their intention of joining the women's division of the City League; and, later that season, they defeated the Harvey Bloomers, a white team, to win the *Defender* trophy before a large crowd of 4,500, including many black socialites in decorated boxes. Isadore Channels contributed nine baskets in a 19-3 rout. The following year, the team entered the tournaments of the Jewish Peoples' Institute and the Amateur Athletic Union. In the latter they were soundly beaten by the white Tri-Chis, described by the *Defender* as the "best in the country."[37]

Shortly thereafter Isadore Channels retired and a number of players defected to start their own teams. Virginia Willis captained the Olivet Baptist team, chief rivals of the Roamers within the African-American community; and Corinne Robinson, an emerging young star, opted to play for the Mid-City A.C. in the AAU tournament. The *Chicago Whip,* another black newspaper, entered the scene when its sports editor, Al Monroe, offered to sponsor a game with the white Taylor Trunks, the national women's champions. Since Sol Butler, the Roamers' manager and sports editor of the *Chicago Bee,* was engaged in men's games, Olivet played the game without his guidance. The Olivet team represented the African-American community in a 32-16 loss, as the Taylor Trunks proved too fast.[38]

The popularity of the women's game mushroomed as interracial games and the number of teams increased. Like the men, women jumped teams often until the Roamers managed to monopolize most of the black talent for the 1927–28 season and an eight-team black women's league brought some stability. A second women's league, with Corinne Robinson as director, followed in 1929, and a women's church league initiated play with 10 teams a year later. That 1930 season witnessed the return of Isadore Channels to the Roamers, who defeated Olivet in an invitational tournament. When a return match a week later between Olivet and the Taylor Trunks was billed as one against the "colored champs," the Roamers protested vehemently, noting that they had never lost to Olivet in six years of competition. Despite such objections, Olivet played, and the major newspapers covered the game, reporting that Violet Krobacek, the Trunks' center, poured in 21 points in an easy 35-10 victory.[39]

The proliferation of women's teams continued despite the Depression, many of them composed of schoolgirls who had learned the game in high school physical education classes. By 1931 the Whippets from black Phillips High School reached prominence by defeating Olivet, and former Roamers players took third place in the AAU tournament as the Oberlin girls. Despite such pretentious titles, the women's teams displayed democracy on the court, particularly in church leagues, where working-class domestics mixed with clerks and teachers. By 1934, the Club Store Coeds team featured a 6'7½" center and Tidye Pickett, an Olympic track qualifier, in dominating other teams. They embarked on a national tour before returning to challenge the Spencer Coal Company, the national women's champions.[40]

Male teams found even greater opportunity to promote racial pride and reap profits. The Union Park Grenadiers, a black team from the growing African-American community on the West Side, brought in the Blueitt brothers to defeat their Irish rivals from Trumbull Park in 1922. Four years later, they succeeded in winning the West Side Parks championship by defeating the Poles of Eckhardt Park. Likewise, the St. Monica's team won the Catholic Order of Foresters League title by using black high school stars, "many of whom never saw the inside of a Catholic church in their life," as the *Defender* readily admitted. High school stars found ready solicitations for their services at black colleges and on local semi-pro contingents.[41]

With an increasing number of teams competing for limited dollars within the black community, promoters sought to provide greater entertainment value by sandwiching their games between rollerskating and dances at neighborhood ballrooms. Other teams employed well-known athletic stars, such as DeHart Hubbard, Paul Robeson, or Joe Lillard, to arouse fan interest. Such promotions fostered a transition from the southern rural culture of many newcomers to the urban black culture of the north, as they tied African-Americans to a national sporting culture that exhibited common sport forms within the capitalist framework.[42]

With both black and white entrepreneurs seeking the limited opportunities for profit within that commercialized culture, many teams were forced to seek greater rewards on the road, following the model of the established baseball teams. The most profitable of such barnstormers, later to become the Harlem Globetrotters, embarked on their initial odyssey to Wisconsin in 1927 amidst charges of fraud. With Dick Hudson, a former pro football player, acting as manager, and a coach who masqueraded as the famous Sol Butler, who had held a world record in the long jump, the team advertised its players as college all-stars. While espousing credentials from such institutions as Colgate, Amherst, and USC, most, in fact, were former Phillips High School stars who had never been to college. The *Defender* charged that the team capitalized on such subterfuge at the expense of unwary whites who paid to see the impostors. Such guile, reminiscent of the trickster in black oral culture and music, was also employed by barnstorming black baseball players to outwit whites. Among the basketball players was Joe Lillard, who would later lose his college eligibility due to professionalism and his professional football career due to the color of his skin.[43]

While the 1920s seemingly portrayed a heyday for black basketball, that was not the case in the schools. Unlike the independent teams, interscholastic players could not isolate themselves on homecourts within the black community or escape discrimination and racism in the city. Despite the YMCA's idealistic proclamations of fair play, teamwork, respect for others' rights, and the integrative benefits of interracial competition, reality often proved otherwise.[44] Although individual blacks were accepted on athletic teams at several schools, they often felt isolation outside of the black belt. Even at Phillips High School, predominantly black by 1922, extracurricular clubs remained white only. When the mixed basketball team traveled to Tilden High School, the Tilden team refused to play. A Tilden student explained that "we nearly laid them [the three blacks] out. When they went home our boys waited and chased them . . . the whites weren't hurt, but the coons got some bricks."[45]

Phillips earned revenge when it defeated Tilden, 26-22, with "rapid and bewildering passing" to win the Central Division title in 1922.[46] Ruben Spears, the black Phillips center, was carried off the court by the winning fans. During the 1924 season, Phillips players were tripped and kicked in their defeat of Lindblom. In rough games for the divisional championships against Englewood, the lightweight team faced biased officiating as numerous foul calls allowed Englewood to tie, then win. Despite their tarnished victory the Englewood players refused to shake hands. In the heavyweight contest a fight ensued and police had to clear the floor. Phillips prevailed and went on to the city title game, where it lost to Lane Tech, a school of 3,000 students, ironically led by a black star, Bill Watson. The outcome seemed a foregone conclusion when the referees disallowed Phillips' baskets for alleged violations and Spears, the star center, fouled out. Not a single foul was called on Lane.[47]

The *Defender*, sensing a chance to promote racial pride and capitalize on Phillips' success, sponsored inter-city matches, in particular, a game against Armstrong High School in Washington, D.C., deemed the country's top black team by the African-American press. When Phillips won handily, the *Defender* offered a return match in Chicago the next year, which drew 4,500 paying customers and thousands more turned away, in a game billed as the "Annual Winter Classic." The following year the *Defender* rented the Chicago Coliseum, as Phillips narrowly defeated a team from Louisville.[48]

Commercialization marred Phillips' 1927 season. Despite another playoff berth, the school forfeited all of its games for using an overage player and for playing against an alleged pro team in Cleveland. Not content with punishment, the white school principals bickered over the rights to Phillips' playoff profits.[49]

The Phillips Junior High School team drew 2,500 fans when it reached the championship game the next year. When the lightweight team advanced to the championship game as the South Side champs, they faced an uncertain opponent, as the north siders deadlocked in a three-way tie. The white principals proposed that all four teams, Phillips included, be picked from a hat to decide the two opponents for the championship. Phillips refused the blatant disregard for its accomplishment and traveled to Indianapolis for a game while awaiting the outcome of the debate. Upon their return, they rejoiced in a 23-10 victory over Harrison "with whirlwind, precision passing," being the first fully black team to win a city championship.[50] The team held the ball and played its subs to hold down the score in an act of sportsmanship; and even the *Chicago Tribune* acknowledged that "dazzling speed, accurate and amazing shooting, and stout defense" made it "the best lightweight contingent in the city league in several years." Jubilation reigned at the awards ceremony, as students snake danced through the school and out into the streets. Albert "Runt" Pullins, the team star and a dribbling ace, soon graduated to the Globetrotters.[51]

The Globetrotters, still playing as the Savoy 5 in 1929, had reason to opt for the road in search of fair play. In a game in which they led the white Golde Clothiers at the half, Golde supporters still offered 2-1 odds. The reason became evident as the refs started calling fouls on Savoy with the opening tip. Joe Lillard, the Savoy star, fouled out early, and a white player was awarded a basket and two foul shots even though he had not been shooting. Unruly fans and the Savoy team left the court with the game tied and greater support for the ongoing campaign for black referees. Blacks charged that racism, collusion, or both, unduly biased the officials' judgment.[52]

The Phillips High School team fared better, with both the lightweight and heavyweight teams advancing to the city championship in 1930. While the lights lost in overtime, the heavyweight game provided a drama that characterized the black urban culture that revolved around religion, sport, and hope. With 16 seconds left to play and Morgan Park leading, 19-18, Agis Bray, the Phillips' star and a future Globetrotter, intercepted a pass and headed for the basket but was promptly fouled. The Morgan Park fans booed as Bray stood at the line until a referee courageously required that they desist. In the dead silence that followed, a young Phillips girl, a recent southern migrant, prayed out loud, "Oh Lawdy, Mr. Jesus, please let Bray make the basket." When Bray obliged she looked skyward and asked for "just one more." She promptly fainted as the ball fell through the basket, ensuring a 20-19 win for Phillips.[53]

Despite their championship victory, the team remained uninvited to the national championship tournament held annually at the University of Chicago. Fearing a southern boycott, Amos Alonzo Stagg invited Morgan Park, the white runner-up, instead, despite a vehement protest by the *Defender*. Throughout the remainder of that decade and into the next, black newspapers crusaded against exclusionary practices in organized sports, professional baseball in particular.[54]

When both Phillips teams reached the finals the next year, the lightweights found themselves in a familiar situation. Phantom fouls cost them their best player in the first half and turnovers inevitably went to the opponent. A last-minute foul resulted in a one-point loss. The heavies couldn't find anyone willing to give them a practice game, so they traveled to the national black tournament in Hampton, Virginia, which they won easily. Upon their return home, they dropped the title game to Crane Tech and its 6'8" center before an overflow crowd of 5,000.[55]

The lightweights avenged their loss in 1932. The *Defender* described the victory over "the white boys" of Crane Tech as one in which "most of Crane's tallies . . . were made on free throws, the fairest of referees being seemingly unable to proportionately balance the fouls when a largely white team is contesting against one mostly colored."[56] With the departure of Stagg from Chicago, and a new tournament director, the Phillips team finally received an invitation in 1935 to what had become a local tournament. As a local affair there was no longer a need to appease Southerners or fear a boycott. By that time African-American athletes appeared on many teams throughout the country. The Xavier University team of New Orleans, which compiled a 67-2 record from 1935 to 1938, featured as many as five Phillips players from Chicago.[57] Throughout the 1930s, the black press clamored for the inclusion of black athletes in the mainstream sporting culture, but the reality of discrimination and the failed hopes of the talented tenth proved obvious for baseball and football players.[58] The loosely organized state of professional basketball, however, still allowed some hope for black males. By 1941 both the New York Rens and the Globetrotters had won world championships, and the Rens were even able to force desegregated seating at their games.[59]

By 1940 basketball had come to serve several functions in the African-American community. Unable to fully integrate with the dominant white culture, African-Americans adopted its sport forms, such as baseball, football and basketball, but adapted their own particular playing styles to fit a black urban culture that assimilated southern rural migrants and incorporated them into a parallel national sporting culture. While such developments were largely organized by northern middle-class blacks, they included working-class participants and gamblers by the mid-1920s. As much as they assimilated, they also gave vent to protest, for all blacks, regardless of their class consciousness, suffered a deep race consciousness. For, while some African-Americans gained wealth, prestige, and socioeconomic status within the black community, none could deny that their color limited true progress outside of it.[60]

Team names, such as the Cheetahs, Flashes, and Bullets, were meant to connote a particular image matched by a particular style of play that featured speed, intricate passing, and clever ballhandling. Joe Lillard's Hottentots recalled a pride in African roots, not unlike the appeals of Marcus Garvey. Traveling teams such as the Harlem Globetrotters or Chicago Collegians gave pretense to a level of sophistication, independence, opportunity, and self-empowerment. Not only did they possess the means to escape the ghetto and demonstrate equality, or even superiority to the white man, at least on the basketball court, but also success provided a piece of the American dream for players like "Fat" Jenkins, who reputedly earned a $10,000 salary in 1930.[61]

It is probably no coincidence that the popularity of the blues paralleled the growth of basketball in Chicago during the 1920s. One gave vent to black frustrations, the other to black hopes. The merger of both was clearly seen in the deportment of spectators who cheered, chanted, sang, and even prayed exuberantly at games, not unlike an evangelical church service.[62] Both church and basketball assumed characteristics of festival, celebrating temporary feelings of power and a sense of community that reinforced pluralism as much as assimilation. Raymond Williams has termed such activities residual practices, in that they are retained from the past and serve to reinforce the values of an alternative culture.[63] Nelson George asserts that the blues even served as a form of resistance to the dominant culture by celebrating black heroes and emphasizing their virility.[64]

The celebration of black heroes, at times, transcended the African-American community and engaged the mainstream white society, as in the cases of Jesse Owens and Joe Louis. Owens's Olympic fame proved transitory, however, and he was soon relegated to carnival-like exhibitions, racing against horses. Joe Louis, too, despite a long and spectacular reign as heavyweight champion, died in poverty. While the interracial basketball contests of local teams or the national championships of the Rens and Globetrotters proved the abilities of black athletes and the potential of sport as a means to social harmony, Jackie Robinson still required the subterfuges of Branch Rickey to gain his place in baseball.[65]

Eventually the black style of play would come to dominate basketball. But when success threatened white perceptions of superiority, the best black players were integrated into the professional white circuit; or, in the case of the Globetrotters, required to become clowns, despite players' objections, in order to fit a white racist image that allowed blacks to entertain them.[66] Once again, the efforts of African-Americans to throw off the shackles of the slave mentality, to free their sharecropping brethren who had come north for salvation, enjoyed only limited success. For most, who remained mired in the ghetto, basketball resulted in just another blocked shot, providing psychic rewards for many but delivering salvation to a relative few. The failure of even that "talented tenth" to win wholesale acceptance in the larger American society would lead to a more aggressive and sometimes hostile approach, first evident in the Detroit riot of 1943, and progressing to the civil rights movement of the 1950s and 1960s. Whereas violent revolution could not overcome white dominance, some sport practices could. Within another generation the black style of basketball with its exuberant expressions of the African-American culture, characterized by powerful dunks and joyous expressions of physicality, predominated in the game.[67]

The experience of African-American basketball players in Chicago was just one part of a more complete cultural fabric woven out of many interconnected threads. Other case studies of Eastern cities indicate some parallel developments.[68] The promise of opportunity in the North allowed urban middle-class blacks and religious groups to organize teams for pride and profit. Women, as well as men, played the game in organized leagues and barnstorming teams. Residential segregation and other exclusionary practices by the white majority forced the development of a parallel sporting culture of African-Americans. Sporting events helped assimilate rural migrants from the south into the urban culture of the north. In the process, distinct black cultures coalesced and transformed the American mainstream popular culture. Though racism blocked their efforts, African-Americans ultimately changed the nature of basketball.

Notes

Gerald R. Gems, "Blocked Shot: The Development of Black Basketball in the African-American Community of Chicago," *Journal of Sport History* 22:2 (Summer 1995): 135–148. Copyright 1995 by the North American Society for Sport History and Gerald R. Gems. Reprinted with permission.

I wish to acknowledge the research assistance of Ray Fetters in this project and to explain the seeming overreliance on the *Defender* as a resource. While sources are limited in general, other black newspapers did exist in New York, Pittsburgh, and Baltimore, but they gave primary coverage to local sporting events.

1. Among basketball histories which do examine the African-American experience, but largely in the East, see Robert W. Peterson, *From Cages to Jump Shots* (New York: Oxford University Press, 1990), and Nelson George, *Elevating the Game* (New York: Harper Collins, 1992).

2. Olivia Mahoney, "Black Abolitionists," *Chicago History* 20 (Spring/Summer, 1991): 22–37, discusses the 1848 constitution and its restrictive "black codes." James R. Grossman, *Land of Hope: Chicago, Black Southerners, and the Great Migration* (Chicago: University of Chicago Press, 1989), 23–24; Thomas C. Cox, *Blacks in Topeka, Kansas, 1865–1915* (Baton Rouge: Louisiana State University Press, 1982).

3. Allan H. Spear, *Black Chicago: The Making of a Negro Ghetto, 1890–1920* (Chicago: University of Chicago Press, 1967), 12.

4. Grossman, *Land of Hope*, 81.

5. Dempsey J. Travis, *An Autobiography of Black Chicago* (Chicago: Urban Research Institute, 1981), 1, 13; Grossman, *Land of Hope*, 81; Spear, *Black Chicago*, 4, 12, 15.

6. Mahoney, "Black Abolitionists," 34; Grossman, *Land of Hope*, 129–30; Travis, *Autobiography of Black Chicago*, 37–39, 42.

7. *Chicago Defender*, November 12, 1910, 1, November 19, 1910, 1, November 9, 1912, 5. Frederic H. Robb, ed., *The Negro in Chicago, 1779–1929* (Chicago: Washington Intercollegiate Club, 1929), 80, 281, 195, 311; Carroll Binder, "Chicago and the New Negro," *Chicago Daily News*, reprint, 1927, 23.

8. Archie Oboler, ed., *The Oski-Wow-Wow: A History of Hyde Park High School Athletics* (Chicago: Hyde Park High School, 1924), 12–18; John Carroll, *Fritz Pollard, Pioneer in Racial Advancement* (Urbana: University of Illinois Press, 1992).

9. Spear, *Black Chicago*, 12.

10. Quintin Hoare and Geoffrey N. Smith, eds., *Selections from the Prison Notebooks of Antonio Gramsci* (New York: International Publishers, 1971).

11. Raymond Williams, *The Sociology of Culture* (New York: Schocken Books, 1981).

12. Spear, *Black Chicago*, 110 and 117, cites the *Broad Ax*, November 2, 1907, May 9, 1908, May 21, 1916, December 31, 1910, January 21, 1911, and May 18, 1912, on the development of a separate black baseball league.

13. W. E. B. DuBois, *The Souls of Black Folk* (New York: Vintage Books, 1990), 68–82.

14. St. Clair Drake and Horace R. Cayton, *Black Metropolis: A Study of Negro Life in a Northern City* (New York: Harper Torchbooks, 1962), 55, cites the *De-*

fender, December 26, 1908, on the 1909 league; and St. Clair Drake, *Churches and Voluntary Associations in the Chicago Negro Community* (Chicago: Work Projects Administration, 1940), 131, cites the *Defender*, September 7, 1912, on the church league.

15. *Defender*, January 28, 1911, 2. The game took place on January 21, 1911.

16. *Defender*, December 7, 1912, 8, March 1, 1913, 8, November 29, 1913, 7; *Lane Tech Yearbook, 1914*, 210–11, 215, show the contributions of black athletes, including Virgil's brother, Napoleon. As Evanston had black athletes on its football and track teams, the refusal to play may have reflected Blueitt's skill as well as his color. Earlier racial incidents are reported in Special Parks Commission, *Annual Report, 1907* (Chicago, 1908), 6, 19–20, 22, 24; and William L. Katz, ed., *The Negro in Chicago* (Chicago: University of Chicago Press, 1922), 288, 291.

17. Steven A. Riess, *City Games: The Evolution of American Urban Society and the Rise of Sports* (Urbana: University of Illinois Press, 1989), 115; Grossman, *Land of Hope*, 4, 200–201, 218–19; Travis, Autobiography of *Black Chicago*, 14.

18. Spear, *Black Chicago*, 46–47, cites Barnett's letter to the *Record-Herald*, January 26, 1912; 205–206 on parks. Smaller pockets of black settlement existed on the west and north sides.

19. *Defender*, February 14, 1914, 7, March 7, 1914, 6, February 16, 1915, 4 (Evanston Quote).

20. *Defender*, February 6, 1915, 4.

21. March 13, 1915, 4.

22. *Defender*, October 30, 1915, 7, November 6, 1915, 8, November 13, 1915, 8, December 18, 1915, 8, November 12, 1921, 10.

23. *Defender*, December 18, 1915, 8.

24. *Defender*, January 15, 1916, 9, November 18, 1916, 7, December 2, 1916, 6.

25. Rob Ruck, *Sandlot Seasons: Sport in Black Pittsburgh* (Urbana: University of Illinois Press, 1987), 14, addresses the development of a national black sporting culture. *Defender*, February 17, 1917, 8, March 3, 1917, 8, March 10, 1917, 8, March 24, 1917, 5, March 31, 1917, 7, April 7, 1917, 8, December 29, 1917, 1, 10.

26. *Defender*, March 4, 1919, 9; William L. Katz, *The Negro in Chicago*, 143.

27. On racial tensions, see Vivian Palmer, *Community History Studies at the Chicago Historical Society*, History of Douglas, interviews 12–13; History of Grand Boulevard, Documents #3–4; Spear, *Black Chicago*; Katz, *The Negro in Chicago*, 272, 274, 282–83, 287–88, 290–91, 295; Travis, *Autobiography of Black Chicago*, 15, 20, 25–26; Grossman, *Land of Hope*, 118–27; Michael W. Homel, "Negroes in the Chicago Public Schools," (Ph.D. diss., University of Chicago, 1972); *Defender*, January 9, 1915, 8, January 16, 1915, 2, January 23, 1915, 4, March 17, 1917, 1. On the race riot, see Katz, *Negro in Chicago*; and William M. Tuttle, *Race Riot: Chicago in the Red Summer of 1919* (New York: Atheneum, 1978).

28. Martin Bauml Duberman, *Paul Robeson: A Biography* (New York: Ballantine Books, 1989), 72.

29. Athletes such as Jay Mayo "Ink" Williams, Paul Robeson, and Fritz Pollard often served as producers, promoters, or agents in the thriving black entertainment industry; see John Carroll, *Fritz Pollard*, 91, 189, 216, 110–14, 224–22; Duberman, *Paul Robeson*; and Stephen Calt, "Anatomy of a 'Race' Label: The Mayo Williams Era," *78 Quarterly* 1 (1989), 9–30. Katz, ed., *The Negro in Chicago*, 266–86, 323, on white control; Riess, *City Games*, 118.

30. On the growth of Olivet Baptist, see Tuttle, *Race Riot*, 98; and Carroll

Binder, "Chicago and the New Negro," 18. See Robb, *Negro in Chicago*, 263, on the relationship of athletic teams and church attendance. *Defender*, March 4, 1919, 9, November 1, 1919, 11, indicates church teams in two divisions. See *Defender*, December 3, 1921, 10, and November 25, 1922, 10, on community efforts to promote athletics.

31. Cornel West, cited by bell hooks, *Yearning: Race, Gender, and Cultural Politics* (Boston: South End Press, 1990), 27. Also see Judith Stein, "Defining the Race, 1890–1930," in Werner Sollars, ed., *The Invention of Ethnicity* (New York: Oxford University Press, 1989), 77–104.

32. *Defender*, April 2, 1921, 10 (quote). See November 6, 1920, 9, December 25, 1920, 6, January 8, 1921, 6, February 26, 1921, 6, March 5, 1921, 6, March 22, 1921, 6, on the eastern tour.

33. *Defender*, April 2, 1921, 10.

34. *Defender*, April 2, 1921, 11.

35. *Defender*, December 2, 1916, 6, December 30, 1916, 7, January 27, 1917, 7, February 17, 1917, 8, March 3, 1917, 7, March 10, 1917, 8, March 17, 1917, 1, March 24, 1917, 5, October 20, 1921, 10, December 24, 1921, 10, February 11, 1922, 10, February 18, 1922, 10, February 25, 1922, 10, March 18, 1922, 10, April 8, 1922, 10.

36. The Roamers were sometimes referred to as the Romas or Romeos. *Defender*, January 17, 1920, 9, states an intended game; March 16, 1921, 6; gives the first game account; December 24, 1921, 10; A. S. "Doc" Young, *Negro Firsts in Sports* (Chicago: Johnson Publishing, 1963), 198; Arthur R. Ashe, Jr., *A Hard Road to Glory: A History of the African-American Athlete, 1919–1945* (New York: Warner Books, 1988), 45; *Polk's Directory of Chicago, 1923*, lists Channels, national tennis finalist, and; later, a champion; and school teachers Margrete Lewis, Nettie Hall, and Esther Henderson.

37. *Defender*, December 20, 1924, II: 8, February 21, 1925, 12, January 16, 1926, II: 5, March 20, 1926, II: 5 (quote).

38. *Defender*, April 10, 1926, II: 9, October 23, 1926, II: 7, January 29, 1927, 10; Robb, *Negro in Chicago*, 309, *Polk's Directory of Chicago, 1928–29*.

39. *Defender*, January 29, 1927, 10, February 6, 1927, II: 6, February 13, 1927, II: 6, 7, February 19, 1927, II: 6, November 26, 1927, II: 6, March 10, 1928, II: 8, November 2, 1929, 18, January 18, 1930, 11, January 25, 1930, 11, 17, December 13, 1930, 8, *Chicago Evening American*, January 15, 1930, 15, January 16, 1930, 14, *Chicago Tribune*, January 16, 1930, 22.

40. Wilma L. Pesavento, "A Historical Study of the Development of Physical Education in the Chicago Public Schools, 1860–1965" (Ph.D. diss., Northwestern University, 1966), 137, states that such instruction started for girls in 1921. Nine of the 27 females who could be identified through Polk's Directory of Chicago were listed as schoolteachers or students, 10 were domestics, and eight clerks or office workers. *Defender*, March 14, 1931, 10, April 4, 1931, 16, December 22, 1934, 9, March 2, 1935, 8, March 16, 1935, 10. Women's teams require a fuller examination. Among the burgeoning literature that analyzes women's sport experiences amidst hegemonics relationships, such as patriarchy, religious influences, and class factionalism, see Lois Bryson, "Sport and the Maintenance of Masculine Hegemony," *Women's Studies International Forum* 10 (1987): 349–60; Gerald Gems, "Sport and the Americanization of Ethnic Women in Chicago," in George Eisen and David Wiggins, eds., *Ethnicity and Sport in North American History and Culture* (Westport, Conn.: Greenwood Press, 1994), 177–200; James

A. Mangan and Roberta Park, eds., *From Fair Sex to Feminism: Sport and the Socialization of Women in the Industrial and Post-Industrial Eras* (Totowa, N.J.: Frank Cass, 1987); and Michael A. Messner and Donald Sabo, *Sport, Men, and the Gender Order: Critical Feminist Perspectives* (Champaign, Ill.: Human Kinetics, 1990).

41. *Defender*, March 18, 1922, 10, January 16, 1926, II: 5, March 6, 1926, II: 7, April 3, 1926, 9 (quote).

42. *Defender*, December 12, 1922, 10, February 2, 1924, 11, February 19, 1927, II: 6, January 11, 1930, 11.

43. *Defender*, December 12, 1908, April 23, 1910, February 20, 1915, for accounts of baseball barnstormers. See *Defender*, January 27, 1917, 7, for the already established eastern basketball circuit. On Globetrotters, see *Defender*, March 14, 1931, 10, February 20, 1932, 8, January 21, 1933, 9. On Lillard, see Ocania Chalk, *Pioneers of Black Sport* (New York: Dodd, Mead, 1975), 228–30. Lawrence W. Levine, *The Unpredictable Past: Explorations in American Cultural History* (New York: Oxford University Press, 1993), 36–39, 45, 60–66, 83, 96–105, on oral culture and music as protest.

44. Wabash YMCA Records, Special Collections, University of Illinois at Chicago, 68–44, Box 3, folder 3–1, Report of Physical Section for 1925, Board of Directors Meeting, January 22, 1926.

45. Katz, *Negro in Chicago,* 249–54.

46. *Defender*, February 18, 1922, 10.

47. School teams competed on two levels, designated by weight to equalize competition. *Defender*, January 19, 1924, II: 2; March 1, 1924, 10; March 15, 1924, 10.

48. *Defender*, April 5, 1924, 1, April 26, 1924, 1, 13, February 21, 1925, 12, February 28, 1925, 11, January 2, 1926, 1, January 9, 1926, II: 4.

49. *Defender*, February 12, 1927, II: 6.

50. *Defender*, January 14, 1928, II: 9, March 3, 1928, II: 8, March 10, 1928, II: 8, March 17, 1928, II: 10 (quote), March 14, 1931, 10.

51. Robert Pruter, "Early Phillips teams paved way for DuSable," *Illinois High School Sports Historian* (January 1990), 4, cites the *Tribune; Defender*, March 17, 1928, II: 10.

52. *Defender*, January 12, 1929, II: 5.

53. *Defender*, March 22, 1930, 13.

54. *Defender*, March 29, 1930, 16; William A. Brower, "Has Professional Football Closed the Door?" *Opportunity* 18 (December 1940), 375–77; David Wiggins, "Wendell Smith, the *Pittsburgh Courier-Journal,* and the Campaign to Include Blacks in Organized Baseball, 1933–1945," *Journal of Sport History* 10 (Summer 1983): 5–29.

55. *Defender*, March 7, 1931, 11, March 21, 1931, 10, March 28, 1931, 16, April 4, 1931, 17. Bob Pruter, "Early Phillips Teams." 5, has pointed out that the rules of that time required a jump ball after each basket, giving Crane Tech a distinct advantage. Bob Gruenig, the 6'8" center, went on to a Hall of Fame career.

56. *Defender*, March 19, 1932, 10; Claude A. Barnett Papers at the Chicago Historical Society, Box 397, file 21, cites the *Defender*, March 4, 1932, for the quote.

57. I want to thank Bob Pruter for noting the decline of the tournament between 1930–1935, and for his analysis of conditions, April 18, 1994.

58. *Defender*, March 4, 1939, clipping in Wabash YMCA Scrapbooks, Special

Collections, University of Illinois at Chicago; Carroll, *Fritz Pollard*, 196–206, Wiggins, "Wendell Smith."

59. *Defender*, February 11, 1933, 10, November 16, 1935, March 14, 1936, 14, Ashe, *Hard Road to Glory*, 51; Claude A. Barnett Papers, Box 397, file 21, newspaper clipping, February 27, 1939.

60. DuBois, *Souls of Black Folk*.

61. *Defender*, February 18, 1922, 10, March 4, 1922, 10, December 27, 1924, II: 6, January 9, 1926, II: 4, October 23, 1926, II: 7, March 17, 1928, II: 10, April 7, 1928, II: 10, January 15, 1930, 8, February 3, 1934, 11, March 27, 1937 clipping in YMCA Scrapbooks. Donn Rogosin, *Invisible Men: Life in Baseball's Negro Leagues* (New York: Atheneum, 1983), 35, makes the point of athletics as one sphere where blacks might challenge whites. *Chicago Evening American*, January 15, 1930, 15, on Jenkins's salary.

62. DuBois, *Souls of Black Folk*, 180–90, on "sorrow songs" among southern blacks; Angela M. S. Nelson, "The Persistence of Ethnicity in African American Popular Music: A Theology of Rap Music," *Explorations in Ethnic Studies* 15 (January 1992), 47–57; Levine, *Unpredictable Past*, on the construction of an African-American culture. *Defender*, January 9, 1924, 2:2, March 1, 1924, 10, March 22, 1930, 13, for examples of fan behavior.

63. Williams cited in Alan G. Ingham and Stephan Hardy, "Introduction," in Alan G. Ingham and John Loy, eds., *Sport in Social Development* (Champaign, Ill.: Human Kinetics, 1993), 3–4.

64. George, *Elevating the Game*, 11–12.

65. Jules Tygiel, *Baseball's Great Experiment: Jackie Robinson and His Legacy* (New York: Oxford University Press, 1983).

66. Frank Waldman, *Famous American Athletes of Today* (Boston: L.C. Page, 1951), 91–92; George, *Elevating the Game*, 60, 72–76, likens the improvisational style of black players to jazz and discusses the Globetrotters, 41–42, 49.

67. The film, and its title, *White Men Can't Jump*, offers a parody of stylistic differences and abilities relative to basketball.

68. John M. Carroll, "The Origin of Black Basketball in New York," and James Coates, "Basketball: The Baltimore and Washington Experience," presentations made at the North American Society for Sport History Convention, May 29–June 1, 1993, Albuquerque, New Mexico.

The All-American Girls Baseball League was set up in 1943 by Chicago Cubs owner Philip K. Wrigley to maintain interest in the national pastime. Wrigley, at the request of President Franklin D. Roosevelt, set up a committee to consider what should be done if major league baseball had to be halted for lack of players. By 1943, most stars were in the military, and rosters were being filled with men physically exempt from service, older players, and boys too young to be drafted. One idea the committee developed was to set up a women's softball league to keep the fans interested. This was a pretty radical notion, because sport was then a male sphere, and women athletes, with the exception of a few "feminine" sports like tennis, golf, and diving, were not supported by the middle class. The AAGBL originally played softball, a very popular sport among industrial women workers in the Depression, but the rules evolved to become virtually identical to men's baseball. The teams were located in the Midwest, including the Rockford Peaches, who won four championships in the league, which lasted through 1954. The promoters recognized the prevailing attitude about women athletes and carefully addressed that by emphasizing femininity, requiring players to attend charm school, wear lipstick, and wear short skirts. The league was largely forgotten after its demise until the motion picture A League of Their Own *(1992) generated interest in these pathbreaking athletes.*

11 | No Freaks, No Amazons, No Boyish Bobs

SUSAN K. CAHN

In 1943 Chicago Cubs owner Philip K. Wrigley launched a bold new baseball enterprise. Fearful that major league baseball might collapse under wartime manpower shortages, he proposed a professional women's baseball league. The All-American Girls Baseball League (AAGBL), as it came to be called, served a dual purpose for Wrigley. He promoted the league as a form of entertainment for a war-weary public in need of wholesome, outdoor recreation. At the same time, he used women's baseball as a temporary replacement for the men's game, keeping stadiums occupied and fan interest alive.

The AAGBL celebrated women's strength and energy, but it also kindled anxieties about traditional gender arrangements in American society. Since the early twentieth century, critics of women sports enthusiasts had cast them in the negative image of "mannish athletes," an image that questioned their femininity and raised the specter of lesbianism. Sport was considered a male activity, the domain of traditional masculine virtues of aggressiveness, competition, physical prowess, and virility. Women athletes were seen as intruders into this male realm.

The AAGBL used the gender issue in sports to its advantage as an ingenious way to market its brand of baseball to the public. By demanding that its players combine "masculine" athletic skill with a very feminine appearance, the AAGBL maintained a clear distinction between male and female roles while providing the fans with skillfully played and exciting baseball. The league thus avoided the mannish image that plagued other women's sports.

League managers could assure audiences, amazed at seeing a woman play a "man's game," that the players were feminine and "normal" in every other respect. Although the AAGBL did not fundamentally challenge existing concepts of masculinity and femininity, it gave a group of gifted women athletes a unique opportunity to compete with the best players in the nation in a game they loved.

The league opened in four midwestern cities: Kenosha and Racine, Wisconsin; South Bend, Indiana; and Rockford, Illinois. After a slow start, attendance climbed steadily, and Wrigley's experiment gained a foothold in the professional sports world. The AAGBL later expanded to include teams in Kalamazoo, Grand Rapids, and Muskegon, Michigan; Fort Wayne, Indiana; and Peoria, Illinois, with short-lived attempts in Chicago, Milwaukee, and Minneapolis; Battle Creek, Michigan; and Springfield, Illinois. It became much more than a wartime surrogate— spanning the years 1943 to 1954—and at its peak operated in ten cities and drew nearly a million fans.

As it became clear that the major league men's game would survive the war, Wrigley lost interest and sold his share of the AAGBL to Arthur Meyerhoff, his close associate and advertising agent. Meyerhoff created the Management Corp. to publicize and coordinate league teams, which typically were owned by businessmen from the sponsoring city. From 1944 through 1950 Meyerhoff's Chicago-based office managed the league with assistance from a board of directors and a league commissioner. In 1951 disgruntled team owners bought out Meyerhoff and decentralized the league's organization during its last four seasons.

The AAGBL's eventual collapse in 1954 should not obscure its remarkable accomplishments. For twelve seasons the league played a four-month schedule of 120 games plus a championship series. Attendance during peak years ranged from 500,000 to one million as fans eagerly turned out to root for local teams named the Daisies, Lassies, Peaches, Blue Sox, and Comets. The league recruited women from nearly every state and several Canadian provinces. Often championship athletes in several sports, players received $40 to $85 per week in the league's early years and up to $125 per week in later years. They grabbed at the chance to play ball professionally, seeing it, as did Fort Wayne player Jean Havlish, "like a dream . . . to get paid for doing something you liked so well." For credibility and name recognition, the AAGBL hired ex-major league baseball managers. Among them were Jimmie Foxx, Marty McManus, and Max Carey (who also served as commissioner for several years). Though constantly beset by financial problems, high manager turnover, and franchise failure, league teams that survived the initial trial period drew well and commanded tremendous loyalty from hometown fans. For instance, the Racine Belles attracted more spectators than any local male sports team had ever drawn. And when the Rockford Peaches threatened to go under in the 1950s, fans raised the money to keep the team afloat. Former Rockford and Kenosha player Mary Pratt remembered, "The fans thought that we were the best thing that ever came down the pike. They really looked up to us."

No other women's team sport before or since created such a viable professional organization. Even tennis and golf, the most successful women's professional sports, were still primarily amateur in the 1940s, without professional tours or associations. In order to succeed, a women's professional sports enterprise had to overcome the cultural perception of sport as a masculine activity. Since the development of organized sport in late nineteenth-century America, men had dominated virtually all athletic events and associations, except for brief periods when women's tennis and swimming commanded a share of the limelight. College football, professional baseball, men's track and field, and boxing enjoyed large popular followings, while administrative bodies like the National Collegiate Athletic Association, the Amateur Athletic Union, and the National and American baseball leagues were led by men with little interest in women's athletics.

Americans saw sport as a male activity, and they associated athletics with masculine ideals of aggressiveness, competitiveness, physical strength, and virility. Virtues for men, such traits raised the specter of "mannishness" in women. Doctors, scientists, and exercise specialists cautioned that sport posed grave emotional and physical dangers to women, issuing ominous warnings about female hysteria and damaged maternal capacity. However, some women braved the criticism and enthusiastically engaged in sports—from the 1890s bicycle craze to gymnastics classes, swimming, track and field, basketball, and especially softball in the 1930s and 1940s. Advocates viewed sport as a step toward emancipation that granted them physical freedom and competitive experience denied under restrictive Victorian notions of femininity.

By World War II, women athletes had established a solid institutional base in community recreation programs, industrial leagues, and intramural school programs. Although proponents had by this time settled on a philosophy of "modified athletics" for women, with special rules, uniforms, and chaperone systems in place to differentiate women's athletics from men's, critics continued to evoke the image of the "mannish athlete." Media portrayals frequently referred to successful athletes as "Amazons" with masculine skills and body types. At the organizational level, efforts to curtail women's competitive sports and to eliminate female track and field events from the Olympic Games persisted through the 1950s.

To overcome resistance to their venture, Philip Wrigley and Arthur Meyerhoff did not try to reduce the tension between sport and femininity but instead decided to accentuate it. Meyerhoff especially sought to promote women's baseball by capitalizing on the contrast between "masculine" baseball skill and feminine appearance, describing the league as a "clean spirited, colorful sports show" built upon "the dramatic impact of seeing baseball, traditionally a men's game, played by feminine type girls with masculine skill." Meyerhoff speculated that the novelty of women's baseball would attract first-time customers intrigued by the "amazing spectacle of beskirted girls throwing, catching, hitting and running like men. . . ." Unlike barnstorming teams that occasionally featured women players competing against men, the AAGBL needed to sustain interest after the initial effect wore off. Meyerhoff again linked success to the combination of feminine charm and masculine activity. He believed that "the sight of girls playing baseball remains a constant source of amazement and wonder to most fans; and "the fact that the All-American players are 'nice girls'" would give women's baseball an edge over men's in winning fan interest and sympathy.

The management did not consider athletic ability within the boundaries of femininity; they described baseball as a masculine activity and the girls' league as a spectacle. The principal logic behind the league was to find women who played ball "like men," not "like girls," and who looked like "nice girls," not like men. Why did Wrigley, Meyerhoff, and the team owners insist on this distinction? The answer lies in the broader history of sport as a male arena and, specifically, in the tarnished image of women's softball.

Invented in the early 1900s as a derivative of baseball for indoor play or in restricted outdoor space, softball came into its own as a game in the 1930s. The Amateur Softball Association (ASA) was organized in 1933, and after only one year 950,000 men, women, and children participated in ASA-sanctioned leagues. New Deal programs like the Works Progress Administration poured money and workers into facility construction projects and community recreation programs. The depression-era boom caused the *Christian Science Monitor* to note that softball was fast "becoming a national recreation for the masses." When the war came, softball's popularity continued to soar so that by the mid-1940s the *New York Times* estimated the sport had grown to include nine million players, 600,000 teams, and 150 million spectators in the United States. Though popular nationwide, softball's strongest roots lay in the Midwest. Chicagoans showed a special zeal for the sport. The city hosted several of the first ASA national tournaments and catered to all ages and abilities through park, YMCA, church, business, industrial, and athletic association leagues.

Girls and women eagerly joined the throng. Unlike baseball, softball had no masculine stigma at first. If anything, the use of a softer ball, the smaller field dimensions, and early names like "kitten ball" and "mush ball" cast softball in a slightly feminine light as a game appropriate for women, youngsters, and men not rugged enough to excel in baseball.

On the local level, any criticism of female athletes usually paled next to the popular support given to teams by neighbors, family members, friends, and co-workers. Softball thrived in rural areas and urban working-class neighborhoods. In both settings, notions of femininity were expansive and flexible enough to encompass the broad range of women's physically demanding domestic work and wage labor. Unlike middle-class culture, rural and working-class cultures had traditionally defined womanhood more in terms of family and community roles than prescribed feminine attributes and activities. Such flexible definitions allowed for the "outdoor girl" or "tomboy" with an avid interest in softball. In addition, by organizing leagues through neighborhood parks, churches, service organizations, and businesses, supporters of softball built upon existing community institutions. During the depression and wartime eras, when money, gas, and leisure hours were in short supply, people flocked to their local playing field for an inexpensive evening's entertainment. When women's teams met success, winning in their leagues and advancing to city, state, regional, and national competitions, they continued to excite loyalty and enthusiasm among hometown fans who were more concerned about players' batting averages than femininity quotients.

However, by the late 1930s, good women's teams began to attract attention as much for their "masculine appearance" as for their superior ability. Within a decade women's skill levels had increased dramatically with the best teams often defeating men's teams in fundraisers and exhibition games. Skilled women players demonstrated speed, power, and competitive zest previously associated only with male athletes. In addition, as women developed physically through training, the size, weight, and musculature of some players evoked negative images of "mannish athletes." During the depression these stereotypes were fueled by cultural anxieties about female intrusion into male realms. High male unemployment and the resulting family disruptions caused many Americans to fear that working women were supplanting men in jobs and in the role of family provider.

Media accounts of women's softball took a more critical approach by 1940, labeling softball a masculine sport and eyeing skilled women players with suspicion. In their book *Softball! So What*, Lowell Thomas and Ted Shane took an apparently positive view; applauding the women's game as an activity that didn't "bunch muscles, give girls a weightlifter's figure, develop varsity-club leg, the usual penalty of fiendish exercise . . ."

Yet the authors also observed that women failed to exhibit ladylike manners on the field and resisted "anything effeminate" in the rules, letting out "such a holler as could be heard from Sappho to Amazonia" when men tried to modify the rules for women. In this case, the authors defended the sport as compatible with femininity. Yet at the same time they introduced element of ridicule by referring to general prohibitions against women athletes and intimating an association between softball and lesbianism through allusions to Sappho and Amazons.

Robert Yoder barely contained his scorn in a 1942 *Saturday Evening Post* feature on women's softball, which described Olympia and Frieda Savona, star players on the national champion team, the New Orleans Jax. "Olympia runs like a man, slides like a man and catches like a man" but "though built like a football halfback, looks frail compared to Miss Frieda." Revealing a sense of threatened manhood, he contrasted women players who "may occasionally play like, and occasionally even look like men" with "the frailest creature on the field [who] is frequently that undeveloped shrimp, the male umpire."

Wrigley sensed that to make women's baseball attractive to a mass audience beyond the neighborhood appeal of softball, he would have to overcome such negative portrayals and circumvent charges that, as a "male sport," baseball led to masculine women. He devised a strategy that served as the guiding principle of the AAGBL long after his own involvement ended. Insisting that the women play baseball, not softball, Wrigley hoped to sustain interest in baseball as a spectator sport. And by demanding players combine masculine skill with feminine attractiveness, he kept the ideal of feminine womanhood constantly before the public eye. In this way the league would try to establish itself as cut above women's softball, avoiding its mannish image and reputation for rougher, tougher players with less audience appeal.

In 1944 the founding of the National Girls Baseball League (NGBL) in Chicago challenged the AAGBL's preeminence and undermined its unique status as the only professional baseball league for women. The NGBL initially consisted of four semipro teams that had dominated women's softball in the Chicago area. Anchored by mainstays like the Parichy Bloomer Girls, the Music Maids, the Rockola Chicks, and the Match Corp. Queens, the league expanded to six teams and attracted 500,000 annual spectators by the late 1940s. Like the AAGBL, it faded out in the early 1950s, but in the meantime the NGBL acted as a constant thorn in the side of its rival. Competition between them for publicity and for players led to salary wars, talent raiding, and an eventual lawsuit. The NGBL remained closely tied to softball, keeping the underhand pitch and shorter base paths of softball as well as the traditional softball uniforms of shorts or knickers. It placed no special emphasis on femininity, though it did not refrain from using sexual appeals in advertising.

The existence of a rival deepened the AAGBL's commitment to its unique brand of feminine baseball. The league had used the underhand pitch in 1943 but quickly legalized a side-arm delivery and eventually switched completely to overhand pitching. Meyerhoff's Management Corp. sought a competitive advantage by continuing to stress femininity and a unique style of ball to contrast with the rough, masculine image of softball. A beauty consultant hired for spring training in 1944 captured the spirit when she substituted the feminine nickname "marygirl" for the more masculine "tomboy" moniker to describe "the type of young womanhood" desired by the AAGBL.

By associating masculinity with athletic skill and femininity with appearance, the AAGBL maintained a clear sense of appropriate divisions between male and female, even as it gave women an unprecedented opportunity to enter a male sports preserve. The AAGBL adhered to this principle both in the concrete daily operations of the league and in the ideology of women's sport it promoted. The league's dress and conduct codes, its public relations campaigns, and its playing rules all reflect this overarching philosophy.

In the AAGBL handbook, Meyerhoff's Management Corp. spelled out the logic behind the accentuated contrast of feminine charm with masculine athletic ability. The section called "Femininity with Skill" instructed recruiters to weigh both ability and femininity in prospective players because it was "more dramatic to see a feminine-type girl throw, run and bat than to see a man or boy or masculine-type girl do the same things. The more feminine the appearance of the performer, the more dramatic the performance." The guide further explained that the league's rules must go hand in hand with players' own efforts to project the desired image. The manual continued:

> For the benefit of self and game every player devotes himself to cultivation of both skill and femininity. Management reinforces this standard faithfully. It is for the purpose of keeping constantly before the spectator the feminine elements of the show that the All-American girls are uniformed in tennis-type skirts. Conversely, boyish bobs and other imitations of masculine style and habit are taboo. Masculine appearance or mannerisms produce an impression either of a masculine girl or an effeminate boy, both effects prejudicial to the dramatic contrast of feminine aspects and masculine skill.

The carefully crafted impression of femininity included a sexual element. AAGBL officials absolutely forbade bawdiness or sexual antics reminiscent of barnstorming teams, often named "Bloomer Girls," from an earlier era. Consistent with its "nice girl" image, the league boasted of All-American Girls' "high moral tone," further safeguarded by the watchful eye of the chaperone. Nevertheless, Meyerhoff understood that the ideal feminine ball player would attract customers with her sex appeal as well as her slugging average. By insisting on short skirts, makeup, and physical attractiveness, he attempted to capitalize on an ideal of wholesome, feminine sexuality. A description of the league in the major league Baseball Blue Book captured the essence of the ploy, explaining on the one hand that players did not reflect sex-consciousness. On the other hand, if by "sex" is meant the normal appeal of the feminine mode and attitude, then most certainly it was an important source of interest and a legitimate element of the league's success.

To ensure that players did in fact embody the desired "feminine mode and attitude," the league's first few spring training sessions featured not only tryouts and preseason conditioning but an evening charm school as well. Led one year by beauticians from the Helena Rubenstein salon and another year by *Chicago Tribune* beauty editor Eleanor Mangle, the clinic coached players on makeup, posture, fashion, table manners, and "graceful social deportment at large." Guidelines on personal appearance accompanied the beauty tips. Management ordered players to keep their hair shoulder length or longer, to wear makeup and nail polish, and never to appear in public wearing shorts, slacks, or jeans.

The league dropped the charm school after its value as a public relations stunt ebbed. However, management's stress on feminine dress and manner never wavered. In fact, as the league's popularity declined after 1948, written dress codes took on a shrill, urgent tone. A 1950 directive from the main office announced: "This league has only two things to sell to the public, baseball and femininity." Stating that most players needed no prodding to appear feminine, the memo warned "others who will feel the sting of a shortened pay check if they don't comply. . . ." After buying out Meyerhoff in 1951, team owners adopted a new constitution that further elaborated dress guidelines, stating: "*Always appear in feminine attire*. This precludes the use of any wearing attire of masculine nature. MASCULINE HAIR STYLING? SHOES? COATS? SHIRTS? SOCKS, T-SHIRTS ARE BARRED AT ALL TIMES."

The league introduced several other measures to create the desired effect. The management rejected players it perceived as too masculine. Even after making a team, a player might be fined or released if she violated league rules. Infractions included not only neglecting dress and hair requirements but "moral lapses" ranging from a bad attitude to negotiating with the NGBL to obvious lesbianism.

The AAGBL also had an unwritten policy against hiring minority women, although it did employ several Cuban players. Not until 1951 did the league openly discuss hiring black women, eventually deciding against the idea "unless they would show promise of exceptional ability." This policy reflects the pervasive racism in American society at large and in sport during the 1940s and 1950s. But it can also be understood in relation to the league's special emphasis on femininity, an image rooted in white middle-class beliefs about beauty, body type, and female nature. This feminine ideal tended to exclude or depreciate black women, making black athletes inherently less likely to meet league standards.

In addition to guidelines on dress and recruiting, the league instituted a player conduct code that forbade most public drinking and smoking, required players to obtain prior approval for social engagements and living arrangements, and imposed an evening curfew. To enforce the rules, each team hired a chaperone responsible for reporting violations to the management. Chaperones were typically, but not always, older than the players. Some had no athletic background and were hired through personal connections to local management. Others, like Rockford chaperone Dottie Green, were former players who stepped into chaperone positions after their playing careers ended. Despite their disciplinary role, chaperones often forged strong alliances with players, serving as mediators, advisers, and even as player advocates when conflicts arose with management.

With these regulations, the league aimed to surround women's baseball "with such safeguards as to warrant public confidence in its integrity and method." Public relations wizard Meyerhoff developed several promotional schemes. He varied spring training sites annually in order to increase media and audience exposure. In later years, the league established two traveling teams of young players not yet skilled enough for regular league play. The idea grew out of a failed expansion attempt in 1948. To thwart the NGBL's own expansion plans, the AAGBL established a Chicago team to occupy a stadium the NGBL had hoped to use. The team, the Colleens, failed immediately as did its expansion twin, the Springfield Sallies. To stave off embarrassment and further financial loss, the league used the team names and uniforms to form two traveling squads. The summer touring teams exhibited the AAGBL brand of ball to enthusiastic crowds in midwestern, northeastern, and southern states, functioning at the same time as a minor league program to hone the skills of potential league players.

Other publicity efforts aimed at gaining national media attention and at establishing good community relations in league cities. A film crew from Movietone News followed the league to its 1947 spring training in Havana, Cuba, to shoot a preseason game before a crowd of 25,000.

Later released as a newsreel called "Diamond Gals," it exposed millions of moviegoers in theaters around the country to the spectacle of All-American Girls Baseball. Articles in national magazines like *Colliers*, *Saturday Evening Post*, and *Holiday* reported on the league's novel brand of baseball and growing popularity. Meyerhoff's office carefully orchestrated contacts with the media, providing glossy photos of the league's most beautiful players, issuing copies of the league's dress and conduct codes, and emphasizing the difference between baseball and softball. To stress the femininity of the league and quickly silence any suggestions of masculinity or lesbianism, AAGBL officials stressed to the media that league rules allowed "no freaks or Amazons." As proof, it proudly drew attention to the married players and mothers in the league, though due to the young age of most players this group never comprised more than a tiny fraction of the AAGBL players.

While national feature stories highlighted the sex appeal and sensational quality of the league, local promotions stressed the team's contributions to community life and the players' "girl next door" image. Meyerhoff's Management Corp. was a profit-making enterprise, but individual teams incorporated as nonprofit organizations and returned a portion of their proceeds to the community by supporting local recreation programs and facility maintenance. Ownership by local businesses provided one source of civic backing, while teams gained additional support from local chapters of the Elks, the woman's club, and similar service organizations. Players made personal contact with community members by rooming with local families, giving clinics, attending banquets, and making public appearances at community events.

AAGBL teams fared best in medium-sized cities like Rockford and Fort Wayne, where such personal contacts could be cultivated. Unlike the larger cities of Chicago, Milwaukee, and Minneapolis where franchises failed, these small industrial centers combined a keen interest in baseball with the absence of other professional sports ventures to compete for the limited market. Daily newspapers in league towns provided excellent regular coverage, and local radio stations broadcast games in some league cities. In contrast to the national media, the local press rarely resorted to the femininity angle, employing it only in feature articles and preseason publicity spots. Once the season began, straightforward reporting prevailed without gendered headlines such as "Pretty Blonde Wins Again" or "Lady Blue Sox."

It is not clear whether the femininity concept advocated by the league was instrumental in a team's success or failure in a particular city. Many factors contributed to a team's fortunes, including financial backing, competition for the entertainment dollar, team strength, and management ability. While spectators may have responded positively to the feminine style and wholesome values projected by the league, skilled play, intense competition, and intercity rivalries also won the enthusiastic support of baseball fans. The continued popularity of semipro and amateur softball teams suggests at least that alternative approaches, less concerned with expressions of femininity, could succeed alongside the AAGBL's intense focus on female image. In Peoria, for example, for several seasons the AAGBL Redwings struggled to stay afloat while the powerhouse women's softball team, the Peoria Dieselettes, remained a popular favorite. And in Chicago, the NGBL offered a legitimate alternative to the Wrigley-Meyerhoff brand of baseball, though never reaching as wide an audience as the AAGBL.

Nevertheless, league officials remained firmly convinced that the contrast between feminine appearance and masculine skill formed the core of the league's appeal. While promotional efforts and dress and conduct codes guaranteed the feminine side of the equation, the impression of "masculine skill" rested on maintaining the distinction between baseball and softball. Management constantly adjusted the rules to more closely conform to the rules of men's baseball. Over the years the league increased the length between bases from 65 to 85 feet, shrunk the ball size, and introduced overhand pitching.

This strategy came back to haunt the AAGBL. The league wanted to highlight the fact that the women could play a man's game—baseball—at the same time denying any resemblance between the All-American Girl and the "pants-wearing, tough-talking female softballer." Eventually this distinction caused the AAGBL to lose contact with its greatest source of talent, semipro and amateur softball players. After the early years the league fought a constant battle to find quality pitching and young talent. Many of the best softball pitchers were unable or even unwilling to make the transition to pitching overhand. Ironically, the very popularity of organized sport, with youth softball and baseball programs springing up everywhere, may have created unforeseen problems. Organized leagues, especially Little League baseball, tended toward strict gender segregation. By the 1950s fewer girls grew up playing neighborhood baseball on sandlot and playground teams. To compensate, the league hatched several player development schemes: summer and winter baseball schools, summer traveling teams, regional tryouts, and junior AAGBL teams in league cities. They did not produce the hoped-for results, causing league commissioner Fred Leo to lament, "We have too many oldtimers." Seeing rookies as "our salvation," the league introduced a rookie rule requiring each team to play at least one first-year player in order to develop recruits who otherwise could not break into the lineup.

Beyond the pitching shortage, the league faced a general problem competing for talent with the NGBL and top amateur softball teams. Though the AAGBL forbade jumping leagues, a few players did cross back and forth. Bidding wars for star players raised salaries and added to the bitterness between the two leagues. When league finances deteriorated in the 1950s, personnel shortages forced the league into a onetime "amnesty" offer to lure former players back to the AAGBL. Other women used the threat of jumping leagues to gain leverage in salary and trade negotiations, prompting the owner of the South Bend Blue Sox to complain, "These girls have no idea of loyalty. . . . They are sure a bunch of tough actors and will gouge you regardless. . . ." The talent shortage may explain the heightened concern over dress and feminine image expressed in league communications during its last years. The league began signing very young players of fifteen and sixteen as well as courting softball veterans like the Savona sisters, noted in the media for both their "mannish" appearance and physical prowess. Forced to relax its standards of age and femininity in recruitment, management may have stepped up efforts to control player behavior and monitor appearance, hoping to reassure the parents of young recruits and to preserve the league's carefully cultivated feminine image.

Women joined the AAGBL from all over the United States and Canada, some heavily recruited, others traveling miles on the slim hope of getting a tryout. The young women shared a common childhood passion for sports and a particular excellence at softball or baseball. Interviews with former AAGBL members suggest that issues of femininity rarely concerned players, who overwhelmingly viewed the league as a fantastic opportunity to do something they really loved—play baseball. Yet looking back, opinion varies about the value of dress codes, rules of conduct, and the AAGBLs overarching femininity principle.

Some players found the league's concern with femininity ridiculous, while others believed it helped the league and improved the image of women athletes. Pragmatic rather than ideological considerations shaped players' views on the pastel skirted uniforms. In a 1985 *Sports Illustrated* interview, Shirley Jameson, one of the first players ever signed, recalled her feelings as "ambivalent," noting that "They were very feminine, and you could do the job—most of the time." But they offered little leg protection when sliding: thus, Jameson recalls, "I spent most of the season with strawberries on both legs." Some players believed that if the uniforms created a good public impression, contributing to the league's survival, they benefited the players regardless of personal taste. Still others, like Kalamazoo player Nancy Mudge Cato, loved the sharp look of the uniform and spoke of it with pride. "I loved that uniform. . . . When

I'd see girls in the softball uniforms, jocks, running around, I didn't like it nearly as much. I was really thankful for the skirt. I thought they were just charming."

Players displayed a similar range of opinion about dress and conduct codes. Nancy Mudge Cato and Jean Havlish, who played in the 1950s and described themselves as more innocent than most, found the rules agreeable. Personally comfortable with the feminine style cultivated by the league, they also recognized that because of the discredited image of women athletes, "You had to be careful so you wouldn't give someone a bad impression, so you wouldn't hurt the gate. . . . You had to be . . . above reproach in everything so you wouldn't hurt the league."

Others chafed under the regulations but conformed out of a calculated estimation of the risks. Pepper Paire explained to *Sports Illustrated* reporter Jay Feldman, "You have to understand that we'd rather play ball than eat, and where else could we go and get paid $100 a week to play ball? So, if some of the girls liked to wear their hair a little bit short, or liked to run around in jeans, they bent with the rules." Yet Paire also remembered that "there were a few little ways of getting around the rules, as long as you were discreet and didn't flaunt it." And Faye Dancer, one of the league's more flamboyant players, regaled Sheldon Sunness of *Z Magazine* with her own approach to the rules. "I always respected the rules. I broke them all, but I respected them."

Shirley Jameson admitted that the charm training served a purpose but also found that the lessons often conflicted with the more important matter at hand—playing baseball. The charm teachers "didn't seem to be tuned in to what we had to do. Some of it was appropos [sic], but a lot of it you just couldn't use playing baseball:" Dottie Schroeder saw charm training as "a joke, it was a promotional deal," while Irene Hickson rankled at the implied criticism of women ball players. Describing charm school as "sickening," she told historian Sharon Roepke, "It was silly, it really was. But everybody felt there was something wrong with you because you could play ball. You were masculine and all that. . . ."

Players like Hickson had grown up in communities where baseball, basketball, and even fistfighting and football were unorthodox but still acceptable activities for girls. Physical strength, competitiveness, and personal toughness were qualities admired in women and men alike. Moreover, in many working-class and rural areas, women's clothing styles were not as restrictive as dominant modes of fashion. To AAGBL players from such backgrounds, the league's dress code and concept of femininity may have appeared strange, irrelevant, or even offensive. Nevertheless, the practical tips on etiquette and social presentation could provide helpful instruction for players unfamiliar with formal dining or public speaking. And for players who wanted more than anything else to play ball, the league's philosophy made pragmatic sense. New Englanders Mary Pratt and Dottie Green admitted that they never questioned the rules at the time because "we were a little square, we were Puritans." But in hindsight, they still found the league's logic convincing, echoing management's reasoning that if fans "want to go out and see a bunch of tomboys play, they can go out to the park for nothing, but they have to pay 90 cents to get in here so they want to see girls with finesse."

Despite this range of opinion, former players seem not to have experienced sport as a masculine endeavor or to have personally felt a tension between sport and female identity. They regarded competitiveness, a love of sport, and the constant quest for improvement as integral aspects of their personalities, neither feminine nor masculine. Players did not express any sense of themselves as less womanly than nonathletes, even though they were aware that to some, baseball was a masculine game requiring masculine qualities. Their love of sport pushed questions of femininity into the background. Sport's masculine connotation presented problems only when it provoked negative responses from others or posed barriers to playing opportunities. In contrast to the Wrigley-Meyerhoff concept of the AAGBL as a unique blend of masculinity and femininity, players did not see the league as a dramatic novelty of gender contrast. Rather, they found drama in the thrill of competition and novelty in the rare opportunity to work, travel, and meet people while pursuing their passion for baseball.

While the All-American Girls played tirelessly and enthusiastically over the long summer months, the management waged a constant battle against financial woes and franchise collapse. By the early 1950s even the most solid teams were in debt. Mainstays like Racine and South Bend withdrew from the league, which shrunk to five teams in 1954. By the end of the season league directors conceded that they could not maintain even this skeleton structure. The board of directors cancelled the 1955 season, promising to reorganize the league in the future.

Many factors contributed to the AAGBL's decline. As urbanites joined the postwar suburban exodus and television took the entertainment world by storm, home recreation became the order of the day. Major spectator sports like football and baseball continued to draw large audiences, but attendance suffered at all other levels. Both local and national media expanded their coverage of major sports, nurturing a national sports culture that gradually supplanted small-town boosterism and local loyalties. Softball remained a popular sport, especially in the city and industrial leagues. However, as returning veterans replaced women in the work force, industrial sports as well as jobs once again became the province of men. Girls' and women's leagues continued to operate, but as very minor programs. And while topnotch amateur and semipro women's softball teams never ceeased providing skilled athletes a place to develop and compete, in most communities Little League baseball, industrial softball, and minor league men's baseball commanded an overwhelming share of funds, facilities, and civic backing.

Finally, the novel combination of "feminine attraction" and "masculine athletics" clashed with the conservative culture of the 1950s. In contrast to the giddy sense of workplace competence and freedom women experienced in the war years, the 1950s witnessed a swift turnabout that propelled women back into domesticity. The emphasis on home, family, and marriage was rooted in return to older, restrictive definitions of femininity. Virulent homophobia—the fear and hatred of gays and lesbians—accompanied the change in gender roles. An upsurge of media interest in sexual crime and "perversion" intensified public hostility toward homosexuality. Police raids on gay bars, military purges, and the firing of homosexual government employees under Cold War "security" policies added to the homophobic atmosphere of the 1950s. Neither of these trends boded well for the AAGBL. With baseball firmly re-established as the national (men's) pastime and femininity once again defined in terms of domestic life, the league's innovative effort to combine sport and femininity and its affirmation of female athletic ability were at odds with the dominant culture. Moreover, in an era of political, legal, and media attacks on homosexuals, the association of women's sport with Amazons or lesbianism jeopardized any attempt to market women's baseball as mass entertainment.

The legacy of the AAGBL lies less in its success or failure than in its fascinating approach to women's sports. The AAGBL management chose to promote the league by accentuating the tension between masculine sport and feminine charm. By continuing to see athletic ability as masculine skill rather than incorporating athleticism within the range of feminine qualities, the league's ideology posed no challenge to the fundamental precepts of gender in American society. In its concern with preserving the distinction between softball and baseball, the AAGBL disparaged women's softball as unfeminine. Yet it ultimately preserved baseball as a male realm by promoting "feminine baseball" as a spectacle.

Attempting to present an image of femininity consistent with popular and marketable ideals, the AAGBL nevertheless played a part in undermining those ideals. The league's philosophy highlighted the contrast between masculine sport and feminine appearance. But the actual experience of playing and viewing AAGBL baseball challenged the idea that athletic skill belonged in the province of men. The league provided women a once-in-a-lifetime opportunity to develop their skills and to pursue their passion for sport aided by financial backing, quality coaching, and appreciative fans. The players returned the favor. They offered eager crowds the chance to view highly skilled competitive baseball played by women. Whether "tomboys" or "marygirls," the All-American Girls' aggressive, superior play challenged social conventions, defied athletic tradition, and offered the public an exciting and expanded sense of women's capabilities.

The Chicago Cubs are much beloved by their fans, who attend their games religiously, whether they are winners or not, enjoying the marvelous ambiance of Wrigley Field. The lovable losers are the darlings of Chicago despite a remarkable history of failure. They have not been to the World Series since 1945, the longest absence of any major league team, and they have not won the World Series since 1908. The team was particularly poor in the period 1953 through 1966, when they never came in higher than sixth, with a tenth-place finish in 1966. The team then was second in the hearts of Chicagoans to the White Sox, who won the AL pennant in 1959. Fans stayed away in droves and from 1963 through 1967, the team failed to draw a million fans. The fiery and experienced Leo Durocher became manager in 1966, and in his second year as skipper brought his young team up to third place. After a second third-place finish in 1968, his now experienced team seemed poised for a shot at the pennant in 1969, the first year of divisional play. The team started out like gangbusters, and a championship seemed certain, with a lead of nine and a half games in August. But the squad faded badly and ended the season behind the charging Mets by eight games.

12 | 1969 and the Chicago Cubs

DAVID CLAERBAUT

"The Cubs are now ready to go for all the marbles."
—*Leo Durocher, on the prospects for 1969*

The title of this chapter, a simple number, need not be embellished. The season was the agony and ecstasy of the second half of the twentieth century for the Chicago Cubs. The memory of that year seems scorched eternally into the psyches of Cub fans and those who played during that fateful season. Ken Holtzman, a pitching cornerstone of the three-time world champion Oakland A's and later of the champion New York Yankees, captured the impact of that year in telling Rick Talley, "I must admit that from start to finish, that season had more excitement than did any of my seasons in Oakland or New York."

No year in the second half of the Cub century has received even remotely as much attention as 1969. Not 1984, not 1989, not 1998's wild card playoff campaign. Not one comes within light years of the attention the 1969 near championship run receives. The *Chicago Tribune* dedicated a near total sports section to it a decade later (June 8, 1979), a former Chicago sportswriter wrote a delightful then-and-now book on the 1969 team, and myriad baseball fans continue to discuss and debate 1969.

It was the summer of the Woodstock Music and Art Festival, where 400,000 camped out near White Lake, New York. It was also the summer of Chappaquiddick and of Charles Manson. People were just getting used to calling Richard Nixon "President Nixon." Riots had given way to rock festivals, and Chicago's near north area, called Old Town, reminded tourists and city residents of parts of San Francisco, with its nightly throngs of youth walking the streets, eating in the restaurants, attending lectures in the coffeehouses, and listening to music in the lively bistros. For those among the largest Opening Day crowd since 1929, a standing-room-only throng of 40,796, it was clear 1969 was the year of destiny for the Cubs. On that brisk April 8, I was one of the standing. The electricity of the moment was fed by the presence of fabled funnyman Jimmy Durante, popular Governor Richard Ogilvie, famed sportswriter Edgar Munzel, and 38–year-old Mr. Cub's 73–year-old father, who received a standing ovation when introduced. The pregame festivities were stimulating but also suspenseful. It was time to play ball.

After the Phillies plated a single run in the top of the 1st, it was the beloved Cubs' turn to flex their muscles and deliver a taste of Cub power. And flex them they did. With two Cubs aboard, the #5 hitter, Ernie Banks, stepped to the plate. Banks eyed Phillie ace left-hander Chris Short, then picked out the pitch he wanted, and drove it over the ivy-covered left-field wall for a three-run circuit shot. It was Cubs 3, Phillies 1, and pandemonium.

Cub fans settled in, excited and relieved. They were thrilled to witness a dramatic Cub homer and were comforted that their aging hero Ernie Banks had demonstrated he still had it in 1969. Now it was up to two-time 20–game winner Ferguson Jerkins to do what they were all certain he would do, tame the Philadelphia bats. In the 3rd inning, however, there was bonus excitement. With a teammate aboard, a Cub rocketed another Chris Short offering over the left-field barrier to make it 5-1. That Cub was Ernie Banks.

With that, the scoring abated for the next 3 innings. With a single Phillie tally in the 7th, Jerkins took the mound in the 9th, up 5-2, and with certain victory in hand. Then disaster hit. Jerkins allowed two base runners, then threw the home-run ball to Phillie shortstop Don Money, his second of the game. With the score now tied, Durocher summoned ace fireman Phil Regan. The Vulture mowed down the enemy in the 9th and 10th. The Cubs, shut out for 7 straight innings, took the field in the 11th, hoping this would be the winning frame.

It was. With Johnny Callison aboard, nemesis Don Money reached Regan for a two-bagger, sending the visitors ahead 6-5. The mood was one of shocking disbelief. Not only had Banks's two-homer, five-RBI game not been enough, but no less a personage than complete-game ace Ferguson Jerkins had yielded a three-run lead in the 9th. Furthermore, the Phillies had even gotten to Phil Regan, pinning him with now undeniable defeat, with the lower half of the order due up in the Cub 11th.

With one out, Randy Hundley managed to get aboard. With that, Durocher—needing a left-handed bat—instructed former boxer, sometime singer, and utility outfielder Willie Smith to hit for the 0 for 4 right fielder Jim Hickman. Barry Lersch, having shackled the Cubs for 4 innings, readied to dispose of the crooning batsman. For Cub fans, no song of Smith's would ever be as sweet as the sight of his swing, one that sent Lersch's slant flying over the right-field wall for a 7-6 Cub triumph.

It was absolute bedlam. The ultimate Opening Day. The players mobbed Smith and the fans rejoiced deliriously. The final three lines of the Cubs' much-played unofficial theme song, which rocked out of the jukeboxes of Windy City watering holes all summer long, said it best.

> Hey, hey, holy mackerel,
> No doubt about it,
> The Cubs are on their way.

Anyone who didn't believe, believed now. According to Ron Santo, "I confess that I never had the feeling that we were certain to win every game in 1967 or 1968," he relates. "When the Dodgers or Giants would come in to Wrigley Field, there was a sense they had the guns to beat us every time. That all changed in 1969. Every time I went out there, I thought we would win. Every game."

Early in the season, realizing that the world champion Detroit Tigers would be following them into Philadelphia for an exhibition game, an unknown Cub wrote on the visiting clubhouse's blackboard, "See you in the World Series if you can make it."

The victorious opener led to triumphs in the next three games. A loss to the expansion Expos in game five was a mere interruption. The Bruins then reeled off seven more wins in succession. The season barely started, the Cubs were 11 and 1. And on top.

And it was fun. Ernie Banks, echoing Holtzman's sentiments, said, "It was the most joyous time of my life. For five hours a day—clubhouse, field, back in the clubhouse—we were like a bunch of brothers. Billy and Randy and Nate cut that record 'Hey, Hey, Holy Mackerel' [actually Smith, Nate, and Gene Oliver]. Willie Smith would sing it on the bus or plane, and we'd all join in. I never in my life experienced that kind of fun."

A fresh epidemic of Cub fever engulfed Chicago. Cub-glorifying bumper stickers again adorned legions of vehicles, while similarly labeled T-shirts sold wildly. The popularity of autographed drinking mugs and baseballs, along with pictures and posters, gained momentum throughout the summer. Any event featuring a personal appearance by a Cub player was a certain hit. A self-styled marketer, Jack Childers, drove the memorabilia and personal-appearance machine. In this pre-agent, pre–free agent era, income from this marketing bonanza was distributed across the roster, not unlike postseason shares, all of which was overseen by player rep Phil Regan.

After bagging 11 of their first dozen outings, the Cubs embarked on a four-game losing snag. When the Cardinals handed the Cubs their fourth straight downer 3-2 in Wrigley on April 24, Redbird skipper Red Schoendienst laid down the gauntlet. "The next time we leave Chicago, we'll be in first place," he challenged. The Cubs answered Schoendienst with wins in their next seven games. Chicago closed the books on April at 16-7, two in front of Pittsburgh, the only other divisional foe with a winning log.

The hysteria was palpable. A huge throng greeted the team at the airport upon their return from their first lengthy road trip. Independent "good ol' Channel 9" was now a ratings winner amid network competition. Ernie became a Sunday sports reporter and later a *Tribune* columnist. Though still spring, October was around the corner in the fans' minds, as 2,000 letters and 600 daily phone calls requesting World Series tickets deluged Wrigley Field offices. Fans lined up in the early morning every day to purchase one of those precious 23,000 unreserved seats on sale each game day. A substantial number of those ticket buyers were part of a now nationally famous group—the Bleacher Bums. Clad in yellow hard-hats, the boisterous throng cheered and celebrated game long.

Columnist Bill Gleason remembers them well. "The yellow construction helmets were real at first. This caught on in the bleachers, such that everybody started to buy these yellow helmets. The guys who wore them at the beginning were part of the original Bleacher Bums, and they were construction workers. These were big, brawny, profane people who would insult the other team's outfielders and threaten them. 'You want to come back of the stands after the game? I'll meet you.' They were originals. *Sun-Times* columnist Jack Griffin really made the Bleacher Bums. He ran with them, going over to Murphy's [a bar near the park] after games. He wrote many columns and immortalized a few of those nuts."

Soon the Bleacher Bums were in full fashionable boom. "They were 17–25–year-olds in the left-field bleachers," explains Craig Lynch. "I remember being there in 1969. There was nonstop cheering—not because the Cubs were winning, but like a college atmosphere."

And they had an impact, according to Santo. "They were rabid and loud: They actually became our tenth man on the field. I truly believe they were a catalyst for success from Opening Day," he claims. Dick Selma, acquired in late April to provide the team with that much-needed fourth starter, became the Bums official cheerleader, as he waved a bullpen towel to incite their vocal passions.

Relations between the bleacher denizens and the Cub players were truly cordial. Author George Castle relates a memorable example: "I saw a drunken fan fall out of the bleachers onto the warning track, and Willie

Smith actually hoisted him back up over the wall—this was before the basket existed—and back into the bleachers before the security officers got to him."

"People falling out of the stands in the heyday of the Bums was why they put up the basket," claims Gleason, with good humor. "The net was not for baseballs, it was to keep those idiots from killing themselves."

WSCR talk-show host Mike Murphy, who became famous for tooting his call-to-action bugle, eliciting a mighty "Charge!" loves to tell of a Bums' excursion to St. Louis: "We stayed at the team hotel, the Chase Park Plaza, downtown," says the former horn blower. "It was an expensive, first-class hotel, pretty steep for a bunch of students and Vietnam vets. We all chipped in, staying 20 to a room. In the lounge we'd try to make a twenty-five-cent beer last as long as possible. One night Durocher laid down a twenty-dollar bill and declared the drinks were on him for the night. The players partied along with us. Santo, Beckert, Jenkins—guys our age—would take us with them to the racetrack."

Les Grobstein's charity softball experience illustrates the bond the fans had with the players. "In July of 1969 I was involved in a softball benefit at Thillens Stadium, a local park in the city. We got Ernie Banks and Fergie Jenkins to come and sign autographs before the game. Ernie left after the session, but Fergie stayed around for our game. Then he offered to pitch on my team and did for two or three innings. He started the next day in Wrigley Field against the Mets.

"Fergie Jenkins and Billy Williams were my favorites," says Grobstein: "Fergie had the whole package, he was the classiest guy on the planet."

Opposing players found the Bums less winsome. "They drove Willie Davis to distraction," recalls Lynch. And for good reason. The fans had unearthed the name of Dodger outfielder Davis's Chicago girlfriend and proceeded to chant "Ruthie" at him throughout the contest. The usual non-power-hitting Davis responded with two opposite field jacks over the left-field wall.

Fox broadcaster and former Giant catcher during the 1980s Bob Brenly refers to Wrigley Field denizens as "very knowledgeable." "In some parks the fans will rag on you, they'll call you by your number and tell you that you stink," he says. "These fans do their homework. 'Hey, you hit into 18 double plays last year, for crying out loud, how slow are you?' They don't just tell you that you stink. They'll tell you why you stink."

Though he enjoyed coming to Wrigley as a visiting player, Brenly can relate well to the Davis experience. "Chicago's a great nightlife town and a lot of the fans are out on the streets," he explains. "If they run into you there, they may remind you the next day as you do your work in the outfield before the game. 'Hey, I saw you at the Lodge last night. You think you'll get any hits today?' they'll yell."

Writer George Castle, in his well-researched book *The I-55 Series*, describes the pregame guerrilla warfare in which Cardinal pitcher Jim "Mudcat" Grant engaged during a midseason series with the Redbirds. Mike Murphy, standing above the 368–foot sign in left center tooted his attention-getting bugle, evoking a voluminous "Charge!" from the throng. That, and some good-natured barbs, hit the right-hander's threshold point. "Grant snapped," noted Ned Colletti, who later served in the Bruins' front office.

Young Mr. Murphy found himself at a disadvantage. According to Murphy, "Mudcat walked to the warning track and looked up at me. He was standing no more than 12 feet away from me. He had a back pocket full of baseballs. I was wearing the open-toed sandals that were popular at the time. He took the first ball and cocked his arm. I thought he was just going to fake a throw. But he fired a 90–mile-an-hour fastball, and it hit the top inch of the wall, just below my toe. The ball ricocheted halfway back to second base. The next ball, he did the same thing, hitting the wall one inch below my sandals. He had perfect aim." With that, Murphy took off like a broken-field runner, weaving his way through the masses. Grant didn't give up, rifling four more throws in his direction, three of which hit innocent fans.

The Bums weren't through. The following day Ron Grousi purchased seven white mice with the intention of scaring Cub nemesis-outfielder Lou Brock. When the fans hurled the rodents fieldward while the game was in progress, a cool Brock remained unfazed. Cub outfielder Willie Smith, however, was so unnerved when he took his position that he ran to the dugout, halting the game while the grounds crew rounded up the unwelcome guests.

The team roared through the first half of May, going 8-4 with a five-game winning skein. Despite losing Beckert when the second baseman was hit in the cheek with a pitch in a May 13 19-0 shellacking of the San Diego Padres, the club didn't slow down. Nate Oliver stepped in and immediately contributed offensively. They closed the month with machine-like consistency, posting eight wins in their remaining 13 contests. May was pitching month for the Cubs, with the team hurling nine shutouts, three by Ken Holtzman. Dick Selma, who won the May 13 19-0 rout, came back 10 days later with a 6-0 whitewash of the Padres in San Diego.

The Cubs had won 16 games in April and 16 more in May. For the book, their two-month log was now 32-16, lengthening their lead to seven and a half games over the 1–over-.500 Pittsburgh Pirates.

* * *

The Lip was feeling his Cheerios like never before. Impatient with the slow-recovering Adolfo Phillips, in early May the lion roared that the centerfielder was ready "but doesn't want to play." When questioned about ripping one of his charges publicly, Durocher, never wanting for an answer, said, "In three years, I've tried everything else. I'll do everything I can to wake him up." More troubled than awakened, Phillips appeared in just 28 games, hitting just .224 in 49 at bats.

By early June Phillips was gone, having left the Cubs in a deal with Montreal for utility infielder Paul Popovich. Durocher had effectively cut Phillips off, reportedly scarcely speaking to him during his final month with the club. "One day Leo said, 'He's out of here,'" relates Randy Hundley, looking back. "We used to play Crazy 8's on the plane, Adolfo, Leo, and myself. One day Leo said, 'Get him out of here. Back up the truck.'"

Phillips, once a regular and Durocher favorite, refused to shake the manager's hand upon his departure. The once budding star left the Cubs a broken young man. He was never the same, batting only 430 more times in the major leagues and out of baseball at 30 years old.

Clearly, Durocher's impatience and impulsivity were costly in the case of Phillips. By failing to establish any rapport with the sensitive Phillips, Leo mishandled him badly, squandering the ability of a player that teammates thought was exploding with potential. "Adolfo could have been a great player," states Hundley. "I don't know exactly what happened to him." Fergie Jenkins did. "Adolfo, a hawk-nosed, slenderly built Panamanian, was an overly gifted ballplayer," wrote Fergie. "He had great talent and did things easily, without struggling or strenuous effort. He had a strong arm, he could run, and he hit for both power and average. One-handed, he could hit the ball out of the park. He was only twenty-three [when he came over from Philadelphia with Jenkins], and it seemed as if he would become a great ballplayer." Unfortunately, Adolfo was not in good health. Few people were aware of it, but Adolfo had a kidney problem. When he caught a cold, it would settle in his kidney, and he had a lot of blood in his urine. His back also ached because of the kidney ailment.

"Adolfo got the reputation of not wanting to play and was accused of 'jaking.' I got to know Adolfo well, rooming with him for a while, and he always wanted to play. He just couldn't because of his health, and it was unfair fair of people to accuse him of being a quitter." "People did not find out what was the matter with Adolfo until after he had been traded from the Cubs to Montreal in 1969. The following year he had to undergo an operation for a stomach tumor. He also had an ulcer caused by worry, pressure that had been put on him by his teammates and Durocher. Adolfo was extremely sensitive. He had to take tranquilizers to settle his nerves."

While many players did not take well to the banishment of their popular teammate, Popovich would prove to be a contributor. Moreover, games were being won, and an air of ongoing celebration permeated the city.

Still but a nose in front of the on-charging Cardinals in June, Santo noted a pivotal game: "Trailing 3-1 to the expansion Expos, I was giving in to negative thoughts. Then Jim Hickman, the oldest starter on the club other than Ernie, came up in the bottom of the ninth with two outs and two on. Hickman never received big attention for his hitting, particularly for the way he could hit the long ball—maybe that's because he played on the same team as a Billy Williams or an Ernie Banks. But on this day, Hickman was Babe Ruth. He hit a towering home run to leftfield, giving us 4-3 victory and allowing us to stay in first place.

"There may have been another time in my career when I was more excited, but if so, I can't remember it. When Hickman arrived at home plate, there was the usual mob scene congratulating him. But I was leading the pack, and pounding on his helmet, hugging, slugging, yelling, and screaming like a Little Leaguer. Hickman later told me he had a migraine headache from the pounding he took from me. . . . I don't know what was going through my mind at the time, I ran down the leftfield line, listening to the cheers from the fans, and for no particular reason, I jumped in the air—and clicked my heels," explained the third baseman.

Santo was apprehensive about Durocher's reaction to the heel-clicking. Leo didn't approve of actions that would show up opponents and give them an angry incentive. Surprisingly, however, Leo loved it. He approached Santo and said, "Golly, Ron, this has been an exciting year, hasn't it? I've got an idea, Ron. Why don't you make this little clicking bit our victory symbol. Just at home. I think it would be dynamite."

The manager had his own rituals, according to Jenkins. "Leo had certain habits or superstitions, as most ballplayers do. For instance, the same player had to pick up the infield ball and start throwing it around every day while we were winning. Nobody else could touch it. After a victory, the next day Leo made sure the same bats were sitting in front of him in the bat rack in Wrigley Field. If a certain player had been sitting next to him on the bench when we won, that player had to be sitting there the next day."

June 29 was Billy Williams Day at Wrigley Field. Over 10,000 would-be witnesses were turned away as 41,060 packed the yard to honor Billy, and not coincidentally to observe a twin bill against the defending champion Cardinals.

Billy and the Bruins rose to the occasion in the opener as the North-siders beat Gibson 3-1 behind Fergie's pitching and a big two-bagger by Williams. Jenkins dispensed with the Cardinals in just 126 minutes. Five days later, in 95–degree July 4 St. Louis heat, he would beat Gibby again 3-1, this time in a 10–inning tilt lasting just 2 hours and 32 minutes.

"I want to thank the Almighty God for the ability to play major league baseball. I want to thank God for protecting me over all the games I played," the humble ironman said to the appreciative fans between contests. He then went on to bang out four hits in game 2, helping the Cubs to a 12-1 drubbing of their hated rivals. When he struck out in his last plate appearance in the 8th, he walked to the dugout amid the deafening roars of a goosebump-generating standing ovation.

I remember the husky-voiced Harry Caray, then still the "King of the Ozarks" Cardinal announcer, regaling the Cubs for their consistency after Jenkins throttled the Redbirds in the opener. The Cubbies had won 16 in April, 16 in May, and now 16 more in June, he intoned. Moreover, they were now nearly 15 games ahead of the defending National League champions.

After one more June triumph, the team was 49-27 and running away from the pack They were seven games in advance of the upstart Mets, who were a surprising 40-32 through the first three months. Things were well in hand with the perpetual failures from New York, the only team in the division within 11 games of the hard-charging Cubs.

It was becoming a season of signal individual achievements. In early June, seemingly ageless Ernie Banks was on a 31–home run, 153–RBI pace. By the end of May, Kenny Holtzman was already 10-1. On June 15 Don Kessinger played a record 54 consecutive games at shortstop with nary an error. On June 29 Billy Williams became the National League ironman, having played in 846 consecutive games.

The Cubs were now firmly ensconced as the darlings of all major league baseball. Their all-afternoon home schedule and national charisma made them a near weekly feature of Saturday NBC Game of the Week. There were few more popular interviews than that of Leo Durocher. Derisively referred to as "the dandy little manager" by Cub announcer Lou Boudreau, Leo played hard to the big-time national press while snubbing the Chicago print and electronic media. Moreover, few could appreciate the joy in Wrigley Field better than NBC play-by-play announcer Curt Gowdy, having served a long tenure behind the mike for the similarly championship-starved Boston Red Sox.

The All-Star game figured to be a virtual coronation for the divisional leaders. In late May a highly impressed Walter Alston had said, "If they left it up to me, I'd pick the entire Cub infield and their catcher for the all-star team." In fact, those five players—slick-fielding keystone combo Kessinger and Beckert along with sluggers Banks and Santo, plus catcher Randy Hundley—were named to the senior circuit's squad.

Ron Santo was leaping up and clicking his heels after each Cub victory. With the Bleacher Bums, Santo's theatrics, and the novel experience of watching the team run away with the Eastern Division championship, Wrigley Field contests were now becoming events rather than mere games.

July opened with three straight wins after a surprise defeat at the hands of the woeful Expos, elevating the team's record to 52-28. Now in the middle of an 11–game road trip, the team went down three consecutive times, once in a twin bill in St. Louis. Though both Hands and Holtzman were beaten by the Cardinals, the Cubs had ace Fergie Jenkins ready to open against the Mets in New York.

Crazily enough, the employees of Shea, left for dead in May, entered the game just five games behind the indomitable Cubs. The game moved to the 9th with Chicago in front 3-1. A bizarre set of events then took place. Journeyman Ken Boswell opened the final frame with a seeing-eye two-bagger to right center, falling among Kessinger, Beckert, and seemingly frozen centerfielder Don Young. The estimable Jenkins, who entered the game at 11-5 and en route to another 20–win campaign, shook off the misfortune, retiring Tommie Agee on a foul fly to Banks.

With that, Gil Hodges sent Donn Clendenon up to pinch-hit. A right-handed slugger, Clendenon hammered a shot deep to left center where Young grabbed it, only to let go of the ball as he slammed into the wall. With runners now on second and third, New York's top hitter Cleon Jones laced a double to tie the game. Still tied, Jenkins bore down with even greater intensity. He intentionally walked Art Shamsky to set up a possible inning-ending double play for his next would-be victim, Wayne Garrett. Garrett did ground out, but managed to move both runners into scoring position in the process.

It was now Jenkins against the lone original Met on the roster, Ed Kranepool. Bamboozled by a low-and-away pitch, Kranepool threw his bat at the offering, only to have it connect with the sphere and send it floating over Don Kessinger's head to drive home the winning run. Unreal. Incredulous. The weak-hitting Mets had pushed over three 9th-inning runs against Jenkins.

Frustrated, humiliated, and enraged, the Cubs headed for the clubhouse. Durocher, once described by baseball Olympus Branch Rickey as having the unique capacity "to make an already bad situation immediately worse," lived up to Rickey's tag. He openly blamed the inscrutable Don Young for the loss, claiming that it was "tough to win when your centerfielder can't catch a blankety-blank fly ball. He stands there watching one and then gives up on the other, it's a disgrace," lamented Durocher, only to continue within earshot of the devastated outfielder. "My three-year-old could have caught those balls."

With Durocher unhinged, Jerome Holtzman of the *Sun-Times* approached Santo, asking whether he had heard Leo's exclamations. Santo remembered that earlier in the game the usually quiet Jim Hickman had told the captain to settle down a riled Don Young, who had thrown his bat and helmet in the dugout after an unsuccessful plate appearance. Santo, who had then grabbed Young and told him to do his job, felt Young had tucked his hitting frustrations in his glove, contributing mightily to the loss.

Young's frustrations had already been in evidence as he positioned himself in the outfield. When Clendenon stepped to the plate, Jenkins motioned him over to the left center alley, but Young didn't budge. "Fergie called me over from third," according to Santo. "'What's with this guy? Why isn't Young moving?'" Fergie wondered aloud.

From the mound, Santo waved Young over. As Santo was motioning, an agitated Durocher headed to the mound and asked what was going on. Once aware of the matter, the manager was rankled. "Get his butt over there," Leo barked angrily and headed for the dugout. But the problem wasn't solved. Young moved only a few strides, and the now distracted Jenkins wanted more. "I waved, and again he was stationary," recalled Santo. "Finally, Young took a few more steps, and at last we're set to face Clendenon."

Young fed his teammates' ire by dressing swiftly and abandoning the clubhouse. Mistaking his instant exit for apathy rather than utter humiliation, Santo stated, "He was just thinking of himself, not the team. He had a bad day at the plate, so he's got his head down. He's worrying about his batting average and not the team. All right, he can keep his head down, and he can keep right on going out of sight for all I care. We don't need that kind of thing."

A firestorm ensued. Santo was awakened in his Waldorf Astoria room at 3 A.M. by a friend, informing him that the *Sun-Times* had boldly stated that he had crossed the unwritten line of publicly criticizing a teammate for losing the game. To Santo's credit, he called a press conference in his tenth-floor room that afternoon and publicly apologized to Young, a player he had conscientiously taken under his professional wing throughout the season. Reiterating his conviction that Young had let his hitting woes rule his glove, Santo spoke empathically. "I know this is true because it has happened to me. I have fought myself when I wasn't hitting and, as a result, messed up in the field. But I know I was wrong. . . . I want everyone to know my complete sincerity in this apology."

No apology, however, ever came from the lips of Durocher.

Back in the hotel the night of the defeat, Young was in no better condition than Adolfo Phillips was earlier in the campaign. Referring to Clendenon's projectile, a distraught Young took total responsibility stating, "I didn't run into the wall on Clendenon's double until I had dropped it. I should have had that ball, but I dropped it. It hit my glove, and I dropped it. I just lost the game for us, that's all I did." That game apparently broke the sensitive youth emotionally. It more than marked Young's career. It effectively ended it.

The next night the on-charging Mets sent their best to the mound, Tom Seaver. More than 59,000 fans watched the right-hander throw a perfect game for 8⅓ innings. It was broken by .243 hitting Jimmy Qualls, who delivered a clean single to left center. Qualls's position? Center-field.

Banks was impressed with the Mets' poise. "Look at them. They're calm for such a young team. That's pretty strange," he said before the final game of the three-game set. In that one, Bill Hands reached the halfway mark to a 20–win season, besting an error-ridden Met bunch 6-2. A reenergized Santo departed the Big Apple feeling unchallenged by the Mets. "Wait'll we get them in Wrigley Field," were his sentiments.

The team seemed unaffected by the misadventures in Shea. After losing the opening game of the home stand to the Phillies, they reeled off three straight wins in preparation for a three-game set with New York, commencing on July 14. They entered the Mets series having split their first 14 games in July.

The fans sensed the threat of the Mets and were arriving as early as 6 A.M. to cheer their heroes. By 9:30, a half-hour before the park opened, 215 Andy Frain ushers were at Wrigley for crowd-control purposes. For the game itself, the Chicago police added 28 extra patrolmen and 3 sergeants to the usual contingent. Bill Hands, now emerging as the ace of the staff, beat Seaver 1-0 in a heart-stopping series opener. With the triumph, Santo danced a jig and the Bleacher Bums roared, "ABEEBEE! UNGOWA! CUB POWUH!" mimicking a cheer of the Black Panthers.

"Yes, sir, that was a World Series game," chortled Durocher, subtly suggesting which team had handled the pressure victoriously, as the Bruins moved a more comfortable 5 1/2 games in front of the Eastern Division pack. The Mets seemed less troubled by the loss than by Santo's Fred Astaire–like antics. When Coach Joe Pignatano hollered "Bush," at Santo before the following afternoon's game, Santo responded nonverbally with a middle finger thrust skyward. When exchanging lineups at home plate, Santo, sensitive chap as he is, had a request for manager Gil Hodges. "Tell Piggy that the only reason I click my heels is because the fans will boo me if I don't."

"You remind me of Tug McGraw," Hodges responded, matter-of-factly. "When he was young and immature and nervous, he used to jump up and down, too. He doesn't do it anymore," said Hodges to the 29–year-old, 10–year veteran. Santo had nothing to say.

Santo paid dearly for his heel-clicking. "The rest of the league wasn't so enthralled," he writes. "Once they started catching on to my act, the fastballs seemed to get a lot closer to my head. The brushback pitches seemed to come a lot closer to my chin."

Long before the Mets series, Santo had been informed of opponents' displeasure. Before a game with St. Louis, Tim McCarver told Santo "a lot of guys around the league know what you're doing and they don't like it." During that game, a messenger in the form of a fastball zipped past his chin.

Another rabbit emerged from the New York hat in the game when backup infielder Al Weis hit only his second home run in two years off Dick Selma with two mates on. The dinger accounted for the lion's share of the New York runs in a 5-4 Met win. The Mets then pulled within 3 ½ spaces the following day when Cub reject Cal Koonce availed himself of the opportunity to stick the spear into Leo, topping Ferguson Jenkins 9-5. Jenkins, whose record fell to 12-7, was in the shower room before the close of the 2nd inning. After the game, Tom Seaver crossed the first-base line, did a dance, leaped, and clicked his heels. For Santo, it was a humiliating afternoon. "They beat us, you have to give them credit for that. Two out of three in our park. I still don't believe it," confessed the humbled third baseman.

When the Cubs packed their bags for their impending trip to Philadelphia, they left their memories of the embarrassment by the Mets behind, taking three of four in Philly. They finished out July with eight home games, four with the Dodgers and four more with the Giants. The Cubs split the two sets to close the month with a mediocre 15-14 mark. At 64-41, Chicago was averaging 16 wins a month and back in front of the Mets by six games overall, three on the loss side.

The soap opera that was July included one more life-on-the-edge caper involving Durocher. Claiming a stomach disorder, Durocher surreptitiously left a nationally televised game in the 3rd inning on Saturday the 26, sneaking off to Camp Ojibwa in Eagle River, Wisconsin, to attend Parents' Weekend in honor of his new bride's 10–year-old son.

Columnist Bill Gleason recalls with amusement how the one-in-a-million story of Leo's AWOL behavior came to be reported by a Durocher adversary, *Chicago Today* sportswriter James Enright. "One of Enright's pals had a kid up there and he was visiting the youngster," Gleason explains, laughing. "He then called Jim and said, 'Jim, what the blazes is Durocher doing up here?' Jim said, What!' That's one of the great baseball stories of all time—the audacity of this guy that he could just sneak away, and nobody would know the difference."

P. K. Wrigley was not similarly amused. He was so angry that he was close to waxing Leo. A profusely apologetic Leo returned to manage a victory over the Giants on July 28. The players seemed unaffected by their manager's unapproved sabbatical, but likely enjoyed seeing their fearless field leader publicly humbled.

The Cubs simply tore through early August with six straight triumphs, burying their concerns of the erstwhile contending Mets. By the morning of August 14, the Chicago Cubs—now 9-2 for the month—were 9½ games ahead of flagging New York. The team returned to Chicago after dividing a twin bill at San Francisco with the Giants on the night of August 17. They had a date the following day with the White Sox to play their annual charity game. Though wanting to rest Banks, Beckert, Kessinger, Santo, Williams, and Hundley, Durocher relented and let them play—for the most part, briefly—before a largest-of-the-season 33,333 Comiskey Park crowd. The Cubs won 2-0 on home runs by Banks and Williams.

Up to this point, the team's Big Six had scarcely been rested. Moreover, most were living off the adrenaline of the season and didn't want to sit. In any case, the 75-45 team was now home, where they were a whopping 40-17 and would play 24 of their remaining 42 outings.

Lingering doubts as to whether 1969 was the Year of Destiny for the Cubs were pretty well expunged on August 19 when Ken Holtzman threw a no-hitter against the eventual Western Division champion Atlanta Braves. The most memorable event in the game occurred in the Atlanta 7th when the great Henry Aaron banged one over the leftfield wall, or what seemed like over. Billy Williams stood looking up, with his right arm against the ivy as the sphere headed for Waveland Avenue. Amazingly, at that instant the ball appeared to stop, hang in the wind, and then simply drop into Williams's glove just inside the park.

Holtzman's recollections of the game are sharp. "When we got to the ballpark that morning, people were lined up all the way around the block trying to get tickets for a game with the Braves. It took a great play by Beckert in the first inning to save it. And the wind blew back a hit by Hank Aaron that normally would have been a homer. Billy Williams caught it with his back to the vines." So certain was Hammer that his wallop would enable him to touch them all, he went into his home run trot. He was nearly at second base before Williams grabbed it. "I'll never forget the look Hammer gave me," says Holtzman.

The celebration in Chicago had all the effects of a high school homecoming. "The fans knew the players used a side street—Berteau Avenue— as a secret shortcut to drive home," relates Castle. "After Kenny Holtzman's no-hitter, they were lined up all along Berteau to cheer Holtzman and the rest of the players. It was like a motorcade." "That day seemed to summarize everything that had been going good for us that year," said the victorious pitcher.

The Cubs, though dropping three straight and seven of the next nine after Holtzman's history-maker, closed August with four consecutive victories. Now 82-52, the squad had won 18 and dropped just 11 in the heat of August, the winningest month of their season. On the 26th, they were given the nod to print playoff tickets.

The Mets, however, having triumphed in 21 of their 31 August encounters, now trailed Chicago by four games. They were not going away. In fact, they were gaining. From May 1 through the end of August, the New Yorkers had actually outplayed the Cubs, going 67-43 while the Chicagoans registered a game and a half weaker 66-45.

On September 2, Leo's squad hung two on Cincinnati, one the completion of a suspended game from June. The Mets, having split their first two games of the month, were now five back. Met mentor Gil Hodges talked as though the curtain was falling on his gamers. 'We're just playing average ball, and hardly that at times," lamented the former Dodger great, quoted in the *Chicago Tribune.* Concerned about their glovework, Hodges pressed on, "We've come this far because of pitching and defense, but we haven't been playing well defensively of late and our pitching staff has a lot of tired arms."

Met lefty Jerry Koosman reportedly had a tender arm, changing his approach from one emphasizing velocity to control. In addition, hard-hitting Cleon Jones had to sit out several games, owing to a painful hand injury. All was not bleak. Donn Clendenon had picked up the offense of late and was verbally challenging the Cubs. "The pressure is still all on the Cubs. This club has learned winning ways and will stay close to Chicago," stated the first baseman. *"They* know if they fall, we will be right there."

On September 3, fireballing Jim Maloney beat Bill Hands 2-0 in the Queen City. No matter. The road trip was over and the Mets had been taken in LA 5-4. Now 44-24 at Wrigley, the team would be sending Holtzman, Jenkins, and a 10-5 Dick Selma against the visiting Pirates.

Bewilderingly, the first two games were 9-2 and 13-4 Pittsburgh blowouts. Meanwhile the Mets, by winning on the sixth, were just 3 ½ games away. After the second loss to Pittsburgh, the *Chicago Tribune,* surveying Cub fans, ran an article entitled, "They're Not Going to Fold; Cub Fans Confident."

The series finale, however, was the one that unhinged Durocher. On the strength of a Hickman homer in the 8th, Phil Regan needed just three outs to ice the game. He got two outs and two strikes. Then future Hall-of Famer Willie Stargell hammered a shot into the teeth of what seemed to Hundley a 35 mph lake wind, over the right-field wall and on to Sheffield Avenue. Game tied, 5-5.

There was plenty of player discontent over Durocher's strategy of leaving Regan in to face the left-handed Stargell. Hank Aguirre, unscored upon in 9 innings by Pittsburgh, was ready. Leo, who apparently could not imagine that Stargell could belt one out against that stiff wind, stayed with his 12–game-winning relief pitcher. Then, after blowing a scoring opportunity in the 10th, in part because Willie Smith failed to sacrifice runners into scoring position, the game went to the 11th. When Don Kessinger committed a critical error in the top of the frame, leading to two Pirate runs, the Cubs' fate was sealed 7-5. With the relentless Mets easily disposing of the Phillies in Shea, 9-3, the Bruins lead had melted to just two and a half.

"To me, that was the pivotal game of the 1969 season," wrote Santo. You could hear a pin drop as we walked into the clubhouse. Everyone's head was down. Nobody said a word. Our usual routine of staying around and talking about the game was abandoned; we got out of there as quickly possible."

Durocher, however, was incensed, and aired his charges soon after. The manager seemed to imply that Jenkins—shelled just two days previous—was a "quitter." Players varied in their interpretations. Some felt Leo had aimed his tirade at Fergie, others felt the meeting was "for all of us." Still others felt the heated speech was "constructive criticism," hardly a likely possibility for the acidic Durocher. Jenkins acknowledged that Durocher "got all over me" for not challenging the Bucs' hitters after a defensive lapse in the outfield, involving Williams and (you guessed it!) Don Young.

Players wondered aloud what impact the skipper's lacing would have on their 19–game winner. Remaining quiet during the outburst, Jenkins seemed to shake it off, later pointing out that, as usual, "the slate was clean the next day" with Durocher. Nonetheless, Jenkins flatly denied the quitter charge, saying, "I definitely did not quit Saturday. I lost a little concentration, but I never quit on this club."

There could not be a more inopportune time for the Cubs to head for New York for a two-game set than right then, September 8 and 9. But that was what the schedule mandated.

The series opener, before 43,274 howling New Yorkers, could not have been more cruel. Now with a 16-12 record to go with a 2.55 ERA, Bill Hands was ready to face Jerry Koosman, having been held back for just this game. The score was 2-2 in the 6th. Then in a pivotal play in this critical contest, one that Randy Hundley flatly calls the biggest play of the year, Wayne Garrett singled to right with Tommie Agee—having delivered a two-bagger—on second. Jim Hickman fired an arrow to the plate as Agee tried to score. Hundley, with a sweeping motion, tagged Agee out, and then, knowing he had nailed Agee, reflexively positioned himself to throw out Garrett at second, should he try to advance.

The score, however, was no longer 2-2. Home plate umpire Satch Davidson called Agee safe, making the score 3-2. It was to be the winning run. Hundley executed an incredible shock and rage-driven high jump. Still agitated 20 years later, when recounting the play to Rick Talley, the forthright Hundley asserts, "I tagged him so hard I almost dropped the ball."

The game had another key subplot. Hands had a less than harmonious relationship with the Mets, due to some knockdown exchanges throughout the season. Hands drew a line in the sand when on the first pitch of the game, he sent Agee sprawling. It was not a prudent pitching decision, because Koosman hit Santo on the forearm to open the second frame. The forearm stiffened and the third baseman's power was gone.

Worse, however, in the minds of a number of Cubs was that the team did nothing about Koosman's smack. No emptying of the bench, no charging the mound, no shouting. Nothing. The late Hank Aguirre recalled it distinctly, telling Talley, "That's when we should have gotten into a fight. It hurt me deeply that Santo just walked to first base, and nobody did anything. That's when I knew we were hurting. Leo or Santo or somebody from the dugout should have started a fight. I wish I hadn't been stuck out in the bullpen or I would have started it."

"We were easily intimidated. It was a degrading incident . . . the club just folded," agreed Rich Nye.

The lead was now one and a half games, and a date with Tom Seaver was in the offing for the following evening.

Partly because of a need to juggle the rotation, owing to Holtzman's unavailability on upcoming Rosh Hashanah as well as his having been knocked out so early in his previous start, Durocher sent the chastised Jenkins to the mound on two days' rest. It was all Seaver, 7-1, as 58,436 screaming fans watched in joy. The spread was now half a game, as Mets owner Joan Payson exclaimed, "Oh, this is wonderful," after having witnessed her charges' conquest.

A sullen Durocher, humiliated with choruses of "Goodbye, Leo," to the tune of "Goodbye, Ladies," sung by the fans in New York—the city of his greatest triumphs—had nothing to say. Dispirited, the team couldn't get to Philadelphia soon enough. There was to be no solace in the City of Brotherly Love, where a Phillie team, heading for 99 losses, defeated the Cubs and Holtzman 6-2 on the strength of Rick Wise's right arm.

The Mets swept the Expos 3-2 and 7-1 at Shea that same night to take the Eastern Division lead from the Cubs by one game. It was the first time in 156 days that the Cubs were not a first-place team. The doors remained closed for 15 minutes after the Cub loss. When they were opened, Durocher had nothing to say, although Santo offered a less than convincing, "I'm optimistic, very optimistic."

Yet another defeat followed the next night, as Rick James, just up from the minors, pinned a 4-3 loss on Dick Selma. Another Met victory over Montreal drove the Cubs two games back. Moreover, another misadventure marked this loss. With the Bruins up 1-0, Philadelphia's Richie Allen had a 3-2 count with two on and two out in the 3rd. Knowing the runners would be moving, Selma lifted his leg off the rubber and whipped the ball to third for what he thought would be an easy pickoff out.

Except that Santo was not there. Tony Taylor scored the tying run as the ball skittered into leftfield foul territory. Durocher hit his head on the dugout roof as he leaped in disbelief at the gaffe. The play was simply the result of a missed sign on a designed play. The pickoff sign for Santo was for Selma to yell, "It's two out, knock the ball down." It was a too well disguised signal. Santo failed to register it as a signal, inasmuch as that particular planned pickoff maneuver had yet to be attempted in 1969. He simply took Selma's words at face value and hollered "Yeah," in response—amazingly the exact verbal signal confirming the play was on.

"Durocher went nuts," recalled Santo. "Selma was so afraid of what Leo might do, he wouldn't go into the clubhouse after the game." Years later, Leo concluded his own explanation of the skull session in his book by saying, "And that's how it goes when everything is collapsing around you."

Gleason remembers a poignant scene after the game. "We couldn't find Selma in the clubhouse, so we thought he was giving an exclusive to TV," says writer Gleason. "There were about twenty-five people in the dressing room, so the New York guys came to me and said, what's going on? Is there anything you can do?'

"'I'm as hot as you are about this,' I said. Phil Regan was the Cub player rep and I called him aside. 'I'm not blaming you for this, Phil,' I said, 'but if you don't get Selma down here to talk to us, you are really going to get ripped in the papers.'"

"Connie Mack Stadium had an alcove—a mini attic. As it turned out, Selma had hid there. Ultimately, he did come down. He had been up there weeping."

And things were collapsing. The Cubs had lost eight straight. Moreover, each of their Big Three hurlers had been beaten twice. Those eight consecutive defeats had cost them seven games (from five up to two down) in the standings, as the Mets went 8-2 in the same nine-day span.

Although the spell was broken the following night in St. Louis when Hands won his 17th game at the hands of the Cardinals, 5-1, the scribes in Chicago were ready to serve Leo his literary lunch. Robert Markus suggested that if the Cubs were in fact to come up short, "Leo Durocher is in for a savage roasting in the local press. A better loser than he is a winner, Durocher has made nothing but enemies on his way back to the top. And every one of them is going to be ready with a verbal knife to stick in Leo's ribs on the agonizing plunge back down."

Surcease from defeat was short-lived, however, as the Redbirds broke a 4-4 tie in the eighth inning en route to a 7-4 win at Jenkins's expense the next night. This was the third time the right-hander came up short in an attempt to get win number 20. Winning hurler reliever Jim Grant said of the Cubs, "The monkey's tail ain't long now, and it's not as short as it's gonna be."

This set up the series finale, a Bob Gibson/Ken Holtzman confrontation. After nine complete, the score was 1-1. With the Mets having lost, the Cubs could climb within two and a half with a win. Although the Cubs failed against Gibby in the top of the 10th, Cub fans took comfort in knowing that Gibson (or perhaps better, a pinch hitter) would open the St. Louis half of the frame. It was Gibson who grounded out. The next hitter however, hammered the sphere over the right-field fence, ending the conflict. His name? Lou Brock. Who else?

St. Louis Globe-Democrat writer Harry Mitauer captured the back-breaking nature of the loss. "A disconsolate group of Cubs . . . looked downhearted as they slowly walked off the field to their gloomy clubhouse," wrote Mitauer. Now three and one-half out, the Bruins took comfort, knowing they were heading to Montreal certain to make up ground against the expansion dead enders.

Durocher then opted to go with Selma to start the Montreal series and then likely have his Jenkins-Hands-Holtzman triumvirate go the rest of the way. A bizarre defensive breakdown in the 1st inning started the Cubs on the path to a 8-2 defeat. The locker room was funereal after the game, which pushed the Cubs four and one-half games behind. Banks, Williams, Beckert and Santo sat lifelessly 30 minutes after the carnage had ended. The brave personas were gone. There were no "we'll get 'em tomorrow" "we'll be all right" bromides.

The Cubs had been certain that they would reverse their fortunes once having snapped their earlier eight-game losing skein. Instead they had dropped three of four. Put the two losing runs together and it was 1 of 12, while the Mets went a sizzling 12-3.

Montreal mentor Gene Mauch, who had presided over the legendary 1964 Phillie collapse, drew a parallel or two. "It's no fun," he said.

"We were a highly emotional bunch just like the Cubs and with a real emotional team, let me tell you, from high to low emotional is a big, big gap." He saw a specific symptom that reminded him of his doomed Philadelphians of years previous. "One thing I saw was that there was a concentrated effort on the part of everybody on the team to relax. Let me ask you something. How can you work at relaxing?" the skipper offered.

Kessinger acknowledged the team was tight. "Sure, we're pressing," admitted the shortstop. "We wouldn't be human if we weren't."

The Cubs left Canada for home the following evening on the heels of Bill Hands's 18th win, 5-4. Interestingly, Durocher made a bold lineup change that evening, playing Willie Smith at first and Paul Popovich at short.

There were no Bleacher Bums when the Cubs returned to the Friendly Confines to defeat the Phillies 9-7, giving Fergie his 20th win before only 6,062 fans. Banks hit the century mark in RBIs. Leo started a rookie the next day, but Joe Decker got no decision. Regan did, a loss, 5-3. The Cubs were five down with just 11 games left. The club split a pair with St. Louis on the 19th, while the Mets dropped two to the tough Pirates.

Bill Hands then lost his 14th the following day, as Steve Carlton handcuffed the Chicagoans 4-1. The Mets, in turn, were no-hit by Bob Moose. Still four back, Jenkins won his 21st in the series finale, 4-3. New York snapped their three-game losing streak, however, sweeping two from the Pirates. The Cubs dropped five back when Seaver won his 24th game at the expense of the Cardinals while the Cubs were idle.

There were just seven games left.

Montreal then came to town and defeated the Cubs and Holtzman 7-3. The victory was particularly sweet for Durocher-reject Bill Stoneman. "I don't talk to anyone named Leo," stated winning pitcher Stoneman.

His reaction was similar to another Durocher castoff, "There goes 'garbage'" Cal Koonce, after the latter threw 5 shutout innings for the Mets in a key game earlier against Chicago. Koonce claimed he "wanted to send a little love to Leo." He stated, "It's the longest I've pitched this season, but the incentive was there. Look around the clubhouse—everybody is enjoying this because they know that big-shot Leo will be unhappy."

In any case, the loss to the Expos was all but lethal because the Mets clinched a tie for the divisional title with a 3-2 win over St. Louis. Just 2,217 watched as Bill Hands notched number 19 the following day with a 6-3 defeat of the Expos, but that evening Gary Gentry shut the Cardinals out 6-0.

It was over.

On September 25, *Tribune* writer George Langford wrote a Cub obituary entitled "Those were the days, my friend," recounting the summer's glories past. The Cubs were it. They were the 'in thing.' They were thrilling the Second City as no one had since who can remember. First place. The Cubs were there, man," he wrote. Langford described more than the weather when he followed with, "Now the cold autumn wind hits you in the face. . . ."

The Cubs won just two of their remaining five games, splitting a two-game set with the Mets as the season mercifully ended. The Mets—100-62 for the year—went a stunning 24-8 for September/October. Moreover, the men of Shea had won 38 of their final 49 games. The Cubs won but 10 of their 28 September/October tilts. Their 92 wins (against 70 losses) gave the Bruins more wins by far than any season had yielded since 1945.

Plugging in the research formula, the 1969 squad actually projects as a 94-68 contingent. Again, bullpen failings (only 27 saves, almost 9 less than the league average), bringing about close defeats, did much to pull the team back.

Though ranking third in runs scored (720), the Cubs actually scored 53 fewer runs than could be statistically expected when one adjusts for the Wrigley factor. They were only slightly above the league in hitting and OBP [on-base percentage] and 15 points over in slugging. Although Kessinger was fourth in the league in runs (109), one wonders just how many more the leadoff might have tallied had his OBP been substantially higher than .335 (just 14 points above the NL norm). Number-two man Beckert's OBP was just .328.

Other than Santo's runner-up placement in RBIs (123), no Cub hitter finished in the top five of any major offensive category. Williams, Santo, and Banks's 324 RBIs accounted for 45% of the team's total. The running game was all but nonexistent—30 steals in 62 attempts.

Pitching, particularly starting pitching, was the foundation of the team. The team's ERA was just 3.34, twenty-five points under the league average. Moreover, factoring in the Wrigley Field adjustment, the staff yielded an incredible 110 fewer runs than might be expected.

Jenkins (21-15) and Hands (20-14) combined for 41 wins against 29 losses, with ERAs of 3.21 and 2.49, respectively. Holtzman added 17 wins (against 13 defeats) and a 3.59 ERA. The Big Three's total of 58 wins was the best of any threesome in all of baseball. Hands's year was so outstanding, he was fifth in the league in TBR [total baseball ranking; this statistic ranks pitchers and position players by the total of wins they contributed by all their activities].

Moreover, the 1969 season generated an attendance of 1,664,857, the organization's largest gate ever. It also yielded more memories.

Ken Holtzman summed up the season as well as any. "It seems that the 1969 season was the ultimate Cub season," he told Talley. "Baseball is always portrayed as a serene, pastoral game with hopes high in the spring, leading to eventual heartbreak in August and September, and what team better personifies that image over the history of baseball than the Chicago Cubs? It's the story of the Cubs franchise. The ultimate lovable losers."

David Claerbaut, *Durocher's Cubs: The Greatest Team That Didn't Win.* (Dallas: Taylor Publ. Co., 2000), 83–104. © 2000, Taylor Trade Publishing. Reprinted with permission.

Chicago fans have had many iconic stars to root for in the past fifty years, including Ernie Banks of the Cubs, Gale Sayers, and Dick Butkus and Walter Payton of the Bears, and Bobby Hull of the Blackhawks, but the brightest star was Michael Jordan of the Chicago Bulls, who led his team to six world championships (1990–1993, 1995–1998), capturing the Finals MVP each season. His fame was worldwide and supplanted Al Capone as the most famous Chicagoan around the world. In a career of fifteen NBA seasons, he averaged 30.1 points per game, the highest in NBA history. He not only led the league in scoring ten times, but was also NBA MVP five times and the best defensive player of his era. In 1999 ESPN named him the greatest athlete of the twentieth century. Jordan utilized his athletic skill, charming personality, good looks, and intelligence to become one of the most successful corporate spokesmen of all time. He became fabulously rich through his endorsements of products for Hanes, Gatorade, and especially Nike. The following article is drawn from the book Michael Jordan and the New Global Capitalism *(1999) by the renowned diplomatic historian Walter LaFeber, which examines Jordan's career, his worldwide celebrity, his impact upon the spectacular growth of Nike, and more generally, on the effect of transnational corporations upon global commerce and industry.*

13 | Bittersweet Championships
Michael Jordan, the Chicago Bulls, and International Sports Marketing

WALTER L. LeFEBER

In 1989, *Time* magazine called Michael Jordan, "the hottest player in America's hottest sport." Sportscasters were labeling him "Superman in Shorts." Although at 6'6" he was a full inch shorter than the average NBA player, Jordan, *Time* breathlessly proclaimed, moved in a world of his own, "a world without bounds. He gyrates, levitates, and often dominates. Certainly he fascinates. In arenas around the country, food and drink go unsold because fans refuse to leave their seats for fear of missing a spectacular Jordan move to tell their children about."[1]

This superman had no problem using his powers to create money magically. The Bulls sold out more games in eighteen months than they had during their entire history before Jordan arrived. Personally, he made many times his Bulls' salary by endorsing Chevrolet, McDonald's, Coca-Cola (then later Gatorade), Johnson Products (one of the largest and most profitable corporations run by African-Americans), and, of course, Nike. He became the first basketball player to appear on a Wheaties cereal box.

If, however, Jordan's skills translated into basketball records and wealth, they had not translated into a team championship. Americans, for all their immodest individualism, saved their highest praise for the Mikans, Russells, Johnsons, and Birds who raised teammates to a championship level. Many could score, but only a few could transcend individualism (that too often in sports, as elsewhere, was only a disguise for selfishness) to win it all. When legendary coach John Wooden was asked in 1990 to rank the greatest players, he chose Larry Bird and Magic Johnson, but not Jordan: "He's a show within himself, he's not a team player."[2]

Jordan's fans placed the fault on a lack of a good supporting cast. That might have been a problem in the mid-1980s, but by 1989, the Bulls had a talented team. Pippen was becoming the second-best all-around player in the league. It went, however, beyond the team. Chicagoans chafed when their hometown was called "The Second City." Given the history of the Cubs and the White Sox, Chicagoans never glimpsed even second place most baseball seasons. While Boston won sixteen NBA championships between 1947 and 1989, and even Minneapolis won five, Chicago's professional basketball teams had twice gone bankrupt and had reached exactly one conference championship (1972–1973—when they lost), in twenty-seven years.[3]

No one felt the failure more sharply than Jordan, simply because no one was as competitive. By 1989–1990, he was not only adjusting to Jackson's demands for a team offense, but making his own personal adjustments. For years this athlete who could not get dates in high school had been pursued by numerous women. It was not unknown for Bulls' practices to be interrupted by well-known actresses who were meeting him for dinner. Nor was it unknown for women to lie in front of his car and refuse to move until he talked with them. Jordan decided to eliminate such distractions.

In 1985, Jordan had met Juanita Vanoy, an independent-minded executive secretary for the American Bar Association. By 1987, they were making wedding plans, only to cancel them by mutual agreement. In November 1988, Jeffrey Michael was born. Ten months later, Michael and Juanita were married. On Christmas Eve morning of 1990, another son, Marcus James, arrived. The Jordans began planning a 26,000–square-foot house on eight acres in a Chicago suburb where the family could find refuge. Michael too seldom said no to the incessant demands on his time. Juanita, he knew, was more careful. "I have no problem saying no," she told *Ebony* magazine. "If someone doesn't step up and say no, there would be no time for his family. Everyone wants a piece of Michael. . . . I know it makes me look like a bitch," but "if that is what I have to be, then I will be a bitch."[4]

With his personal life in order, Jordan set out in the autumn of 1990 to prove John Wooden wrong. The season began badly. The Bulls lost their first three games. Then they won two in a row, including a rout of Larry Bird's Celtics. When the Bulls returned to Boston in February 1991, they were at full speed. Jordan scored 39 points, Pippen 33, as they whipped the Celtics by 30 points. "The Bulls are the best team I've ever seen," Bird announced. With a record 61 wins, 21 losses, and Jordan's fifth straight scoring title, the Bulls cruised into the playoffs, where they demolished the New York Knicks in three straight. They then defeated Philadelphia four games to one and, finally, humiliated their long-time intimidators, the former champion Detroit Pistons, in four straight games.[5]

Jordan and the Bulls then faced Magic Johnson and Los Angeles in the championship series. The Lakers won Game One. The second contest turned out to be pivotal.

The Bulls destroyed the Lakers 107-86, as Jordan sank fifteen of eighteen shots to score 33 points. During a 15-2 run that won the game, Jordan made a shot that became famous. He soared to the basket to dunk with his right hand, in midair encountered a Laker blocking his path, brought the ball back down, switched it to his left hand, then somehow glided to the left of the basket and banked the ball in to score—all before returning to the ground. Magic Johnson admitted that "he did the impossible, the unbelievable."[6]

The Bulls won the next three games and the championship. Even with a painfully bruised toe, for which he used a specially slit shoe to obtain some relief, Jordan dominated the games. He and the Bulls finally had their championship. He clutched the Most Valuable Player trophy after the final game, hid his head in Juanita's arms, and cried before tens of millions of viewers. He then apologized to reporters: "I never showed this kind of emotion before in public." The *Chicago Tribune*'s Sam Smith wrote that Jordan did not have to apologize: "He really is human" after all.[7]

Selling a Championship

New York essayist and literary critic Stanley Crouch could say that Jordan played with "disciplined audacity."[8] Americans liked that kind of play because "the improvisational hero is the great American hero. Louis Armstrong, Fred Astaire, or Michael Jordan conceiving some sort of remarkable play while in motion." As if comparing a basketball player to an inventor of jazz (Armstrong) or a creator of modern dance (Astaire) were not sufficient, *Time* believed Jordan surpassed the *Mona Lisa*: "Modern life suffers from the Mona Lisa complex," the magazine gushed, "the idea that when you finally see a legendary work of art, it inevitably disappoints, appearing somehow smaller . . . than you had imagined it. Except Michael Jordan." Only the Bulls' star united "hard-court fundamentals with the improvisational creativity of the blacktop"[9] In other words, he played in the ordered commercialism of the twenty-thousand-seat auditorium, but with the imagination and seldom-seen skills exhibited on inner-city (or rural) playgrounds.

All in all, Paul Sullivan wrote in the *Chicago Tribune*, Jordan did not have "a bad year. He welcomed his second son into the world, had a hamburger named after him [McDonald's McJordan] . . ., agreed to let a network use his likeness in a Saturday morning cartoon, earned his second Most Valuable Player award, cut a commercial with [famed rock-and-roll musician] Little Richard . . ., hit a free throw with his eyes closed," and finally could wear "the championship ring."[10]

Sullivan's list was only part of the story. When *Sports Illustrated* gave Jordan its coveted "Sportsman of the Year" award for 1991, the article's subtitle read: "The consummate player and the ultimate showman, Michael Jordan has captivated America and is about to conquer the world." A leading sports advertising agent declared, "He has a level of popularity and value as a commercial spokesman that is almost beyond comprehension. It is a singular phenomenon. It never happened before and may not ever happen again."[11]

In 1992, Jordan earned about $25 million. Only $3.8 million came from his Bulls salary. The rest came from endorsements, including new deals with the Illinois State Lottery Commission, Guy Laroche (for making Time Jordan watches), and a restaurant bearing his name in Chicago. Not all the gloss turned to gold. Time Jordan attracted few customers. Other markets, however, seemed to be infinitely elastic. An unbelievable six million Wilson basketballs bearing Jordan's signature had been bought. Nike's Air Jordan remained the world's most profitable sports shoe.[12]

It was his success in the global market that set Jordan apart from the earlier commercial triumphs of Kareem Abdul-Jabbar and Magic Johnson. The NBA broadcast the Bulls-Lakers finals to more than seventy overseas countries. Nike featured six advertisements teaming Jordan and filmmaker Spike Lee, which had been widely acclaimed when initially shown several years later. The commercials worked well overseas. Rated the most "likable" and "familiar" of all performers in America, according to one poll, Jordan was becoming equally popular in some overseas countries.[13]

Soon after the Bulls won the championship, calls started coming in from Japan. "They want him for commercials," his agent explained. "I was just speaking to a broadcaster in Yugoslavia," a friend told Jordan, "and he told me you're the biggest star there. They see the games on tape delay."[14] Especially remarkable was Jordan's and the NBA's popularity in such countries as Italy, Spain, and Hungary, for they had long, successful basketball traditions of their own. Some of their leagues were considerably older than the NBA. But tradition seemed to be no match for communication satellites, global-minded advertising executives, the drive of David Stern's NBA marketing powerhouse, and Nike commercials.

Another dimension of Jordan's cross-cultural popularity in 1991 was revealed by a sports goods dealer in Skokie, Illinois, a Chicago suburb. "Michael Jordan is the same for everyone who walks in here. He is a hero," said Pradip Baywe, who had been born in India. "Anybody. Germans. Russians. Poles. Indians. Koreans. They are all looking for Michael Jordan, No. 23." The famous, sometimes infamous and bloody, ethnically divided communities in Chicago had found something in common. Meanwhile back in India, Pradip Baywe noted, his nephew wore Air Jordan shoes.[15]

This movement of commerce and culture went both ways. Europeans and Japanese flooded U.S. markets with their goods in the 1980s and 1990s. Gucci, Chanel, Benetton, Armani, and Italian-designed jewelry reached well over $2 billion annually in exports to the United States. And these upscale goods brought with them styles and smells that many Americans considered the standard for international elegance. But with the important exception of some Japanese and European automobiles and electronic goods, these products were styled and priced largely for the elite. American society showed increasingly wide gaps between the rich, the middle class, and the poor. The new post-industrial, information-technological revolution acted like earlier radical technological changes of the mid-nineteenth and late nineteenth centuries: they further widened the gaps between the classes and especially hurt the poor.[16]

Meanwhile, the NBA, Nike, McDonald's, Gatorade, Bugs Bunny, and other products associated with Jordan conquered the United States and spread across the mass cultures of Europe, Asia, and Latin America, made newly accessible by cable and satellites. European exports to the United States set some fashion standards, while American sports set new standards in reaching untold numbers of potential buyers. The $2 billion or so of the high fashion exports into the United States were dwarfed by the many billions of revenue generated overseas by Nike, McDonald's, and Disney.

One major nation chose to fight this Americanization of its mass culture. France had long been proud of its own cultural accomplishments, not least its language—which, before World War II and the ascendancy of English, had been the language usually accepted as standard for conducting international relations. As early as the 1920s, many French complained that U.S. films, business techniques, architecture, and music were corrupting their culture. Americans noted, however, that most French did not complain. As writer Matthew Josephson observed while living in Paris, he found "a young France that . . . was passionately concerned with the civilization of the U.S.A., and stood in a fair way to be *Americanized.*" One of the great authors of the century, F. Scott Fitzgerald, followed out the logic while he lived in France in the 1920s: "Culture follows money," so Americans "will be the Romans in the next generation as the English are now." The French ambassador to the United States seemed to show little delight when he had to admit to Americans, "Your movies and talkies have soaked the French mind in American life, methods, and manners. American gasoline and American ideas have circulated throughout France, bringing a new vision of power and a new tempo of life. . . . More and more we are following America."[17]

Some sixty years later, in 1982, a French culture minister dropped the politeness. Culture, as Fitzgerald noted, still followed capital. The French official warned of "American cultural imperialism." A cartoon appeared in 1986 showing the noble European continent defended by the great literary figures of d'Artagnan, Don Quixote, and Shakespeare against a U.S. attack—from the skies—led by Mickey Mouse, E.T., Marilyn Monroe, and a hamburger. The cartoon caught the problem rather accurately: culture was indeed becoming international, but it was not becoming harmonious. Europe's elite traditions were being blitzed from the skies (where the communication satellites roamed) by American mass culture. One critic put it bluntly: "The success of American popular culture abroad is due in part to the populist values on which it is based, [and is] more attractive to many of the common people . . . than the traditional values of their own countries."[18] The United States, moreover, possessed the capital and technology to ensure that the "common people" saw that culture.

Michael Jordan represented a movement not only threatening to overthrow the basketball dynasty of Magic Johnson and the Los Angeles Lakers. He and the products he endorsed also endangered traditional dress and even eating habits around the world.

Basketball Is My Escape . . . Everything Else Is So Complicated

In 1991–1992, the Bulls set another record by winning sixty-seven of their eighty-two games as they conquered a second straight championship. After Jordan also won his second consecutive Most Valuable Player award, *Sports Illustrated*'s Jack McCallum wrote that he "stands alone on the mountain top, unquestionably the most famous athlete on the planet and one of its most famous citizens of any kind. . . . He *transcends* sports."[19] Jordan's dominance was tragically enhanced on November 7, 1991, when Magic Johnson announced that he had been infected with the HIV virus that causes AIDS, and that he would retire from the Lakers. Having become a close friend of Johnson's, the news devastated Jordan.

The 1991–1992 season was again a smashing commercial success for the Bulls' star. During the January 1992 Super Bowl, Nike ads gained international acclaim when they teamed him with Bugs Bunny on a basketball court. Critics ranked this "Hare Jordan" advertisement as the best of the day—a day that had become a kind of Super Bowl for hotly competitive U.S. advertising executives and their clients (who paid a million dollars for mere seconds of ad time during the game's time-outs). Phil Knight later said the Super Bowl ads had been "a big risk." "We invested in six months worth of drawings and a million dollars in production costs to show Michael Jordan, probably the most visible representative of Nike, paired with a cartoon character." But it worked: "We got thousands of positive responses."[20]

When *Newsweek* magazine listed the hundred most influential people in American culture, Jim Riswold was one of the select. Riswold was hardly a household name. But he was the writer who had turned out dozens of Nike advertisements since the late 1980s. Knight and Riswold so fine-tuned Nike's marketing that they had divided their global sales for basketball shoes into three segments. One was Air Jordan, by far the most popular. When that shoe lost sales, however, Nike produced "Force," which was represented by the burly Charles Barkley of the Phoenix Suns, and "Flight," represented by the balletic Scottie Pippen. "Instead of one big glop," Knight bragged, "We have the number one, the number two, and the number four brands of basketball shoes."[21] Adidas, Reebok, and the others had to take whatever Knight, Riswold, and Jordan left them.

In 1992, the United States put together the greatest-ever basketball team to represent the country at the Olympic games in Barcelona, Spain. The "Dream Team," as it was soon called, was led by Jordan, Pippen, Bird, Johnson (who came out of retirement for the games), and Barkley. As the Olympics approached, media attention grew so intense that the Dream Team chose to live in high-security seclusion apart from the other athletes.

Jordan was the focal point of the media and public. Each month, hundreds of babies in the world were being given the first two names of Michael Jordan. When Nike threw a mammoth press conference in Barcelona, a Japanese correspondent asked, "Mr. Jordan, how does it feel to be God?"[22]

Julius Erving knew something about public adulation, but he was nevertheless stunned when he arrived in Spain. Jordan, "Dr. J" concluded, was less a person than "something of a 24–hour commodity." Erving and Jordan tried to get away from the crush by taking a helicopter out of Barcelona to a private golf course in the Pyrenees Mountains. By the time the two reached the fifth and sixth holes, however, the local inhabitants had spread word that Jordan was playing the course. People "started coming out of the bushes, down the hills," Erving marveled. By the time the two left there were "200 or 300 people waving goodbye to the helicopter. . . . I realized he needed some time to get away from the game and find some peace."[23]

Given Nike's genius in exploiting communication satellites and cable, it was not obvious where that peace could be found. At his last open public appearance, his biographer Jim Naughton records, Jordan went to a Dallas shopping mall where he signed autographs for an hour and a half, yet satisfied only a small number of the five thousand who overran both tight security and the mall. At a Memphis golf tournament for charity, huge crowds followed him in hundred-degree heat, while men tried to offer him hundred-dollar bills in return for an autograph.[24]

Several years earlier, Jordan had begun to try to retreat from such a crazy world. Once gregarious and spontaneous, he moved behind security, living in secret hotel suites. Sports columnist Mike Lupica later compared Jordan's determined attempt at finding privacy with similar attempts by the most legendary, and reclusive, baseball star of the post-1930s era, Joe DiMaggio. The New York Yankee great, however, had destroyed any chance to find seclusion by marrying Marilyn Monroe, who rightly considered the media and cameras to be her best friends. Not surprisingly, the marriage lasted less than a year. Jordan, on the other hand, had married in part to ensure his privacy. "Regardless of how available he is," Lupica wrote, "it's as if there is a line he has drawn between himself and the world. And he does not want that line crossed."[25]

Trying to draw such a line while being the center of global media attention during a long, nine-month season, or while he daily appeared in global living rooms through the power of Jim Riswold's advertising and the new technology that raced across boundaries—all this seemed to be a contradiction. As the new media developed after the early 1970s, as television moguls learned how to gain audiences and riches by exploiting this technology, they revealed the most private of experiences, then transmitted these revelations instantaneously around the globe. It sometimes seemed to be a symbiotic relationship. One partner maintained its celebrity and wealth by revealing deep secrets to the other, which, in turn, demanded more such secrets to maintain its audience. The media happily and lucratively kept the information and fascination flowing in both directions, while developing new devices to deepen the dependency. Given Jordan's fame and the squeaky-clean image he (and Nike, and his other endorsements) had so labored to create, it was only a matter of time before the media that helped make him would try to profit by breaking him.

As Jordan later admitted, he'd brought some of it on himself. In October 1991, President George Bush invited the Bulls to the White House for a celebration of their first championship. Jordan decided not to attend the ceremony. He said he had already met the President. Nor did he want to be the center of attention and take the limelight away from his teammates. The media speculated, however, that his absence might have more to do with Jordan being a registered Democrat who was not enthusiastic about the Republican President. Other media alleged that at the time of the White House ceremony, Jordan was playing golf at his retreat in Hilton Head, South Carolina, where bets on each hole supposedly reached four figures. When reporters caught up to ask why he had snubbed the President of the United States, Jordan uncharacteristically lost his control: "It's none of your business," he blurted out.[26]

Criticisms over missing the President's party had barely quieted before another barrage occurred. Jordan, his agent, and Nike threatened to sue the NBA for using the star's image without either their permission or their access to the profits generated by the wildly popular likeness of the Bulls' leader. The NBA backed down, but Jordan emerged looking to many like a greedy multimillionaire who willingly attacked the very system that had made him rich and famous.

Then, in late 1991, Sam Smith published *The Jordan Rules*. The star emerged from Smith's account as a selfish, mean, ghoulishly demanding egoist who physically beat, or launched tirades against, teammates when he thought they let him down. At one point, Smith charged, Jordan had punched teammate Will Perdue in the face when he decided the giant center had not played up to Jordan's standards. Of course no one, especially the earthbound Perdue, could approach Jordan's standards. Smith also claimed that he had been bitterly sarcastic in complaining about Bulls General Manager Jerry Krause. Jordan apparently made fun of both Krause's plump physique and some of his deals for players. As observers pointed out, however, in a half-dozen years, Krause had assembled a team that already owned two championships and had made Jordan not merely a scorer but a winner.

Coach Phil Jackson recalled that when the book appeared, "Michael was furious." Jordan had been careful to follow a discipline and a set of values that made him respected as well as popular. In 1984–1985, he had quickly taken off the gold chains and fur coat when he realized these might be misunderstood by the audiences he wanted to reach. Reporters noted that Jordan never allowed himself to be seen in public without fashionable, usually conservative, clothes. He did not even let himself be seen in the Bulls' dressing room without being fully and well dressed. He showered and dressed in the trainer's room, which was off-limits to the media, so he could always appear appropriately before the cameras. Jordan declared with conviction that if a person only saw him once for a fleeting moment in a hotel lobby, he wanted that person to remember him as proper, well dressed, and respectable—which, indeed, he seemed to be.

That he had to endure growing criticism of his actions on and off the court was therefore most painful. He told *Sports Illustrated* that he always tried to be a "positive image" and a "positive influence." "I never thought a role model should be negative," Jordan declared. "If you want negativity, then you wouldn't have asked for Michael Jordan. You might've asked for [heavyweight boxing champion] Mike Tyson or somebody else."[27]

But trying to be a role model twenty-four hours a day in the televised fishbowl that seemed to be his life was, not surprisingly, difficult. As Erving had seen firsthand, there seemed to be no place to escape. "I look forward to playing now, more than ever," Jordan said in 1991, because it was the only place he could avoid the constant spying into his private life. "Basketball is my escape, my refuge," while "everything else is so . . . busy and complicated."[28]

Within another year, however, not even basketball could be a refuge from alleged scandal and personal tragedy. Every allegation against Jordan, every sorrow he endured was, moreover, relayed to global audiences by cable and satellite. Nike was also coming under bitter attack. The gap between image and reality in the new media-made world of the 1990s was growing so wide that not even Michael Jordan could leap across it.

Notes

From *Michael Jordan and the New Global Capitalism* by Walter LaFeber. Copyright c. 1999 by Walter LaFeber. Used by permission of W. W. Norton & Company, Inc., 1999), 49–54, 75–89.

1. *Time* (Jan. 9, 1989): 50–52.
2. Jerome Holtzman, "Jordan Finds Teammates," *Chicago Tribune*, June 11, 1991, IV: 1.
3. Roger G. Noll, "Professional Basketball: Economic and Business Perspectives," in Paul D. Staudohar and James A. Mangan, eds., *The Business of Professional Sports* (Urbana: University of Illinois Press, 1991), 33.
4. *Ebony*, 47 (Nov. 1991): 72–74.
5. *Chicago Tribune*, June 17, 1991, VII: 3, conveniently ran the highlights of the 1990–1991 season.
6. Paul Sullivan, "747: A Fitting Time to Fly—and Unveil the Movie," *Chicago Tribune*, June 17, 1991, VII: 5.
7. *Chicago Tribune*, June 13, 1991, IV: 1, 5.
8. Jim Naughton, *Taking to the Air: The Rise of Michael Jordan* (New York: Warner Books, 1992), 10–11.
9. *Time* (June 24, 1991): 46.
10. Paul Sullivan, "Living Legend Zaps Off a Splendid 1990–91 Season," *Chicago Tribune*, June 13, 1991, IV: 1.
11. *Sports Illustrated*, Dec. 23, 1991, 65–66.
12. Naughton, *Taking to the Air*, 149.
13. *Los Angeles Times*, June 1, 1991, D1.
14. Ira Berkow, "Air Jordan and Just Plain Folks" *New York Times*, June 15, 1991, I: 29.

15. *Chicago Tribune,* June 2, 1991, I: 1, 18.

16. Nicola and Marino de Medici, "Foreign Intervention: Europe Invades America," *Public Opinion* 9 (Feb.–Mar. 1986): 17–20.

17. Frank Costigliola, *Awkward Dominion: American Political, Economic, and Cultural Relations with Europe, 1919–1933* (Ithaca, N.Y.: Cornell University Press, 1984), 19–20, 175–76.

18. Richard Grenier, "Around the World in American Ways," *Public Opinion* 9 (Feb.–Mar. 1986): 58.

19. Jack McCallum quoted in *Current Biography* 58 (Feb. 1997): 24.

20. Geraldine E. Willigan, "High-Performance Marketing: An Interview with Nike's Phil Knight," *Harvard Business Review* 70 (July 1992): 99.

21. Ibid., 96–98.

22. Donald Katz, *Just Do It: The Nike Spirit in the Corporate World* (New York: Random House, 1994), 41.

23. Mark Vancil, ed., *The NBA at Fifty* (New York: Park Lane, 1996), 239.

24. Naughton, *Taking to the Air,* 3, 15.

25. Mike Lupica, "Let's Fly Again," *Esquire* 123 (May 1995): 52.

26. Bob Greene, *Hang Time* (New York: Doubleday, 1992), 286.

27. Phil Jackson and Huge Delehanty, *Sacred Hoops: Spiritual Lessons of a Hardwood Warrior* (New York: Hyperion, 1995), 157; *Chicago Tribune,* March 21, 1992, III: 1.

28. Jack McCallum, "Everywhere Man," *Sports Illustrated* (Dec. 23, 1991): 69.

Contributors

GEORGE D. BUSHNELL was the author of *Wilmette: A History* (1976).

SUSAN K. CAHN, associate professor of history at SUNY, Buffalo, is the author of the acclaimed *Coming On Strong: Gender and Sexuality in Twentieth-Century Women's Sport*, which was recognized as the best book in sports history in 1994 by the North American Society for Sport History. She is co-editor with Jean O'Reilly of *Women and Sports in the United States: A Documentary Reader* (2007).

JOHN M. CARROLL is Regents Professor at Lamar University (Beaumont, Texas), where he teaches courses on U.S. military history, the Vietnam War, the Cold War, and sport in America. He has written *Red Grange and the Rise of Modern Football* (1999) and *Fritz Pollard: Pioneer in Racial Advancement* (1992) and is currently writing a biography of all-time star running back Jim Brown.

DAVID CLAERBAUT has taught at a several universities and is president of Dr. David Claerbaut and Associates, a sales training consulting firm. He is the author of several books including *Urban Ministry in a New Millennium* (2005), *Bart Starr: When Leadership Mattered* (2004), *Recruiting Confidential: A Father a Son, and Big Time College Football* (2003), and *Durocher's Cubs: The Greatest Team That Didn't Win* (2000).

BRUCE J. EVENSEN, of the Department of Communication at DePaul University, is the author of *When Dempsey Fought Tunney: Heroes, Hokum, and Storytelling in the Jazz Age* (1996) and *Truman, Palestine, and the Press: Shaping Conventional Wisdom at the Beginning of the Cold War* (1992).

GERALD R. GEMS has been a professor in physical education at North Central College in Naperville, Illinois, since 1988. He is the author of numerous books, including *The Athletic Crusade: Sport and American Cultural Imperialism* (2006), *Viet Nam Vignettes: Tales of the Magnificent Bastards* (2006), *For Pride, Profit, and Patriarchy: Football and the Incorporation of American Cultural Values* (2000), and *Windy City Wars: Labor, Leisure, and Sport in the Making of Chicago* (1997).

WALTER L. LeFEBER is a distinguished historian of diplomatic history. A two-time winner of the prestigious Bancroft Prize, he taught for forty years at Cornell University. Among his major books are *America, Russia, and the Cold War* (1966), *The New Empire: An Interpretation of American Expansion, 1860–1898* (1963); *Inevitable Revolutions: The United States in Central America* (1984), and *The Clash: U.S.–Japanese Relations throughout History* (1997).

ROBIN DALE LESTER was headmaster at several outstanding independent schools, including Trinity in New York City and the Latin School of Chicago. He received a PhD in American history from the University of Chicago in 1975 and revised his dissertation into his stellar monograph *Stagg's University: The Rise, Decline, and Fall of Big-Time Football at Chicago*, which won the North American Society for Sports History Book Award for 1996.

MICHAEL E. LOMAX is associate professor of health and sport studies, University of Iowa, where he teaches classes in inequality in sport, marketing, finance, and entrepreneurship in sport, and twentieth-century American sport. He is the author of the definitive *Black Baseball Entrepreneurs, 1860–1901* (2003), which won the Robert Peterson Award in 2004, and is currently writing a follow-up volume.

DANIEL A. NATHAN, associate professor of American studies, Skidmore College, is the author of the prize-winning book *Saying It's So: A Cultural History of the Black Sox Scandal* (2002), which won the Best Book Award from the North American Society for Sport History and the Society for the Study of Sport Sociology. He has published in several scholarly journals, including *Aethlon, American Quarterly, American Studies, Journal of American Studies, Journal of Sport History, OAH Magazine of History*, and *Sociology of Sport Journal*.

STEVEN A. RIESS is the Bernard Brommel Research Professor of History at Northeastern Illinois University, Chicago, where he has taught American history for more than thirty years. His books include *Sports in the Industrial Age, 1850–1920* (1995), *City Games: The Evolution of American Society and the Rise of Sports* (1989), and *Touching Base: Professional Baseball and American Culture in the Progressive Era* (1980, rev. ed., 1999). The former editor of the *Journal of Sport History*, his books have won three citations from *Choice* as outstanding academic books, and he has received several grants from the National Endowment for the Humanities.

CORD SCOTT, a PhD candidate in history at Loyola University, Chicago, is an instructor of history at the International Academy of Design and Technology in Chicago.

JOHN CHI-KIT WONG is assistant professor of sport management at Washington State University, Pullman. He is the author of *Lords of the Rinks: The Emergence of the National Hockey League, 1875–1936* (2005).

Index

Sport and Society

The University of Illinois Press
is a founding member of the
Association of American University Presses.

Composed in 9.5/12.5 Trump Mediaeval
with Myriad Pro display
by Jim Proefrock
at the University of Illinois Press
Designed by Dennis Roberts
Manufactured by Cushing-Malloy, Inc.

University of Illinois Press
1325 South Oak Street
Champaign, IL 61820-6903
www.press.uillinois.edu